STUDIES IN

AFRICAN AMERICAN HISTORY AND CULTURE

edited by

GRAHAM HODGES
COLGATE UNIVERSITY

A GARLAND SERIES

BENEATH THE IMAGE OF THE CIVIL RIGHTS MOVEMENT AND RACE RELATIONS

ATLANTA, GEORGIA, 1946–1981

_____

DAVID ANDREW HARMON

GARLAND PUBLISHING, Inc.
NEW YORK & LONDON / 1996

Library of Congress Cataloging-in-Publication Data

Harmon, David Andrew, 1961–
    Beneath the image of the civil rights movement and race
relations : Atlanta, Georgia, 1946–1981 / David Andrew Harmon.
        p.   cm. — (Studies in African American history and
culture)
    Includes bibliographical references and index.
    ISBN 0-8153-2437-5 (alk. paper)
    1. Afro-Americans—Civil rights—Georgia—Atlanta—
History—20th century. 2. Civil rights movement—Georgia—
Atlanta—History—20th century. 3. Atlanta (Ga.)—Race relations. I. Title. II. Series.
F294.A89N443   1996
305.896'0720758231'09045—dc20   95-52439

Printed on acid-free, 250-year-life paper
Manufactured in the United States of America

Contents

Introduction

Most examinations of the Civil Rights Movement have been written from a national perspective. These studies have presented local African American protest movements as part of a national campaign for civil rights that lasted approximately from 1955, the Montgomery Bus Boycott, to 1968, the assassination of Dr. Martin Luther King, Jr. In this context, demonstrations in Montgomery, Greensboro, Albany, Birmingham, Selma, and Memphis have been viewed as prototypical African American protest movements and milestones in this national campaign for civil rights.

In reality, almost every southern community experienced sustained protest movements that lasted, in many cases, for several years. These local protest movements were unique and developed independently of national civil rights organizations and leaders. Historical examinations of specific local protest movements such as William Chafe's study of Greensboro, Robert J. Norrell's examination of Tuskegee, and John Dittmer's work on Mississippi provide a fuller understanding of the local context of the freedom struggle and a new approach to the study of the Civil Rights Movement.

This study is the story of the local Civil Rights Movement and race relations in Atlanta, Georgia from 1946 to 1981. Atlanta, perhaps more than any other southern city, was the embodiment of Henry Grady's New South ideology. White Atlantans desired to combine progress and modernity with the grace and civility of the Old South. The African American community of Atlanta included an intellectual, politically sophisticated middle-class leadership that wanted political and civil rights. The Civil Rights Movement in Atlanta thus presented a unique challenge to white Atlantans and their desire for progress and civility.

Between 1946 and 1981 the image of Atlanta that dominated the public's perception was that of a New South city, relatively free from the region's prejudices. Atlanta took pride in its reputation for progressive race relations. The city's white leadership boasted of the racial cooperation that existed between white and African American citizens and the achievements of Atlanta's African American community.

Yet throughout this period the city's image of racial progress existed side by side with social, political, and economic realities that contradicted this perception. African American citizens often had to use political pressure, litigation, and direct action to initiate racial reform. Residential segregation actually increased during this period. Perhaps the most obvious contradictions between Atlanta's image and reality were in regard to economic equality. Despite the presence of a sizable African American middle class, a large majority of African American citizens lived near or below the poverty level. Thus, while Atlanta had a reputation for being racially progressive, social and economic realities for many African American residents were profoundly different.

This study is an examination of this paradox for it lies at the heart of the story of the local Civil Rights Movement in Atlanta. Central to understanding this paradox was the prime role played by the governing interracial coalition which controlled the response to and pace of racial and social change in the city. The commitment of this interracial coalition to the economic growth of Atlanta and the maintenance of an image of racial progress often took priority over racial beliefs and attitudes. The major accomplishment of this coalition was its ability to adapt to changing racial relations, most noticeably the transition from white to African American political power. The major weakness was that its policies favored the interests of the upper-economic strata of both communities. African American participation in this coalition produced few benefits for African Americans of lesser economic means.

The first four chapters of this work examine the origins and development of the Civil Rights Movement in Atlanta, the formation of the interracial coalition, and the response of the white community to the protest movement. The last three chapters assess the impact of the Civil Rights Movement on poor African American communities and the policies and internal dynamics of the interracial governing coalition.

Acknowledgments

All works are collaborative efforts and during the course of doing research and writing this study, I have benefitted from the expertise and help of many individuals.

I am indebted to a large number of archivists and librarians, especially for the skillful and invaluable assistance given me at the manuscript divisions and libraries of Emory University, Clark-Atlanta University, the Martin Luther King, Jr. Center for Nonviolent Social Change, and the Atlanta History Center.

Several individuals took the time to speak to me about their observations about race relations in Atlanta and their involvement in the Movement. Their names are listed alphabetically in the bibliography. These observations and personal accounts enriched my perspective on the events described and conclusions reached in this work.

Many friends and acquaintances have provided assistance and have been a source of support. Andy Doyle read a portion of my manuscript. His editorial suggestions and thoughtful critique as well as his friendship have been of immeasurable value. Mark McQuire has always been a source of encouragement and a good friend over the past ten years. I owe special thanks to Millie Weaver of the School of Liberal Arts at Auburn University at Montgomery for preparing this manuscript for publication.

I first began research for this work while a graduate student at Emory University. James Roark and LeRoy Davis provided a penetrating and extremely useful critique of my dissertation. I am fortunate in that I can refer to Dan Carter as my mentor and friend. His faith in my ability and his encouragement and support are in a large measure responsible for this study.

Finally, I could not have completed this work without the guidance and the emotional and financial support of my parents, Allen and Betty Harmon, and my brother, James Harmon. It is a special pleasure to dedicate this work to my family.

Beneath the Image of the Civil Rights Movement and Race Relations

I

The Second Real Emancipation

On a cloudy and rather cool Fourth of July 1944, Atlantans flocked to the polls to vote in the state Democratic primary. Four African American citizens went to Precinct E in the city's third ward. Following standard procedure, they filled out slips with their names and addresses. Along with his slip, A.T. Walden, an attorney and leader of this group, presented to the precinct manager a receipt from the tax collector's office which certified that he had paid the state's poll tax and was qualified to vote in the general election in November. A clerk compared Walden's slip with her records and informed him that his name and address did not appear on the registrar's list. The omission of the names of Walden and other African American citizens was not a mistake or an oversight. The state Democratic Party barred African Americans from voting in the primary. Rather than creating a disturbance, Walden and the members of his group said "thank you" and left. They vowed, however, to continue their struggle for the ballot.[1]

The action undertaken by this small group was part of an ongoing struggle for African American franchisement in the South. This struggle began shortly after African American citizens first won the right to vote. During Reconstruction, most adult African American males became voters for the first time. Under the supervision of federal troops, approximately 700,000 African Americans, most of whom were former slaves, qualified as voters. The Military Reconstruction Acts of 1867 permitted African Americans to participate in the framing of new state constitutions and the formation of new governments.

A majority of white southerners denounced these governments. They referred to resident northerners who held office in the new governments as "carpetbaggers," a term suggesting that these officials had no stake in southern society. Southern whites who cooperated with the reconstructed governments and supported Republican policies were denounced as "scalawags" (a scalawag is an animal of little value and breeding). African American participation in this political coalition shocked most white southerners. While African Americans were politically influential in every southern state, they did not dominate the new governments. Only in South Carolina did African Americans comprise a majority of the state legislators. No state ever elected an African American governor and only a small number of blacks served as lieutenant governors. African Americans generally occupied lesser state offices. Although African Americans never held office in proportion to their numbers in the region, their presence generated complaints of "Negro rule."

The spectacle of African American citizens holding office was loathsome to southern whites. Southerners (as well as northerners) considered African Americans innately inferior. Southern whites resorted to both extralegal and political means to halt the political empowerment of African Americans. Several secret organizations such as the Ku Klux Klan, the Knights of the White Camelia, the Pale Faces, and the '76 Association were formed to terrorize African American voters, disrupt Republican Party meetings, and threaten government officials. While many "respectable" southerners publicly condemned the excessive use of violence and physical force directed at African American citizens, they sympathized with and privately condoned the activities of these organizations.

The Democratic Party manipulated the racial fears of white voters by utilizing white supremacy rhetoric. Democratic partisanship was associated with white domination. Many scalawags returned to the Democratic Party resulting in small and ineffective black-majority Republican organizations in many southern states. In 1869 conservative white southerners regained political control of the government in Tennessee. During the next two years, the state governments of Virginia, North Carolina, and Georgia were "redeemed." In the mid-1870s, conservative whites regained political control of Alabama, Arkansas, and Mississippi.

Congress passed two constitutional amendments and a series of federal statutes designed to protect the rights of African Americans. The Fourteenth Amendment defined United States citizenship and prohibited states from passing laws which would "abridge the privileges or immunities of citizens of the United States," "deprive any person of life, liberty, or property without due process of law," and "deny to any person within its jurisdiction the equal protection of the laws." The second section of this amendment required all states either to enfranchise all male citizens or else lose seats in the House of Representatives proportionate to the number that they excluded. The third section disqualified former public officials who had supported the Confederacy from holding office at the state and federal level.

The Fifteenth Amendment stipulated that states could not invoke race as a ground for disenfranchising citizens otherwise eligible to vote.

In 1870 and 1871, Congress enacted legislation to punish those who interfered with suffrage rights. The Enforcement Acts prohibited state officials from discriminating among voters on the basis of race, forbade individuals from conspiring to interfere with a person's right to vote, and outlawed the use of physical threats and economic intimidation against voters. Congress authorized the appointment of officials to examine election irregularities, investigate registration procedures, and certify election results. The president was given authority to dispatch federal troops and marshals to implement court decrees. Under the provisions of the Enforcement Acts, the Justice Department annually prosecuted an average of over seven hundred voting rights cases.[2]

These actions, however, proved inadequate. The United States Congress never invoked the second section of the Fourteenth Amendment despite evidence of disenfranchisement by southern states. Due to political considerations, the wording of the Fifteenth Amendment was purposely ambiguous. States could circumvent the intent of the amendment as long as suffrage restrictions were not overtly racial. Two decisions by the United States Supreme Court in 1876 severely weakened the effectiveness of the Enforcement Acts. In the *United States v. Cruikshank*, the Court distinguished between the rights of national and state citizenship. According to this decision, the Fourteenth Amendment protected only the rights of national citizenship; it limited the actions of states, not those of individuals. The states safeguarded the rights of state citizenship. This ruling would require African Americans who had complaints against private individuals to seek redress from hostile local and state authorities.[3] In the *United States v. Reese*, the Court held that the Fifteenth Amendment did not confer the right of suffrage, but merely prohibited exclusion on the basis of race.[4] The legal technicalities that these decisions imposed made prosecutions of voting rights cases almost impossible. Following these decisions, indictments by the Justice Department declined to less than two hundred cases per year.[5]

The Compromise of 1877 marked the formal end of Reconstruction and the federal government's commitment to the principle of civil and political rights for African Americans and the use of federal power to guarantee these rights (this commitment was expressed in the Thirteenth, Fourteenth, and Fifteenth Amendments). In the 1876 presidential election, Democratic candidate Samuel Tilden won 185 electoral votes to Republican candidate Rutherford Hayes' 166 with twenty electoral votes in dispute. Tilden was only a single vote shy of the 186 electoral votes required for a victory. Congress established an Electoral Commission to decide who would receive the disputed votes. By a partisan vote of eight to seven, the Commission awarded all disputed votes to Hayes. Many Democrats refused to abide by the decision and promised to stage a filibuster to prevent Hayes' inauguration.

Northern Republicans and Southern Democrats, however, reached a compromise. Republicans promised that Hayes would withdraw the remaining federal troops from the South. The Democrats agreed to support Hayes, protect the rights of freedmen, and refrain from partisan reprisals against Republicans in the South. Other informal promises were made. Republicans promised support for southern internal improvements such as the construction of Mississippi levies and a transcontinental railroad along a southern route. Hayes agreed to name a white southerner to his cabinet. In return, Southern Democrats promised to elect Republican James A. Garfield as Speaker of the House. While both sides broke many of these agreements, Hayes removed the federal troops from the South. The remaining Republican governments collapsed, and Democratic regimes regained political ascendancy. On a goodwill tour of the South in the fall of 1877, President Hayes told a group of African Americans in Atlanta that "their rights and interests would be safer" if southern whites were "left alone by the general government."[6]

The end of Reconstruction did not immediately result in the establishment of one-party politics and African American disfranchisement in the South. Democrats faced considerable opposition from various Independent and Republican candidates. The Democratic Party, for example, temporarily lost political control in Tennessee and Virginia. Part of the success of non-Democratic candidates was due to the African American vote. Most Independent and Republican candidates openly appealed for black votes. According to estimates compiled by Morgan Kousser in *The Shaping of Southern Politics...1880–1910*, African Americans in at least seven southern states gave a majority of their votes to Republican and Independent gubernatorial candidates during the 1880s (a sixth to a third of the white vote also went to opposition candidates).[7]

In response to this challenge, Democrats again played on racial fears. The Democratic Party was the "white man's party." They warned that the election of Republican and Independent candidates would lead to "Negro domination" and a return to Reconstruction. Democratic candidates, however, were politically pragmatic. In areas where the African American vote was crucial to victory, they solicited black votes and made concessions to African American leaders. Due in a large measure to political competition, African Americans continued to hold office and vote during the 1880s.

A more formidable challenge to the Southern Democratic Party than Independent and Republican candidates, and one that would serve as a stimulus to African American disenfranchisement was the Populist insurgency of the 1890s. The weakness of the southern economy led to the formation of several agrarian protest organizations such as the Wheel and the Brothers of Freedom in Arkansas and the Farmers Alliance in Texas. In the late 1880s these groups merged to form the Alliance. This agricultural interest group encompassed Democrats, Republicans, and Independents. Upon the formation of the Populist Party in the late 1880s, a number of Alliance leaders such as Leonidas Polk of North Carolina and Thomas Watson of Georgia joined this new organization. They argued that the solutions to the South's problems lay with the Populist and not the Democratic Party. The Populist Party thus presented a viable political alternative to the Democrats.

The Populists courted Southern Republicans and African Americans. In 1892 Republican and Populist organizations entered fusion tickets against Democratic candidates in nearly every southern state. Through the Colored Alliance, the Populist Party appealed to African American farmers.[8] It hoped to form a class-based political alliance between small white and African American farmers. In 1894 the Populist Party gained control of both legislative houses in North Carolina. That state sent a Populist to the United States Senate and three party members to the House. In Georgia, the Populist-Republican ticket won over forty-five percent of the vote.[9]

Southern Democrats countered this opposition by incorporating Populist issues and rhetoric and utilizing the litany of white supremacy. In the 1890s Democratic candidates began to speak out against the railroads, Wall Street, and the trusts. Fearing the possibility of a biracial political alliance of small farmers drawn together by their common economic interests, Democrats warned that the African American vote could easily become the political balance of power between competing white factions in the region. A vote against the Democratic Party was a threat to white supremacy.

When these tactics failed, the Democratic Party could and did rely on fraud and, eventually, on disenfranchisement to eradicate political opposition. Democratic election officials stuffed ballot boxes, altered and manipulated returns, tampered with registration lists, and changed polling places without prior notification. They purposely tried to confuse African

American (and poor white) voters. South Carolina's Eight Box Law, for example, required a separate voting box for each office and disallowed ballots placed in the wrong receptacle. Many officials moved these boxes around in order to confuse illiterate voters. In addition to fraud and trickery, Democratic partisans also used physical and economic intimidation to control or discourage African American voting.

Southern states began to experiment with disenfranchisement legislation. Early restrictive measures included the poll tax and literacy and property requirements. Legislators carefully crafted these statutes in order that they complied with the letter, if not the spirit or intent of the Fifteenth Amendment. These measures, for example, did not specifically mention race. When Congress, the Courts, and the national Republican Party failed to intervene, southern legislatures felt free to compose or copy from each other legislation restricting suffrage.

State Democratic parties also began to bar African American participation in their primaries. Before the Civil War, county conventions or mass meetings nominated most candidates. The use of the primary by the Democratic Party did not become widespread in the South until the late 1870s. Democratic officials viewed the primary as the best means to unite the party by settling intraparty differences before the general election. Defeated candidates pledged that they would abide by the results of the primary. With suffrage restriction and the white primary, the possibility of attracting enough disgruntled voters to defeat a Democratic candidate became extremely unlikely. Clearly, the institution of the white primary was one of the prime reasons for the South's failure to develop an effective two-party system.

During the 1880s and 1890s there was little controversy over restricting African American participation in Democratic primaries. Democratic leaders maintained that the party was a private association which could prescribe qualifications for voters in the state Democratic primary. The Fifteenth Amendment only prohibited the state from denying citizens the right to vote in general elections on account of race. The white primary, according to Democratic leaders, was a continuation of past practice. They noted that African Americans were generally supporters of the Republican Party or independent political movements.

The white primary served as an effective means to limit the suffrage rights of African Americans (and poor whites) in the South. Because of the dominance of the Democratic Party in the region, winning in the primary was tantamount to victory in the general election. There was little incentive for African Americans to make an effort to register. In some areas of the

South, African Americans were specifically excluded from Democratic primaries as early as 1878. While practices varied from county to county, most state Democratic committees or conventions had adopted the white primary by the early twentieth century.[10]

Georgia was one of the first southern states to pass legislation limiting suffrage rights. The 1868 state constitution required the payment of a dollar poll tax in order to vote. This provision was temporarily suspended during the "Second Reconstruction" of Georgia (1869–1871).[11] When the Democratic Party regained power, it quickly reinstituted the poll tax requirement. The Redeemer-dominated constitutional convention of 1877 enacted a cumulative poll tax to ensure that the Georgia Republican Party would not regain political power.

The new amendment required a voter to pay a poll tax not only for the year in which he registered but for every year since the enactment of the law or his twenty-first birthday. If a voter missed the annual payment, his poll tax would be doubled the following year. This tax had a drastic effect on voting in Georgia. In 1878 only thirty-seven percent of the potential electorate in the state voted as compared to sixty-eight percent in the rest of the South. Between 1880 and 1888, the estimated African American turnout in presidential elections dropped from thirty-nine to nineteen percent. The Republican turnout declined from seventeen to eleven percent. The Republican Party was weaker in Georgia during the 1880s than any other southern state with the possible exception of South Carolina.[12]

The Georgia Democratic Party also began to bar African American participation in its primaries. Many county Democratic committees in the state adopted the white primary as early as 1890. The Atlanta Democratic Executive Committee excluded African Americans from voting in a 1892 primary.[13] While African Americans could still vote in general and special elections, this was largely meaningless because of suffrage restrictions and the dominance of the Democratic Party in the state. After 1900, only about one-in-ten of the qualified African Americans in Georgia voted.[14]

In 1898 and 1901 State Representative Thomas Hardwick proposed a literacy test requirement for voting which included a grandfather clause loophole for illiterate whites. The Georgia House of Representatives twice defeated the Hardwick Disenfranchisement Bill by overwhelming margins. Many legislators believed that the poll tax and the white primary had removed the need for further restrictions. Influential African American leaders such as Booker T. Washington, W.E.B. DuBois, John Hope, and John H. Deveaux opposed the bill. In 1906 Hardwick, now a United States

Congressman, thrust the disenfranchisement issue into the Democratic primary campaign for governor.

Originally, Hardwick endorsed James Pope Brown, the son of a former governor and an advocate of African American disfranchisement. Eventually realizing that Brown could not win, Hardwick persuaded him to withdraw in favor of Hoke Smith, a former owner of the *Atlanta Journal* and secretary of the interior in the Cleveland administration. Smith was a racial "moderate" who had opposed the Hardwick Disenfranchisement Bill, advocated black education, and condemned lynching. Hardwick asked Tom Watson, the influential Populist leader and a friend, to endorse Smith. Watson had previously criticized Smith for his support of the gold standard and opposition to Populism. In order to win his backing, Watson demanded that Smith support African American disfranchisement and railroad regulation. Smith acquiesced to Watson's demands.

African American disenfranchisement became the major issue in the primary. Backing Hardwick's plan for disenfranchisement, Hoke Smith warned that present suffrage restrictions, the poll tax and the white primary, were inadequate. According to Smith, it would be "folly for us to neglect any means within our reach to remove the present danger of Negro domination." He also approved the use of "any means" to purge elected African American officeholders.[15] Trying to use the issue to his advantage, Clark Howell, Smith's major opponent and editor of the *Atlanta Constitution*, warned that the "Hardwick-Smith" plan would disenfranchise more poor whites than African Americans. A literacy test requirement would "draw the Negroes of Georgia out of the cotton patch and into Negro colleges."[16] Howell accused Smith of hypocrisy by noting that Smith had appointed African Americans to federal office while he was secretary of the interior. Hardwick and Watson used the primary to advocate African American disenfranchisement. Hardwick issued a letter to "white voters" urging support for suffrage restrictions. Watson wrote several inflammatory articles on the "Negro issue." The *Atlanta Journal* (which had previously opposed the Hardwick bill) and the *Augusta Herald* kept up a constant barrage of editorials and articles stressing the need for African American disfranchisement. Smith rode the issue to victory.

In 1907 the Georgia General Assembly proposed a state constitutional amendment to disenfranchise African Americans. In addition to the poll tax, a voter had to meet at least one of these conditions: (1) be able to read, write, and explain any paragraph of the state and federal constitution; (2) be a person of "good character" who understood the duties and obligations of state and national citizenship; (3) had served in the United States or

Confederate armed forces; (4) be a lawful descendent of a person who had served in the armed forces and (5) own forty acres of land or five hundred dollars worth of tax-assessed property. The amendment allowed the registrar wide discretion in determining whether a person met these qualifications. While Smith acknowledged that "the members of one particular race" might find it more difficult to meet these qualifications than others, he argued that "their inability to become voters is not deemed or abridged on account of race or color." In 1908 the citizens of Georgia ratified the constitutional amendment by a two-to-one margin (79,968 votes in favor and 40,260 against).

Thomas Hardwick predicted that the 1908 amendment would "disenfranchise at least ninety-five percent of the negro vote—in fact about all of them."[17] He was correct in this assessment. Disenfranchisement almost completely eliminated African American voting in Georgia. Due to suffrage restrictions and the white primary, the registration of African Americans in Georgia reached an all-time low. As late as 1940, less than five percent of the potential African American electorate in the state were registered.

In April 1944 the United States Supreme Court in *Smith v. Allright* declared the white primary to be unconstitutional. Rejecting the legal contention that primaries were affairs conducted by private organizations, the decision held that they were part of the electoral process and thereby constituted state action. By condoning racial discrimination within primaries, state governments were in violation of the Fifteenth Amendment.

In Georgia, the *Smith v. Allright* decision raised questions about the legality of the state Democratic primary which was scheduled for July Fourth of that year. Reacting to the decision, United States Senator Walter George of Georgia stated that the ruling was "essentially unrealistic" and "would lead into a field where courts ought not to go." He assured his constituents that the decision would not apply to the upcoming primary. According to Senator George, state primaries in Georgia, unlike those in Texas where *Smith v. Allright* originated, were private affairs. Lon Duckworth, chairman of the state Democratic committee, reaffirmed that African Americans would not be allowed to vote in the primary. The decision, according to Duckworth, did not apply to Georgia because the state Democratic Party, not the legislature, established all rules and regulations for the primary.[18]

Other voices in the state urged compliance with the decision. These appeals, however, were generally calls for law and order rather than support for the substance of the decision. While stating that the ruling had to be carefully studied, Governor Ellis Arnall warned that all aspects of the state's electoral process had to comply with the law of the land. An editorial in the *Atlanta Constitution* declared that questions regarding African American participation must be solved within the confines of the Court's decision and without "violence or hysteria." The *Atlanta Journal* acknowledged that the decision was based on "firm legal principles." It warned, however, that "respect and observance can only come from public sentiment." When a ruling involved "political and social revolution," the implementation of the decision must "rest on practical considerations and public opinion."[19]

The greatest potential for social and political change in Georgia due to the *Smith v. Allright* decision was in the city of Atlanta. One reason was the size of Atlanta's African American population. In 1940 African Americans comprised roughly thirty percent of the city's population. At the time of the court's ruling, three thousand African Americans were registered (four percent of the total electorate).[20] The abolition of the white primary in Georgia would inevitably lead to an increase in African American registration. Atlanta's black community would not be able to initiate change through the electoral process by its own votes; however, it would be able to provide crucial support in close elections, especially if it chose to vote as a bloc. In exchange for the votes of black residents, African American leaders could bargain for better living conditions under a system of segregation or for greater social and political equality.

These possibilities did not escape the attention of city officials, especially Atlanta Mayor William Hartsfield. An instinctive politician, Hartsfield knew that the decision would change the voting patterns of the region. He mentioned to several close associates the importance of the ballot and the sweeping political and social change that could result. Immediately after reading a newspaper account of the *Smith v. Allright* decision, Mayor Hartsfield warned Atlanta Police Chief Herbert Jenkins that an African American citizen could use his ballot as "a front ticket to sit on the front seat anywhere he wants to sit, if he knows how to use it." Hartsfield realized that the city's African American community knew "how to use it."[21]

Atlanta's African American community had a tradition of political activity that extended back to Reconstruction.[22] During the early 1870s, two African Americans served on Atlanta's Board of Aldermen. Between 1884 and 1891 the African American community provided the crucial swing vote between the Prohibitionists and the Anti-prohibitionists, the main factions comprising the city's Democratic Party. Representatives of these factions vied with one another for African American support. In return for their electoral support, leaders of Atlanta's African American community often asked for better schools, the employment of African American firemen and policemen, representation on city boards and agencies, and fair treatment for all citizens. Their ability to win these concessions was contingent upon the number of votes that they could deliver to the particular candidate. Ironically, because of this political negotiating in which white candidates willingly participated, many Democratic Party officials began to accuse African Americans of corrupting the political process. "Corruption" thus became a convenient excuse to bar African Americans from voting in the primary.

Atlanta's African American community had long protested suffrage restrictions. Benjamin Davis, a national Republican committee member from Georgia and editor of the *Atlanta Independent*, spearheaded many of these efforts. Davis worked closely with the Equal Rights League, a statewide African American voting rights organization, in an attempt to defeat the 1908 disenfranchisement amendment. In 1909 Davis formed the Organization for Effective Party Work which attempted to reform the state's suffrage requirements. Both of these campaigns, however, were unsuccessful.

Despite suffrage restrictions and the white primary, many African Americans voted in special and general elections. Between 1919 and 1921 Atlanta's African American community was largely responsible for defeating two referenda which would have allowed the Board of Education to issue four million dollars in school bond issues for educational improvements. African American citizens overwhelmingly opposed these measures because no funds were earmarked for the improvement of black schools. Prior to a third referendum, Atlanta's mayor and the president of the school board met with African American leaders. They reached an agreement whereby one-third of the funds would be spent on the construction of African American schools. These funds financed the city's first public black high school as well as the conversion of several white elementary schools into black use and the purchase of new equipment for African American use. The bond issue easily passed due to African American support.

Atlanta's African American community also played an extremely important role in the recall election of Mayor James Key. In 1932 prohibitionists and members of organized labor petitioned to recall the mayor. Since this was a special election, African Americans could vote. Key, who was extremely popular in the African American community, actively solicited its support. The local branch of the NAACP and the Atlanta Teachers Association launched a successful voter registration drive.

The African American community overwhelmingly backed Key. Due to its support, the recall effort failed.

Despite this political activity, many African American leaders were concerned over what they perceived as voter apathy. Voter registration increased when the interests of the African American community were threatened, but sharply declined in politically dormant years. In 1930, for example, only five hundred out of a total African American population of 130,000 were registered to vote. Due to the interest generated by the recall effort, African American registration increased to twenty-five hundred in 1932. This peak figure declined, however, to fifteen hundred by 1935. Poor participation was undoubtedly due in part to voting restrictions and the white primary. Many African Americans, for example, could not afford to pay a cumulative poll tax. Because of the importance of the primary in choosing Democratic candidates, many believed that there was little reason to register to vote in largely meaningless general elections. Many African American leaders believed that apathy was also due in part to a lack of knowledge of the political system and how it operated.

At the suggestion of community activist Lugenia Burns Hope and A.T. Walden, president of the Atlanta branch of the NAACP, African American leaders organized citizenship schools in 1932 to battle voter apathy and stimulate political interest. In addition to teaching the process of registration and voting, this six-week course also taught the structure of local, state, and national governments. Instructors, many of whom were faculty and students at Atlanta University, urged those in attendance to register despite suffrage restrictions and the white primary. To encourage participation in these schools, students who attended four of the six classes received certificates in special graduation ceremonies. Attendance at these schools averaged around 150 at each session.[23]

In 1934 John Wesley Dobbs, a retired mail clerk and prominent statewide fraternal leader, organized the Atlanta Civic and Political League (ACPL). This organization sponsored several voter registration rallies throughout the African American sections of the city. At these community rallies, John Wesley Dobbs and other leaders argued that African American civil rights would only come through registration and voting. They were well aware that the bonds of second-class citizenship would never be broken as long as the vast majority of African Americans did not vote. In 1936 the ACPL listed several objectives that it hoped to achieve by increasing African American registration and voting. These objectives included the employment of African American firemen and policemen; better working conditions and wages for African American professionals;

and the construction and improvement of public recreational facilities in the African American community. The ACPL claimed credit for increasing African American registration from 500 to 3000 between 1934 and 1939.[24]

The work of the ACPL was only one aspect of the voter registration activities that were occurring in Atlanta's African American community. Between 1932 and 1939 the local branches of the NAACP and the Urban League, the Atlanta Teachers Association, the Alpha Phi Alpha Fraternity, and various other civic, fraternal, and religious organizations sponsored voter registration activities. Martin Luther King, Sr., pastor of Ebenezer Baptist Church, led a rally and voting rights march on City Hall in 1935.[25]

The *Atlanta Daily World* played an important role in these activities. W.A. Scott, II, established this African American daily in 1928. Scott died as a result of a gunshot wound in 1934. His brother, Cornelius A. Scott, took control of the newspaper. In memory of his brother, C.A. Scott continued the editorial policy of supporting voter registration activities. The *Atlanta Daily World* gave wide coverage and publicity to the viewpoints and activities of African American leaders and organizations involved in voter registration at a time when the two major white dailies virtually ignored the African American community. The *Atlanta Daily World* was thus an important means of communication between African American leaders and the masses, especially in terms of conveying the importance of registration and voting.[26]

The activity in Atlanta reflected the growing politicalization of the African American community during the 1930s. Prior to that decade, African American leaders often had difficulty in rallying black citizens for political action because politics had little relevance for the average African American citizen. Disenfranchised, discriminated against, and their racial concerns unheeded, many African Americans felt excluded from the political process. The New Deal dramatically altered this perception of the role of government and politics. Relief programs made the federal government tangible and its activities relevant to African Americans. The New Deal aroused the political interests and hopes of people traditionally excluded from mainstream politics.

This sentiment was especially prevalent among African American southerners. African American leaders began to organize in order to claim their right to participate in the political process. Local organizations such as the ACPL, the North Carolina Committee on Negro Affairs, the Hampton County Civic League (Virginia), and the Huntsville Negro Voters Club (Alabama) were formed to promote voter registration and urge qualified African Americans to go to the polls. Many of these organizations offered adult education courses in subjects ranging from voter registration to black history to personal finance. The national NAACP and Urban League urged its local branches to participate in the struggle for suffrage rights.

This period also witnessed the departure of African Americans from the Republican Party into the Democratic Party. Many African Americans had become disenchanted with the Republican Party by the 1930s. The late nineteenth- and early twentieth century Republican presidents did not fulfill the expectations of African American citizens. During tours of the South in 1898 and 1901, William McKinley stressed national reconciliation at the expense of African American civil rights. While African Americans applauded Theodore Roosevelt for his appointment of blacks to federal office and his public opposition to lynching, they were dismayed by his actions during the 1906 Brownsville riot and his cultivation of southern whites during his 1912 presidential bid.[27] William Howard Taft nominated southern Democrats to office, appointed fewer African Americans to office than his predecessors, and ignored the problems of segregation, disfranchisement, and racial violence. The Harding and Coolidge administrations appointed few African Americans to office and failed to revoke the policy of segregation in the civil service. In the 1928 presidential election, Republican nominee Herbert Hoover was more concerned with attracting white southern support than maintaining ties with the African American community. Once in office, Hoover ignored racial concerns and appointed few African Americans to federal jobs. Efforts by African Americans to secure anti-lynching and enfranchisement legislation during these Republican administrations were unsuccessful.[28]

Despite this rather dismal record, the majority of African American citizens continued to support the Republican Party. The Democratic Party failed to capitalize on African American dissatisfaction with Republican policies; it offered no promising alternatives. Segregation in federal departments increased, for example, under the Democratic administration of Woodrow Wilson. Democratic candidates found the "legacy of Lincoln" that still existed within the African American community difficult to overcome. For the majority of African Americans, the Democratic Party was still the party of oppression due to the political power of its southern wing. For these reasons, conservative African American leaders argued that it was safer to stay within the Republican Party than to switch to the Democratic Party.

The New Deal, the image of Franklin Roosevelt, and new political opportunities within the Democratic Party altered the political allegiance of African Americans to the Republican Party. By the 1936 presidential election, African Americans were overwhelmingly supporting the Democratic Party. Federal relief programs attracted many African American citizens. While racial discrimination existed within the majority of these programs, many African American citizens were able to survive the depression due to this limited economic assistance. The simple inclusion of African Americans within these programs marked a departure from past practice. Economic assistance thus provided large political dividends for the Democratic Party. While Roosevelt, like his Republican predecessors, failed to address the racial concerns of the African American community, many African Americans responded to the New Deal and the Democratic Party for purely economic reasons.[29]

Due to this economic assistance, the activities of Eleanor Roosevelt, and the president's magnetic personality, many African Americans perceived Roosevelt to be a genuine friend to the black community. African Americans began to transfer to Roosevelt the affections that had previously been reserved for Abraham Lincoln. While Lincoln was "Father Abraham," Roosevelt was the "Father of the New Deal." He inherited Lincoln's mantle. Roosevelt personified a government that was now becoming more tangible and relevant to African Americans.

The national Democratic Party offered new political opportunities for many African Americans. While many Republican leaders were encouraging the formation of "lily-white" party organizations in the South and taking the African American vote for granted, Democratic candidates began to court actively the huge concentration of African American voters in northern urban centers. Many African American politicians obtained both elected and appointed positions in local and state organizations in these areas. Many federal agencies began to appoint "racial advisors." For these reasons, many younger African American leaders began to perceive the Democratic Party as a means by which they could advance their own political goals and the interests of their race. The national Democratic Party offered black leaders opportunities that did not exist within the Republican Party.[30]

The *Smith v. Allright* decision was thus delivered during a period of intense political activity within the African American community and at a time when a majority of African Americans had recently abandoned their historical allegiance to the Republican Party. The demise of the white primary presented opportunities for African American participation in elective politics in the South missing since the 1890s. The decision cracked the barriers to the most important election in the South, the Democratic primary. The African American community was ready to take advantage of these new political opportunities.

Atlanta's African American community recognized the importance of the *Smith v. Allright* decision. The day after the Supreme Court's decision was handed down, C.A. Scott announced that he would attempt to vote in the upcoming primary. In the following weeks, social, political, business, and religious leaders announced their intention to vote in the July Fourth primary and urged all African American citizens to register.[31] In May 1944, C.A. Scott and A.T. Walden founded the Fulton County Citizens Democratic Club. Its stated purpose was "to support and participate in the activities of the Democratic Party."[32] The Citizens Democratic Club's first objective was to register African Americans to vote in the primary. A.T. Walden helped to organize eleven Democratic Clubs across the state under an umbrella organization known as the Georgia Association of Citizens Democratic Clubs. These clubs sponsored voter registration drives in their respective communities. By the registration deadline for the primary, approximately ten thousand African Americans across the state had registered.[33]

In early June, a subcommittee of the Georgia Democratic Party Executive Committee asserted its intention to continue to bar African Americans from the July primary. Faced with the prospect that African Americans would be excluded despite their activities, the members of the Fulton County Citizens Democratic Club passed a resolution stating that only officers and members of the club's executive committee would attempt to vote in the upcoming primary. This effort would lay the foundation for a court challenge to Georgia's white primary. Following the passage of this resolution, black leaders urged African American citizens not to attempt to vote in the primary. An editorial in the *Atlanta Daily World* referred to the resolution of the Democratic Club as "a sound course of action, good strategy and indicative of the sober and sound leadership so vitally imperative in these critical hours of world chaos and tension." It urged those who were not members of the Citizens Democratic Club to "accept the action and follow the course outline by officials and thus minimized the cause for misunderstanding and allay fears."[34]

Tension existed in Atlanta in the immediate period before the primary. Rumors circulated the city about possible racial violence. Former Governor Eugene Talmadge, who was already planning another gubernatorial bid, warned of possible violence if African Americans attempted to vote.[35] Prior to the primary, the *Atlanta Constitution* and the *Atlanta Journal* gave brief coverage to the activities of the Citizens Democratic Club. They assured their readers that the attempt to vote on the part of certain officials was simply an action to initiate litigation. Both newspapers urged restraint. The *Atlanta Constitution* warned that "only the most ignorant class of either race would attempt to cause trouble under such conditions."[36] In order to ease tensions and strengthen its legal position, the Executive Committee of the Fulton County Democratic Party instructed precinct clerks to follow the same procedures with African Americans attempting to vote as with white citizens until the actual point of casting a ballot. At this point clerks were to deny African Americans the ballot. Instead of supplying the precincts with complete registration lists, the Executive Committee supplied only the names of those eligible to vote in the primary.

On the day of the primary, three hundred African Americans attempted to vote in nine communities across the state. In addition to Walden and his group, sixteen African Americans appeared at six different polling places in Fulton County. When they attempted to vote, the clerk informed them that their names were not on the registration lists. With the exception of white crowds who gathered at some of the precincts, there were no signs of open hostility or reported incidences of violence.[37]

After consulting with representatives of the national NAACP, the Fulton County Citizens Democratic Club, the Georgia Association of Citizens Democratic Club, the local chapter of the NAACP decided to delay legal proceedings. Thurgood Marshall was trying to persuade the Justice Department to enforce the *Smith v. Allright* decision. He believed that pending litigation would give the Justice Department a reason to postpone criminal indictments. Marshall presented the Attorney General with affidavits detailing suffrage violations in Florida, Alabama, and Georgia. Leaders of the Fulton County Citizens Democratic Club called for a federal probe of violations in Georgia.[38]

African American citizens in Columbus, Georgia decided to file suit after Primus King, an African American minister, was denied the right to vote. While wishing them success in their endeavor, leaders of the Fulton County Citizens Democratic Club called the action of these citizens "both untimely and unwise." Without proper legal representation and documentation, they warned that the suit would be unsuccessful.[39] In October 1945 Judge T. Hoyte Davis, using the legal precedent of *Smith v. Allright*, found the Georgia white primary to be unconstitutional. The state decided to appeal the decision thus temporarily delaying its implementation.

To achieve better communication within the African American community and exchange ideas with the white community, a group of African American citizens decided to establish a public forum at the Butler

Street YMCA, a center of social and political activity within Atlanta's African American community. This organization decided to hold luncheons to be served at minimal cost. It invited social, political, and religious leaders to address the group on issues of concern to the city. While its participants were initially African American, members of all races were welcomed. Established in 1945, this forum became known as the Hungry Club, "hungry for food and ideas." The Hungry Club was not a formal organization or an action group. It did not endorse leaders or their causes. Rather this forum became an acceptable means by which white leaders and citizens could exchange ideas with their counterparts in the African American community.

In January of 1946 U.S. Representative Robert Ramspeck of the Fifth Congressional District of Georgia (DeKalb, Fulton, and Rockdale counties) decided to vacate his seat in mid-term. Rather than appointing someone to fill this vacancy, Governor Ellis Arnall called for a special election to be held in early February. While the white primary was still in effect in Georgia, African Americans could participate in this special election. The Atlanta NAACP, the ACPL, the Fulton County Citizens Democratic Club, and the *Atlanta Daily World* sponsored a voter registration drive. By the time of this election, approximately 6876 African Americans were registered to vote.[40]

Nineteen candidates announced their intention to run in the election. The contest quickly narrowed to two main candidates, Thomas Camp and Helen Douglas Mankin. Thomas Camp had served as Ramspeck's executive secretary and as a lobbyist for the Railroad Association of Georgia. Although regarded as a conservative and endorsed by the politically reactionary "Talmadge crowd," Camp also drew support from moderate individuals and organizations. As the leading candidate throughout the campaign, Camp generally avoided comment on specific issues. Like most southern politicians at this time and on the advice of an African American supporter, Camp ignored the African American vote. He refused to meet with African American leaders for question-and-answer sessions.

Helen Douglas Mankin was an attorney who had served five terms as a state representative from Fulton County. As a state legislator, she supported the progressive reform legislation proposed by the gubernatorial administrations of E.D. Rivers and Ellis Arnall. Mrs. Mankin favored reforms in such areas as child labor, suffrage restrictions, and the operation of prisons and state-supported mental institutions. In her campaign for Congressman Ramspeck's seat, her political support came from white liberals, New Dealers, organized labor, and foes of Eugene Talmadge. In her tenure as state legislator and during the campaign, she did not directly address the race question. She stated on several occasions, however, that social and economic reforms in Georgia would benefit citizens of all races. Unlike Camp, she did not completely ignore the African American vote. She met secretly with African American leaders. Mrs. Mankin and African American leaders feared a public endorsement would hurt her politically.[41] Prior to the election, an editorial in the *Atlanta Daily World* stated, "There is one candidate we favor on the basis of the record above the others...but we think it would be unwise to express our preference in these columns."[42] While the editorial did not mention Helen Douglas Mankin by name, politically informed black voters understood the "coded" language.

On the eve of the election, African American leaders held a mass rally at Wheat Street Baptist Church in order to discuss the candidates' backgrounds and their positions on specific issues. Officially, citizens were urged to vote for the candidate of their choice. At the end of the meeting, African American leaders endorsed Helen Douglas Mankin by name. This late endorsement was made in order to convey their decision to the African American community without informing the city's white voters. Word spread quickly throughout the community that leaders had endorsed Helen Mankin. As to the public record of the election, no African American leader or organization formally endorsed her. The *Atlanta Daily World*'s coverage of the meeting made no mention of an endorsement.[43]

The turnout for the election was extremely light. By early evening, all precincts had reported except for Ward 3-B, an African American precinct. This precinct was adjacent to Atlanta University and included two African American housing projects. Voting had been extremely heavy at this precinct. Officials turned away late arrivals. The voter turnout at Ward 3-B was approximately fifty percent, the highest in the city. Before the votes at this precinct were counted, Thomas Camp led Mrs. Mankin by 156 votes. The outcome of the election depended upon the votes of Ward 3-B. Mrs. Mankin received 956 votes of the 1040 votes cast at the precinct. Thomas Camp received only seven votes.[44]

The national media widely covered this election and the role of the African American vote. *Time* and *Newsweek* magazines credited Mrs. Mankin's victory to the African American vote.[45] Possibly in an effort to allay racial tensions, local coverage of Mrs. Mankin's victory was rather subdued. While both the *Atlanta Journal* and *Atlanta Constitution* acknowledged the role of the African American vote, they stressed that Mrs. Mankin was the choice of both white and African American citizens. In the days immediately following her election, both newspapers downplayed the decisive impact that the African American vote had on the election. The *Atlanta Daily World* also gave only limited coverage to the story. It simply stated that the African American vote determined the outcome of the election. There was no further comment; none was needed. While she publicly thanked her supporters, Mrs. Mankin did not directly comment on the role of the African American vote in her election. She simply spoke of her election as a sign of progress in the South.[46]

In order to capitalize on the momentum generated by the election of Helen Douglas Mankin and mobilize opposition to gubernatorial candidate Eugene Talmadge, leaders of Atlanta's African American community met informally to discuss ways to increase voter registration. They concluded that better coordination between organizations involved in voter registration activities was needed. These leaders decided to pool their resources under a single organization, the All Citizens Registration Committee (ACRC). While this organization was placed under the auspices of the local chapter of the NAACP, the ACRC represented a cross section of the various groups involved in voter registration activities. Members of the ACPL, the Fulton County Citizens Democratic Club, the local chapters of the NAACP and Urban League, and the Alpha Phi Alpha Fraternity participated in this nonpartisan organization.[47]

The ACRC launched a massive registration drive that lasted from early March to early May, the state's deadline to register for the 1946 elections. The goal of this committee was to register twenty-five thousand African American citizens. The heart of this campaign was a door-to-door canvass of Atlanta's African American neighborhoods. Because of its expertise in community organization, the Atlanta Urban League largely directed this effort. Grace Hamilton, Executive Secretary of the League, and R.A. Thompson, the League's Industrial Secretary, organized a detailed survey of the city indicating the precincts, census tracts, and blocks where African Americans resided. Approximately 875 volunteers canvassed these areas urging citizens to register. The ACRC carefully selected ward leaders, precinct captains, and census tract leaders to aid and supervise the activities of the volunteers. The committee stationed workers at the Fulton County Courthouse to direct citizens to the Registrar's Office. The ACRC established a Speaker's Bureau to supply discussion leaders for church groups, private social affairs, and mass meetings.[48]

This campaign was a community effort. At the request of the ACRC, African American churches held "Citizenship Sundays." On these occasions, ministers devoted time in their services to ask members to register.[49] Many black-owned businesses made financial contributions to the drive and urged their employees to register. Labor unions, fraternal organizations, tenant associations, and other social and professional groups requested members to register and participate in the drive. Many of these groups also organized carpools to transport people to the Fulton County Courthouse. The *Atlanta Daily World* gave prominent coverage and strong editorial support to these events. WERD, an African American owned radio station, ran spots urging registration. The Alpha Phi Alpha Fraternity supplied "We Are Registered Voters" stickers. Registered voters proudly placed these stickers on the window frames and doors of their homes. The ACPL supplied "I Have Registered" buttons to members of the community.[50]

In their efforts to register, African American citizens in Atlanta faced little overt white resistance. Two major problems, however, were the accessibility to and operational hours of the Registrar's Office. Atlantans were required to register at the Fulton County Courthouse. A trip to the courthouse was extremely burdensome and time-consuming for African American citizens because public transportation and major street arteries did not extend into the poorer African American neighborhoods. The operational hours of the Registrar's Office were from eight-thirty in the morning to five o'clock in the evening, Monday through Friday, a schedule which made it extremely difficult for working-class applicants, particularly African Americans, to register. The registration drive compounded these problems. The Registrar's Office could not handle the excess crowds generated by the campaign. In late April, the *Atlanta Daily World* noted that hundreds of African Americans attempting to register had been turned away by the Registrar's Office. They were unable to register before the office closed.[51]

In order to solve this problem, African American leaders requested the Registrar's Office to extend its hours of operation. The Registrar's Office established limited hours on Saturday. African American leaders also asked for special registration stations to be established in African American neighborhoods. Prior to this request, the Registrar's Office had used neighborhood registration stations in white areas of the county. Due to excess crowds, officials decided to allow a special "mobile" registration station to open in various African American neighborhoods. Over a three-day period, this station went to three different locations. In each of these neighborhoods, the station opened for three hours. Volunteers from the *Atlanta Daily World*, the Atlanta Urban League, and local African American colleges aided county registrars in handling the crowds. The response was overwhelming. Over a three-day, nine-hour period, approximately 2,383 African Americans registered at these stations. This success marked the end of the registration campaign.[52]

When the overwhelmingly successful campaign ended in early May, over 21,000 African Americans were registered in Atlanta. This figure represented an increase of slightly more than fourteen thousand registered voters over a two-month period. When the campaign began, African American citizens comprised approximately eight percent of the total electorate. When it ended, African American citizens comprised approximately twenty-seven percent of the total electorate.[53] The success of this campaign was largely due to community organization. This drive would serve as an organizational model for future registration drives in Atlanta's African American community.

The success of the registration campaign was also due in part to reform in state suffrage restrictions and the end of the white primary. In February 1945 Georgia became the fourth southern state to abolish the poll tax. In August the Georgia General Assembly lowered the voting age requirement from twenty-one years to eighteen. In April 1946 the United States Supreme Court affirmed the district and appellate court's decision that Georgia's white primary was unconstitutional. Governor Ellis Arnall announced that the state would abide by the Court's decision. He blocked attempts on the part of conservative state legislators to circumvent the decision by repealing all state primary laws. As a result of these reforms, voting in the state increased. The vote in the 1946 primary more than doubled that of the 1942 primary. African American registration in the state increased from 20,000 in 1940 to 125,000 in 1947.[54]

The leaders of Atlanta's African American community realized that increased voter registration would not directly lead to desired changes in race relations. Political education and a program to achieve racial reform were also needed. During the registration campaign, the local chapter of the NAACP reopened its citizenship schools. In order to prepare newly registered voters for the upcoming primary, African American leaders stressed that the intelligent use of the ballot would bring about greater social and political equality.[55] With the ballot, African American leaders believed that they could win concessions from the white community.

One of the major concessions desired by Atlanta's African American community was the employment of African American policemen to patrol black neighborhoods. Relations between the police department and the African American community were extremely poor at this time. One major reason was the lack of proper law enforcement. While black-on-white crime was given a high priority, the police department was largely indifferent toward black-on-black crime. Many policemen refused to patrol African American neighborhoods or respond to emergency calls from these areas. Police indifference contributed to the extremely high crime rate in the African American sections in the city. Disturbed by the high crime rate and motivated by the murder of his brother, C.A. Scott attempted to bring this issue before the public through articles in the *Atlanta Daily World*. City officials ignored his pleas for better law enforcement and the employment of African American officers.[56]

Relations were also poor due to a persistent pattern of police brutality. During the 1930s, the Commission on Interracial Cooperation (CIC) began to document and publicize cases of police brutality. It hoped that these cases would pressure city officials, the police department, or civic and religious groups into addressing this issue. In 1933 the CIC released a report documenting thirty-one instances of police brutality against African American citizens. Of these cases, five resulted in death.[57] A less violent, but perhaps more oppressive, form of brutality was the police department's sweeping use of the city's loitering ordinances. During the 1930s, policemen stopped African Americans who were on the streets past midnight. If these African American citizens could not produce proof of employment, they risked imprisonment for loitering. African American women could be charged with violating the "sundown law," a measure originally designed to control prostitution in the city.[58]

Another intimidating factor in the relationship between Atlanta's African American community and members of the police department was the influence of the Ku Klux Klan. Police membership in the Klan was widespread. Admission to the force and future promotion depended upon the individual's willingness to join the Klan and participate in its activities. Herbert Jenkins, a racial moderate and later to be Atlanta's police chief, felt compelled to join the Klan in order to advance in the department.[59] Several members of the police department openly participated in Klan ceremonies and parades. On one occasion, police officers escorted a Klan parade through the heart of Atlanta's African American community in order to intimidate African American citizens.[60] The Klan was also influential within the Police Committee, the actual governing body of the police department, and the departmental police union.

African American leaders believed that the employment of African American policemen to patrol black communities would be an effective deterrent to the high crime rate and would begin to improve the racial attitudes of the department. Perhaps more importantly, they believed that African American officers would instill a sense of communal and racial pride among African Americans. African American leaders believed that the effective use of the ballot would provide the political leverage to force this concession.

The issue of hiring African American policemen was addressed as early as the 1880s. African American leaders used this demand as a concession for their political support. This effort largely failed because white candidates could renege on their promises without suffering political repercussions. African Americans also could not deliver enough votes to politically warrant this concession. With the advent of the white primary and other voting barriers, leaders were forced to use moral persuasion to press this issue. In an age of white supremacy and racial separation, city officials ignored their pleas.

In 1934 several African American leaders decided to approach Mayor James Key. Because of his "progressive" racial views and the role played by the African American vote in the recall effort, they felt that Key would be sympathetic to the issue of African American police officers. The issue of police brutality had also received attention due to the publication of the CIC report. While he expressed sympathy for their cause, Key told them that white Atlantans and the police force would not accept African American officers at this time. According to Key, a period of racial education was needed. When the time was right, Key pledged that he would authorize the employment of African American policemen.[61]

James Key was unable to keep his pledge. In the 1937 mayoral election, William Hartsfield, a former alderman and state legislator, defeated Key. A major campaign issue was the ineffectiveness and corruption that existed within the police department. Upon assuming office, Hartsfield replaced Police Chief Thurman Sturdivant with Lieutenant Marion Hornsby. As police chief, Hornsby initiated a series of reforms that weeded out corruption and improved the performance of the department. The employment of African American policemen, however, was not one of these reforms. Hornsby opposed the employment of African American officers. He believed that they would be ineffective, create division within the department, and lower morale. During his tenure, Chief Hornsby effectively blocked any action which would lead to the employment of African American police officers.[62]

Mayor Hartsfield tried to avoid the issue of African American policemen. While calling for the fair treatment of all citizens and endorsing Hornsby's reforms, Hartsfield praised and defended the operations of the police department. None of these reforms, however, directly addressed racial concerns. In private meetings with African American leaders,

Hartsfield gave them little hope that African Americans would be employed. He bluntly informed one African American leader that he would listen when "you get me ten thousand votes."[63]

Hartsfield's initial response to the issue of African American policemen was shaped by political considerations and reflected his previous positions on racial issues. The actual power to employ African American police officers rested with the Board of Aldermen, the Police Committee, and Chief Hornsby. Mayor Hartsfield could thus avoid taking a stance on this politically volatile issue. Also due to the political infighting that had previously occurred within the department over his replacement of Sturdivant, Hartsfield could not publicly rebuke the decision of his police chief. He also had little to fear from the electorate. At this time, the majority of white Atlantans were either opposed or indifferent toward this issue. The only political threat to Hartsfield on this particular issue came from the African American community. With the white primary and voting restrictions in place, this threat was minimal.

Mayor Hartsfield's response also reflected his previous positions on race-related issues. As a city alderman in 1926, Hartsfield introduced an ordinance prohibiting African American barbers from cutting the hair of white customers. In 1942, while trying to gain support for the annexation of the adjacent Buckhead community, he privately warned residents of the possibility of African American political control if the city did not increase in size.[64] In 1944 Hartsfield urged the chairman of the House Un-American Activities Committee to investigate the NAACP. He claimed that the organization was secretly supporting "professional white agitators...who were...stirring up racial questions in the South, especially among educators, church groups, and women's groups."[65] While these positions reflected the views of a majority of his constituents and white southerners, they hardly marked him as a white liberal.

Undeterred by Hartsfield's indifferent response, Atlanta's African American community accelerated its campaign for black police officers. In 1945 the United Negro Veterans Organization sponsored a public demonstration in support of hiring African American policemen. Over one hundred participants marched from Auburn Avenue, the "heart" of Atlanta's African American community, to City Hall. They carried signs which called for "Employment to Negro Police." Afterwards the demonstrators held a mass meeting in front of City Hall. The demonstration was peaceful and orderly. While certainly capturing the attention of the white community, the demonstration drew criticism from many African American leaders. The *Atlanta Daily World* characterized the demonstration as being "ill-advised" and "inopportune." It called upon the United Negro Veterans Organization to stop "appealing to mass pressure and prejudices in the achievement of its objectives." The editorial stressed that only a "practical education plan" would lead to the employment of African American officers.[66]

Instead of public demonstrations, African American leaders urged citizens to register for the upcoming mayoral election. In order to protest Hartsfield's handling of the police issue, several leaders endorsed the mayoral candidacy of G. Dan Bridges, a city alderman and chairman of the Police Committee. During the campaign, Bridges promised to address the issue of police brutality if elected.[67] The African American vote was not yet sufficient to influence the election. Hartsfield was re-elected in 1945.

Due to the increasing activism in the African American community and the city's high crime rate, the demand for African American policemen to patrol black neighborhoods began to receive attention from the white community. Continuing the work of the CIC, the Southern Regional Council (SRC) provided city officials and local organizations with surveys illustrating the successful employment of African American policemen in other large southern cities. To reach a wider audience, the Southern Regional Council published surveys and articles supporting the use of African American policemen in its publication, the *New South*.[68] SRC officials hoped that education on the issue would lead to the peaceful employment of African American officers. The SRC served as an important link between leaders of both races. It also gave advice to organizations, both white and African American, as to how petitions should be written.[69]

Religious and professional women organizations also became involved in the issue. Concerned over the high crime rate, women from Methodist churches in the area petitioned the Board of Aldermen for the employment of African American policemen.[70] The Atlanta Council of Church Women also petitioned the Board. In 1946 the Atlanta Chapter of the American Association of University Women sponsored forums to discuss the issue. The issue of employing African American policemen also drew the support of newspaper editors and professional organizations. Ralph McGill, editor of the *Atlanta Constitution*, advocated the employment of African American policemen in his daily columns and magazine articles. Eventually, the Atlanta Bar Association and the Fulton County Grand Jury expressed their support.[71]

White proponents of this issue believed that the employment of African American officers would be the single most effective means of combating the city's high crime rate and mending strained racial relations. Increasingly, petitions began to list southern cities where the employment of African

American policemen proved successful.[72] While these cities were presented as models to follow, these listings clearly insinuated that Atlanta was not as racially progressive as its peers. Many of these petitions also expressed the concern that the high crime rate was damaging to the city's image. The petition of the Atlanta Council of Church Women stated that its members were "both shocked and disturbed over the inevitable smirch that has come upon the name of the city and its listing as almost leading the nation in the number of murders committed each year."[73] This last reference could have been to an article which appeared in *Newsweek* magazine. Entitled "Atlanta's Junior Hoodlums," the article noted Atlanta's high crime rate, particularly among its youth.[74] Several organizations were concerned and embarrassed by this type of national exposure. Racial reform was not directly mentioned in these petitions as a reason for the employment of African American police officers.

Support within the white community provided the opportunity for Mayor Hartsfield to change his position without suffering major political repercussions. Eventually realizing the necessity of the employment of African American officers, Hartsfield cautiously began to encourage this support. In late 1945 he suggested to Guy Johnson, Executive Director of the Southern Regional Council, that civic and religious organizations, rather than civil rights agencies, should bring this issue to the public. The mayor also suggested that newspaper editors be solicited for their support.[75] Hartsfield shrewdly realized that a majority of white citizens would oppose the employment of African American policemen if it was presented as a civil rights issue. The hiring of African American policemen on the grounds of racial reform would be a direct criticism and violation of southern mores. Hartsfield believed that white citizens would approve of the hiring of black officers if it was presented as a "law-and-order" issue or a "progressive" reform. When African American leaders met with Hartsfield following the 1946 registration campaign, he indicated his support for the employment of African American officers to patrol black communities.[76]

Upon the sudden death of Marion Hornsby in 1947, Mayor Hartsfield appointed Herbert Jenkins, a proponent of African American officers, to be police chief. Jenkins had served within the department for more than fifteen years. As a police aide and chauffeur to Mayor Key in the 1930s, he attended meetings in which leaders discussed the issue of African American policemen. In 1946 Jenkins had suggested that a departmental survey of southern cities employing African American policemen be conducted in order to examine their use. Stating that no African American policemen would be employed in Atlanta, Chief Hornsby vetoed this proposal.[77] Upon assuming office, Jenkins' major goal was to modernize the department. He introduced uniform training procedures for all police officers; sought court approval to establish a mandatory retirement age; established an internal affairs committee to investigate charges of police brutality and misconduct; and discouraged police membership in the Ku Klux Klan and other hate organizations. Improving relations with the African American community was an important component of Chief Jenkins' plan to modernize the police department.[78] Jenkins realized that better relations depended upon the employment of African American officers.

Mayor Hartsfield and Chief Jenkins did not have the authority to hire African American officers. Responsibility rested with the Board of Aldermen. Several members of the Board publicly expressed support for the proposal. When the issue was presented before the Board in November 1947, it decided to refer the matter to the Police Committee with instructions that a hearing be held to determine public reaction to the measure. While there was probably sufficient support within both bodies to pass the proposal, the Board of Aldermen provided the opportunity for the opposition to express its position.

The forum was held in late November 1947. Private individuals and representatives from civic, business, and religious organizations appeared before the Police Committee. Opponents of the proposal argued that the employment of African Americans would lower the morale and reputation of the department. Many viewed the proposal as an attack on southern values and attitudes. One speaker voiced his opposition on the ground that "Negroes are incapable of showing equality with the white man." Two political figures, former Atlanta Mayor Walter Sims and Georgia Commissioner of Agriculture Tom Linder, condemned the proposal. Voicing the concerns of many local and state politicians, Walter Sims argued that the proposal was a political measure brought about by increasing African American registration in the city.

Proponents of the measure countered these arguments. Chief Jenkins and African American leaders argued that the high incidence of crime within the African American community threatened the city if ignored. Supporters tried to soothe racial fears. They stressed that African American officers would patrol only black neighborhoods and would not have the authority to arrest white citizens. Many pointed to the success of other southern cities in employing African American policemen. African American leaders stressed that the proposal would lead to better relations between the police department and the black community.[79]

After the hearing, the Police Committee decided that it would not approve of the proposal unless Chief Jenkins wrote a public letter of recommendation. The purpose of this letter was to alleviate racial fears. Clearly the letter also served as a means by which members of the Board of Aldermen and the mayor could protect themselves from controversy. Members of the Board could use the recommendation of the police chief as a convenient excuse to vote for the proposal. While cautiously building support for the proposal behind-the-scenes and urging Jenkins to write the letter, Mayor Hartsfield kept a low profile throughout the debate. Because of his prominent role in the approval of the decision, Jenkins would have served as the scapegoat if racial problems developed.

In his letter of recommendation, Jenkins listed several "conditions" under which African Americans "could successfully be employed." African American police officers "would not be allowed to exercise police power over white people." They were to be denied Civil Service status "until their success has been proven." A separate precinct station for African American officers was to be established by the department. Chief Jenkins promised to send a delegation to other southern cities to study their use of African American officers.[80] These requirements directly addressed many of the concerns of white Atlantans. Before suggesting these conditions, Jenkins discussed this issue with several southern chiefs of police. The conditions suggested in the letter were almost identical to requirements established by other southern police departments.

The carefully worded resolution to hire African American policemen sought to ensure white Atlantans that the employment of African American officers would pose no threat to southern racial conventions. According to the resolution, a "large number of citizens and civic organizations as well as both daily newspapers" supported the employment of African American policemen in order to halt "the mounting crime and murder rate in negro sections of the city." African American officers would be "approved on a trial basis, with the distinct understanding that they are to be used in negro sections only, under such rules and regulations and under conditions as will not create any friction or tensions between the races." The resolution called for the certification of at least eight officers.[81] In December 1947 the Board of Aldermen approved the resolution by a ten-to-seven vote. Mayor Hartsfield signed the resolution without fanfare.

Immediately following the passage of the resolution, posters denouncing Mayor Hartsfield and members of the Board of Aldermen appeared throughout the city. In an attempt to discredit municipal officials, completely unfounded rumors circulated the city that the Rosenwald Fund had secretly bribed the mayor and Chief Jenkins to employ African American police officers.[82] Many members of the police department also opposed the employment of African Americans. Jenkins later estimated that ninety percent of the department's personnel opposed the decision.[83] To calm this dissension, he appeared before each watch to discuss the issue. Jenkins also transferred some white policemen who could not accept the black officers. While racial tensions on the police force were evident for a period of time, this opposition declined as African American policemen proved their value to the department.

The most serious public opposition was a suit filed in Superior Court challenging the legality of the resolution. This suit, *Yarn v. Atlanta*, contended that the restrictions placed upon the territorial assignments and arrest powers of black officers were unconstitutional. The Georgia State Supreme Court eventually dismissed the case on the ground that the chief of police had the sole authority to assign duties and territories to officers.[84] Many police chiefs in the state used this decision as a legal justification for the various restrictions placed upon the duties of African American police officers.

Despite this initial opposition, the Police Committee with the assistance of C.A. Scott chose eight African Americans to serve as police officers. They paid careful attention to choosing the eight best-qualified applicants. Chief Jenkins and members of the Police Committee spent over two months interviewing and selecting those chosen. These candidates underwent the same recruitment process and training procedures as white officers.[85] In April 1948 African American policemen first began to patrol black neighborhoods. The first day was one of celebration within the African American community as black citizens lined the street to observe the new officers. They cheered and paraded behind the black policemen.[86] African American leaders considered the employment of black officers to be a major civil rights victory.

Jenkins established a separate precinct station for African American officers at the Butler Street YMCA. Because of the fear that isolated attacks might be directed against them, African American officers were required to dress and keep their police equipment at the "Y". They patrolled only African American neighborhoods and basically operated as a separate unit within the department. While restrictions on arresting white citizens remained in effect, African American officers occasionally arrested white citizens. They also presented these cases in court. Regulations, however, required African American policemen to obtain the signature of a white officer on the arrest charges.[87]

As African American policemen proved their value to the community, restrictions on their duties and number were gradually removed. In 1950, the police department discontinued its use of the Butler Street YMCA as a separate precinct station and moved the African American officers into the main headquarters. The department began to allow African American policemen to wear their uniforms home and to court. The number of African Americans employed by the Atlanta Police Department slowly increased. By 1957 twenty-seven officers and four plainclothes detectives were African American. In 1959 there were forty African American officers, roughly six percent of the police force. By 1968 twenty percent of the department's personnel were African American, the highest percentage of African Americans on a major metropolitan police force in the nation.[88]

During the 1950s professional and civil rights organizations began to request the removal of all restrictions on African American police officers. Despite the support of several municipal officials, local newspapers, and Chief Jenkins, the Board of Aldermen and members of the Police Committee were reluctant to remove all restrictions.[89] Faced with this hesitancy, Chief Jenkins unilaterally removed all remaining restrictions in April 1962.[90] He used the *Yarn* decision as the basis for his authority.

The end of the white primary and the employment of African American police officers were milestones in the relations between Atlanta's African American and white communities. Increasing registration augmented the political power of Atlanta's African American community. Using this newfound political power, the African American community was able to pressure city officials for concessions. During the campaign for police officers, African American leaders developed new strategies to bring about social and political change and established new lines of communication with the white community. These events inaugurated a new approach to ease racial tensions in the city.

This approach involved the use of private negotiations between African American and white leaders as a means to ease racial problems. An important second component, and one often ignored, was education. Many African American leaders believed that an awareness on the part of the white community of the needs and desires of the black community would lead to greater racial understanding. By discussing immediate racial problems and working together to solve them, leaders of both communities could facilitate changes in race relations.

This approach had limitations as to the tactics and strategies utilized by African American leaders and organizations, the demands that could be made, and the pace of racial change. While various African American leaders and organizations had conducted demonstrations and boycotts in Atlanta prior to this time, the majority of African American leaders did not approve of these tactics. They feared that public demonstrations would be harmful to the negotiating process, create greater racial strife, or possibly lead to a conservative white backlash. Leaders urged citizens to show their discontent by voting. Rather than the use of public demonstrations, most favored litigation if political pressure and negotiations proved unsuccessful.

As shown in the private negotiations and public debate regarding the employment of African American policemen, black leaders worked for improved social and political conditions within the framework of segregation. They were temporarily willing to settle for "half-a-loaf." Leaders of both races were bound by existing racial attitudes and political realities. James Key and William Hartsfield repeatedly warned African American leaders that moderate white officials would be defeated by conservative candidates if the African American community pressed too quickly for reforms.

By using this approach, racial reform would necessarily be a gradual if not glacial process. Without adequate bargaining power, Atlanta's African American community was unable to place its demands on the white community's political agenda. For example, the employment of African American policemen was intermittently discussed over a period of sixty years. Because the focus of the discussion was on the conditions under which the African American policemen would operate instead of addressing the more fundamental issues of civil and political rights, these negotiations were conducted in a piecemeal fashion. Without the application of direct pressure by the African American community, negotiations were long and tedious processes. By utilizing a strategy of negotiations and litigation, the wait for justice was extremely long and often disappointing.

With the exception of those adamantly opposed to any type of racial reform, the use of negotiations to ease racial tensions received the approval of various segments of the white community. To those who supported gradual racial reform and those who foresaw racial change as inevitable, negotiations had several advantages. The use of negotiations drew upon the progressive belief that gradual racial reform could be achieved through constructive dialogue between white and African American leaders. Various religious and human relations organizations called for such discussions. Negotiations, according to these groups, allowed for the gradual transformation of racial attitudes. By discussing racial problems, they believed that racial change could be achieved without violence. "Good race relations" came to be defined among these organizations as an absence of violence and racial conflict. Overt acts of racial hostility on both sides were harmful to relations between the races and the social and economic progress of the region.

Atlanta's white leadership structure favored the use of negotiations to ease racial tensions. By using this approach white leaders controlled the pace of racial change in the city while maintaining their social and political control. Negotiations were generally limited to "moderate" white business and political leaders and "acknowledged" African American leaders. Militant viewpoints on the race question—white and African American, liberal and conservative—were excluded. Bound by prevailing social customs, racial attitudes, and political realities, a small group of leaders made decisions regarding the scope and pace of race reform in Atlanta. Public forums were held at various times to discuss racial issues. Rather than utilize as a means to formulate policy, leaders generally held rallies and mass meetings in order to build support for decisions already made or for opponents to constructively vent their frustrations. Clearly, white leaders also used negotiations as a means to delay racial reform.

As shown in the campaign for the employment of African American police officers, the use of negotiations at this time had advantages for Atlanta's African American community. Negotiations were a means by which Atlanta's African American community could effectively air its grievances. Race reform, if limited, was achieved and reform often led to more changes. By using negotiations, Atlanta's African American community was able to broaden its lines of communication with the white community. African American leaders began a new and constructive dialogue with representatives of white professional, religious, and civic organizations in the city. These organizations would probably have been hesitant to support the employment of African American police officers if more militant tactics had been employed. Increased African American registration augmented the political bargaining power of Atlanta's African American community enabling it to wrest increasingly significant concessions from white officials. Finally, the use of negotiations created a peaceful, if somewhat artificial, atmosphere in which racial reform could occur.

One of the major disadvantages to the use of negotiations was that the pace of racial change largely remained under the control of the white community. For this reason, African American leaders debated the efficacy of negotiations. Reverend Martin Luther King, Sr., a frequent participant in the negotiating sessions, believed that picketing and public demonstrations were sometimes necessary to pressure city officials. A.T. Walden supported the use of negotiated settlements and litigation. John Wesley Dobbs advocated hard political bargaining. C.A. Scott believed that racial tensions could be solved through constructive dialogue between the races. Despite these differences, all leaders stressed the primacy of the ballot. The majority supported negotiations or discussions as a first step in easing racial tensions.

Prior to the adoption of a systematic strategy of negotiations with moderate whites, African American leaders met with city and business leaders on an ad hoc basis. Without adequate bargaining power, these initial meetings were unsuccessful. In order to capitalize on the African American community's newfound political power, leaders realized that they needed a more formal organization. The goals of this organization were to educate the community as to the major racial issues and unite it behind desirable political candidates.

In the fall of 1949, A.T. Walden, a Democrat, and John Wesley Dobbs, a Republican, organized the nonpartisan Atlanta Negro Voters League (ANVL). While members were free to participate in the activities of their respective national parties, they were required to publicly support the local candidates endorsed by the ANVL. The net result of these activities was a large and effective African American voting bloc. With one or two exceptions, the majority of the candidates endorsed by the ANVL were successful in their bids for office. The ANVL had to place a special logo on its endorsed slate of candidates in order to thwart other organizations or individuals from creating bogus tickets. City officials recognized the political strength of the ANVL. The white leadership structure regarded officials of the ANVL as the principal negotiators and spokespeople for Atlanta's African American community. While many of Atlanta's African American leaders disdained the concept of bloc voting, they found it to be a pragmatic and effective defense against racial oppression.[92]

The formation of the ANVL reflected the changes occurring in the relations between the two races. The major catalyst behind these changes was the end of the white primary. With increasing African American registration, leaders were able to pressure the white community for limited concessions. Largely for this reason, African American leaders adopted the use of negotiations to solve racial problems. The ANVL became the conduit through which the grievances and desires of the African American community were expressed.

In an editorial entitled "Our Second Real Emancipation," C.A. Scott stated that the *Primus King* decision "gives us political equality and will prove to be the beginning of real democracy in Georgia."[93] While Atlanta's African American leaders realized the long struggle ahead, they believed that the mechanisms to achieve racial change were in place. Armed once again with the ballot, African American leaders believed that racial change would occur.

Notes

1. *Atlanta Constitution*, 5 July 1944.

2. Stephen Lawson, *Black Ballots: Voting Rights in the South, 1944–1969* (New York: Columbia University Press, 1976), p. 4.

3. The *Cruikshank* case arose when an armed white mob in Louisiana murdered over one hundred African Americans over a disputed gubernatorial election in 1873. These men were found guilty of violating section six of the Enforcement Act which forbade conspiracies to deny the suffrage rights of citizens. The plaintiffs appealed on the grounds that their indictments on federal charges were faulty. Lucy E. Salyer, "*United States v. Cruikshank*," in *The Oxford Companion to the Supreme Court of the United States*, ed. Kermit L. Hall (New York: Oxford University Press, Inc., 1992), p. 209.

4. *The United States v. Reese* arose when a Kentucky electoral official refused to register an African American citizen for a municipal election. He was indicted under the Enforcement Act for refusing to register a citizen on the basis of race. This suit was the Supreme Court's first suffrage case under the provisions of the Fifteenth Amendment and the Enforcement Act. Ward E.Y. Elliot, "*United States v. Reese*," in *The Oxford Companion to the Supreme Court of the United States*, ed. Kermit L. Hall (New York: Oxford University Press, Inc., 1992), p. 714.

5. Lawson, pp. 4–5.

6. Southern Democrats did not deliver the votes necessary to elect James Garfield Speaker of the House. Hayes withdrew his support for the Texas and Pacific Railroad. C. Vann Woodward, *Origins of the New South, 1877–1913*, 2nd ed. (Baton Rouge: Louisiana State University Press, 1971), pp. 23–47.

7. J. Morgan Kousser, *The Shaping of Southern Politics: Suffrage Restriction and the Establishment of the One-Party South, 1880–1910* (New Haven: Yale University Press, 1974), p. 28.

8. African American farmers formed the Colored Farmer's National Alliance and Cooperative Union as a parallel organization to the white Southern Farmers Alliance in 1888. By 1891 this organization claimed more than a million members in twelve state organizations. See Lawrence Goodwyn, *The Populist Movement: A Short History of the Agrarian Revolt in America* (New York: Oxford University Press, Inc., 1978), pp. 118–123.

9. Kousser, p. 36.

10. Earle and Merle Black, *Politics and Society in the South* (Cambridge: Harvard University Press, 1987), pp. 84–87; V.O. Key, *Southern Politics in State and Nation* (New York: Alfred A. Knopf, 1949), pp. 619–643; Kousser, pp. 28–36; Lawson, pp. 23–44; Donald R. Matthews and James R. Prothro, *Negroes and the New Southern Politics* (New York: Harcourt, Brace, and World, 1963), pp. 16–17; and C. Vann Woodward, pp. 235–290, 321–349.

11. In 1869 the United States Congress reinstituted military rule in Georgia after the state legislature expelled twenty-eight African American members from both houses. Georgia had to ratify the Fifteenth Amendment before she could be restored to the union. In 1870 the state legislature restored the seats of the African American members and expelled twenty-nine white conservatives. That same year, the state ratified the Fifteenth Amendment. In 1871 Georgia was restored to the Union. In a special election in December, Democrat James W. Smith was elected governor. With the Democrats in control of both houses, Georgia was "redeemed."

12. Kousser, p. 211.

13. The Atlanta Democratic Executive Committee allowed African American participation in the 1896 city elections due to the strength of the Populist Party in Georgia. It readopted the white primary in 1897. C.A. Bacote, "The Negro in Atlanta Politics," *Phylon* XIV (Fourth Quarter, 1955), pp. 337–339.

14. Kenneth Coleman, ed., *A History of Georgia* (Athens: University of Georgia Press, 1977), p. 279.

15. Dewey W. Grantham, Jr., *Hoke Smith and the Politics of the New South* (Baton Rouge: Louisiana State University Press, 1958), p. 150.

16. Grantham, p. 151; and Kousser, pp. 218–220.

17. Grantham, p. 159.

18. *Atlanta Journal*, 4 April 1944; and Atlanta Urban League, "Good News From Georgia," 25 April 1944; p. 3, Grace Towns Hamilton Papers, Box: 7, Folder: 2, Atlanta History Center, Library and Archives, Atlanta, Georgia.

19. *Atlanta Constitution*, 5 April 1944; and *Atlanta Journal*, 4 April 1944.

20. Bacote, p. 344.

21. Interview with Herbert T. Jenkins, May 14, 1969, p. 47, by Thomas H. Baker, LBJ Oral History Collection, Lyndon B. Johnson Presidential Library, Austin, Texas.

22. Sources used for the discussion of past political activity in Atlanta include: C.A. Bacote, "The Negro in Atlanta Politics," *Phylon* (Fourth

Quarter, 1955), pp. 333–350; Paul Bolster, "Civil Rights Movements in Twentieth Century Georgia" (Ph.D. dissertation, University of Georgia, 1972); John H. Calhoun, "Some Contributions of Negro Leaders to the Progress of Atlanta" (Master's thesis, Atlanta University, 1968); Irene Hill, "Black Political Behavior in Atlanta, Georgia: An Analysis of the Politics of Exchange, 1908–1973," (Master's thesis, Atlanta University, 1980); Herbert Jenkins, *Keeping the Peace: A Police Chief Looks at His Job* (New York: Harper and Row, 1970); Martin Luther King, Sr. with Clayton Riley, *Daddy King: An Autobiography* (New York: William Morrow, 1980); Clifford M. Kuhn, Harlon E. Joye, and E. Bernard West, *Living Atlanta: An Oral History of the City, 1914–1948* (Athens: University of Georgia Press, 1990); Benjamin Mays, *Born to Rebel: An Autobiography* (New York: Scribner, 1971; reprint edition, Athens: University of Georgia Press, 1987); Sharon Mullis, "The Public Career of Grace Towns Hamilton: A Citizen too Busy to Hate" (Ph.D. dissertation, Emory University, 1976); Jacqueline Rouse, *Lugenia Burns Hope: Southern Reformer* (Athens: University of Georgia Press, 1989); and Michael Suber, "The Internal Black Politics of Atlanta: An Analytic Study of Leadership Roles and Organizational Thrusts," (Ph.D. dissertation, Atlanta University, 1975).

23.   Bacote, pp. 342–343; and Rouse, pp. 119–120.

24.   Bolster, p. 86; and Hill, pp. 28–29.

25.   King with Riley, pp. 100–101.

26.   Author's Interview with C.A. Scott, 20 February 1991.

27.   In 1906 three companies of the Twenty-Fifth Regiment, composed of African Americans, were involved in a riot in Brownsville, Texas. In November, on the basis of an inspector's report which blamed the African American soldiers, Roosevelt dismissed the entire battalion and disqualified its members for service in either the military or the civil service of the United States. This action outraged African American leaders.

28.   George Brown Tindall, *The Disruption of the Solid South* (New York: W.W. Norton Company, 1972), pp. 1–21; and Nancy Weiss, *Farewell to the Party of Lincoln: Black Politics in the Age of FDR* (Princeton: Princeton University Press, 1983), pp. 4–5, 15–17.

29.   In her study of African American political activity during the New Deal period, Nancy Weiss makes the convincing argument that African Americans became members of the Democratic Party largely in response to the economic benefits of the New Deal.

30.   Weiss, pp. 209–235.

31.   These leaders included: F.B. Washington, Director of Atlanta University's School of Social Work; A.T. Walden, legal counsel for the

NAACP; Reverend Martin Luther King, Sr., pastor of Ebenezer Baptist Church; C.L. Harper, President of the local branch of the NAACP and Executive Secretary of the Georgia Teachers and Education Association; Clarence Bacote, history professor at Atlanta University; and Grace Towns Hamilton, Executive Secretary of the Atlanta Urban League. *Atlanta Daily World*, 5 April–5 May 1944.

32.   Author's Interview with C.A. Scott; and *Atlanta Daily World*, 24 May 1944.

33.   Atlanta Urban League, "Good News from Georgia," p. 2.

34.   *Atlanta Daily World*, 30 June 1944, 4 July 1944.

35.   Kuhn, Joye, and West, *Living Atlanta*, p. 322.

36.   *Atlanta Constitution*, 1 July 1944; and *Atlanta Journal*, 2 July 1944.

37.   *Atlanta Constitution*, 4–5 July 1944.

38.   Despite appeals by Thurgood Marshall and leaders of the Fulton County Citizens Democratic Club, Attorney General Francis Biddle decided not to prosecute suffrage violations. Lawson, pp. 48–49.

39.   *Atlanta Daily World*, 26 August 1944.

40.   Bacote, p. 344.

41.   Lorraine Spritzer, *The Belle of Ashby Street: Helen Douglas Mankin and Georgia Politics* (Athens: University of Georgia Press, 1982), pp. 63–74.

42.   *Atlanta Daily World*, 10 February 1946.

43.   The *Atlanta Daily World* asked citizens to vote for the candidate of their choice. The coverage of the mass meeting simply noted speakers. There was no mention of any political endorsement. *Atlanta Daily World*, 12 February 1946.

44.   Spritzer, p. 72, and *Atlanta Constitution*, 13 February 1946.

45.   "Georgia's Black Ballots," *Newsweek*, 27 (29 February 1946): 28; and "Precinct 3B," *Time*, 47 (25 February 1946): 22.

46.   *Atlanta Daily World*, 13 February 1946; and *Atlanta Journal*, 13 February 1946.

47.   *Atlanta Daily World*, 12 March 1946.

48.   *Atlanta Daily World*, 13 March 1946; Bacote, p. 346; and Kuhn, Joye, and Bernard, pp. 334, 337.

49.   Walter Van Jackson, Letter to Pastors, 21 March 1946; Clarence Bacote, Letter to Pastors, 12 April 1946, Grace Towns Hamilton Papers, Box: 7, Folder: 1; and *Atlanta Daily World*, 17 March 1946.

50.   *Atlanta Daily World*, 21 April 1946, and Bacote, p. 347.

51.   *Atlanta Daily World*, 25 April 1946.

52.   On 1 May, 678 African American citizens registered at the Butler Street YMCA. On 2 May, 750 African Americans registered at the University and John Hope Homes. On 3 May, 955 African Americans registered at the Pollard Funeral Home in the Pittsburgh-Summerhill area of the city. *Atlanta Daily World*, 2–4 May 1946; and Bacote, p. 348.

53.   Jack Walker, "Negro Voting in Atlanta, Georgia, 1953–1963," *Phylon* XXIV (Winter 1963): 380.

54.   Lawson, p. 134.

55.   Bacote, p. 348.

56.   Author's Interview with C.A. Scott; and Jenkins, pp. 24–25.

57.   Commission on Interracial Cooperation, "Police Brutality in Atlanta," Commission on Interracial Cooperation Papers, Woodruff Library, Atlanta University, Atlanta, Georgia.

58.   Kuhn, Joye, and West, pp. 338–339.

59.   Jenkins, p. 4.

60.   Jenkins, pp. 4, 19, 23–24; and Kuhn, Joye, and West, pp. 313–317.

61.   Jenkins, pp. 9–10; and Kuhn, Joye, and West, p. 340.

62.   Charles L. Rosenzweig, "The Issue of Employing Black Policemen in Atlanta," (Master's thesis, Emory University, 1980) pp. 36–38, 40–41, 53.

63.   Harold Martin, *William Berry Hartsfield: Mayor of Atlanta* (Athens: University of Georgia Press, 1978), p. 50; Kuhn, Joye, and West, p. 341; and Rosenzweig, pp. 63–64.

64.   Kuhn, Joye, and West, pp. 329–330.

65.   Martin, p. 46.

66.   *Atlanta Daily World*, 5 March 1945.

67.   Kuhn, Joye, and West, pp. 341, 347–349.

68.   See Harold Fleming, "How Negro Police Worked Out in One Southern City," *New South* 2 (October 1947): 3–5, 7; John A. McCray, "South Carolina Police Chief Praises Work of Negro Officers," *New South* 2 (November 1947): 3,5; and Margaret Price, "South Finding Negro Police Valuable, SRC Poll Shows," *New South* 2 (October 1947): 2.

69.   Interview with Harold Fleming conducted by Jed Dannenbaum and Kathleen Dowdey, Ralph McGill Papers, Woodruff Library, Emory University, Atlanta, Georgia.

70.   Petition from Methodist Women Requesting Negro Policemen, 5 February 1943, Southern Regional Council Papers, 1:42:1448, Woodruff Library, Atlanta University, Atlanta, Georgia.

71.   Rosenzweig, pp. 58–62.

72. Petitions from Methodist Women, the United Negro Veterans Organization, Atlanta Council on Church Women, and Women from Various Churches in the Atlanta East and Atlanta West Districts listed southern cities which had successfully employed African American policemen. These petitions are located in the Southern Regional Council Papers, 1:42:1448.

73. Petition from the Atlanta Council of Church Women, Southern Regional Council Papers, 1:42:1448.

74. "Atlanta Junior Hoodlums," *Newsweek*, 27 (1 April 1946): 25.

75. Guy Johnson, letter to C.L. Harper, 30 November 1945, Southern Regional Council Papers, 1:42:1448.

76. Jenkins, p. 25; Kuhn, Joye, and West, p. 341; and Rosenzweig, pp. 65–67.

77. Rosenzweig, p. 53.

78. Jenkins, pp. 18–24.

79. *Atlanta Constitution*, 28 November 1947; *Atlanta Daily World*, 28 November 1947; Rosenzweig, pp. 65–67; and "Race Hatred Gets A Hearing," *New South*, 2/3 (December/January, 1947/1948): 7.

80. Herbert Jenkins, Letter to the Chairman, Police Committee, Atlanta Board of Mayor and Alderman, 1 December 1947, Herbert Jenkins Papers, Box: 5, Atlanta History Center, Library and Archives, Atlanta, Georgia.

81. Resolution by Alderman Ralph Huie to the Board of Aldermen, 4 December 1947.

82. Rosenzweig, pp. 77, 81–82.

83. Herbert Jenkins, address, "Understanding the Community: Community Changes As It Affects Police-Community Relations," Michigan State University, 23 May 1961, transcript, Herbert Jenkins Papers, Box: 15.

84. Rosenzweig, pp. 77–81.

85. Author's Interview with C.A. Scott; and Jenkins, *Keeping*, pp. 26–27.

86. *Atlanta Constitution*, 4 April 1948.

87. Jenkins, *Keeping*, pp. 27–28; and Rosenzweig, p. 72.

88. Ronald H. Bayor, "Race and City Services: The Shaping of Atlanta's Police and Fire Departments," *Atlanta History*, 36 (3/Fall 1992): 19–24; and Jenkins, *Keeping*, p. 31.

89. Mayor Ivan Allen, the *Atlanta Journal* and *Constitution*, and organizations such as the American Civil Liberties Union, and the Atlanta Council on Human Relations supported the removal of restrictions on the duties of African American officers. Upon request of the Board of

Aldermen, Jenkins wrote a letter recommending the removal of all restrictions. The Police Committee sponsored a public hearing to discuss the issue. Members of the Police Committee, however, took no course of action upon the completion of the hearing.

90.   Jenkins' order removing the restrictions appeared without fanfare in the Daily Bulletin of the Atlanta Police Department. "Atlanta Police Department Daily Bulletin," 30 April 1962, #at-102, Herbert Jenkins Papers, Box: 5.

91.   Author's Interview with LeRoy Johnson, 13 November 1990; and Author's Interview with C.A. Scott.

92.   *Atlanta Daily World*, 14 October 1944.

II

The Politics of Race

Atlantans re-elected William Hartsfield to a fourth term as mayor in 1949.[1] The key to his victory was his ability to obtain the political and financial backing of Atlanta's white business community, white voters on the north side of the city, civic and good government organizations, and the leadership of the African American community. Representatives of these interests formed the nucleus of Hartsfield's administrations. This carefully constructed political coalition not only dominated the city's political leadership, but to a large extent controlled the response to and pace of racial and social change in Atlanta during the 1950s.

Representatives of the business community were ardent and long-time supporters of Mayor Hartsfield. The mayor established close personal and political ties with most of the city's prominent business leaders even though he was not of the same social background and economic status. In the early 1900s, Hartsfield met Robert Woodruff, later to be president of the Coca-Cola Company. As a city alderman in the 1920s, Hartsfield served with Everett Millican of the Gulf Oil Company. Woodruff and Millican introduced Hartsfield to other members of Atlanta's business community. Because of their own social status and reputation within the community, the support of these two men influenced other business leaders to back Hartsfield's political ambitions. In return for their support, Hartsfield regularly sought the advice and guidance of a "kitchen cabinet" of business leaders on matters relating to municipal policy.[2]

Atlanta's white business community had a definite agenda. Its major goals were to attract new industries to the area and revitalize the downtown business district. During the 1920s the Atlanta Chamber of Commerce began actively to pursue these goals. In 1925 it initiated an $825,000 advertising campaign known as Forward Atlanta. This campaign promoted Atlanta as a regional distribution center. By the time Forward Atlanta ended, approximately 762 enterprises with 20,000 new jobs and payrolls totaling $34.5 million had moved into the area.[3]

In 1933 Charles Palmer, a prominent businessman and real estate developer, recognized the potential of slum clearance as a means to revitalize the downtown business district. A slum clearance program would increase downtown property values and provide employment opportunities. Federal funds for low-cost public housing were available due to the passage of the National Industrial Recovery Act. Palmer selected a substantially white residential area south of Georgia Tech University and Beaver Slide, an African American neighborhood east of Atlanta University, for slum clearance. Both areas contained extremely deplorable housing and living conditions. Techwood Homes, the nation's first public housing project, was built for white residents in the area south of Georgia Tech University. Developers built University Homes, an African American housing project, on the site near Atlanta University.

Concerned about deterioration in areas surrounding the city, downtown business and property owners formed the Central Atlanta Improvement Association (CAIA) in 1941. Representatives from the Coca-Cola Company, financial institutions, the city's newspapers, public utilities companies, downtown retail stores, and real estate firms participated in this organization. The CAIA encouraged support for programs that fostered the economic growth and redevelopment of the downtown business district.[4] Because of the economic resources and political influence of its members, the CAIA was frequently able to bypass formal channels when initiating redevelopment projects.

During the 1920s ward politics produced a municipal administration which was unsympathetic to the goals of the business community. Rather than downtown redevelopment, city politicians were more concerned about the interests of their particular wards. The Ku Klux Klan and trade unions wielded great influence in municipal affairs and politics at this time. These organizations professed to champion the interests of the common workingman.

The business community was not completely united behind the goal of downtown revitalization. Owners of small neighborhood firms feared that the revitalization of the downtown area would harm their businesses. Rather than investment in downtown redevelopment, they favored projects which would improve city neighborhoods. Many of these business leaders formed organizations to focus on neighborhood concerns. While these organizations were able to delay or halt certain projects, they were unsuccessful in shifting the emphasis of the larger business community from downtown redevelopment to neighborhood revitalization. These organizations did not have the political influence, economic resources, or unity of the larger business community. While many of these businessmen were active in the Chamber of Commerce (as well as members of the CAIA), the Chamber generally supported programs which emphasized downtown redevelopment.[5]

The 1937 mayoral campaign of William Hartsfield provided an opportunity for the business community to wield greater influence in municipal affairs. Distancing himself from ward organizations, Hartsfield relied on the political and financial support of the business community. During this campaign, Hartsfield presented himself as a good government candidate as he spoke against government corruption and ward politics. In running on this platform, Hartsfield was voicing the concerns of the business community. The Chamber of Commerce and the Atlanta Real Estate Board had sought revision of the ward system since the 1920s. During his administration, Hartsfield initiated reforms in city management and the budgetary process. The agenda of the business community replaced that of the ward politician and the Klan. This cooperation led to an alliance between the city's political leadership and the business community.

One of the main motivations for the involvement of the business community in municipal affairs was economic self-interest. The revitalization of the downtown business district and promotion of the city as a center of commerce financially benefitted business and property owners. In general, slum clearance and urban renewal projects were economic bonanzas for the larger financial institutions, real estate firms, development corporations, and construction firms. These programs also increased downtown property values and attracted outside investment to the city. Community projects such as expressway and airport construction were closely connected to business interests.

This motivation, however, was more complex than simple profit. The business community of Atlanta perceived its interests as being the same as those of the city. This belief had some legitimacy. Programs advocated and initiated by the business community were responsible for the building and redevelopment of the city's infrastructure. These programs, which included the construction of a downtown expressway, an air terminal, and newer municipal facilities, attracted outside investment. Between 1946 and 1954, approximately 800 new industries and 1200 branch offices of national corporations were established in the area.[6] Under business leadership, Atlanta grew from an "overgrown country town" into a city.

The business community of Atlanta also had a long tradition of civic involvement. During the Great Depression, Rich's was the first major department store in Atlanta to accept scrip from municipal employees and provide currency as change. In 1934 the Coca-Cola Company advanced the city $800,000 for its budget. In December 1936 it agreed to back the city's payroll for that month. Because of this action, local banks honored city scrip at face value. During his tenure as president of Coca-Cola, Robert Woodruff made generous contributions to the city. His philanthropies included endowments for local universities, land purchases for city parks, funding for various municipal facilities, and donations to various charitable organizations such as the Community Chest (later renamed the United Way of Metropolitan Atlanta). Most of the community projects initiated in Atlanta during the 1940s through 1960s were directly or indirectly connected to the activities of Richard Rich of Rich's or Robert Woodruff. These two men set the standard for the business community's involvement in civic affairs. Due to their example and influence, other business leaders and enterprises made contributions to charitable and civic causes in Atlanta. This involvement in civic affairs gave business leaders a sense of personal investment in the well-being of the city.

The involvement of the business community in political and civic affairs was also due in part to shared values and concerns. In his memoirs, Ivan Allen, Jr., a prominent business leader and a mayor of Atlanta, described the business-civic leadership that emerged in Atlanta during the 1950s. His description was applicable in many ways to the earlier generation of businessmen in Atlanta and illustrative of the continuity of shared values that existed in Atlanta's business community.

Ivan Allen described this establishment as "the leaders of the top fifty or so businesses in the city." They were "white, Anglo-Saxon, Protestant, Atlantan, business-oriented, nonpolitical, moderate, well-bred, well-educated, pragmatic, and dedicated to the betterment of Atlanta as much as a Boy Scout troop is dedicated to fresh milk and clean air." According to Allen, these men "constituted a separate social set—common backgrounds, common interests, and common goals." The older generation of business leaders expected the "successors to the throne" to "function just as they had: to love Atlanta, to cherish her, to guide her, to make her a better place than she was when we 'inherited' her."[7]

The decision-making process in Atlanta reflected these values and attitudes. Decisions involving downtown redevelopment or municipal policy were usually made in private discussions and negotiations between members of the business-civic leadership. Once decisions were made, business or civic leaders recruited the personnel and collected the resources necessary to implement the projects. When all of these elements were in place, these leaders conducted a campaign to generate political and public support. This process involved limited public participation. In making these decisions, the business community of Atlanta believed that it was acting in the best interests of the city.[8]

The political power of the business-civic leadership, however, was not omnipotent. A program of downtown redevelopment could not have been implemented without a sympathetic municipal administration and political support within the community. This political backing came from the north side of the city. Residents in this area were mainly white and middle-class. Many had lived in the city before moving to the suburbs. Several businessmen lived in this area. Most residents politically supported William Hartsfield. Within the white community, this area of the city provided the mayor's margins of victory. Hartsfield's program of municipal reforms and his "progressive views" won the support of residents in this area.

The business-civic leadership of Atlanta involved representatives from the north side of the city in the planning of urban renewal and redevelopment projects. Mayor Hartsfield frequently appointed aldermen from this area to serve on the aldermanic committee on urban renewal. Representatives from this section of Atlanta also served on the Citizens Advisory Committee on Urban Renewal (CACUR). Generally, these representatives favored a program of redevelopment.[9] Expressways, for example, provided north side residents easy access to the downtown area. Since redevelopment and urban renewal projects were unlikely on the north side of the city, residents in this area could enjoy the benefits of downtown redevelopment without suffering from the problems caused by these projects. They did not have to endure the dislocation or disruption in neighborhoods that resulted from redevelopment and urban renewal. Representation on committees dealing with redevelopment projects also served as a means of protection for residents living on the north side of the city. These representatives blocked attempts to relocate citizens or build low-cost public housing on the north side of the city.[10]

Hartsfield viewed the participation of middle-class white voters in this coalition as crucial in maintaining Atlanta as a white majority city and in improving race relations. Due to white migration to the suburbs and an increase in the African American population during the 1940s and 1950s, the inner-city neighborhoods were becoming increasingly African American. Hartsfield feared that this shift in the racial balance would hurt the city economically and increase racial tensions. He believed that Atlanta should remain a white majority city under the control of the middle-class. Annexation became his chosen method to counteract this racial imbalance. Atlanta attempted to annex adjacent white suburbs in 1938, 1943, and

1947. Privately, the mayor warned white property owners that the defeat of annexation attempts would result in African American political control of the city. He assured African American leaders that affluent whites were dedicated to improving relations between the races.[11] In most instances, these arguments were unconvincing. The three annexation attempts were unsuccessful.

In addition to white voters on the north side of the city, members of good government organizations supported the reforms initiated by William Hartsfield. During the 1920s and 1930s, organizations such as the League of Women Voters had attempted to revise the ward system. During the 1950s, good government organizations and business associations combined their efforts to challenge the constitutionality of Georgia's county unit system. While these campaigns were unsuccessful, reform and business leaders established channels of communication. A small, but significant, "liberal" element existed within Atlanta's business community. A number of businessmen's wives were members of reform organizations such as the Southern Association of Women for the Prevention of Lynching, the Atlanta Council of Church Women, the Fellowship of the Concerned, and the YWCA.[12] While this liberal element was unable to persuade the larger business community to embrace many of its causes, a continuing dialogue existed between reform organizations and the business-civic leadership.

In mayoral elections, Hartsfield won the political support of business leaders, affluent whites, and the "liberal" or reform element. Political opposition generally arose from the less affluent, working-class residents of the city. In general, these voters were more provincial, financially conservative, and racially intolerant than their white counterparts. Most of these residents opposed downtown redevelopment. Located mainly in the south, west, and central sectors of the city, their neighborhoods would first face the dislocation and disruption resulting from downtown redevelopment. Protecting the north side of the city, developers targeted sites in south, west and central Atlanta for low-cost public housing. These neighborhoods were also beginning to face the effects of an increasing African American population. These areas of the city would be the first to experience conflict resulting from racial transition. Hartsfield's policies were thus unpopular in these communities.

Prior to the 1930s, working-class whites wielded greater influence in municipal affairs due to ward politics. With the advent of Hartsfield's first administration, their political fortunes began to decline. This loss of influence was largely due to the inability of these residents to unite behind a single political candidate or platform.[13] Nevertheless, they were formidable opponents to business interests. Aldermen from these areas were able at times to halt, delay, or change the plans of certain redevelopment projects. With the flight of middle-class whites to the suburbs, the political influence of the less affluent whites would apparently increase.

The end of the white primary in Georgia added, however, a new dimension to this political environment. The African American vote would once again be a decisive factor in local elections between two competing factions within the white community. A political alliance with either side would have provided benefits for the African American community. The problems facing white working-class neighborhoods were similar to those of inner-city African American communities. Many heavily populated African American neighborhoods were located in areas earmarked for redevelopment, slum clearance, and urban renewal. These projects would result in disruptions in established African American communities and the displacement of their citizens. As C.A. Scott noted in the *Atlanta Daily World*, slum clearance and urban renewal "could mean 'Negro clearance'."[14] Common bonds thus existed between working-class white and inner-city African American neighborhoods. Years of racial prejudice and emerging conflicts over limited housing, however, cast doubts over an alliance between African American and white working-class leaders.

An alliance with the business-civic leadership also had certain benefits to offer Atlanta's African American community. Whether resulting from personal convictions or economic and political considerations, members of the business-civic leadership appeared willing to accept gradual racial reform. As part of this governing coalition, certain segments of the African American community would be expected to benefit financially from redevelopment and urban renewal projects. While many of these projects would result in the displacement of African American residents, city officials promised that quality low-cost public housing would be built. Since the business-civic leadership was already in power, African American leaders had established communication links with business and reform leaders. Despite some early disagreements with Hartsfield, African American leaders felt that they could conduct business with him. No such relationship or understanding existed between African American and white working-class leaders.

The decision as to which alliance to join and the conditions of such a coalition rested in part with the leadership of Atlanta's African American community. The political power of these leaders depended upon their ability to deliver or influence African American voters. This ability was due to the sense of unity or cohesiveness that existed within the African American community.

This cohesiveness was forged in an era of white supremacy and racial segregation. Like other southern cities, Atlanta was strictly segregated. State laws required segregation in common carriers, schools, and state-endowed institutions. Local ordinances supplemented state segregation laws. The city of Atlanta required segregation in places of public assembly (theatres, public halls, stadiums, and auditoriums); street cars, taxi-cabs, and cars-for-hire; parks (with the exception of the Grant Park Zoo, the only zoo in the city); cemeteries; establishments selling alcoholic beverages for on-premises consumption; and barber shops. As African American residences became more concentrated in the east, west, and south sections of the city, the Atlanta Board of Aldermen passed ordinances legalizing residential segregation in 1913, 1917, and 1922. Even though the courts declared these laws invalid, municipal officials used racial zoning to halt the migration of African American residents into certain areas of the city and create buffer zones between white and African American residential neighborhoods.

The white community of Atlanta also used violence and other forms of intimidation to maintain white supremacy and racial separation. After sensationalized and unconfirmed accounts of attempted assaults of white women by African American men appeared in city newspapers over a period of several months, a white mob attacked African American citizens in downtown Atlanta. After four days of rioting in September 1906, approximately twelve people were killed (ten African Americans, two whites) and seventy (sixty African Americans, ten whites) were injured. At the peak of its popularity in Atlanta, the Ku Klux Klan conducted marches in African American communities for purposes of intimidation. In 1930 a gang of white men murdered Dennis Hubert, an African American student, for allegedly assaulting a white woman. After the conviction of these men for murder, a white mob burned down Hubert's home, assaulted his cousin, and threw rocks at the Spelman College Chapel. The tensions caused by Hubert's murder were exacerbated by an organization known as the American Order of Fascisti (commonly referred to as the "Black Shirts"). The "Black Shirts" advocated the employment of white citizens at the expense of African American workers. During the mid-1940s, many former members of the "Black Shirts" participated in the Columbians, Inc., another white supremacist organization. The Columbians stopped and questioned African Americans traveling through white neighborhoods in the city. This organization was connected to a series of bombings, beatings, and other acts of violence directed against African Americans during the 1940s.[15]

One incident which particularly shocked Atlanta's African American community was the lynching of two young couples outside Monroe, Georgia, a small town located about forty miles east of Atlanta. The victims were Roger Malcolm, his brother-in-law George Dorsey, and their wives. In July 1946 Roger Malcolm was jailed after an altercation with a white man. After Malcolm was released on bail, an armed group of white men stopped the car containing the two couples. This mob subsequently killed the African American couples. Upon an examination of the four bodies, the coroner estimated that they had been shot at least sixty times.

The *Atlanta Daily World* gave prominent coverage to the case and leaders of Atlanta's African American community called for a mass meeting at Wheat Street Baptist Church. Community leaders formed a Permanent Committee of Action under the leadership of Reverend William Holmes Borders in order to raise funds for the victims of racial reprisal. Members of the community raised over $10,000. A portion of this money paid the funeral expenses of the victims. Reverend Borders selected the coffins, oversaw the funeral arrangements, and provided comfort for family members.[16] Despite reward offers by the Permanent Committee of Action and the state and investigations by state and federal law enforcement agencies, no arrests in this case were made.[17] Two weeks following the lynching, a student at Morehouse College in a letter to the *Atlanta Constitution* noted that African Americans "want and are entitled to the basic wants and opportunities of American citizens: the right to earn a living at work for which we are fitted by training and ability; equal opportunities in education, health, recreation, and similar public services; the right to vote; equality before the law; and some of the courtesy and good manners that we ourselves bring to all human relations."[18] The young student was Martin Luther King, Jr.

While city officials, the two major newspapers, and various segments of the white community condemned the activities of these white supremacist groups, these organizations were products of the racial attitudes and oppression that existed within the city. Because of these attitudes and the separation of the races, the African American community of Atlanta turned inward. Residents depended upon community institutions and organizations to provide for their emotional, social, material, educational, and civic needs. These institutions provided not only the needs of Atlanta's African American community, but also its leadership. Leaders basically emerged from four main sectors of Atlanta's African American community. These sectors were the churches, the colleges, the business community, and women organizations.

The Church was an important institution in Atlanta's African American community. It attempted to fulfill the religious, social, economic, and civic needs of its parishioners. In the early 1900s the First Congressional Church operated a health care center, organized a temperance society, established an employment bureau, gave financial assistance to the needy and neighborhood charities, and provided recreational facilities for children. Wheat Street Baptist, Big Bethel A.M.E., Ebenezer Baptist, and other African American churches had similar programs. At this time, the white community was not providing these services for African American residents. These programs thus provided a refuge from a hostile environment. While many churches later curtailed these programs due to increasing costs and the advent of federal and state relief programs, the African American Church in Atlanta was one of the city's main providers of social welfare.[19]

Many African American ministers played an important role in easing the tensions between the races and achieving racial reform. After the 1906 race riot, African American ministers formed an advisory board (eventually called the Atlanta Civic League) to meet with city officials in order to abate racial violence and hostility. African American ministers were also at the forefront of the struggle for civil rights. Due to derogatory characterizations of African Americans in one newspaper in 1910, local ministers launched a boycott against businesses which advertised in the paper. Citing "nigger troublemakers who were taking over Atlanta," this newspaper, the *Georgian*, financially collapsed a few months after the boycott began.[20] Many of Atlanta's most prominent ministers and their congregations participated in voter registration activities, the campaign to obtain African American police officers, and boycotts against merchants who failed to employ African American sales clerks. The Church thus served as an important channel of communication between civil rights leaders and the masses. For this reason, the participation of African American ministers was crucial in the battle against racial oppression.

Atlanta's African American colleges were important in fulfilling the educational needs of the African American community. Atlanta University, Morris Brown, Clark, Morehouse, Spelman, and the Interdenominational Theological Center (formerly Gammon Theological Seminary) were established in the decades immediately following the Civil War. The African Methodist Episcopal Church established Morris Brown. White missionary and religious societies were associated with or founded the other institutions.[21] In 1929 Atlanta University, Morehouse, and Spelman formed the Atlanta University Center. Clark, Morris Brown, and the

Interdenominational Theological Center later joined this consortium. This consortium allowed the institutions to develop a cooperative program of studies through the pooling of resources and the exchange of students and staff. Its establishment also reduced direct Church influence on the schools, thus enhancing its own particular influence on community affairs.

Prior to 1924 Atlanta provided no public high schools for its African American residents. Black colleges in Atlanta compensated for this lack of educational opportunity by sponsoring high school "academy" departments. These programs often served as conduits for the students' entry into the college. On the college level, the schools of the Atlanta University Center offered its students a diverse curriculum. While training students in the traditional fields of teaching and the ministry, these universities offered courses in the sciences, business, and law. In 1920 the Atlanta University School of Social Work opened. This institution's main orientation was toward coping with African American issues and problems.[22] The schools of the Atlanta University Center provided an educated African American leadership. Many leaders had educational ties to these colleges. A.T. Walden was a graduate of Atlanta University. C.L. Harper graduated from Morris Brown. Reverends Martin Luther King, Sr. and William Holmes Borders attended Morehouse College. Most of Atlanta's business leaders were either graduates of the Atlanta University Center or taught at one of the institutions.

While trying to provide their students with a sheltered environment from the humiliations of a segregated society, these institutions encouraged their students and staff to participate and become involved in community activities. Students and faculty participated in voter registration drives and citizenship schools. Activities on these campuses were opened to all races. The schools of the Atlanta University Center were one of the few places where biracial meetings could occur in Atlanta. Students from Agnes Scott, Emory University, Georgia Tech, and the African American institutions frequently met to discuss local and national issues. The faculties of these colleges encouraged their students to discuss the racial situation. In 1948, for example, the sociology departments of the schools of the Atlanta University Center in conjunction with the Southern Regional Council sponsored a two-day civil rights conference. Workshop groups discussed issues such as segregation, education, and economic opportunity. A panel discussion was held on the state of race relations in the South. Over 1500 students participated in these sessions.[23]

Atlanta's black business community provided for the economic needs of its residents. In the late 1890s and early 1900s, African American businesses were located near the downtown business district. According to a 1899 survey of African American businesses in Atlanta, nine of the twenty-five firms closely studied had considerable white patronage (fourteen establishments exclusively depended on black trade).[24] After the passage of segregation ordinances and the Atlanta race riot of 1906, these firms relocated in African American residential and business districts and catered to an all-black clientele. "Sweet Auburn" Avenue became the heart of this black business community. By 1911 the city of Atlanta had some two thousand black owned establishments representing over a hundred types of businesses. The earliest business establishments were primarily financial enterprises, particularly insurance and banking. In 1905 Alonzo Herndon founded the Atlanta Mutual Insurance Association (later renamed Atlanta Life Insurance Company). In 1909 Heman Perry organized the Standard Life Insurance Company. At this time, the main objective of these companies was to provide sick, accident, and life insurance benefits to African American policyholders. These policies could not be obtained easily from white institutions. In 1925 the Citizens Trust Company opened. This enterprise was the first African American bank to become a member of the Federal Reserve System. The Citizens Trust Company financed most of the business enterprises on Auburn Avenue and provided mortgage and loan policies which allowed African American families to purchase homes.[25] For most African American residents, loans would have been difficult to obtain from a white institution.[26]

Most of Atlanta's black businesses were small retail and service establishments which served the daily needs of the community. African American customers could enter these establishments without facing the humiliations that often occurred in downtown stores. These firms also provided employment opportunities for African American residents at a time when most African American workers were restricted to menial or domestic labor.

Business leaders were active in civic affairs. They used their positions within the business community to inspire other African Americans to greater economic success. Many African American leaders made generous contributions to civil rights organizations, charitable causes, and local institutions. For example, Norris Herndon, president of the Atlanta Life Insurance Company, contributed to the NAACP, the National Urban League, the United Negro College Fund, the United Way, Atlanta University, Butler Street YMCA, and other organizations.[27] Business leaders participated in voter registration activities by making financial contributions and urging employees to register. Others performed a more active role. Eugene Martin, an executive at the Atlanta Life Insurance Company, was an active member of the NAACP, the Georgia Interracial Commission, and the Fulton-DeKalb Commission on Interracial Cooperation. L.D. Milton, president of Citizens Trust Company and co-owner of Yates and Milton's Drugstores; J.B. Blayton, president of the Atlanta Mutual Federal Savings and Loan Association and owner of radio station WERD; T.M. Alexander, an insurance agent and a realtor; and W.L. Calloway, a realtor, were members of various local and national civil rights organizations. African American Atlantans regarded these gentlemen as community and race leaders.

In 1942 the Atlanta Life Insurance Company became a party to the struggle for the equalization of teacher salaries in Georgia. The salaries of African American educators in Atlanta ranged between sixty-two to seventy percent of the pay of white teachers in the various school classifications. William Reeves, a junior high school teacher and a former employee of Atlanta Life, filed a suit asking that African American teachers employed by the city be paid the same salary as white teachers. Reeves had the support of the Atlanta Life Insurance Company, the local NAACP, the Atlanta Citizens Committee for the Equalization of Teacher Pay, and several local civil rights agencies. The Atlanta Life Insurance Company agreed to employ any teacher fired as a result of the suit.

In October the school superintendent suspended Reeves alleging that he was physically incapacitated and morally unfit to be a teacher. While these charges lacked substance, the School Board approved of the superintendent's action and Reeves was fired. When the case was brought before the Court, attorneys for the School Board asked for its dismissal on the ground that Reeves was no longer an employee of the school system. The judge granted a continuance in the case so that the NAACP could find a substitute plaintiff. Honoring its pledge, the Atlanta Life Insurance Company rehired Reeves.

Atlanta Life agreed to offer the substitute plaintiff the same commitment that was offered Reeves. While the Federal Court ruled in favor of the plaintiff, this decision was reversed upon appeal. The Court eventually dismissed the case in 1951. Throughout these legal proceedings, Atlanta Life remained a firm supporter of the suit and honored all of its commitments to the community.[28]

Women organizations were also at the forefront of meeting the needs of Atlanta's African American community. These organizations included the Gate City Free Kindergarten Association, the Neighborhood Union, the Atlanta branch of the Southeastern Federation of Colored Women, and the

Women's Committee for Improvement in Colored Public Schools. Members of these organizations were usually middle-class African American women who were concerned about the future of their children, the "moral uplift" of Atlanta's African American community, and the promotion of racial and ethnic pride. In the early 1900s the Gate City Free Kindergarten Association maintained five free kindergartens for African American children. In 1908 African American women founded the Neighborhood Union. Under the leadership of Lugenia Burns Hope, this organization established and maintained a health care center, provided recreational facilities for African American children, petitioned city officials for improved public facilities and services, investigated conditions in African American schools, and offered courses in home hygiene, and nursing and infant care.[29] In the 1950s African American women clubs campaigned for better bathroom and restaurant facilities in downtown department stores.[30]

Through these activities women became more politically aware of the issues facing Atlanta's African American community. Many of these women became members of the CIC, the Urban League, the NAACP, and the YWCA. In many instances, the social programs of these organizations were extensions of activities that originated with local women groups. For example, the Atlanta Urban League and the Atlanta School of Social Work incorporated many of the programs that originated with the Neighborhood Union. Due to their role in these organizations, women became an important part of Atlanta's African American leadership structure.

The leadership of Atlanta's African American community emerged from these sectors of the community. These individuals did not simply proclaim themselves as leaders. While its recognition was important to a certain degree, the white community did not simply handpick certain African American residents as leaders. Rather, the influence and power of Atlanta's African American leaders derived from the institutions and organizations that they represented. African American citizens respected these leaders for the services that they rendered for the community.

In many ways, Atlanta's African American leaders were similar to their counterparts in the white community. They were from the upper-economic strata of the African American community. Most had college degrees. Because of these advantages, these individuals believed that they had a special responsibility to speak for the masses. In doing so, these leaders felt that they were acting in the best interests of the community.[31] Decisions were made in discussions among leaders. While mass meetings and rallies were frequently held, African American leaders used these public forums to generate support and enthusiasm for decisions already made. Atlanta's African American leaders stressed the importance of unity in the struggle against racial oppression.

In the 1949 mayoral election, Atlanta's African American leaders politically supported William Hartsfield. This election signified the beginning of a political alliance between Atlanta's African American community and the business-civic leadership. The terms of this alliance were quite simple. The African American community would politically support the business-civic leadership. With this support, the white business community could retain political power and pursue a program of economic growth and downtown redevelopment. In return, the business-civic leadership promised a more congenial racial climate. White leaders would check any racial violence directed against the African American community. While segregation was to remain intact, the business-civic leadership appeared willing to accept gradual racial reform. The African American community would receive a share of the benefits resulting from a program of economic growth and redevelopment. Both sides agreed that behind-the-scenes negotiations to solve racial problems were preferable to open conflict.[32]

Within this governing coalition, the most pivotal organization was the Atlanta Negro Voters League. The business-civic leadership credited the ANVL for organizing the African American vote. Because of its success, the ANVL became the major communication channel between Atlanta's African American community and the business-civic leadership. William Hartsfield established a close working relationship with A.T. Walden, one of the original founders of the ANVL. The two men met frequently to discuss racial concerns. The ANVL, with only modest success, pressed for improved municipal facilities, a Commission on Human Relations to handle racial tensions, representation on city boards and agencies, an upgrading of African American employees, and the desegregation of public facilities.[33] The membership of the ANVL comprised the leadership of the African American community's most prominent institutions. Members included Warren Cochrane, director of the Butler Street YMCA; C.A. Scott, editor of the *Atlanta Daily World*; Grace Hamilton, Executive Secretary of the Atlanta Urban League; C.R. Yates, chairman of the board of Citizens Trust and co-owner of Yates and Milton's Drugstores; W.J. Shaw, Secretary of the Republican Party Organization; C.L. Harper, principal of Washington High School and president of the local NAACP; Walter Aiken, a realtor and independent contractor, and Martin Luther King, Sr., pastor of Ebenezer Baptist Church.

The political relationship that existed between the business-civic leadership and the ANVL did not initially result in the appointment or election of African Americans to municipal office. While African Americans voted for white candidates endorsed by the ANVL, the majority of white Atlantans would not vote for an African American candidate. The ANVL and biracial politics in Atlanta won a major victory, however, when city voters elected Rufus Clement to the Board of Education in 1953. While he eventually won a decisive victory, Clement had several obstacles to overcome during the election.

Clement, who was in his sixteenth year as president of Atlanta University, announced that he was running for the post of Third Ward representative. While this ward was predominately an African American district, candidates for the Board were elected citywide. T.H. Landers, who had served on the Board of Education for twenty-six years, was Clement's opponent. Clement actively solicited voters in both white and African American neighborhoods. Believing that an African American candidate could not win, Landers did not actively campaign for the position.

When conservative members on the Atlanta Democratic Executive Committee heard that an African American candidate was seriously running for the Board, they mounted their own campaign to ensure that he would not represent the Democratic Party. The Executive Committee wrote to the chairman of the House Un-American Activities Committee requesting any information that the house committee might have on Rufus Clement. Two days before the election, the Democratic Executive Committee called a special meeting to consider disqualifying Dr. Clement on the ground that he was a member of nine "subversive" organizations including the American Civil Rights Conference, the Southern Conference for Human Welfare, and the Southern Negro Youth Conference. When white supporters informed him of the Executive Committee's intentions, Clement went before it prepared to defend his record. A.T. Walden and Hughes Spalding, a prominent white attorney, accompanied him. Clement argued that he had withdrawn his membership and support from these organizations when he had learned that they had been infiltrated by Communists. After questioning Clement for several hours about his personal and organizational associations, the Atlanta Democratic Executive Committee, by a vote of five to four, decided that Clement could not properly be disqualified.[34]

Rufus Clement won election to the Board of Education by nearly 10,000 votes (22,259 to 13,936). He captured forty-eight of the city's fifty precincts. Ironically, two African Americans, A.T. Walden and Dr. Miles Amos, were elected to the Atlanta Democratic Executive Committee in the same election. National news publications characterized Clement's election as a "victory" for the city and region.[35] While they were overwhelmed and heartened by Clement's election, the majority of African American leaders remained willing to work behind-the-scenes (at least temporarily) to protect African American interests.

In addition to the Atlanta Negro Voters League, the Atlanta Urban League was an important communication link between the business-civic leadership and the African American community. Founded in March 1924, this organization was concerned with the daily needs of African American residents. Its goals were to provide jobs, better schools, health and recreational facilities, and decent housing for African American residents. The League's approach to these problems was conservative. It relied on the tools of education, persuasion, and negotiations. The Executive Board of the League was biracial; its staff was all-black. The Atlanta Urban League was dependent upon the Community Chest, the white business community's leading charitable cause, for its funds. Almost ninety percent of the League's budget came from Community Chest funds.[36]

Between 1943 and 1961 the Atlanta Urban League was under the leadership of Grace Hamilton. Rather than challenging segregation, she believed that conditions could only improve by enlisting the aid of both white and African American leaders.[37] Her method of improving race relations in Atlanta was education. She wanted to make the white community aware of the problems that African American residents in the city faced. Under her leadership, the Atlanta Urban League conducted large-scale fact-finding surveys in the areas of African American education, housing, hospital care, and recreation.[38] With this information, she hoped to enlist the aid of white leaders in solving the numerous problems that existed. While her success was only modest, she gained the approval of many white leaders in her activities.

In 1956, 1957, and 1959, white supremacist groups attacked the activities of the League. In 1956 the States Rights Council of Georgia demanded that the Community Chest drop the Atlanta Urban League from its recipients. It charged that the League was "inimical to the best interests of our society in the field of race relations."[39] In 1957, the Council accused the League of transferring the funds of the Community Chest to its national headquarters and the NAACP. This action would have violated a funding agreement between the League and the Community Chest.[40] In 1959 the "White Sentinel," a group based in Florida, accused the Community Chest of supporting the "anti-white conspiracy of the Urban League."[41] In each instance, the business community and the Community Chest came to the defense of the League. After a careful investigation of the charges, the president of the Community Chest denied that any transfers of funds had occurred. An editorial in the *Atlanta Journal* informed its readers that the leadership of the Atlanta Urban League "is composed of conservative local citizens and its policies conform to local patterns and traditions."[42]

In order to maintain political control, this governing coalition had to adhere to "local patterns and traditions" while slowly moving the city toward limited racial reform. The greatest threat to this coalition was racial violence. Hostility between the races had the potential to heighten racial distrust among coalition members. At least, a semblance of racial peace was needed in order that negotiations between coalition members could occur. White leaders faced the opposition of those opposed to any racial change. Many of those opposed to racial change were prone toward intimidation and violence. For this reason, white leaders argued that racial reform had to be gradual. African American leaders faced similar problems. While pressure on the white community was needed to initiate reform, most African American leaders feared that racial conflict would increase tensions and lead to a conservative white backlash. These African American leaders believed that a delicate balance between pressure and compromise was needed. White and African American leaders realized that issues with potential racial overtones had to be solved through quiet negotiations rather than violence.

One such issue was housing.[43] Following World War II, Atlanta experienced a housing shortage, particularly in the African American community. An increase in the demand for housing was largely due to the migration of African Americans seeking wartime employment. During the wartime period, Atlanta's African American population increased by approximately 17,000. A secondary reason for the shortage was the rising economic status of many African American residents. These citizens desired decent housing. Most African American dwellings were of poor quality.

Segregation exacerbated the housing shortage. As the African American population increased in size, the white community tried to regulate the mobility of African American residents and the areas in which they could reside. Various methods of regulation were used. Zoning created buffers between white and African American communities. For example, cemeteries and vacant land zoned for commercial enterprises were used as buffers. When the expansion of an African American community "threatened" a white residential and business district on the west side of Atlanta, city officials located Joel Chandler Harris Homes, a white housing project, between the two communities.[44] Roads served as a means to restrict the mobility of the African American population. In many areas, neighborhood leaders designated certain roads as boundaries between white and African American communities. Many streets in Atlanta suddenly changed names as they passed from an African American to a white neighborhood. In many areas, access between adjacent white and African American communities was difficult because of no direct road connections. Isolation of African American residents in remote areas of the city was a serious problem.[45]

Because of segregation, African Americans received less land than whites for residential dwellings. By 1946 African Americans comprised over one-third of the city's population, but they were restricted to approximately ten percent of the city's developed residential land.[46] The housing situation was especially precarious on the west side of the city. By 1940 forty percent of Atlanta's African American population lived in this area of the city. Residents in this area made the maximum use of existing housing facilities. Many African Americans were forced to seek existing housing units in fringe areas of white communities.

As African Americans moved into these fringe areas, racial conflict developed. Racist and neighborhood organizations threatened African Americans who purchased homes in formerly all-white communities. During the mid-1940s, Columbians attempted to physically block African American families from occupying their newly purchased homes. A gang of white men would suddenly appear at these houses carrying signs which read, "Zoned for Whites" and "White Community Only."[47] During the late 1940s and 1950s, sporadic bombings occurred in areas of racial transition. As African American families began to move into the Edgewood and Bankhead areas in the eastern and western sectors of the city, unknown terrorists detonated explosives near several newly purchased fringe area homes. Many African American families in racial transition areas were exposed to cross-burnings, phone threats, and physical intimidation. More "sophisticated" white residents raised funds with which they hoped to purchase property from whites who were threatening to place their homes on the African American market.[48] While these activities did not halt racial transition, they often served as strong deterrents to African American residential expansion.

White and African American leaders quickly acted to ease racial tensions. In 1945 William Hartsfield urged the Atlanta Real Estate Board to discourage its members from selling homes in white communities to African Americans.[49] In 1946 the Atlanta Urban League convened a meeting of representatives from the business community, social agencies, and the government to discuss ways to increase African American housing. This meeting resulted in the formation of a Temporary Coordinating Committee on Housing (TCCH). The TCCH organized three committees to launch a housing program. A land committee was charged with the responsibility of obtaining sites for African American housing. A second committee was responsible for studying the feasibility of organizing a corporation which could build on these sites. The purpose of the third committee was to work closely with county and city planning agencies, the Atlanta Chamber of Commerce, and other organizations in the launching of this program. Working within a system of segregation, the land committee targeted six areas which it felt was suitable for African American residential expansion. All of these areas were either owned by or already contained some African American residents. With the help of the Urban League and other municipal agencies, African Americans resided in all six areas by 1955.[50]

In 1952 the white leadership of Atlanta approved the concept of new African American residential areas. The Metropolitan Planning Commission, a commission organized by the General Assembly to recommend a plan for Atlanta's orderly growth, issued a major planning document. This report accepted and suggested new areas of the city for the expansion of African American residences.[51] While no African Americans served on the Commission, it was aware of the activities of the TCCH and the Atlanta Urban League in the field of housing. While the report was attacked by whites who objected to the concept of relinquishing land for black residential areas and by African Americans who resented the designation of segregated residential districts, four of the areas cited in this report became locations for African American housing.

Despite these efforts, racial conflict on the west side of the city persisted as African American residents moved into formerly all-white neighborhoods. A major area of contention was Mozley Park, a white lower middle-class neighborhood located on the west side of the city about three miles from the downtown business district. Attempts by African Americans to establish residences in this area proved unsuccessful due to racial violence and intimidation. By the early 1950s, African American neighborhoods had begun to bypass and encircle this community. As residents from these African American communities began to enter the fringe areas around Mozley Park, many white residents decided to leave the area.

In 1952 Mayor Hartsfield appointed a special biracial committee, the West Side Mutual Development Committee (WSMDC), for the purpose of "promoting the orderly and harmonious development" of the west side of Atlanta. The WSMDC was to seek solutions to the problems of housing and racial transition through fact-finding and mediation between white and African American residents. It was also to serve as an ex-officio mediating board for future conflicts in the area and a model for similar committees in other areas of racial transition. The WSMDC consisted of six members, three whites and three African Americans. All members were residents of the west side of Atlanta.[52]

The major accomplishment of the WSMDC was an agreement between the Empire Real Estate Board, an organization of African American realtors, and the real estate committee of the Chamber of Commerce. African American brokers agreed not to accept any house listings from the south side of West View Drive. This drive became the boundary between the African American and white communities on the southwest side of the city. Since Mozley Park was inside the established boundary line, it quickly became an African American neighborhood. Between 1954 and 1955 approximately 737 homes in the Mozley Park area became available for African American residents. The park and elementary school in this area became African American facilities. City officials expressed their satisfaction with the agreement.[53]

This settlement served as a model for other areas of the city. When white homeowners in Collier Heights, a fashionable white community in Northwest Atlanta, learned that vacant land beyond their community was to be developed for African American housing, they began to negotiate with African American brokers. The two parties reached an agreement. The brokers promised those wishing to sell that their homes would be purchased at a reasonable price and "For Sale" signs would not dot their community. Racial transition in this area was extremely peaceful. Approximately 300 homes passed from white to African American occupancy.[54] City officials cooperated with and supported the transfer. Various agreements were made throughout the city to mark the limits of African American expansion.

In April 1959, the United States Commission on Civil Rights held a hearing to investigate minority housing opportunities in Atlanta and the South. While presenting a picture of racial progress and cooperation in Atlanta, the underlying messages relayed by African American and white witnesses were quite different. White witnesses stressed that the integration of public and private housing would increase racial tensions and decrease minority housing opportunities. A white member on the WSMDC stated that "it has never been the custom or public policy for Negroes to live side-by-side whites in the same community."[55] According to the president of the

Atlanta Real Estate Board, residential integration would "destroy the progress of recent decades toward solving the minority housing problem here and would deal a tragic blow to race relations and to the local economy in the city of Atlanta."[56] Rather than integration, the president of Atlanta Savings and Loan suggested that "private enterprise in the field of housing is doing the job—under separate markets."[57]

African American witnesses condemned residential segregation. An African American member on the WSMDC argued that the housing problem was the "result of a traditional pattern of segregation in housing and the separation of the two races." He warned the committee "that the problems we have handled need not have existed, nor do the statements that we are making indicate a satisfaction on our part or an endorsement of a segregated housing pattern."[58] The president of the Empire Real Estate Board noted that federal agencies "had a continuing responsibility in helping to remove the barriers of segregation from housing."[59] The remarks made by African American witnesses were tempered with an awareness of the prevailing racial conditions in the city. An executive officer of the Atlanta Urban League noted that if an African American needed "a decent house he must at the present time work within the system of segregation." He could not "wait for the Millennium to come."[60]

In meeting these short-term housing needs, all elements of Atlanta's governing coalition participated. The crucial catalyst was the Atlanta Urban League. It organized the TCCH and served as a vital communication link between white and African American leaders. Representatives of the mayor, the Atlanta Chamber of Commerce, city and planning agencies, the Atlanta Life Insurance Company, the Citizens Trust Company, the Atlanta Real Estate Board, and the Empire Real Estate Board participated in various discussions concerning the housing situation. African American financial institutions provided mortgages and loans for families moving into areas of racial transition. The WSMDC allowed limited citizen participation in the decision-making process. African American and white leaders supported the various agreements reached.

A major motivation for the governing coalition was to prevent racial violence. In the process, white leaders acknowledged the need for more African American housing. They were able, however, to maintain boundaries between white and African American communities. The African American community was able to obtain more areas for residential expansion on the south and west sides of the city. While voicing their concerns, African American leaders were forced to work within the framework of segregation. A "compromise" between coalition members was thus reached. Community leaders at this time hailed these various agreements as model examples of how white and African American leaders could work together to solve racial problems.

Cooperation on the housing issue drew members of the coalition closer together, both politically and personally. White leaders lauded the educational and business achievements of the city's African American community. While acknowledging that problems existed, African American leaders generally praised the city's white leadership and the state of race relations. White and African American leaders developed communication links and personal working relationships. African American leaders used these connections to obtain better facilities for their communities.

One facility particularly cited by leaders as a product of racial cooperation was the Hughes Spalding Pavilion, an African American teaching hospital. In 1947 the Atlanta Urban League published a survey of medical problems and facilities in the African American community. This survey, "Report on the Hospital Care of the Negro Population of Atlanta, Georgia," noted the urgent need for African American medical personnel and a hospital catering to non-indigent African Americans.[61] Grace Hamilton sought the support of Hughes Spalding, Sr., chairman of the Fulton-DeKalb Hospital Authority. Spalding addressed a letter to 250 prominent citizens expressing his support for the construction of a hospital. In this letter, he stressed the "responsibility" of the city's white leadership to "adequately look after the health of our negro citizens and make this a better community for them to live."[62] The city's newspapers extensively covered the findings of the League's survey and expressed editorial support for the construction of a hospital. Emory University donated a piece of land adjacent to Grady Memorial Hospital as a site for the medical facility and agreed to assume responsibility for a program to train African American personnel.

White and African American leaders promoted the hospital as a biracial effort. In 1950 the Fulton-DeKalb Hospital Authority appointed a biracial Advisory Board of Trustees to oversee the construction and operation of the hospital. This board had ten members, five whites and five African Americans. Funding for the hospital came from a wide variety of federal, state, and local agencies. Sixty percent of the hospital's funding came from Hill-Burton funds (federal funds made available to local communities for hospital construction); twenty percent from the state government; and ten percent from Fulton and DeKalb counties.[63] In June of 1952, a biracial audience was present for the hospital's dedication services. Governor Herman Talmadge officially dedicated the Hughes Spalding Pavilion.

Benjamin Mays, president of Morehouse College, received the medical facility. A semblance of racial peace and harmony was established for the audience and national media.[64]

Despite this biracial effort, Hughes Spalding Pavilion was a segregated institution. The hospital was limited to African American patients. Even though the hospital was directly adjacent to Grady Memorial, it maintained separate kitchen and laundry facilities. State funding for the hospital was noncontroversial because the facility perpetuated segregation. Despite voicing approval for the hospital's training program, the Dean of Howard University warned Grace Hamilton that "we must get away from the established pattern [segregation] and that now is the time to make the start."[65] This project was not a deviation from the established pattern of segregation.

During the 1950s, direct negotiations between Atlanta's white and African American leaders did not lead to the end of segregation. On this particular issue, the majority viewpoint of Atlanta's white leadership conformed to that of the general public. In testimony before the U.S. Commission on Civil Rights, white leaders referred to the segregation of the races as "the overwhelming public opinion of the South," "our custom and tradition," and "an established fact."[66] Leaders warned that integration would lead to increasing hostility between the races and a white conservative backlash. Politically, those opposed to racial reform posed the greatest threat to the power of the business-civic leadership. As long as African American leaders appeared willing to work within the framework of segregation and did not apply overt pressure, concessions relating to the integration of segregated housing patterns or public facilities did not have to be made.

In 1951 a group of African American citizens filed a suit requesting the city to desegregate its golf courses. Atlanta maintained seven segregated courses. It provided no separate golfing facilities for its African American residents. In June of 1955 the Fifth Circuit Court of Appeals upheld the separate-but-equal doctrine. The Court ruled that the city could maintain segregated golf courses if the city provided equal facilities for its African American citizens. According to the Court, the recent decision in *Brown v. Board of Education* did not apply to public facilities. The Court ordered the city to provide a golfing facility for its African American residents. On 7 November 1955 the Supreme Court reversed the decision of the Fifth Circuit Court of Appeals. It ordered the desegregation of Atlanta's golf courses. The Court also handed down a similar ruling ordering the city of Baltimore to desegregate its public bathing facilities.[67]

Reaction to the Court's decisions in Georgia was instantaneous. Because of the similar decision rendered in the Maryland case, widespread fears existed that the court decree would require the city of Atlanta to desegregate all of its public recreational facilities. State Attorney General Eugene Cook charged that the NAACP "is able to obtain from the Court any decision that is designed to further its program to force intermarriage." Governor Marvin Griffin announced that the state would sell or lease its parks before allowing integration. Members of the state legislature offered to revoke a provision in Atlanta's city charter which forbade the city from selling or leasing large recreational facilities to private citizens. The *Atlanta Journal* suggested that the Supreme Court should have "taken into account customs and traditions of people, as well as mathematics and the law."[68]

The reaction of Mayor Hartsfield was quite different. Even though many citizens urged him to close the courses, Hartsfield ordered that they be opened to African American residents. The mayor argued that closing the courses would "disrupt white citizens from playing and would result in putting 100 city employees out of work." Compliance with the decision, according to Hartsfield, was "simply the right thing to do." City officials undertook several actions to ease racial tensions. They reassured citizens that the Court's decision applied only to golf courses. City employees examined buildings, benches, and locker rooms to ensure that no racist remarks were inscribed on surfaces. The city personnel department warned park department employees that insulting African American citizens would be a ground for job dismissal. The city closed shower facilities at the golf courses. Hartsfield maintained that "since most people travel to and from the courses today, the showers were just not needed anymore."[69]

After the Supreme Court handed down the decision, Mayor Hartsfield met with Police Chief Jenkins, the city attorney, the head of the Parks Program, and African American leaders to discuss the peaceful integration of the city's golf courses. African American leaders pledged to make no attempts at integration until the city officially received the court decree and an orderly plan of desegregation could be arranged. On 22 December, District Judge Boyd Sloan officially ordered the desegregation of the city's golf courses. No mention was made as to other public facilities. On Christmas Eve 1955, five African American citizens peacefully played golf at Atlanta's North Fulton Golf Course. In commenting on Atlanta's decision to comply with the Court's ruling, Governor Marvin Griffin warned that "this is but a foretaste of what people can expect in those communities where the white people are divided at the ballot box and where the NAACP holds the balance of power on election day."[70]

While important symbolically, the desegregation of Atlanta's golf courses affected only a small portion of the African American community. Only one African American golf club, consisting of 150 members, existed in the area. In 1957 a movement to desegregate Atlanta's buses posed a greater challenge to the city's pattern of segregation. State and local ordinances required segregated seating on common carriers. As in other southern cities, African American passengers faced the humiliations of sitting in the back section of buses and entering and existing the vehicle through the rear doors. Racial conflict frequently occurred between African American passengers and the bus operator. Despite these conditions, approximately fifty-three percent of Atlanta's bus passengers were African Americans.[71]

Encouraged by bus boycotts in Baton Rouge, Tallahassee, and Montgomery, African American ministers organized the "Law, Love, and Liberation" Movement to desegregate the city's buses. This movement claimed the participation of over 100 local ministers. Its chairman was William Holmes Borders. Instead of a mass boycott of the buses as used in Baton Rouge and Montgomery, the basic strategy of this movement was simply to establish a test case of Georgia's segregation statutes. Only African American ministers participated in the initial stages of the campaign. Leaders urged other African American citizens to refrain from participating until they were "notified for help."[72]

In January 1957 a group of African American ministers boarded a local bus in an effort to desegregate public transportation in Atlanta. The ministers sat in various sections of the bus, including vacant front seats. In order not to unnecessarily heighten racial tensions, the ministers took special precautions. They announced their plans to integrate the buses at a mass meeting at Wheat Street Baptist Church and in the *Atlanta Daily World*.[73] The ministers chose a relatively empty bus. They decided not to sit next to white passengers, particularly women. After the ministers entered the bus, the operator changed the sign on the front of his vehicle from the name of the route to "Special." He returned the bus to the garage. With the exception of a minor confrontation between a white passenger and a photographer, no incidents of violence were reported. On this particular day no arrests were made. At a mass meeting that night, William Holmes Borders announced that members of the "Law, Love, and Liberation" Movement "would be on the buses the next day and the day thereafter until Atlanta enforced Georgia's law on segregation."[74]

The following day, Police Chief Herbert Jenkins issued warrants for the arrest of six African American ministers.[75] He charged the ministers with violating the state segregation laws. After being fingerprinted, questioned, and charged, the ministers were released on a $1000 bond. If convicted the maximum punishment was twelve months in a public works camp or a $1000 fine and six months in a camp. Upon being informed that African Americans were trying to desegregate Atlanta's buses, Governor Marvin Griffin placed the state militia on standby alert. William Hartsfield and Chief Jenkins stated that they had to uphold the law including the state's segregation statutes. Robert L. Sommerville, head of the Atlanta Transit Company, said that the company was bound by state law. He suggested, however, that "if the law is wrong, it should be changed."[76] After their arrests, the ministers urged African American citizens to refrain from further attempts at integration until the courts could dispose of the matter.

Preferring not to face future demonstrations or a boycott of the buses, the business-civic leadership and the Atlanta Transit Company were willing to accept a court challenge of Georgia's segregation laws. Eventually, two court cases developed. The six African American ministers faced state charges. In June of 1957, Reverend Sam Williams, current president of the local chapter of the NAACP, and Reverend John Porter filed a suit in Federal Court seeking an injunction against segregation on Atlanta's buses. Nearly two years later, Federal Judge Frank A. Hooper declared segregated seating on Atlanta's buses unconstitutional.[77]

Immediately after the Court handed down its decision, Mayor Hartsfield urged citizens to use "sound common sense and civil decency."[78] The Atlanta Transit Company printed circulars advising passengers of the court decision and explaining proper behavior. It also began to paint over or remove the signs that had previously defined racial boundaries within the buses. William Holmes Borders stressed that bus desegregation was the result of cooperation between the races. He urged patience by those who desired greater reform. The buses were desegregated without violence.

In his memoirs, Reverend Martin Luther King, Sr. noted that the desegregation of Atlanta's golf courses and buses was achieved through the "Atlanta Plan." According to King, the "Atlanta Plan" consisted of "one nonviolent direct action, arrests, and subsequent integration through court decree." Because segregation could not be solved through direct negotiations between white and African American leaders, the court decree became the means by which the white leadership of Atlanta could grant these particular concessions. It served as a means by which white leaders could rationalize and justify their actions. Because this total process generated little conflict, communication and trust between white and

African American leaders were maintained. This sense of cooperation appealed to leaders of both races.

While noting that "there was nothing basically wrong with this approach," King identified two critical problems with this strategy. First, the total process was too time-consuming. The suit to desegregate Atlanta's golf courses required four years of litigation. The bus case was resolved in two years. To a young African American citizen, this "was an eternity." Secondly, the "Atlanta Plan" never "got to the roots of segregation, those deeper places in the human soul where the law did not reach." Hidden behind the handshakes, kind words, and smiles were the humiliations and pent-up frustrations of living in a segregated society. As King suggested, these "emotional time bombs" had "to be defused rather than hidden even further away."[79]

These problems largely remained hidden from the governing coalition. Judging by appearances, the policies and programs of the coalition were extremely successful. The coalition initiated an ambitious and economically profitable downtown redevelopment program. It was successful in creating, at least, the semblance of racial peace and harmony. Working within the framework of segregation, white and African American leaders achieved limited racial reforms without arousing overt racial violence. They were able to work together to solve temporarily the housing shortage and provide facilities for the African American community. While problems and disagreements existed between members of the coalition, they were able to develop strong communication networks and personal working relationships. Leaders of both races believed that negotiations and the "Atlanta Plan" would eventually solve outstanding racial problems.

These "achievements" captured the attention of the national press. With the South rocked by violence and an increase in the number of civil rights protests during the 1950s, journalists began to perceive Atlanta as being different from other southern cities. Atlanta was an "oasis of racial tolerance" in a state that was committed to a policy of massive resistance. In an article on the city, a journalist for *Time* magazine noted that Atlanta was "still a Jim Crow city, but on the whole ashamed of violent racial prejudice."[80] In *Fortune* magazine, a columnist wrote that Atlanta "is often called an 'Oasis in the South'—not just because you can get a legal drink of bourbon in Atlanta, but because there is in Atlanta, a surprising remission of Little Rocketry that is found in many cities and almost all non-metropolitan areas of the South." The article also noted that in "street after street of the Negro residential sections there are homes indistinguishable from upper-class homes in neighborhoods altogether white."[81] The national press favorably reported the desegregation of Atlanta's golf courses and buses, the construction of Hughes Spalding Pavilion, and the negotiations to solve the housing shortages.[82] Several articles praised the business and educational achievements of the city's African American community.[83] Douglas Cater of the *Reporter* noted that "it is easy to come away from a tour in the South with a conviction of total gloom." However, the use of negotiations to solve racial problems in Atlanta, according to Cater, "provides at least some grounds for hope."

Mayor Hartsfield was aware that a reputation for good race relations made favorable national press for Atlanta. He was masterful in his handling of the press and the promotion of the city. He coined the phrase, "a city too busy to hate," to describe Atlanta during the 1950s. When visiting reporters or businessmen came to Atlanta, the mayor frequently took them on a personal nocturnal tour of the city which included projects under construction, the Atlanta University Complex, and African American middle-class neighborhoods. On these tours, Hartsfield frequently visited African American leaders.[84] These sights and Hartsfield's charming personality made a favorable impression on his guests.

Concerned about violence in Little Rock, Arkansas in 1957, Hartsfield and city leaders began to stress the economic and civic benefits of maintaining a reputation for racial progress. In fact, the maintenance of this reputation became a justification for racial reform. In 1957 Hartsfield warned a gathering of white civic leaders that "if Atlanta loses control of peaceful race relations we are gone." The mayor noted that "it is of special importance to downtown businessmen to maintain decent race relations and avoid violence."[85] After African American leaders attempted to desegregate Atlanta's public transportation system, Hartsfield stated that the city's record in race relations "was a desirable thing, not only for the sake of decency, but from the standpoint of business as well."[86] This economic justification was often combined with an appeal to civic pride. Atlanta, according to this line of reasoning, was a "New South" city; it would be the model and set the standard for better race relations in the region.

Atlanta's reputation and image were largely based upon symbolic gestures. In the decade following the formation of the governing coalition, Atlanta's African American community made few concrete gains. Despite the negotiated agreements, housing within the African American community remained in short supply. Most dwelling units were in poor condition. Residential segregation in the city actually increased. Between 1940 and 1960, the city's residential segregation index rose from 87.4 to 93.0.[87] City services and facilities in the African American community remained inadequate. African American workers were largely confined to domestic or menial labor. Atlanta remained a segregated city. The desegregation of the city's golf courses and buses, were accomplished through court decree. While politically members of the coalition, few public officials were African American.

In an era of racial segregation and low expectations, symbolic gestures were important. African American leaders perceived these actions as first steps toward greater integration. In this respect, the coalition was successful. During the 1950s, it was largely able to meet the demands of the African American community. In an era of raising expectations, symbolic gestures, however, would not be enough. A younger generation of African American citizens began to demand more concrete results and greater concessions. The continuing success of the coalition would depend upon its willingness and ability to address these concerns.

Notes

1.   Roy LeCraw, a former president of the Atlanta Chamber of Commerce, defeated William Hartsfield by 83 votes to win the 1941 mayoral election. In 1942 LeCraw resigned as mayor due to military service. Hartsfield was elected mayor in a special election. With the exception of this brief period of time (1941–1942), Hartsfield served as mayor of Atlanta from 1937 to 1961.

2.   This "kitchen cabinet" of business leaders included Ivan Allen, Sr., Miss Helen Bullard, Clarence Haverty, Bob Maddox, Everett Millican, Frank Neeley, Richard Rich, Bob Strickland, Jack Tarver, and Robert Woodruff.

3.   Figures are cited in Clifford Kuhn, Harlon E. Joye, and E. Bernard West, *Living Atlanta: An Oral History of the City, 1914–1948* (Athens: University of Georgia Press, 1990), p. 92.

4.   In 1967 the Central Atlanta Improvement Association and the Uptown Association, an organization formed to promote the Ponce de Leon Avenue/North Avenue Corridor, merged to form Central Atlanta Progress. Clarence Stone, *Regime Politics: Governing Atlanta, 1946–1988* (Lawrence: University Press of Kansas, 1989), p. 16; and Central Atlanta Progress, "Fifty Years of Leadership and Progress, 1990 Annual Report," p. 2.

5.   Stone, *Regime Politics*, pp. 16–17.

6.   Figure is cited in Norman Shavin and Bruce Galphin, *Atlanta: Triumph of a People* (Atlanta: Capricorn Corporation, 1982), p. 225.

7.   Ivan Allen, Jr. with Paul Hemphill, *Mayor: Notes on the Sixties* (New York: Simon and Schuster, 1971), pp. 29–31.

8.   My interpretation of the decision-making process in Atlanta is quite similar to that of Floyd Hunter in *Community Power Structure*. While one may disagree with some of his observations, his basic argument that the policy-making role is formally divided between governmental and economic leaders appears valid. As Clarence Stone has recently noted, Hunter did not argue that a "power structure" rules in command fashion. Rather, Hunter suggests that a coalition with advantages and resources guides the community's response to social change.

9.   Clarence Stone, *Economic Growth and Neighborhood Discontent: System Bias in the Urban Renewal Program of Atlanta* (Chapel Hill: University of North Carolina Press, 1976), pp. 35–38.

10.   Author's Interview with Cecil Alexander, 9 April 1991.

11.   Harold H. Martin and Franklin Garrett, *Atlanta and Environs: A Chronicle of its People and Events: Years of Change and Challenge 1940–1976*, Vol. III (Atlanta: Atlanta Historical Society, 1987), p. 339; and Stone, *Regime Politics*, pp. 27, 30–32.

12.   Author's Interview with Cecil Alexander.

13.   With the possible exception of Lester Maddox, no effective candidate or public official came forward as a spokesperson for the less affluent whites in Atlanta. One possible reason was the effectiveness of the governing coalition. The combined votes of citizens on the north side of the city and the African American community provided almost the majority needed to win. After the 1949 election, most candidates at least made an effort to win a portion of the African American vote.

14.   *Atlanta Daily World*, 23 March 1950.

15.   Kuhn, Joye, and West, pp. 158, 314–316; J. Wayne Dudley, "'Hate Organizations' of the late 1940s: The Columbians Inc.," *Phylon* XLII (3/September 1981): 262–274; Charles H. Martin, "White Supremacy and Black Workers: 'Black Shirts' and Black Workers Combat the Great Depression," *Labor History*, 18 (3): 366–381; and John Hammond Moore, "Communist and Fascists in a Southern City," *South Atlantic Quarterly*, 67 (Summer 1968): 437–454.

16.   *Atlanta Daily World*, 27 July–18 August 1946.

17.   In May 1992, forty-six years after the lynching, a white eyewitness to the event, Clinton Adams, has stepped forward with new information. Adams claims that he witnessed the event while playing. He was ten years old in 1946. Adams has identified four local white farmers, including the individual who paid Malcolm's bail and was driving the car containing the couples, as being members of this white mob. All of those named by Adams are now deceased.

18.   Quoted in Martin and Garrett, p. 125.

19.   Edyth Rose, "Black Heritage in Social Welfare: A Case Study of Atlanta," *Phylon* XXXVII (Winter 1976): 297–307.

20.   Martin Luther King, Sr. with Clayton Riley, *Daddy King: An Autobiography* (New York: William Morrow, 1980), pp. 86–87.

21.   For a detailed examination of Atlanta University and its impact on Atlanta, see Clarence Bacote, *The Story of Atlanta University: A Century of Service, 1865–1965* (Atlanta: Atlanta University, 1969).

22.   In 1918 the Neighborhood Union organized a Social Service Institute at Morehouse College. The Atlanta University School of Social Work emerged from this Institute in 1920. In 1928 the Association of Schools of Social Work accredited the institution. In 1938 the school

became affiliated with Atlanta University. In 1948 it became an integral part of Atlanta University as one of its graduate schools.

23. Interview with Dr. Lucy Grisby, conducted by Kathleen Dowdey and Jed Dannenbaum, Ralph McGill Papers, Emory University, Atlanta, Georgia.

24. Robert J. Alexander, "Negro Businesses in Georgia," *Southern Economic Journal*, 17 (4/51): 453–454.

25. From 1925 to the mid-1970s, Citizens Trust Bank financed more than eighty percent of all the businesses on Auburn Avenue. W.L. Calloway, *The "Sweet Auburn Avenue" Business History 1900–1988* (Atlanta: Central Atlanta Progress, 1988), p. 10.

26. For a detailed examination of Atlanta's African American business community, see Robert J. Alexander, "Negro Businesses in Georgia," *Southern Economic Journal* 17 (4/51): 451–464; W.L. Calloway, *The "Sweet Auburn Avenue" Business History 1900–1988* (Atlanta: Central Atlanta Progress, 1988); E. Franklin Frazier, *The Black Bourgeoisie* (New York: The Free Press, 1957); Alexa Benson Henderson, *Atlanta Life Insurance Company: Guardian of Black Economic Dignity* (Tuscaloosa: University of Alabama Press, 1990); Emmet John Hughes, "The Negro's New Economic Life," *Fortune* LIV (September 1956): 127–131, 251–262; and Robert Vowels, "Atlanta Negro Business and the New Black Bourgeoisie," *Atlanta Historical Bulletin*, 21 (Spring 1977): 48–66.

27. Henderson, pp. 168–170.

28. King with Riley, pp. 104–105; and Henderson, pp. 176–178.

29. Jacqueline Rouse, *Lugenia Burns Hope: Black Southern Reformer* (Athens: University of Georgia Press, 1989), pp. 20–40, 57–90, 123–129.

30. This letter-writing campaign on the part of women organizations was focused on Rich's department store. These organizations believed that changes at Rich's would influence other retail establishments in the downtown area. As a result of this activity, Richard Rich announced that he would improve African American restroom and restaurant facilities in his department store. Letter from MRS Club to Richard Rich, 24 March 1958; Letter from the Coterie Club to Richard Rich, 28 March 1958; Letter from the Atlanta Chapter of Jack and Jill to Richard Rich, 14 April 1958; Letter from the Colored Women's Club of Atlanta to Richard Rich, 20 June 1958; and Letter (form) from Richard Rich to each of these various clubs. These letters are located in the Richard Rich Papers, Woodruff Library, Emory University, Atlanta, Georgia.

31. Author's Interview with LeRoy Johnson, 13 November 1990.

32.   The terms of this alliance were not formally written or publicly stated. It was a "gentleman's agreement" between white and African American leaders. Past studies have described the terms of this coalition as simply the exchange of votes in return for a peaceful racial climate. In his studies of politics in Atlanta, Clarence Stone illustrates the importance of land use and downtown redevelopment in the formation of this governing coalition and alliance. As these programs were initiated, African American leaders expected a share of the benefits of these various programs. Naturally, African American leaders also believed that gradual racial reform would result from an alliance with the business-civic leadership. See Stone, *Regime Politics*, p. 36.

33.   The Atlanta Negro Voters League was successful in obtaining improved health and recreational facilities for the African American community. City officials promised to hire more African American citizens and upgrade existing employees. The ANVL was unsuccessful in convincing Hartsfield to establish a Human Relations Commission. For a list of objectives desired by the ANVL, see The Atlanta Negro Voters League, "Revised Preliminary Report on the Committee of Objectives," 13 February 1954, A.T. Walden Papers, ANVL files, Atlanta History Center, Library and Archives, Atlanta, Georgia.

34.   *Atlanta Constitution*, 11–12 May 1953.

35.   "Changing South, Negroes Elected to Office," *New Republic*, 128 (25 May 1953): 57; "Victory for Atlanta," *Time* 96 (25 May 1953): 61; and "Victory for the People," *Nation* 176 (30 May 1953): inside cover.

36.   J.B. Blayton, Letter to the National Urban League Board of Directors, January 1960, Grace Towns Hamilton Papers, Box: 4, Folder: 1, Atlanta History Center, Library and Archives, Atlanta, Georgia.

37.   For a detailed examination of Grace Hamilton's life and philosophy, see Sharon Mullis, "The Public Career of Grace Towns Hamilton: A Citizen too Busy to Hate," (Ph.D. dissertation, Emory University, 1976).

38.   These surveys were as follows: "Report on Public School Facilities for Negroes in Atlanta, Georgia" (1944); "Report on the Hospital Care of the Negro Population of Atlanta, Georgia" (1947); "A Report on the Housing Activities of the Atlanta Urban League" (1950); and "A Report on the Parks and Recreational Facilities for the Negro Population of Atlanta, Georgia" (1954). These reports may be found in the Grace Towns Hamilton Papers.

39.   The States Rights Council of Georgia was a statewide organization "dedicated to the preservation of constitutional government and the

maintenance of harmonious race relations." This organization had the support of the governor, the state attorney general, and other political leaders. It claimed a membership of over 150,000 members. *Southern School News*, October 1956, p. 11.

40. According to an agreement between the Atlanta Urban League and the Community Chest, funds had to be spent on projects in the area. The Atlanta Urban League could not transfer funds to its national headquarters or any other civil rights organization. The Community Chest established a special committee to investigate these charges. This committee found the charges to be false. Letter to A.T. Walden from Roger F. Whittaker, chairman of the Urban League Study Commission, 4 February 1957, A.T. Walden Papers, Atlanta History Center, Library and Archives, Atlanta, Georgia; and Letter to William T. Bodenhamner, head of the States Rights Council of Georgia, from William C. Wardlaw, president of the Community Chest, 9 August 1957, Southern Regional Council Papers, 1:71:2166, Woodruff Library, Atlanta University, Atlanta, Georgia.

41. Atlanta Urban League, Meeting Minutes of the Board of Directors, 15 October 1959, Grace Towns Hamilton Papers, Box: 4, Folder: 3.

42. *Atlanta Journal*, 13 October 1959.

43. For detailed examinations of African American residential expansion on the west side of the city, see Samuel L. Adams, "Blueprint for Segregation: A Survey of Atlanta Housing," *New South* 22 (Spring 1967): 77–84; James W. Harris, "This is Our Home: It is not for Sale," (Senior thesis, Princetown University, 1971); Gloriastine Thompson, "The Expansion of the Negro Community in Atlanta, Georgia from 1940–1958," (Master's thesis, Atlanta University, 1959); and Robert A. Thompson, Hylan Lewis, and Davis McEntire, "Atlanta and Birmingham: A Comparative Study in Negro Housing," in *Studies in Housing and Minority Groups*, eds. Nathan Glazier and Davis McEntire (Berkeley: University of California Press, 1960), pp. 14–51.

44. Author's Interview with William Calloway, 22 April 1991.

45. For a detailed examination of the use of highways and roads as a means to enforce racial segregation, see Ronald H. Bayor, "Roads to Racial Segregation: Atlanta in the Twentieth Century," *Journal of Urban History*, 15 (November 1988): 3–21.

46. Figure is cited in Harris, p. 3.

47. *Atlanta Constitution*, 3 November 1946.

48. Adams, pp. 77, 79–80.

49. Harris, p. 6.

50.   The TCCH and the Atlanta Urban League were involved with the following housing projects: (1) The Fairhaven Project, (2) Highpoint Apartments, (3) Magnolia, (4) The Old Marietta Road Project, (5) The Richardson Road Development, and (6) IRE-Ron apartments. Atlanta Urban League, "A Report of the Housing Activities of the Atlanta Urban League" (1950).

51.   The Metropolitan Planning Commission cited seven areas to "handle the expansion of the colored population over the next thirty years." Each area would "contain complete and well-planned neighborhoods." Metropolitan Planning Commission, *Up Ahead: A Regional Land Use for Metropolitan Atlanta* (Atlanta: Metropolitan Planning Commission, 1952), pp. 52–53, 88–90.

52.   Westside Mutual Development Committee, "Public Proposal of the Westside Mutual Development Committee Regarding the Operation of the Real Estate Market with Respect to Race and Occupancy," printed in *Hearings before the United States Commission on Civil Rights, Housing, Atlanta, Georgia, April 10, 1959* (Washington, D.C.: Government Printing Office, 1959), p. 462.

53.   Thompson, Lewis, and McEntire, pp. 28–31.

54.   Harris, pp. 8–10.

55.   *Hearings before the United States Commission on Civil Rights, Housing, Atlanta, Georgia, April 10, 1959* (Washington, D.C.: Government Printing Office, 1959), p. 450.

56.   Ibid., p. 538.

57.   Ibid., p. 519.

58.   Ibid., pp. 455–456.

59.   Ibid., p. 542.

60.   Ibid., p. 527.

61.   The survey, "Report on the Hospital Care of the Negro Population of Atlanta, Georgia" noted that African American medical care "compared unfavorably with that of the white population." The African American community had higher infant mortality and death rates than the white community. There were only 2.6 general hospital beds per 1000 African Americans (this was 1.9 beds/1000 short of the United States Public Health Services' minimum standard). Only 21.7% of the general hospital beds in the area could be used by African Americans. Only one African American physician practiced for every 3,368 citizens (normally there is one physician for every 1000–1500 persons). There were no African American physicians on the staff of Grady Memorial Hospital. No African Americans could serve as interns. African American nurses could work at Grady.

However, training and staff were segregated. African American personnel were unable to join professional medical societies. Indigent Atlantans of both races could receive treatment at Grady Hospital. Due to segregation, medical facilities for middle-class African Americans were limited. With the exception of Grady Hospital and few private health care centers, most medical facilities refused to provide services for African Americans. Although African American citizens received reasonable medical treatment, they experienced severely overcrowded conditions and long waiting lists.

62. Hughes Spalding, Sr., Letter to Mr. B. Authur Howell, 30 January 1948, Grace Towns Hamilton Papers, Box: 177, Folder: 2.

63. Mullis, p. 132.

64. A journalist from *Time* magazine noted the irony of dedicating a segregated institution in the presence of a biracial audience. *Time* 59 (30 June 1952), p. 64.

65. W. Montague, Letter to Grace Hamilton, 16 January 1948, Grace Towns Hamilton Papers, Box: 5, Folder: 1.

66. *Hearings before the United States Commission on Civil Rights, Housing, Atlanta, Georgia, April 10, 1959* (Washington, D.C.: Government Printing Office, 1959), pp. 446, 537, 494.

67. The case to desegregate Atlanta's golf courses was *Holmes v. Atlanta*. The decision to desegregate public bathing facilities in Maryland was *Lonesome v. Maxwell*. *Race Relations Law Reporter I* (1957), pp. 14, 146–151.

68. *Atlanta Constitution*, 8 November 1955; and *Atlanta Journal*, 9 November 1955.

69. *Atlanta Constitution*, 23 December 1955; and *Atlanta Journal*, 23 December 1955.

70. *Atlanta Journal*, 24 December 1955.

71. Figure cited in King with Riley, p. 155.

72. *Atlanta Daily World*, 9 January 1957.

73. The mass meeting occurred at Wheat Street Baptist Church on the evening before the first attempt. At this meeting African American citizens were told that the ministers would attempt to desegregate the buses on the following day. Leaders of the Movement presented citizens with eight basic principles to guide their actions. This meeting was discussed in detail in the *Atlanta Daily World* on the morning of the attempt. It informed readers that ministers were going to attempt to desegregate Atlanta's buses that very day. In interviews, William Holmes Borders has stated that he notified Hartsfield on the morning of this attempt. He had previously warned Police Chief Jenkins and all of the city aldermen that ministers would attempt to

desegregate the buses. In interviews with Harold Martin, Jenkins maintained that he was not aware of the attempt to desegregate the buses on that particular morning. Mayor Hartsfield also expressed surprise.

74.   *Atlanta Daily World*, 9 January 1957.

75.   Arrangements as to the time of the arrest, the charges filed, those arrested, and the means of transportation to the police station were quietly negotiated between white and African American leaders. The ministers arrested were William Holmes Borders, R.B. Shorts, R.W. Williams, A. Franklin Fisher, H. Bussey, and B.J. Johnson.

76.   *Atlanta Journal*, 10 January 1957.

77.   The federal case to desegregate Atlanta's buses was *Williams v. Georgia Public Service Commission*. Because of previous court decisions, the ruling by Frank Hooper was orally delivered in less than a hour. *Race Relations Law Reporter IV* (1960), pp. 166–169.

78.   *Atlanta Journal*, 9 January 1959.

79.   King with Riley, p. 154.

80.   "Oasis of Tolerance," *Time* 69 (20 May 1951): 31.

81.   "Atlanta: Really Springing," *Fortune* 56 (December 1957): 31.

82.   These articles include: "Atlanta Does Itself Proud," *Christian Century* 70 (3 June 1953): 653; "Mayor Hartsfield Uses the Light Touch," *Reader's Digest* 72 (June 1958): 203–207; "Victory for Atlanta," *Nation*, 176 (30 May 1953): 1; and *Time*, 68 (15 June 1957): 21.

83.   These articles include: G.S. Perry, "Atlanta," *Saturday Evening Post* 218 (22 September 1945): 26–27; James Street, "Atlanta," *Holiday*, 9 (June 1951): 26–37; and "Oasis of Tolerance," *Time* 69 (20 May 1957): 31.

84.   Douglas Cater, "Atlanta: Smart Politics and Good Race Relations," *Reporter* (11 July 1957): 19, 21.

85.   Ibid., p. 18.

86.   *Atlanta Journal*, 10 January 1957.

87.   The residential segregation index is a number along the scale from 0 to 100 that represents the average degree of territorial separation between white and black households. If every block is occupied by only households of the same race, the index is 100 which is the maximum possible residential segregation. If every block has exactly the same racial percentage as other blocks, the index is 0 or the minimum possible racial segregation. Karl E. and Alma F. Taeuber, *Negroes in Cities: Residential Segregation and Neighborhood Change* (Chicago: Aldine Publishing Company, 1965), pp. 32–34, 39–41.

III

Challenges to the Coalition: Political Succession and Segregation

During the 1950s African American citizens began to challenge southern racial attitudes through the use of economic boycotts, marches, sit-ins, and other forms of nonviolent, disruptive tactics. In 1953 African Americans in Baton Rouge successfully conducted a boycott of the city's public transportation system. Bus boycotts also occurred in Montgomery (1955–1956), Tallahassee (1956), and New Orleans (1956). Under the leadership of Fred Shuttlesworth, African American citizens in Birmingham used nonviolent direct action to protest discrimination in employment, bus and train segregation, and the segregation of public schools and municipal facilities. During the late 1950s, Reverends James Lawson and Kelly Miller Smith of Nashville organized what they referred to as a "nonviolent workshop." In these workshops, they taught local students the philosophy and tactics of nonviolence. In 1959 these students conducted "practice" sit-ins in two local department stores. In September of that year, the Congress of Racial Equality conducted a sixteen-day workshop in nonviolence in Miami. At this workshop, Dr. Martin Luther King, Jr. participated in the training of local students in nonviolence. These students conducted sit-ins at a local department store. Although they did not capture the attention of the national media, African American citizens conducted sit-ins in sixteen southern cities between 1957 and 1960.[1]

Proponents of nonviolent direct action believed that it was necessary to confront the people and institutions which perpetuated racial oppression. By using direct action techniques to force their oppressors to yield, they hoped that racial reform would immediately be realized. Proponents of direct action believed that their tactics were more effective and could bring about faster results than negotiations, persuasion, or litigation. They cited the early successes in Baton Rouge and Montgomery as evidence that their tactics worked.

In the summer of 1959, the Southern Christian Leadership Conference, the Congress of Racial Equality, and the Fellowship of Reconciliation sponsored a nonviolent workshop at Spelman College in Atlanta. A biracial group of leaders from these organizations decided to eat at a local restaurant. Whether out of shock, uncertainty about the restaurant's policy, or the desire to avoid a public incident, employees served this group.[2] These leaders hoped that others would follow their example of protest. Encouraged by this example, younger African Americans began to desire greater racial reform.

While African American leaders in Atlanta supported this goal, they urged patience and restraint. Most leaders viewed public demonstrations as a means to pressure the white community into negotiations or establish grounds for legal action. Once these processes were initiated, they urged citizens to refrain from further public demonstrations. Black leaders cited the desegregation of golf courses and buses and the city's peaceful racial climate as proof that negotiations and the legal process worked for Atlanta's African American citizens. Due to a series of events that occurred between the mid-1950s and early 1960s, many African American citizens began to question these strategies for reform and the ability of the city's governing coalition to maintain a peaceful racial climate.

One such event was a campaign on the part of state officials to curtail the activities of the NAACP in Georgia. State Attorney General Eugene Cook spearheaded this campaign. In a speech before the Fifth Annual Convention of the Peace Officers Association in Georgia, Cook charged that the NAACP was a "subversive" organization. Its membership, according to Cook, was mainly comprised of "South-hating white people with long records of affinity for, affiliation with, and participation in Communist, Communist-front, fellow-traveling and subversive organizations, activities and causes."[3] The States Rights Council of Georgia distributed copies of this speech throughout the region. In July 1955, the State Board of Education adopted a resolution which would revoke the license of any teacher or school official who was a member of or supported the NAACP or any "allied organization."[4] In 1957 the Georgia General Assembly passed a law defining and providing punishment for the crime of barratry (the "fomenting or inciting of litigation"). In 1958 it passed a resolution creating a joint committee of the House and Senate to investigate the need for further legislation defining and prohibiting barratry. The resolution also gave the committee the right to investigate the activities of all persons and groups encouraging litigation in the state.[5]

Georgia's attack on the NAACP was part of a regional campaign headed by southern officials to disrupt the organization's activities. In 1956 the attorney generals of Alabama, Louisiana, and Texas obtained injunctions halting the activities of the NAACP in their states. Florida, South Carolina, and Virginia also passed legislation specifically designed to hinder NAACP operations. In many southern states, government officials demanded that the NAACP make available its financial and membership records. Local branches refused to comply with this request. They realized that the publication of these records could expose members to economic reprisals and violence and frighten current and potential members from participating in NAACP activities.[6]

In Georgia the NAACP consisted of forty branches with a total membership of more than 13,000 members. Because of its size and activity, the Atlanta branch was a main target of the state's campaign. In November 1956 the State Revenue Commissioner sought access to the financial and membership records of the Atlanta branch and the regional office of the NAACP on the ground that the organization neither filed state income taxes nor applied for state tax exemption. Both offices refused to open their records for state inspection. After the state obtained a court order, Ruby Hurley, the NAACP regional program director, submitted the organization's records to the state agency. Claiming that he was not an official of the NAACP and that the Atlanta branch was an autonomous organization, John Calhoun, the branch's current president, refused to produce any records. Judge Durwood Pye sentenced Calhoun to jail on contempt charges and fined the Atlanta branch twenty-five thousand dollars. After four hours in jail, Calhoun agreed to produce the branch's financial records. The State Revenue Department levied an assessment of $17,459.08 against the Atlanta branch for eleven years of back income tax.[7]

The regional attack on the NAACP had a devastating impact on the organization and the South. Between 1955 and 1958, over 246 NAACP branches in the region disbanded. Its southern membership declined from 128,716 to 79,677 (forty-five to twenty percent of the total membership). Alabama completely halted NAACP operations within its borders for nine years. The state closed the NAACP's Southeast Regional headquarters which was located in Birmingham. This attack financially hurt the organization because local branches provided funds for the activities of the national office. The NAACP also had to expend funds on defending itself from state attacks.

As Aldon Morris notes in *The Origins of the Civil Rights Movement* (1984), the demise of the NAACP in many southern African American communities left "an organizational and protest vacuum." Prior to the attack, NAACP branches initiated and organized protest activities and provided public forums where African American citizens could discuss local grievances and problems. Since the NAACP was no longer in many communities to provide these services, African American citizens had to look to alternative organizations and strategies to fight racial oppression.[8]

While the attack on the NAACP was less severe in Georgia than many other southern states, it had several implications for the Civil Rights Movement in Atlanta. During the 1950s, the local branch in Atlanta had played a major role in the African American community's struggle against racial oppression. The NAACP was involved in the suits desegregating the city's golf courses and buses. Atlanta's leaders adopted the organization's gradualist, legal approach to civil rights. Partly due to the harassment of state officials like Cook, the effectiveness and influence of the Atlanta branch declined. While the NAACP was able to continue its battle against segregated schools, it had to expend some of its emotional and financial resources in defending itself against attacks by the state. These attacks weakened the faith of many young African Americans in the organization and its gradualist, legal approach to civil rights problems. Rather than joining the NAACP, younger African Americans looked toward organizations that favored a less conservative approach.

Incidents of racial violence also raised questions about the governing coalition's ability to achieve racial reform. Racial peace was an important element in the agreement between white and African American leaders. While the racial climate of Atlanta compared favorably with other southern cities, incidents of racial violence were frequent during the 1950s, particularly in areas of racial transition. Between March 1956 and November 1957, for example, an unknown assailant dynamited three homes owned by African Americans in formerly all-white neighborhoods.[9] Despite housing agreements between white and African American leaders, sporadic acts of racial violence continued.

The issues of violence and bigotry were brought to the forefront in October 1958 when terrorists bombed the city's largest synagogue. Evidence tended to link this incident with similar bombings in other southern cities. Between March 1956 and November 1957, terrorists bombed Jewish houses of worship in Gastonia and Charlotte, North Carolina; Jacksonville and Miami, Florida; Nashville, Tennessee; and Birmingham, Alabama. One week before the dynamiting of the Temple in Atlanta, a similar blast occurred at a newly integrated high school in Clinton, Tennessee.[10] Members of the National States Rights Party and the Christian Anti-Jewish Party were indicted for the bombing of the Temple. The first trial for one of the accused resulted in a mistrial. When his second trial ended with an acquittal, the state dropped the charges against the other suspects.[11]

Unlike the bombings of African American homes, the dynamiting of the Temple received extensive press coverage. Mayor Hartsfield came quickly to the scene. While dutifully noting that Atlanta was "a lighthouse of racial and religious tolerance," Hartsfield argued that "every political rabble rouser is the godfather of these cross burners and dynamiters who sneak about in the dark and give a bad name to the South."[12] In his column, "A Church, A School," Ralph McGill wrote that the bombing of the Temple was "the harvest of defiance of courts and the encouragement of citizens to defy law on the part of many southern politicians."[13] For many African Americans, the bombing symbolized the bigotry and racial intolerance that existed in the city.

Violence also occurred in the form of police brutality. Even though Atlanta desegregated its police force in 1948, relations between the police department and the African American community remained poor. In September 1958 an incident which resulted in the shooting of an African American citizen raised questions of police brutality. Police officers arrested a youth for causing racial disturbances in the Perry Homes community. After being arrested, the youth alleged that one of the officers beat him. A witness who came to the youth's aid was also arrested. This witness claimed that she was "roughly handled," and "beaten" by the officers. During the confrontation, the housing manager of Perry Homes alleged that he was "seized" and "roughly handled," and "received one blow" from one of the officers. Another employee approached the policemen. According to witnesses, an officer, without provocation, shot the employee before he reached the scene of the confrontation. The police officers involved denied these charges. They claimed that a large mob tried to interfere with the arrest of the youth. When the white dailies reported the incident based on the accounts of the officers, an "intense excitement" existed in the Perry Homes community and bordering African American neighborhoods.[14]

Due to the potential for racial violence, African American leaders formed a Citizens Committee to address the situation. The Committee wrote letters to the newspapers and city officials detailing the accounts of the African American witnesses and requesting that the officers who used unnecessary force be punished. While carefully noting that it believed that these officers were few in number, the Committee urged the suspension of "trigger-happy" policemen. The police department agreed to investigate the charges.[15]

The response of African American leaders to this particular incident was illustrative of past and future responses to accusations of police brutality. When the potential for racial conflict existed, African American leaders usually formed a committee to deal with the situation. The committee usually requested an investigation of the incident and the suspensions of the officers involved. If charges were filed against an African American citizen perceived to be innocent by the community, the committee would raise funds for the accused's defense. In response, the police department usually agreed to investigate charges of police brutality. Unless hard and convincing evidence was produced, the usual remedy was the reassignment of the officers involved to other duties or patrols. The main objective of the police department and African American leaders was to prevent these incidents from escalating into major racial disturbances. Because of this emphasis, individual cases tended to be dealt with rather than the overall issues of police brutality and the relations between the police department and the African American community.

The excitement generated by nonviolent direct action, state harassment of the NAACP, and continued acts of racial violence and police brutality created serious doubts about the ability of the governing coalition to address racial change. These doubts occurred at a time when the coalition was particularly vulnerable. Disagreements over policy had developed between white and African American leaders. Opposition to the leadership of the coalition was increasing. The leadership structure of both communities was changing as younger leaders began to challenge the policies of their mentors.

The political vulnerability of the governing coalition was evident in the 1957 mayoral election. In the primary, Archie Lindsay, a Fulton County Commissioner, was Hartsfield's main opponent. Despite his accomplishments, Hartsfield was a vulnerable candidate due to his age (sixty-seven years old), some personal and financial problems, allegations of corruption in the police department, and racial tensions stemming from the housing situation on the west side of the city. The mayor won the primary with 37,612 votes to Archie Lindsay's 33,808. Hartsfield won in the more prosperous white districts, carried the predominately African American precincts by heavy majorities, soundly lost in the economically lower-class white neighborhoods, and evenly ran in the other areas of the city. The closeness of the vote was due to an increase in the ballots cast in the economically lower-class white neighborhoods and a poorer showing than usual by Hartsfield in white middle-class communities.[18]

Due to the close vote in the primary, opponents of the mayor suggested the holding of a local Democratic convention. Their goal was to nominate a slate of candidates to oppose Hartsfield and his allies on the Board of Aldermen. Charlie Brown, who ran for mayor in 1949 and 1953, was approached as a possible candidate. He declined to run. The effort to challenge Hartsfield failed because of dissension between the mayor's opponents and the inability to find serious candidates. This challenge, however, concerned members of the business-civic leadership. Twenty civic and business leaders met to discuss the political situation. Despite some reservations, they agreed to support politically and financially Hartsfield against any challenge in the general election.[17]

A challenge came from Lester Maddox, the proprietor of a local restaurant known as the Pickrick. Maddox's notoriety was largely due to a series of humorous ads, "Pickrick Says," which appeared in the local newspapers. These ads enticed working-class families, students from Georgia Tech, local politicians, and others who lived in the vicinity of his restaurant. "Pickrick Says" became a means by which Maddox expressed his political and racial views. He criticized those who would bring about integration through force. While he definitely held racist views, Maddox referred to himself as a segregationist (according to Maddox, a person who believed in the separation of the races, but not in white supremacy).[18]

In the primary, Maddox had supported Archie Lindsay. His campaign was similar to that of Lindsay. He attacked corruption within the police department, Hartsfield's "dictatorial administration," and the mayor's positions on racial matters. In contrast, Hartsfield concentrated on issues relating to the progress of the region. He stressed that racial peace was essential for progress. Hartsfield won the election with 41,300 votes to Lester Maddox's 23,987. His margin of victory was due to the African American vote. In the predominately African American districts, Maddox won only 353 votes out of the 15,562 ballots cast (two percent). In the white community, he won 23,634 votes of the 50,325 ballots cast (forty-seven percent). Hartsfield regained the support of many of the white middle-class neighborhoods that he lost in the primary. Maddox's support was mainly in the white working-class neighborhoods of South and West Atlanta. Hartsfield credited his victory to the desire for racial peace and progress. Maddox attributed the outcome of the election to African American bloc voting.[19]

Despite his margin of victory the 1957 election politically weakened Hartsfield. Perhaps recognizing this fact, Hartsfield hired a director of public relations and an administrative assistant for the first time. Previously, he had jealously guarded all political control. In September 1958 political rivals of Hartsfield defeated two of the mayor's most loyal supporters in their re-election bids to the state legislature. The mayor began to shift his attention from purely local issues to state and regional concerns. He filed a legal challenge to Georgia's county unit system. Hartsfield became more vocal in his call for racial peace and progress in the region. The mayor railed against "rabble rousers" and "racial agitators."[20] Because of these actions, Hartsfield began to receive national attention and praise. In 1957 *Fortune* magazine named him as one of the nation's best mayors even as, ironically, his local power diminished.[21]

Conservative members on the Board of Aldermen began to assert their influence on local policy. These members targeted an important rezoning proposal. In 1958 a survey by the Atlanta Housing Authority estimated that by 1963 government urban renewal projects in Atlanta would dislocate more than ten thousand families. City officials decided that additional public housing units would placate federal officials and African American leaders who were concerned about the displacement of black residents. Small business owners and low-income white residents generally opposed urban renewal projects and objected to the building of housing units in their neighborhoods to accommodate displaced residents. They argued that public housing lowered property values and defaced their communities. Small property owners also objected to the city's use of eminent domain to obtain land for urban renewal projects.

In November 1958 the Board of Aldermen requested the Atlanta Housing Authority to purchase land for the construction of 1000 African American housing units. The Atlanta Housing Authority chose the site of the former Egleston Hospital. While located in a predominately African American neighborhood, the Egleston site was also near the Georgia Baptist Hospital and Druid Hills Baptist Church. Both institutions and white neighborhood organizations opposed the construction of public housing units in the area. The proposal had the support of the governing coalition, the Citizens Advisory Committee on Urban Renewal, and good government organizations. Before housing units could be built, the Board of Aldermen had to rezone the site. In 1959 it rejected the rezoning proposal. After the measure's defeat, the Atlanta Housing Authority obtained a site on the west side of the city where 650 public housing units could be built. In March 1960 the board voted to rezone the site on the west side of the city, but rejected a reconsideration of the Egleston rezoning proposal.[22]

The rejection of the rezoning proposal caused widespread dissension between coalition members. The white business community feared that its rejection would encourage African American opposition to the city's urban renewal program. Before the second vote on the proposal, Richard Rich in a letter to the board president noted that the Egleston site was "such a logical place and a natural place to put displaced families, who must move from urban renewal areas, that it appears your action could set a precedent that would almost sabotage completely the urban renewal program."[23] Many leaders blamed the defeat on Hartsfield's inability to obtain the needed votes to pass the proposal. Previously, the business community had relied on the mayor to obtain board majorities on controversial issues. Many began to question whether new leadership was needed.

The rejection of the rezoning proposal generated discontent among African American leaders. The Atlanta Housing Authority chose the Egleston site largely because it was vacant land within the African American community. Black leaders backed the proposal. At a meeting of the Citizens Advisory Committee on Urban Renewal, Grace Hamilton stated that the committee should simply accentuate the fact that this area is predominately Negro and will remain so."[24] A perceived understanding between coalition members was that the African American community would be able to develop its own areas of the city. Because of the Board's action, many African American leaders began to question the sincerity and validity of previously negotiated agreements. After the proposal's defeat, African American leaders held a mass rally to protest the vote and express concerns. A.T. Walden and other leaders urged the continuation of ties with the business-civic leadership.[25]

The political vulnerability of the governing coalition led to the emergence of new leadership within both communities. Within the African American community, younger middle-class professionals began to challenge the "Old Guard" leadership. While still committed to the use of negotiations to solve racial problems, these leaders recognized the need for other tactics. They also desired a more active leadership. Within the white community, a younger generation of business leaders emerged. While still committed to many of the same values as their mentors, they were more willing to accept limited reform in exchange for racial peace and the economic progress of the region.

Younger African American professionals expressed their discontent with Atlanta's white and African American leadership in 1958 by forming a new organization, the Atlanta Committee for Cooperative Action (ACCA). Following his 1957 reelection bid, Hartsfield spoke to a meeting of African American leaders. In his speech, the mayor emphasized the progress that Atlanta had made in the area of race relations. As evident in the question-

and-answer session following the speech, many younger leaders were more concerned with the discrimination and racism that still existed in the city. They found Hartsfield's answers to be unsatisfactory. Many believed that the mayor was unwilling to undertake the necessary actions to achieve real reform. These younger professionals were concerned that the "Old Guard" leadership seemed to be protective of the mayor.[26]

The goals of ACCA were to energize the city's African American leadership, publicize the existing racial problems in the city, and provide technical assistance to those individuals and organizations involved in the civil rights struggle. The membership of this organization consisted mainly of young professionals and businessmen. Its membership included Jesse Hill, chief actuary and later president of Atlanta Life Insurance Company; Carl Holman, an English professor at Clark University and later president of the National Urban Coalition; Clarence Coleman, a deputy director of the National Urban League; Whitney Young, dean of the Atlanta University School of Social Work and later executive director of the National Urban League; and Samuel Westerfield, dean of the Atlanta University School of Business and later United States ambassador to Liberia.[27]

Members of ACCA became involved in efforts to desegregate colleges in Georgia. Jesse Hill, who was also a member of the education committee of the NAACP, enlisted the aid of other ACCA and NAACP members to desegregate the Georgia State College of Business (now Georgia State University). They needed to recruit creditable candidates for a lawsuit. In June 1959 Hill chose two students from Turner High School, Charlayne Hunter and Hamilton Homes. After determining that the academic program at Georgia State did not meet their particular needs, both students expressed an interest to attend the University of Georgia. Carl Holman aided the students in preparing their applications for the University of Georgia. Fearing possible violence, members of ACCA maintained a nightly patrol of Charlayne Hunter's residence in the weeks immediately following her application.[28]

One of the major concerns of ACCA was to bring attention to the discrimination and racism that still existed in Atlanta. Many members believed that boosterism and Atlanta's reputation as a progressive city hid these problems. ACCA decided to prepare a report on the inequalities that African Americans experienced in education, health services, housing, employment, justice and law enforcement, and policymaking. Members of ACCA collected the data. Carl Holman edited the report. The Atlanta Life Insurance Company financed the study, and the Southern Regional Council agreed to print the report.[29]

In February 1960 this survey, *A Second Look: The Negro Citizen in Atlanta*, was published. ACCA distributed the report to city officials, business, civic and neighborhood organizations, and the daily newspapers. The survey asked "their fellow Atlantans to take a second look at Atlanta: specifically to take a long, hard look at some of the problems which will not simply go away if we wink at them or ignore them long enough." *A Second Look* warned that Atlanta must guard against "complacency" and "self delusion."[30] It presented compelling evidence that the realities experienced by African Americans in Atlanta differed from the general perception of racial conditions in the city.

Many members of ACCA feared that the "Old Guard" leadership would disapprove of the survey because of its harsh criticism of conditions in Atlanta. They worked in secret and did not inform older conservative leaders of the project until it was completed. The "Old Guard" leadership, however, generally praised the report. Many made contributions to another printing. They could not deny the accuracy of the data. The *Atlanta Daily World* described the survey as "sober and factual." It noted that the report contained "no irresponsible rabble-rousing." The *Atlanta Constitution* and *The New York Times* gave detailed coverage to the contents of the report. In an era of sit-ins and public demonstrations, both newspapers noted the survey could serve as a potential platform for a campaign by African Americans to achieve racial reform in Atlanta.[31]

In addition to these activities, ACCA members petitioned for the removal of signs designating segregated restrooms at the airport. They urged the desegregation of public facilities and an end to discrimination in employment. ACCA members participated in a campaign initiated by local women organizations to improve segregated facilities in downtown Atlanta.

While its members often disagreed with the conservative policies and agenda of older African American leaders, ACCA did not directly challenge the "Old Guard" leadership. Rather, members worked quietly to cajole or pressure elder leaders into addressing a broader range of concerns and assuming a more activist posture. While rivalries existed, members of ACCA and the ANVL, the organizational voice of the "Old Guard" leadership, were free to disagree with each other. Some individuals were members of both organizations.[32] Because ACCA members maintained ties to the "Old Guard" leadership, they could serve as communication links and mediators between elder leaders and younger African Americans who favored a more militant approach to the struggle for civil rights.

Another potential rival to the "Old Guard" leadership emerged. In November 1959 Martin Luther King, Jr. announced that he was moving the headquarters of the Southern Christian Leadership Conference to Atlanta. Many conservative leaders opposed this action. While his father was an established leader in the community, King had not been directly involved in local affairs. Because of King's growing reputation as a regional and national leader, many feared that he might try to upstage their power in local affairs. The "Old Guard" leadership realized that campaigns for racial reform in Atlanta would be portrayed in the press as being directed by King rather than local leaders. An active affiliate of SCLC would also drain the resources and membership of existing local organizations.[33]

Concern also existed about the white community's reaction to King's presence in Atlanta. Following King's announcement, Governor Ernest Vandiver stated that "a wave of crimes including stabbings, bombings, and inciting of riots, barratry, destruction of private property and many other crimes" always followed King's presence. King, according to Vandiver, would not be welcomed in the state.[34] Ralph McGill also had reservations about King's decision to move to Atlanta at this particular time. In a letter to Harry Ashmore, McGill noted that he and other white Atlantans were on guard like "citizens of medieval walled cities who heard that the great plague was coming."[35] The potential for violence directed at King by certain elements of the white community existed. Many leaders were concerned that King's emphasis on nonviolent direct action would destroy the trust and communication built between them and leaders of the white community. They believed that nonviolent direct action as a tactic to achieve racial reforms had the potential to hinder negotiations.

Martin Luther King, Jr. realized the difficulties in returning to Atlanta. Most of the city's African American leaders were friends of his father and knew King as a boy. Before his departure for Atlanta, members of King's staff and community leaders held discussions as to what his role would be in local affairs.[36] While King could be a regional and national leader, his role in Atlanta would be limited. King assured community leaders that he was not trying to upstage their power. He attempted to downplay his homecoming and involvement in local affairs. While King participated in various activities at the request of local leaders, he never personally undertook a SCLC campaign in Atlanta. King also muted any direct criticism that he had of Atlanta's black leadership.

Conservative leaders were aware of the growing discontent and divisions within the African American community. Previously, the ANVL had been without viable competition. Neighborhood leaders on the south and west sides of the city formed political and civic organizations. These groups, however, mainly focused on neighborhood issues. On a citywide basis, these organizations did not challenge the authority of the League. While membership in the ANVL was opened to all registered voters in Fulton and DeKalb counties, leadership largely remained in the hands of a few individuals.[37] Younger African American citizens were generally attracted to more active organizations in which they could assume leadership roles.

In 1959 the executive committee of the League discussed the political and organizational divisions that existed within the community. One member suggested that the League should include the participation of all groups in its activities. A.T. Walden noted that the organization was formed "for the purpose of presenting an united front." While conceding that the League needed to cooperate and work with other organizations, he warned that political unity must be maintained. C.A. Scott argued that "some situations" did not require complete unity among organizations. He called for "more democratic" participation in the League.[38]

A more subtle transition in leadership was occurring within the white community. A new generation of businessmen was beginning to assume leadership positions. Many of these individuals were from families which had a tradition of civic involvement. Their power originated from influential family-owned businesses. Others emerged from leading industries and commercial enterprises in the area. Their status in the community was largely due to their position in the enterprise.[39] In many instances, elder leaders had carefully groomed these individuals. During an early phase in their career, many of these future leaders, for example, worked on community and civic projects such as the Boy Scouts Council and the Community Chest fund drive.[40]

Many of these younger businessmen became concerned about the city's future and the ability of the present leadership to meet new challenges. While Atlanta's economy was sound during the 1950s, the city experienced a decline in its growth rate and job production toward the end of the decade. Many younger businessmen blamed state and local officials for not being sufficiently active in their attempts to attract new industry. They perceived the Egleston vote as a temporary setback to the city's urban renewal program. Due to racial tensions in the region, many businessmen were concerned about a strong conservative challenge to the business-civic leadership in the upcoming 1961 mayoral election. Many felt that Hartsfield was simply too old and politically vulnerable to make another bid. The search for another viable candidate began. Due to a school desegregation suit and student unrest, many younger businessmen realized that the potential for racial violence in the city existed. Conflict between the races would disrupt their plans for the economic progress of the city. They believed that all of these issues had to be aggressively addressed.[41]

In December 1960 the Atlanta Chamber of Commerce named Ivan Allen, Jr. to serve as its president for the following year. Ivan Allen, Jr. was a member of this younger generation of business leaders. His father was the founder of a local office equipment firm. During the 1920s, Ivan Allen, Sr. was co-chairman of the Forward Atlanta program. He was a close friend and advisor to Mayor Hartsfield. Ivan Allen, Jr. was the heir apparent to his father. Prior to his appointment as Chamber president, Allen had held various positions in the gubernatorial administrations of E.D. Rivers, Ellis Arnall, and M.E. Thompson. He was a member of the state Board of Education and Chamber of Commerce. During the late 1940s and 1950s he became actively involved in a number of civic and community projects. When his father retired, he assumed the presidency of the Ivan Allen Company.

Like his fellow business peers, Allen was concerned about the "general malaise that the city was in" and "the problems that the city was going to be faced with in the coming years." With the input of other businessmen, he prepared a "Six Point Program." The main goal of these businessmen was to construct an agenda which would address their concerns and guide the city over the next decade. Members of the Chamber of Commerce subsequently endorsed this program, and it appeared in its literature.

This younger generation of business leaders initiated Allen's "Six Point Program" which emphasized business and economic objectives rather than social and welfare needs. Because of the resources and political influence of the business community, these objectives could be achieved without major public participation in the planning and development. The "Six Point Program" called for maintaining open schools, an increase in the pace of local expressway construction, an expansion and acceleration of the city's urban renewal and housing programs, the construction of an auditorium/coliseum and a stadium, the lobbying for a large-scale rapid transit system, and a "Forward Atlanta Campaign."[42] Inherent in the objectives of this "Six Point Program" was the belief that the economic progress of the region would gradually lead to limited social change.

The core of this program was "Forward Atlanta." A successful Forward Atlanta campaign would serve as a justification and a catalyst for the other objectives. Similar to the original Forward Atlanta program of the 1920s, it was a national advertising campaign with the intent of attracting new industries to the area. In its initial phase, approximately 1500 firms pledged $1.6 million to the effort. Half of the money raised during this period went to advertising. Ads promoting the city appeared in *Business Week, Fortune, Newsweek,* the *New Yorker,* and the *Wall Street Journal.* The Chamber of Commerce sponsored *Atlanta Magazine,* a monthly publication that highlighted the city. During the program's first four years, it also hired a traveling representative to visit with industrial and business prospects.[43]

By the time the Forward Atlanta campaign began, business leaders recognized that a good reputation in race relations was helpful in attracting new industries. In particular, southern cities had to have an untainted image in order to be truly competitive for new enterprises and industries. As a result, Atlanta capitalized on its growing reputation for racial moderation. Representatives from the city boasted of the liaison that existed between the white and African American communities; the use of negotiations to ease racial tensions; its African American colleges, businesses, and middle-class neighborhoods; a leadership dedicated to economic and social progress; and an atmosphere of racial harmony. In the area of race relations, the business leadership felt that Atlanta had an enormous advantage over southern cities such as Birmingham and New Orleans.

The white leadership of Atlanta realized that racial conflict could quickly tarnish a city's image. Little Rock, Arkansas was a glaring example. Similar in many respects to Atlanta, the business community of Little Rock embarked on a campaign to attract industries in the early 1950s. The city had a progressive reputation and good record in race relations. In 1957 racial disturbances stemming from the desegregation of Central High School tarnished that city's progressive image.[44] Immediately following the disturbances, outside investment in the city plummeted. The spectre of Little Rock haunted the business community of Atlanta during the early 1960s. Atlanta could not afford to be "another Little Rock."

While the majority of Atlanta's business leaders shared the same prejudices as their fellow citizens, they realized that some change was inevitable. Many believed and hoped that gradual racial reform would be achieved through the economic progress of the region. Economic growth was thus their main priority. Atlanta's businessmen were willing to accept limited racial reform in exchange for the absence of conflict between the races. They were reluctant, however, to affect major racial change due in part to their racial beliefs and opposition from conservative elements within the white community. White leadership thus tended to follow a middle course. Leaders in Atlanta yielded the minimum racial reform necessary to avoid racial conflict. Legal challenges and pressure from the black community would be necessary to bring about major racial reform.

Despite the subtle changes in the leadership of both communities, the governing coalition remained intact. While younger African American leaders desired greater racial reform and a more energetic leadership, they were still basically committed to the use of negotiations with the business-civic leadership and litigation to solve racial problems. Due in part to their desire for economic growth, a younger generation of business leaders appeared more willing than their elders to accept racial reform. The African American community as a voting bloc still did not have enough votes to assume a political majority. Despite some debate among African American leaders as to its true effectiveness, an alliance with the business-civic leadership appeared the wisest course of action.

During the 1950s, one issue that had the potential to cause racial conflict and dissension among coalition members was school desegregation. As in most southern cities, African American students in Atlanta attended overcrowded, dilapidated buildings with no kindergartens, auditoriums, sporting facilities and cafeterias. African American citizens worked to improve these conditions. They supported school bond issues hoping that money would be allotted to African American schools. Citizens petitioned the School Board for better facilities and higher salaries for teachers. In 1944 the Atlanta Urban League conducted a study of the conditions of African American schools. As a result of this study, African American leaders organized a Citizens Committee on Public Education to inform the public on the inequalities and discrimination that existed. Atlantans passed a school bond issue which allotted four million dollars of a nine million dollar bond proposal to African American schools (only a small amount of these funds were actually spent on black schools). In 1950 African American parents filed suit arguing that educational facilities were unequal. In 1952 lawyers for the plaintiffs amended the suit to argue that segregated schools were inherently unequal. Because the case was delayed due to the *Brown* decision, the Court eventually dismissed the suit on the ground of lack of prosecution in June 1956.

In May 1954 the United States Supreme Court declared that segregated educational facilities were inherently unequal. One year later, the Supreme Court ruled that desegregation need only be implemented "with all deliberate speed." Four days following the *Brown II* decision, the Atlanta branch of the NAACP petitioned school authorities to abolish segregation.[45] National and state officials met at the Wheat Street Baptist Church to devise a strategy as to how desegregation could be achieved. The strategy outlined at this meeting included the filing of a petition requesting desegregation with each local school board followed by periodic inquiries. The final step was to be a legal challenge. William Boyd, the state NAACP president, instructed local branches to follow this procedure. He pledged that the state office would commit itself to help those areas where no local branches existed.[46] By September 1955 eight local branches had filed petitions with their local school boards.[47]

Hoping to avoid the *Brown* decision, Georgia officials attempted to preserve public education on a "separate-but-equal" basis. In the early 1950s, the state allotted more money to education. African American schools shared in this increased revenue. The General Assembly also increased and equalized the salaries of teachers. Following the *Brown* decision, the state's response was one of open defiance. Governor Herman Talmadge announced that the state would not accept racially mixed schools. State Attorney General Cook refused to appear before the Supreme Court when it heard briefs as to how and when the *Brown* decision was to be implemented. In 1953 the state legislature had created the Georgia Education Committee to explore ways of circumventing the federal assault on segregation, publicizing the "Georgia way of life," and investigating subversives. In 1956 the legislature passed a resolution declaring the *Brown* decision "null, void, and of no force or effect" and a measure requiring all state law enforcement agencies and employees to enforce segregation laws. The state agreed to defend all public officials charged, accused, or indicted relative to federal statutes that disregarded Georgia's segregation laws.

State legislation also dealt with the closing of public schools and the establishment of a private school system if integration occurred. The Georgia state constitution required separate schools. State law prohibited the payment of state and local funds to any public school system that did not provide separate schools. The elimination of such funds would effectively close a public school system. The General Assembly placed the governor in control of the state's public schools. The state legislature empowered the governor with the authority to close the schools of any one county, city, or independent district. It also allowed the governor to deem whether a school was entitled to state funds. When he judged the action was necessary, the governor also had the authority to suspend the compulsory attendance law on the grounds of "riot, insurrection, public disorder, disturbance of the peace, natural calamity or disaster, the destruction of private property, or to preserve the general welfare of the state."

In November 1954 the citizens of Georgia ratified a "private school amendment" which allowed grants of state, county, or municipal funds to private citizens for educational purposes. The legislature passed a series of laws to codify this amendment. It passed a measure allowing the State

School Building Authority and local governments to lease school property to persons and organizations engaged in the operation of private schools for educational purposes. Individuals who contributed to private schools could claim a tax credit on their state income tax returns. Educators and other personnel who accepted employment in private nonsectarian schools were still eligible for retirement benefits. Legislation, however, revoked benefits to teachers working in racially-mixed schools. Clearly, this legislation was an open attack on the public school system and the *Brown* decision.[48]

Ironically, the passage of this legislation created strategic problems for those opposed to school desegregation. Rather than focusing the debate solely on the question of integration, this legislation raised issues concerning public schools versus private schools, law and order, and the operational control of the public school system. While the majority of citizens in the state opposed integration, many were against the closing of public schools even if desegregation occurred. A small number of individuals were hesitant to disobey the "law of the land." Many officials questioned whether the decision to close public schools should ultimately rest with the state or the community affected. Groups could thus rally around a wide variety of issues.

Integration was a potentially divisive issue in the debate over school desegregation. Proponents of school desegregation in Atlanta could rally, however, behind the issues of open public schools, law and order, and community control. Those who were hesitant to challenge directly or openly discuss racial attitudes could speak freely on these other issues. Proponents of school desegregation were in a unique position. While denouncing the *Brown* decision and defending traditional racial beliefs, they could still speak in favor of open schools.

In November 1957 eighty white ministers in Atlanta released a statement supporting open schools. In the wake of the *Brown* decision, local white ministers had remained silent on the issue of school desegregation, but rising racial tensions in the region placed pressure on them to provide religious and moral leadership.[49] This statement, commonly referred to as the "Atlanta Manifesto," listed six principles which the ministers felt "to be of basic importance for thought and conduct" in the area of race relations: the protection of free speech, an obligation to obey the law, the preservation of the public school system, respect for all races and differing positions, communication between "responsible leaders" of both races, and dependence on prayer and God's guidance to solve racial difficulties. The ministers assured readers of the "Atlanta Manifesto" that they opposed the "amalgamation of the races." Nevertheless, they declared their belief that all

Americans were "entitled to the full privileges of first class citizenship." The statement urged citizens to refrain from the use of violence and economic reprisal. The ministers did recognize, however, the right of citizens to attempt to change the *Brown* decision through legal means.[50]

The following year, approximately 312 ministers representing sixteen different denominations issued a second statement, one which was more direct in its support of school desegregation than the "Atlanta Manifesto" and strengthen the wording of the six principles. In regard to the *Brown* decision, the statement noted that "a policy of obeying only those laws or rulings of the Court which we agree with leads inevitably to anarchy." Citizens had to "face up to the fact, that under the ruling of the Supreme Court made in the discharge of its constitutional authority, enforced segregation in the public schools is now without support in and contrary to national law." The ministers argued that the destruction of the public school system would be "a tragedy of the first magnitude." They pledged that church facilities would not be offered as "a means for denying the constitutional authority of our national government." The statement asked southern officials to avoid inflammatory utterances and establish lines of communication with African American leaders. The ministers urged an intelligent discussion of the issues and the appointment of a Citizen's Committee to resolve the controversy.

Similar to the "Atlanta Manifesto," this second statement contained several conciliatory positions. The ministers denounced the "wisdom of massive integration" and the "amalgamation of the races." The statement argued that mutual esteem between the races had to be maintained on the basis of free choice rather than force. The ministers urged the Supreme Court to give "due consideration to local situations" and avoid the "indiscriminate" desegregation of schools. They asked the federal government to "leave the working out of details in local hands."[51]

These statements largely established the tone of debate in Atlanta. In advocating school desegregation, many religious, civic, and professional organizations drew upon the principles listed in the ministers' statements. These organizations included the United Church Women, the Georgia Council on Human Relations and its affiliate branches, local PTAs, and various medical and professional organizations. The *Atlanta Constitution*, *Gainesville Daily Times*, *Macon Telegraph*, and *North Georgia Tribune* were among the newspapers that editorially supported open schools or legislation giving the power of opening or closing schools to the local community. Conspicuously absent from most of the statements supporting open schools was a discussion of the racial implications of desegregation.

By the end of the 1950s, the proponents of school desegregation in Atlanta had formed an effective movement to save public schools. The organizational core of this campaign was a group commonly referred to as HOPE, Help Our Public Education. In October 1958, two women who were concerned about the school issue organized a morning coffee to discuss ways to preserve public education. Ten women participated in this initial meeting. By November 1958 one hundred people were attending these morning sessions and approximately 400 supporters attended a rally at a local auditorium that month. In March 1959 a HOPE meeting at a municipal theatre attracted 1800 people. William Hartsfield, Ralph McGill, and Sylvan Meyer (editor of the *Gainesville Daily Times*) spoke at the rally. By the end of 1959 HOPE chapters were established in Athens, Gainesville, Rome, and Savannah. HOPE eventually organized ten chapters across the state. While men were active in the organization, the majority of HOPE members were white middle-to-upper class women who were concerned about the education of their children.[52]

A pamphlet published in September 1959 listed the positions which were to guide HOPE supporters in their campaign to preserve public education: (1) Georgia needed a public school system; (2) a private school system could not adequately meet the needs of the state's citizens; (3) the temporary closing of any public school system would "be an extreme and indefensible" action; (4) the organization would not support litigation aimed at closing any public school; (5) HOPE supported the continued operation of public schools in accordance with established laws, "recognizing that any conflict must be resolved," and (6) the decision to continue open schools ultimately rested with the individual citizen. For political and strategic reasons, HOPE adopted three key tactics: (1) membership in the organization was restricted to white citizens; (2) HOPE supporters were not to debate the merits of segregation versus integration or the validity of the *Brown* decision; and (3) HOPE would not encourage or be a party to litigation pertaining to the school controversy.[53]

HOPE's strategy was to educate citizens as to the importance of a public school system. Members encouraged open discussion of the school situation. HOPE organized neighborhood discussion groups, public forums, conferences, and workshops. It established a Speaker's Bureau to meet increasing requests for discussion leaders from church, civic, and social organizations. Parents were encouraged to discuss the issue at PTA meetings. HOPE sent out repeated mailings and literature on open schools to state and local officials. In January 1960 it presented a petition supporting open schools to the state legislature. HOPE was able to amass 10,024 signatures from eighty cities and counties across the state.[54]

Almost from its inception, HOPE was in communication with open schools movements in Virginia, Arkansas, and Louisiana. Representatives from these organizations came to Atlanta to discuss the school situation in their particular communities. Throughout the school debate, the experiences of these communities were vivid examples of what could possibly happen in Atlanta should the open schools movement fail.

In Virginia an organized segregationist grass roots movement combined forces with the Byrd political machine to develop and enact a policy of massive resistance to the *Brown* decision. In 1956 the Virginia General Assembly adopted a set of laws designed to block any effort to desegregate schools. Once a federal court issued an order to integrate schools, these measures required the governor to take control of the affected school, close it, and attempt to reopen it on a segregated basis. Legislation denied state funds to integrated schools, but provided tuition grants for private schools in affected areas. In 1958 the state legislature passed a measure allowing the local School Board and governing body to petition the state jointly if the community desired to operate its schools under local control. When federal courts ordered the desegregation of schools in Charlottesville, Norfolk, and Warren County in September 1958, Governor J. Lindsay Almond, Jr. closed nine public schools in these areas, suspending the education of approximately 12,700 white students. Many of these students, but not all, entered makeshift private schools.

Whether out of fear of the Byrd political machine or simply taken by surprise, effective opposition to the closing of schools in Virginia did not emerge until Almond took action. While organizations such as the Virginia Council on Human Relations, the American Association of University Women, and the Fort Royal Ministerial Association immediately denounced the governor's action, they had little influence. A statewide open schools movement did not emerge until organizations from Norfolk, Charlottesville, and Arlington formed the Virginia Committee for Public Schools in December 1958. Largely composed of white middle-class professionals, the Virginia Committee for Public Schools excluded African American members and focused on the need to maintain open schools, rather than integration, as the key issue. Virginia's business community did not actively become involved in the open schools movement until January 1959. By this time, the effects that the school crisis had on the economy of the state were apparent and the business community began to pressure Almond to open schools.

On 19 January 1959 the Supreme Court of Appeals of Virginia held that the closing of schools and the cutting off of state funds to prevent desegregation violated the state constitution. On the same day, the United States District Court for the Eastern District of Virginia ruled that the denial of state funds violated the Fourteenth Amendment. In a special session of the General Assembly held later that month, legislative forces led by Governor Almond prevented the passage of legislation designed to circumvent these decisions. In February schools in Charlottesville, Norfolk, and Warren County reopened on an integrated basis. Prince Edward County in Southside Virginia, however, continued a policy of massive resistance. Rather than comply with a court order to desegregate their schools by a certain date, the white citizens of that county decided to close the public school system. Beginning in September 1959, white children began attending private schools; African American children were denied a public education. Public schools remained closed in Prince Edward County until a court order required them to open on an integrated basis in 1964.[55]

During this same period, a school crisis also developed in Little Rock, Arkansas. Whether out of the desire to prevent racial violence or win a third term in office, Governor Orval Faubus intervened to halt a local plan for the desegregation of Little Rock's Central High School. On the day before the school opened, he mobilized troops of the Arkansas National Guard to block the entry of African American students. After a period of three weeks in which he met with President Eisenhower and a federal judge enjoined him from interfering further with integration, Faubus withdrew the guardsmen. On the following school day, a white mob gathered around Central High when rumors spread that the African American students were in the building. President Eisenhower federalized the Arkansas National Guard and ordered 1,100 paratroopers from the 101st Airborne Division flown into Little Rock to ensure the safety of the students. Troops patrolled the halls of Central High for the rest of the year. In September 1958 the Supreme Court denied a petition by the Little Rock School Board to delay integration on the ground of community opposition (*Cooper v. Aaron*). In response, Governor Faubus signed legislation that gave him the authority to close all of Little Rock's high schools.

Bound by their own racial attitudes and uncertain as to the proper course to follow, business leaders in Arkansas were slow to respond to the school crisis. Governor Faubus occupied center stage. Initially, business leaders attempted to delay the court order. When this effort failed, the business community of Little Rock, which was increasingly becoming concerned over the economic impact of the school crisis on the city, decided to assume a more visible role. After two unsuccessful attempts, business leaders seized political control of the School Board and installed one of their own as president. This Board was dedicated to reopening the city's high schools. The Women's Emergency Committee aided business leaders in their activities. This organization attempted to use the school issue as a means to build support for improved racial conditions in the city. Largely due to the activities of the business community and the Women's Emergency Committee, schools in Little Rock reopened in 1960.[56]

As events in Little Rock were beginning to return to normal, a school crisis in New Orleans was beginning to reach its climax. In 1956 a federal district judge in New Orleans ordered the city to make arrangements for the desegregation of its schools. In 1959 the District Court ordered the city to file a desegregation plan by May 1960. Between 1956 and 1959 the New Orleans Board of Education made no efforts to construct a plan or prepare the city for the desegregation of its schools. In May the Board informed the Court that it did not have a desegregation plan. The judge ordered the desegregation of all first grades at the opening of the school year in September 1960. Stunned by the decision, the School Board asked Governor Jimmie Davis to intervene in the case.

In August Davis announced that he was in control of the New Orleans public school system and ordered the schools to open in September on a segregated basis. Fearing that Davis would close all city schools, a group of white parents filed a suit requesting an injunction to restrain city officials from enforcing state segregation statutes. In response, the District Court declared all state laws requiring segregation in the schools unconstitutional and nullified the governor's seizure of the School Board. It ordered the Board to proceed with the desegregation of the schools. The Board indicated its willingness to comply with the court order. The judge agreed to delay desegregation until November of that year in order to give the Board time to design a desegregation plan.

After the School Board announced that it had granted transfer permits to five African American female students, Governor Davis called the state legislature into special session. The legislature passed several measures which would block the desegregation of state schools. In early November, four state legislators, accompanied by armed members of the state police, arrived at the New Orleans Board of Education Building and announced that the legislature had assumed authority over the School Board. A few hours later, the District Court issued an order prohibiting state authorities from interfering with the Board's desegregation plan. The Board formally approved the transfer of five African American students into two all-white schools. Another attempt by the state legislature to seize control of the School Board failed.

In November 1960 four African American students (one withdrew her transfer application) integrated city schools. White parents at the integrated schools, however, began to withdraw their children. By the end of the first week, every white child was withdrawn from one school and all but two white children were withdrawn from the second. Segregationist leaders in the city held a large rally at the municipal auditorium. The following day, a white mob, estimated at between one and three thousand people, marched on City Hall, the federal court, and the Board of Education Building. After the police turned away the mob at the Board of Education Building, it grew unruly and began to throw bottles and stones at African American citizens. Sporadic "street battles" between white and African American citizens continued throughout November and December. Every morning, a huge white crowd gathered at the integrated schools to taunt, threaten, and physically harass the African American students and few white pupils who went to the schools despite the boycott.

Largely due to the unfavorable national publicity that the city was receiving, business leaders in New Orleans ran an advertisement in the *Times-Picayune* appealing for an end to the violence and expressing support for the School Board. In January 1961, they participated in a dinner which paid tribute to the school board members for the efforts they made to preserve open schools. While these actions were only symbolic gestures, they provided a needed public display of confidence and support for the School Board. While the school boycott continued throughout the school year, violence in the city began to decrease.

In July 1961 Victor Shiro, the newly appointed mayor of New Orleans, and other community leaders appealed for law and order in the upcoming school year. In September, the School Board, with the support of the mayor and other community leaders, expanded its desegregation plan to include four other white schools. While random acts of violence were reported and the white boycott continued at some of the schools, the desegregation of New Orleans schools in 1961 was peaceful and calm.[57]

As Morton Inger argues in his study of the New Orleans' school crisis, the city's problems were largely due to the lack of leadership. With the exception of an endorsement of a moderate candidate to the Board and the December appeal for an end to violence, the business community remained silent throughout the controversy; it did not prepare the city for the desegregation of its schools. The New Orleans Chamber of Commerce did not express its support for the peaceful desegregation of the schools and compliance with the court order until the summer of 1961.

Two organizations were specifically formed to express support for open schools in New Orleans, the Committee for Public Education (CPE) and Save Our Schools (SOS). CPE urged that schools be kept open even if that meant integration. Because its membership was basically comprised of conservative, native-born citizens, CPE's backing of open schools allowed moderate individuals and organizations to express their support. SOS represented the "white liberal" element in the city. Social workers, Tulane faculty, and relative newcomers to New Orleans largely comprised the membership of SOS. While SOS supported the same position taken by CPE, its members were willing to voice support for integration. SOS members frequently spoke at events sponsored by HOPE.[58]

Atlantans watched these events with interest and concern. They were determined not to make the same mistakes. A 1960 advertisement of HOPE, for example, read, "Police at New Orleans Quell 2000, DON'T LET IT HAPPEN HERE!" HOPE members believed that many of the problems in New Orleans, Little Rock, and Norfolk were due to a lack of leadership and community preparation. After discussions with members of open school movements in Virginia and Little Rock, proponents of open schools in Atlanta realized that they had to launch an effective campaign before any schools were closed. They recognized the importance of focusing on the issue of open schools rather than integration and involving political and business leaders in their activities.

While acknowledging the effectiveness of focusing on open schools, a few individuals and organizations were concerned that the issue of integration was minimized. The Southern Regional Council, the Georgia Council on Human Relations, and the American Friends Service Committee were among the organizations which argued that desegregation was good in itself rather than merely a necessary concomitant to open schools. Many African American leaders expressed concern that the white religious community and advocates of open schools did not denounce segregation.[59] Harry Boyte, a member of the Georgia Council on Human Relations and the American Friends Service Committee, was disturbed that HOPE excluded African American participation. Frances Pauley, a human relations activist and chairperson of the Georgia Council on Human Relations, was initially reluctant to join HOPE for the same reason. She joined only at the urging of Donald Hollowell, an African American attorney and close friend.[60]

The open schools movement found an ally in Mayor Hartsfield. When an Atlanta attorney suggested selling the city's schools to private parties to prevent desegregation, Hartsfield publicly condemned the proposal. He argued that the closing of public schools was unthinkable and a single day's shutdown would do damage to the city.[61] The mayor publicly stated several times that he wanted to avoid the schools closings and violence that occurred in Little Rock, New Orleans, and Virginia. After African American parents filed a school desegregation suit in 1958, Hartsfield asked the state legislature not to interfere with the city's decision to comply with whatever ruling the court reached. He urged the governor and legislature to allow communities to decide whether to integrate or close schools. This proposal created a bitter confrontation between the governor and mayor. The governor rejected his plea and the state continued a policy of massive resistance. Nevertheless, Hartsfield argued that compliance with the court's decision would enhance the city's image and thus be beneficial to its economic growth and progress.

With civic and religious organizations and Mayor Hartsfield at the forefront of the debate, the business community initially played a passive, behind-the-scenes role. In 1958 a steering committee under the auspices of the League of Women Voters approached community leaders in order to enlist their support for open schools. They refused to help.[62] In 1959 "several prominent ministers" and "very important businessmen" met to discuss the role of the business community in the "school crisis." While the businessmen expressed various opinions, the general consensus of these leaders, according to one participant, was that they "were becoming a little weary of talking of it, that there is little that they could do at the present time, and that efforts by them to intervene with the governor might well do more harm than good in increasing the gap between Atlanta and the rest of the state."[63] HOPE members also noted a reluctance on the part of the business community to become involved in the school controversy.[64]

In the early 1960s businessmen decided to take a more active role in the fight for open schools. One reason for this decision was the desegregation crisis at the University of Georgia. For the first time, businessmen realized that the state's segregation statutes could actually close down Georgia's university system. Obviously, this action would have a devastating impact on the state's economy. Business leaders in Atlanta were concerned that school closings would damage their attempts to attract outside investment. The Atlanta Chamber of Commerce voiced its strong support for open schools and pledged to "clearly set forth to the public at large and the business community in particular the full implications of the Little Rock, Norfolk, and New Orleans stories."[65] In a private meeting with Governor Vandiver, business leaders called upon him to keep the schools open regardless of the court decision. They argued that the closing of schools would have disastrous effects on the economic growth of the state.[66] While many of these businessmen undoubtedly still believed in the separation of the races, their desire for economic growth took precedence over their belief in white supremacy.[67]

Despite this rather formidable campaign to save public schools, considerable opposition to school desegregation existed in the city. In January 1959 evangelical ministers organized the Evangelical Christian Council in order "to advance evangelical Christianity and to give Bible-believing Christians a voice." In March 1959 fifty-three ministers of this organization issued a manifesto on the school controversy. While taking no firm position on the closing of schools, the ministers believed that integration was "Satanic, unconstitutional, and one of the main objectives of the Communist Party." Any integration would present "grave moral, social, religious, and constitutional problems." According to the ministers, anything that would lead to the "amalgamation of the races" was a "sin against Almighty God." Nevertheless, the manifesto urged that people of all races be treated in "a moral and Christian manner" and that "all things should be done without strife and vainglory; that each race should maintain its purity and earnestly seek to develop its own members to the highest state of perfection in all things."[68]

In addition to evangelical Christians, prosegregation forces were represented in the debate. One organization specifically formed to fight against school desegregation was MASE, Metropolitan Association for Segregated Education. MASE members urged that schools be kept segregated even if private schools had to be substituted for public schools. Members held rallies, and wrote state and city officials urging that the schools remained segregated. In January 1960 MASE officials asked the plaintiffs in the school desegregation case to withdraw their litigation and cease all integration efforts for the best interests of both white and African American children. In 1960 MASE officials claimed a membership of over five thousand members in Fulton County.[69]

Members of hate organizations, particularly the Klan, participated in the debate over public schools. The state had revoked the Klan charter in 1947, but the U.S. Klan, the Knights of the Ku Klux Klan received a new charter in 1956. Between the mid-1950s and early 1960s, the membership of the Klan grew rapidly in Georgia. In the Atlanta area, three different Klan associations were represented.[70] At a Klan rally in December 1960, a member of the Carroll County Board of Education suggested that all public schools ordered to integrate should be closed. At the same meeting a Klan official noted that the answer to the school controversy would be to "either close schools or burn schools."[71] In addition to the Klan, representatives of such hate organizations as the National States Rights Party, the National White American Party, and the Christian Anti-Jewish Party were present in the city during the school debate. The following of these organizations in Atlanta was small, and they had only a limited impact on the school controversy.

The lines of debate in Atlanta were thus clearly drawn. Proponents of open schools argued that citizens had to obey the *Brown* decision. Unless state laws were changed, public schools in the city had to close. Proponents thus focused their attention on open schools, law and order, and local option. Since the validity of the *Brown* decision and integration were potentially divisive issues, proponents did not discuss them. Those opposed to school desegregation tried to focus the debate on the *Brown* decision and the issue of forced integration. If federal courts ordered schools to integrate, they favored the closing of schools. Most supported the establishment of some type of private education supported by state funds while public schools were closed. White and African American parents simply wanted a decent education for their children.

In June 1959 District Court Judge Frank Hooper declared that Atlanta's segregated school system violated the Fourteenth Amendment. Allowing sufficient time for the Georgia legislature to respond, the Court ordered the Atlanta Board of Education to submit a plan for desegregation by December of that year. In response to the decision, Governor Vandiver stated that he had no recourse under state law but to close any integrated schools. Attorney General Eugene Cook argued that the interests of both races demanded the withdrawal of litigation. Mayor Hartsfield again requested legislation allowing local option. According to a street poll in the *Atlanta Constitution*, most citizens opposed the decision, but were willing to accept it.[72]

Before drafting its proposal, the Atlanta Board of Education studied plans adopted by Charlotte, Dallas, New Orleans, and other southern cities. It eventually adopted a pupil placement plan similar to one used in Alabama. Clearly, the proposal was designed to minimize desegregation. The proposal listed eighteen standards regulating transfers among Atlanta's schools. These regulations included "the available room and teaching capacity in the various schools," "the scholastic aptitude and relative intelligence or mental energy or ability of the pupil," "the effect of the admission of the pupil upon the academic progress of the students in a particular school or facility thereof," "the morals, conduct, and personal standards of the student," and "the choice and interests of the pupil."[73] None of the proposed regulations made a direct reference to race. Desegregation was to begin in the twelfth grade and proceed at the pace of one grade per year, top-to-bottom. The burden of requesting transfer to another school rested with the student.

Attorneys for the African American parents and children had several objections to the plan: (1) the plan placed the duty of desegregation upon the students rather than the school system; (2) no reference was made to the desegregation of school staff; (3) the plan contained delays which made a "prompt" and "reasonable" start toward desegregation impossible; (4) the wording of many of the standards were vague and unclear; (5) two regulations, "the possibility of friction or disorder among the pupils" and "the possibility of breaches of peace or ill will or economic retaliation within the community," were unconstitutional; (6) students were not given adequate time to appeal their placement; and (7) the plan was contingent upon the passage of state legislation. The Court ordered two changes in the plan. Changes were made in the appeal process and "economic retaliation" was removed as a standard regulating transfer (this provision was intended to halt African American boycotts of white establishments).[74]

The order to desegregate Atlanta's school system placed Governor Vandiver in a difficult position. Advocates and opponents of school desegregation began lobbying legislators and other elected officials. Current laws required the closing of integrated schools. A majority of the state's citizens and elected officials supported this position. In an extremely difficult 1958 gubernatorial campaign in which candidates tried to "out-seg" the other, Vandiver stated, "neither my child nor yours will ever attend an integrated school during my administration—no, not one." Despite his campaign rhetoric and public posture, Vandiver was not a rabid segregationist. He was aware that the closing of public schools would be disastrous for the economy and the reputation of the state.

Griffin Bell, Vandiver's chief of staff, offered a solution to the governor's dilemma. He suggested the formation of a committee of respected citizens and leaders to examine the school issue. This committee would be required to hold at least one hearing in each of Georgia's ten congressional districts. The meetings would allow individuals who wished to speak on the issue of school desegregation to testify before the committee. The stated purposes of this committee were to give the people of the state a chance to vent their feelings and study possible alternatives to school desegregation.[75] Obviously, the findings of such a committee would also lessen the political pressure on the Vandiver administration by shifting the responsibility for the decision on whether to keep schools open or close them to the committee. In 1960 the Georgia General Assembly created the Committee on Schools and, upon the recommendation of Governor Vandiver, appointed John Sibley, a respected Atlanta attorney and board member of several local corporations, as chairman.

Beginning in February 1960 the Committee on Schools, generally referred to as the Sibley Committee, held hearings in each of the state's ten congressional districts. Sibley insisted on holding the testimony of the witnesses to the main issue. As defined by the Committee, the issue was whether the citizens of Georgia wanted to maintain current laws that would force the schools to close if ordered to desegregate or to enact local option or pupil placement laws that would allow each community to handle the school situation in its own fashion. Throughout the hearings, Sibley was determined not to permit a debate over segregation or integration to obscure this issue. In each district, advocates and opponents of open schools tried to influence the Sibley Committee by recruiting witnesses to testify in their behalf. Generally, the northern districts of the state supported local option or a pupil placement law; whereas, southern districts preferred maintaining present state laws. Preference for open schools was more pronounced in the urban areas than rural counties and small towns. Witnesses from the Atlanta area overwhelmingly supported open schools.[76]

The Sibley Committee filed both a majority and minority report with the General Assembly. The majority report referred to the *Brown* decision as "an usurpation of the legislation function through the judicial process," "an invasion of the reserved rights of the state," and "a clear and present danger to our system of constitutional government." It acknowledged that a three-to-two majority of committee witnesses favored maintaining segregation even at the cost of public schools. Nevertheless, the report noted that the citizens of Georgia "must recognize that the decision exists, that it is binding on the federal courts, and that it will be enforced." According to the report, an insistence upon total segregation would mean the eventual abandonment of public education. For this reason, the majority report recommended that Georgia repeal its massive resistance laws and adopt a local option policy that would allow local communities to determine their own course of action.[77]

The minority report argued that the purpose of the Sibley Committee was to determine the wishes of the state's citizens. The members found "virtually unanimous sentiment among the people of the state of all races that continued maintenance of separate schools is in the best interests of the state." According to the report, forced integration would cause "serious turmoil, bitterness, rancor, and internal strife, inflicting much harm on the people of Georgia, and accomplishing nothing for the welfare of its citizens." The report recommended that public school systems be preserved on a segregated basis until closed by a federal court decree. As a last resort, it urged that a system of grants be established for private educational purposes on a segregated basis as outlined in the private school amendment.[78]

The Atlanta plan was to be implemented for the 1960 school year. Due to the majority report of the Sibley Committee, Judge Hooper decided to delay the implementation of the plan until 1961 in order to allow the state legislature enough time to repeal existing state segregation laws. He warned that the plan would be implemented in 1961 regardless of state laws. Due to the delay, the desegregation process would involve both the eleventh and twelfth grades.

In the midst of the debate over school desegregation, an unidentified terrorist bombed an African American school in early December 1960. This incident made leaders aware of the potential for racial violence in the city. As in the case of the Temple bombing, Mayor Hartsfield blamed political demagogues and indifferent civic leaders for the racial unrest that existed in the city and region. Following this bombing, the Georgia Council of Churches, a biracial organization, urged the governor to keep the schools open. It also called on Christian churches to welcome all who came to worship services regardless of race.[79]

In January 1961 a federal judge ordered the immediate desegregation of the University of Georgia. Following state law, Governor Vandiver ordered a cutoff of state funds to the university. After the United States Supreme Court upheld a lower court's decision to prohibit the cutoff of funds and a demonstration erupted on the campus protesting the presence of the two African American students (Charlayne Hunter and Hamilton Holmes), Governor Vandiver appeared before the Georgia General Assembly. In his speech, Vandiver recommended legislation which would allow the desegregation of public schools. The legislature passed the proposals by a vote of approximately 240 to 16.

At a mass meeting in April, African American leaders urged students to apply for transfer to white schools. Approximately 129 African American students sought reassignment to white schools. Students were required to score at least the norm on a scholastic aptitude test which was routinely given in all of Atlanta's white schools. Forty-eight of the 129 students were invited back to take an intelligence test which was not used by the school system. The Board of Education notified twenty-four of the forty-eight students to report for an interview. The superintendent for Area I of the Atlanta public school system and the principals of the white schools to which the students sought transfer interviewed the students. At the end of this long process, the School Board selected ten African American students to transfer to white schools.[80] The Board denied widespread rumors that it had planned to limit desegregation to a certain number of students and schools, but a NAACP spokesman argued that "it is easier to go to Yale than to transfer from one public school to another in Atlanta."[81]

After African American students requested reassignment at her school, a white female student asked to transfer to an all-white high school. She listed "to maintain freedom of association" on her application as her reason for desiring reassignment. The Board of Education denied her request. Obviously, the approval of such a transfer would undermine the desegregation plan by allowing white students to leave desegregated schools via transfer. The State Education Board attempted to override this decision. Judge Frank Hooper, however, enjoined the State Board from interfering with the decisions of the Atlanta School Board.[82]

In preparing for school desegregation, local officials had the advantage of learning from other cities. Members of the Atlanta police department and the Georgia Bureau of Investigation, for example, were sent to cities which had desegregated their schools to observe the measures taken by their police departments and law enforcement agencies to preserve law and order.[83] Through contact with their counterparts in cities that had attempted school desegregation, political, business, and civic leaders also became aware of potential problems. The city's leadership was determined that these problems would not occur in Atlanta.

Since 1959 representatives from various statewide organizations had met to discuss and exchange ideas as to how to preserve public education in Georgia. In February 1961 leaders of HOPE called for a meeting of these organizations to discuss ways to secure the peaceful desegregation of schools in Atlanta. HOPE regarded its original goal of maintaining open schools as being fulfilled. From this meeting a coalition known as OASIS, Organizations Assisting Schools in September, emerged. OASIS eventually consisted of some fifty-three religious, civic, professional, and business organizations. White, biracial, and African American organizations could join OASIS.[84]

According to its chairperson, the purpose of OASIS was "to make known to every citizen of Atlanta the facts of the Atlanta plan, its effects upon the public school system, and the contribution each individual can make toward maintaining good will and responsible leadership."[85] OASIS sponsored various meetings with students and their parents about the specifics of the Atlanta plan and the general issue of desegregation. It established a Speaker's Bureau which supplied discussion leaders for civic, religious, and professional groups. The Quaker House (The Friends' Fellowship House), NAACP, Atlanta Council on Human Relations, and HOPE sponsored meetings between white and African American students. One meeting included the transfer students and representatives from three of the four white schools scheduled to be desegregated. The Atlanta Council on Human Relations appointed white members to work with the African American transfer students and their families. African American leaders counseled the students and served as communication links to school officials. On the weekend prior to the desegregation of the schools, OASIS sponsored a "Law and Order Sunday." Ministers of all faiths urged the peaceful desegregation of schools, and some white and African American churches participated in an exchange of members.[86]

A major area of preparation was security. Police Chief Herbert Jenkins was entrusted with keeping racial peace. One of Jenkins' concerns was the performance of his own department. He realized that most of his officers held conventional racial attitudes. Some officers still had ties to the Klan. Relations between the police department and the African American community were poor. In order to combat this problem, Jenkins required every officer to read books and pamphlets on law and order, particularly literature on racial problems and riots. He asked officers to write an evaluation of this reading material. In 1961 the department conducted a police training school on desegregation for all officers. This training included lectures and discussions on the general subject of desegregation and racism within the United States.[87] Jenkins' ultimate weapon to deal with his officers was his power of assignment. He assigned officers who were suspected of having ties to racist organizations or had a history of confrontation with African American residents to duties unrelated to school desegregation. In a conversation with Benjamin Mays, president of Morehouse College, Jenkins noted that "it made a lot of difference who the officer in charge is when calming racial disturbances."[88]

Jenkins' major concern was the safety of the transfer students. The superintendent of detectives established a task force to observe the activities of "troublemakers," "crackpots," and "known members of hate organizations." The department supplied dossiers of these individuals to each officer. Before the school controversy, Jenkins used undercover officers to keep informed of Klan activities.[89] The police department asked dealers of explosives and firearms to inform it of any unusual purchases.

Chief Jenkins assigned a task force to each school scheduled to be desegregated. The members of each task force were to familiarize themselves with the blueprints and personnel of their assigned school. They were to become acquainted with the transfer students and their families. Jenkins assigned a detective to drive each of the transfer students to their schools. A special force was on standby alert at the central station. At the proper signal, ninety percent of the police force could arrive at the schools in fifteen minutes. No adults were allowed to park at the schools, nor spectators and sightseers allowed to assemble in the vicinities of the schools. The police department requested students not to loiter or congregate in cars, parking lots, schoolyards, hall corridors, bathrooms, or stairways. As a legal basis for these extreme measures, Jenkins discovered a city ordinance which outlawed the disturbance of any school or church in session.[90]

City officials were also concerned about the press. In a letter to Burke Marshall, Assistant Attorney General for Civil Rights, Hartsfield noted that he was worried about a "large unregulated press." He asked Attorney General Robert Kennedy to speak "to the heads of radio and television chains about the dangers of arousing mobs through these means."[91] Naturally, elected officials and business leaders were also worried about the portrayal of Atlanta by the media. In order to address these concerns, city leaders attempted to regulate press coverage while appearing to be accessible and receptive to the media.

OASIS provided each reporter covering the school situation with a specially prepared handbook. This booklet contained a brief history of the school desegregation case, the details of the Atlanta desegregation plan, information about the participants involved in the desegregation of the schools, and statements from city officials and noted personalities such as Ralph McGill stressing the city's determination to peacefully obey the law. City officials invited the press on a bus tour of Atlanta's middle-class African American neighborhoods and the Atlanta University Center. Chief Jenkins allowed a journalist for *Life* magazine to observe a police stakeout of a known racist organization.[92] OASIS members scheduled dinners, cocktail parties, and other social functions for members of the press. Since school grounds were closed to reporters, the city provided a press room at City Hall. The room had direct telephone lines to each desegregated school and a police radio hook-up. The city provided the reporters with teletype machines, typewriters, and telephones. The Chamber of Commerce supplied free cokes, hot coffee, pickles, and sandwiches to reporters. Local dignitaries were present to answer questions. To many reporters, Atlanta was a welcomed relief from the turmoil and violence that they experienced in other areas of the region.[93] To the delight of city officials and business leaders, many of the reporters' accounts stressed this particular point.

In August 1961 nine African American students attended four formerly all-white schools.[94] The desegregation of these schools was relatively peaceful. The police arrested six people near the schools on opening day. Charges included "failure to move on," and "carrying a concealed weapon." One week following the desegregation of the schools, detectives arrested several individuals at a Klan-sponsored protest rally in Northwest Atlanta.

Due to the peaceful desegregation of its school system, Atlanta received praises from federal officials and the national media. At a press conference, President John F. Kennedy congratulated the city for the "law-abiding manner in which the high schools were desegregated." He urged "the officials and citizens of all communities which face this difficult transition in the coming months to look closely at what Atlanta has done and to meet their responsibility as the officials of Atlanta and Georgia have done with courage, tolerance, and above all with respect to the law."[95] Mayor Hartsfield and Chief Jenkins received personal calls from Robert Kennedy and Burke Marshall. A *New York Times* editorial praised Atlanta for "providing a new and shining example of what can be accomplished."[96] The major news publications gave special coverage to the city and complemented it on the peaceful desegregation of the school system.[97]

The focus of the media's coverage was the absence of racial violence. While many news accounts noted the small number of students and schools actually involved, the media judged desegregation in Atlanta successful because no violence occurred. Due to racial strife in the region, the absence of overt racial conflict and "civility" between the races became important standards in evaluating the state of race relations in a particular area or city. The media portrayed southern cities which experienced limited racial conflict as "harbingers of racial change." At various times, Atlanta, Dallas, Charlotte, and Durham were some of the cities placed in this category. The peaceful desegregation of Atlanta's schools enhanced its growing reputation as a racially progressive city.

Despite this praise, many proponents of school desegregation criticized the process. A report prepared by the Atlanta Council on Human Relations offered, for example, a contrasting interpretation of school desegregation in the city. The report noted that the School Board took no action to comply with the *Brown* decision until faced with a legal challenge. The School Board contested the suit, and only adopted a plan when ordered by the federal courts. The report charged that the plan was first instituted in the twelfth and eleventh grades because these high school students would be reluctant to transfer to new schools. The plan adopted by the School Board was "such to discourage and slow down the process." Support within the community was for "open schools" and "law and order" rather than desegregation. The community and the press defined the success of the plan as "good discipline outside the schools" and "the physical presence of x students at x schools on x morning." The report noted, however, that "any plan which places the whole burden or the initiative on the student can hardly be expected to bring about any widespread change through the entire system." Widespread desegregation was "obviously not one of the units of measurement of success."[98] In a letter to the *New York Times*, Eliza Paschall, chairman of the Council, questioned whether Atlanta should be praised simply because "we didn't bomb our schools."[99] Other members of HOPE and OASIS expressed disappointment at the small number of students and schools involved in the process.

While acknowledging that the city had "made a significant beginning," Reverend Sam Williams, an African American leader and scholar, noted that "the token acceptance of nine Negro students into previously all-white schools does not really alleviate the many inequalities of Atlanta's segregated school system."[100] Due to the rigors of the procedure, the School Board approved of only eight percent of the transfer applicants in 1961. Clearly, in the opinion of most African American leaders, this small number did not constitute the desegregation of Atlanta's public school system. The NAACP continued its legal challenge by requesting an acceleration of the desegregation process, the integration of staff at city schools, and the removal of all standards governing the transfer of African American students to white schools.

The governing coalition met the challenge of school desegregation. Despite continuing litigation, the school desegregation issue solidified the ties that existed between white and African American leaders. "Old Guard" and emerging new leaders within the community joined efforts to ensure the peaceful desegregation of the city's schools. Mayor Hartsfield, business and civic leaders, the police department, and the media all contributed. These efforts were consistent with their commitments to peaceful race relations and the economic progress of the city. These commitments would guide the response of Atlanta's leadership to changing racial conditions.

Notes

1.   Aldon D. Morris, *The Origins of the Civil Rights Movement: Black Communities Organizing for Change* (New York: The Free Press, 1984), pp. 183–194.

2.   Ibid., p. 192.

3.   *Southern School News*, November 1955, p. 15.

4.   A statewide protest caused the Board to later rescind this action. A substitute resolution required each teacher to sign an oath to "uphold, support, and defend the constitution and laws of Georgia."

5.   Southern Regional Council, "Georgia: Segregation-Desegregation, Current," Atlanta, 1960, p. 7, Southern Regional Council Papers, 3:123:508, Woodruff Library, Atlanta, Georgia.

6.   Numan Bartley, *The Rise of Massive Resistance: Race and Politics in the South During the 1950s* (Baton Rouge: Louisiana State Press, 1969), pp. 185–187.

7.   *Southern School News*, December 1956, p. 10; *Southern School News*, January 1957, p. 16; and Harold Martin and Franklin M. Garrett, *Atlanta and Environs: A Chronicle of Its People and Events: Years of Change and Challenge, 1940–1976*, Vol. III, (Atlanta: Atlanta Historical Society, 1978), p. 9.

8.   Morris, pp. 30–34.

9.   Southern Regional Council, "Georgia," p. 35.

10.   *Atlanta Constitution*, 13 October 1958; and Arnold Shankman, "A Temple is Bombed—Atlanta 1958," *American Jewish Archives*, 23 (1971): 125.

11.   Janice Rothschild Blumberg, *One Voice: Rabbi Jacob Rothschild and the Troubled South* (Macon: Mercer University Press, 1985), pp. 82–108; and Shankman, pp. 141–151.

12.   *Atlanta Constitution*, 13 October 1958.

13.   Ralph McGill, "A Church, A School," *Atlanta Constitution*, 13 October 1958.

14.   "Throng of 500 Seek to Kill Officer," *Atlanta Journal and Constitution*, 14 September 1958, p. 2; and *Atlanta Constitution*, 17 September 1958, p. 33.

15.   Citizens Committee, "A History of the Citizens Committee," 17 September 1958, Southern Regional Council Papers, 1:71:2180.

16.   M.K. Jennings, *Community Influentials: The Elites of Atlanta* (Glenclove: Free Press, 1964), pp. 131–132; and Harold M. Martin, *William*

Berry Hartsfield: Mayor of Atlanta (Athens: University of Georgia Press, 1978), pp. 122–125.

17. Jennings, pp. 134–136; and Martin, pp. 128–129.

18. Bruce Galphin, *The Riddle of Lester Maddox* (Atlanta: Camelot Publishing Company, 1968), pp. 14–20; and Lester Maddox, *Speaking Out: The Autobiography of Lester Maddox* (New York: Doubleday and Company, 1975), pp. 30–35.

19. Jennings, pp. 138–139.

20. Martin, pp. 131–132, 137.

21. "New Strength in City Hall," *Fortune* 56 (November 1957): 156–157.

22. Clarence Stone, *Regime Politics: Governing Atlanta, 1946–1988* (Lawrence: University of Kansas Press, 1989), pp. 40–42.

23. Richard Rich, Letter to Lee Evans, 31 December 1959, Richard Rich Papers, Box: 15, Folder: 16, Woodruff Library, Emory University, Atlanta, Georgia.

24. Citizens Advisory Committee for Urban Renewal, "Minutes of Meeting held 15 December 1959 of the Executive Committee and Invited Members of CAC," Richard Rich Papers, Box: 15, Folder: 16.

25. Stone, p. 42.

26. Author's Interview with LeRoy Johnson, 30 November 1990; Interview with Carl Holman conducted by Jed Dannenbaum and Kathleen Dowdey, Ralph McGill Papers, Woodruff Library, Emory University, Atlanta, Georgia; and Nancy Weiss, *Whitney M. Young, Jr. and the Struggle for Civil Rights* (Princeton University Press, 1989), pp. 62–63.

27. Author's Interview with LeRoy Johnson; Interview with Carl Holman, McGill Papers; and Weiss, pp. 63–64.

28. Interview with Carl Holman, McGill Papers; Calvin Trillin, *An Education in Georgia: Charlayne Hunter, Hamilton Homes, and the Integration of the University of Georgia* (New York: Viking Press, 1964; reprint ed., Athens: University of Georgia Press, 1991), pp. 6–12; and Charlayne Hunter-Gault, *In My Place* (New York: Farrar Straus Giroux, 1992), pp. 124–129.

29. Author's Interview with LeRoy Johnson; Interview with Carl Holman, McGill Papers; and Weiss, p. 64.

30. The Atlanta Committee for Cooperative Action, *A Second Look: The Negro Citizen in Atlanta, Georgia* (Atlanta, January, 1960), Foreword.

31. *Atlanta Daily World*, 13, 16 February 1960; *Atlanta Journal and Constitution* 14 February 1960, p. 12-b; and *New York Times*, 14 February 1960, p. 30.

32. Based on his interview, Carl Holman perceived the formation of ACCA as an alternative organization to the Atlanta Negro Voters League. In her study, Nancy Weiss argues that one of the objectives of ACCA was to "shake up, if not supplant, the old guard leadership that purported to speak for black Atlantans (Weiss, p. 63)." In his interview, LeRoy Johnson argued that ACCA was "not designed to challenge the leadership; it was designed to augment the Voters League (personal transcript)."

33. Interview with Carl Holman, McGill Papers; Taylor Branch, *Parting the Waters: America in the King Years, 1954–63* (New York: Simon and Schuster, 1988), pp. 267–268; David Garrow, *Bearing the Cross: Martin Luther King, Jr. and the Southern Christian Leadership Conference* (New York: William Morrow and Company, 1986), p. 124; and Stephen Oates, *Let the Trumpet Sound: The Life of Martin Luther King Jr.* (New York: Harper and Row, 1982), pp. 150–151.

34. *Atlanta Daily World*, 2 December 1959, p. 2.

35. Ralph McGill, Letter to Harry Ashmore, 15 December 1959, Ralph McGill Papers, Box: 9.

36. In his interview, Carl Holman notes that some meetings were held at Spelman College to discuss King's role in Atlanta. He lists John Calhoun, Ella Baker, and Glen Smiley as participants.

37. Irene Hill, "Black Political Behavior in Georgia: An Analysis of the Politics of Exchange, 1908–1973" (Master's thesis, Atlanta University, 1980), pp. 61–65.

38. "Minutes of the Atlanta Negro Voters League," 26 May 1959, A.T. Walden Papers, Files of the Atlanta Negro Voters League, Atlanta History Center, Library and Archives, Atlanta, Georgia.

39. In his studies of the Atlanta power structure, Floyd Hunter found over twenty-nine families that had connections in both business and civic affairs and had been part of the power structure for over three decades. In each case, a family member was present to "inherit" his family's position in the power structure. These families included the Adairs, Allens, Grants, Havertys, Healeys, Howells, Hurts, Inmans, Massells, Richs, Spaldings, and Woodruffs. The CEOs/business owners of certain major companies have also held long-standing positions in the Atlanta power structure. These companies included Adair Realty Company; Ivan Allen Company; Atlanta Newspapers Incorporated; Citizens and Southern Bank; Coca-Cola; Davison-Paxon; Delta Airlines; Georgia Power; Haverty Furniture Company, Rich's Incorporated, and Trust Company of Georgia.

40. A rising member of Atlanta's business community was expected to be a member of various local art and music societies, the Chamber of

Commerce, the Capital Club, the Piedmont Driving Club, or various ranking civic clubs, and hospital and university boards. All of these memberships provided training and grooming for the city's leadership.

41. Ivan Allen with Paul Hemphill, *Mayor: Notes on the Sixties* (New York: Simon and Schuster, 1971), pp. 21–22, 29–30.

42. Ibid., pp. 31–34.

43. Allen with Hemphill, pp. 149–150; and Curtis Driskell, "The Thrust of Forward Atlanta," *Atlanta Magazine*, 4 (August 1964): 37–40.

44. Tony Freyer, *The Little Rock Crisis: A Constitutional Interpretation* (Westport: Greenword Press, 1984), pp. 15–35.

45. *Southern School News*, July 1955, p. 11.

46. Paul Bolster, "Civil Rights Movements in Twentieth Century Georgia," (Ph.D. dissertation, University of Georgia, 1972), p. 159; Martin and Garrett, p. 223; and *Southern School News* July 1959, p. 11.

47. These eight branches were Atlanta, Augusta, Columbus, Liberty County, Macon, Savannah, Valdosta, and Waycross.

48. For a description of legislation dealing with school segregation during the 1950s, see Bolster, pp. 137–141.

49. Some business leaders were pressuring members of the religious community to address the racial issue. Author's Interview with Reverend Austin Ford, 3 December 1990.

50. Statement was printed in the *Atlanta Journal and Constitution*, 3 November 1957.

51. "Out of Convictions: A Second Statement on the South's Racial Crisis, signed by 312 Ministers of Greater Atlanta," (Atlanta: Georgia Council of Churches, 1958).

52. Mrs. Harold Freedman, Mrs. Thomas Breeden, and Mrs. David Neiman, "The Beginning of Hope: The Struggle for Open Schools," Atlanta, Southern Regional Council Papers, 4:137:57.

53. HOPE Pamphlet, September 1959, Southern Regional Council Papers, 4:137:57.

54. Freedman, Breeden, and Neiman, pp. 2–3.

55. For a detailed examination of school desegregation in Virginia, see Carl Abbot, "The Norfolk Business Community: The Crisis of Massive Resistance," in *Southern Businessmen and Desegregation*, eds. Elizabeth Jacoway and David Colburn (Baton Rouge, Louisiana State Press, 1982), pp. 98–119; Robbins L. Gates, *The Making of Massive Resistance: Virginia's Politics of School Desegregation, 1954–1956* (Chapel Hill: University of North Carolina Press, 1962); Richard Kluger, *Simple Justice: The History of the Brown v. Board of Education and Black America's*

Struggle for Equality (New York: Alfred A. Knopf, 1976; reprint ed., New York: Random House, 1977), pp. 451–507; Benjamin Muse, *Virginia's Massive Resistance* (Bloomington: Indiana University Press, 1961); and Bob Smith, *They Closed Their Schools: Prince Edward County, Virginia, 1951–1964* (Chapel Hill: University of North Carolina Press, 1965).

56. Tony Freyer, *The Little Rock Crisis: A Constitutional Interpretation* (Westport: Greenwood Press, 1984); and Elizabeth Jacoway, "Taken by Surprise: Little Rock Business Leaders and Desegregation," in *Southern Businessmen and Desegregation*, eds. Elizabeth Jacoway and David Colburn (Baton Rouge: Louisiana University Press, 1982), pp. 15–42.

57. Morton Inger, *Politics and Reality in an American City: The New Orleans School Crisis of 1960* (New York: Center for Urban Education, 1969).

58. Inger, pp. 28–29.

59. Benjamin Mays, *Born to Rebel: An Autobiography* (New York: Scribner, 1971, reprint ed., Athens: University of Georgia Press, 1987), pp. 244–245; and Reverend Martin Luther King, Sr. with Clayton Riley, *Daddy King: An Autobiography* (New York: William Morrow and Company, 1980), pp. 112, 121.

60. Author's Interview with Frances Pauley, 9 November 1990; and Author's Interview with Nan Pendergast, 17 December 1990.

61. Inger, p. 72.

62. Freedman, Breeden, and Neiman, pp. 2–3.

63. Paul Rillings, Memorandum to Harold Fleming, 15 December 1959, Southern Regional Council Papers, 1:64:1989.

64. Author's Interview with Nan Pendergast.

65. Allen with Hemphill, p. 32.

66. Interview with Ernest Vandiver conducted by Jed Dannenbaum and Kathleen Dowdey, Ralph McGill Papers.

67. For a discussion of the attitudes of Southern businessmen toward desegregation, see Elizabeth Jacoway, "An Introduction: Civil Rights and the Changing South," in *Southern Businessmen and Desegregation*, eds. Elizabeth Jacoway and David Colburn (Baton Rouge: Louisiana State Press, 1982), pp. 1–14.

68. *Southern School News*, April 1959, p. 7; Ralph McGill, *The South and the Southerner* (Boston: Little, Brown, and Company, 1963), p. 277; and Martin and Garrett, pp. 309–310.

69. *Southern School News*, December 1959, p. 16; *Southern School News*, February 1960, pp. 1–2.

70. The three Klan associations represented in the Atlanta area were: The United Klans of America, Knights of the Ku Klux Klan; The National Knights of the Ku Klux Klan; and the U.S. Klan, Knights of the Ku Klux Klan. Sherman Harris, "Present Status of Klans in the United States," May 1964, pp. 2–3, Southern Regional Council Papers, 1:41:1407.

71. *Southern School News*, January 1961, p. 1.

72. Martin, pp. 134–135.

73. "Resolution of the Atlanta Board of Education adopted November 30, 1959 and Amended January 4, 1960 and Amended January 18, 1960," in Eliza Paschall, *It Must Have Rained* (Atlanta: Emory University, 1975), pp. 22–26.

74. *Southern School News*, December 1959, p. 16; *Southern School News*, February 1960, p. 2.

75. Interview with Ernest Vandiver, McGill Papers.

76. Author's Interview with Frances Pauley.

77. "Majority Report of the General Assembly Committee on Schools," (Atlanta: April 1960), pp. 1, 3, 10, 15–18, John A. Sibley Papers, Files of the General Assembly Committee on Schools, Woodruff Library, Emory University, Atlanta, Georgia.

78. "Minority Report of the General Assembly Committee on Schools and Additional Statement by Render Hill," (Atlanta: April 1960), pp. 3–4, 6–7, John A. Sibley Papers, Files of the General Assembly Committee on Schools.

79. *Southern School News*, January 1961, p. 1.

80. "Trial Brief, *Calhoun v. Latimer*, Civil Action No. 6298, Plaintiff's Proposed Findings of Fact and Conclusions of Law," 30 April 1962, Grace Towns Hamilton Papers, Box: 75, Folder: 2.

81. *Atlanta Journal*, 28 April 1961.

82. *Southern School News*, June 1961, p. 8; *Southern School News*, August 1961, p. 8; *Southern School News*, September 1961, p. 6; and *Southern School News*, January 1962, p. 11.

83. Captain R.E. Little, Memorandum to Police Chief Herbert Jenkins (re: observation of police methods in dealing with the integration of schools in New Orleans), 21 November 1960, Herbert Jenkins Papers, Box: 5, Atlanta History Center, Library and Archives, Atlanta, Georgia.

84. Grace T. Hamilton, "A Record of Progress: Community Preparations for Desegregation of Public Schools in Atlanta," 30 June 1961, pp. 1–4, Southern Regional Council Papers, 4:136:44; and "History of OASIS," n.d., Eliza Paschall Papers, Box: 23, OASIS files, Woodruff Library, Emory University, Atlanta, Georgia.

85. Mrs. John Hamner, Letter to John Adams Sibley, 20 May 1961, John Adams Sibley Papers, Files of the General Assembly Committee on Schools.

86. Grace T. Hamilton, pp. 11–16; and "Activities of the Atlanta Council on Human Relations (re: school desegregation)" Eliza Paschall Papers, Box: 2, Folder: 9.

87. Herbert Jenkins, *Keeping the Peace: A Police Chief Looks at His Job* (New York: Harper and Row, 1973), pp. 57–58.

88. Benjamin Mays, p. 294.

89. Interview with Herbert Jenkins conducted by Jed Dannenbaum and Kathleen Dowdey, Ralph McGill Papers; and "Special Notice to all employees of the Atlanta Police Department: Bulletin H-14-206 (re: list of potentially dangerous individuals)," 29 August 1961, Herbert Jenkins Papers, Box: 5, Folder: 3. Papers relating to the security of the students (maps and blueprints of the schools, list of assigned students, etc.) are found in Box 5 of the Jenkins' collection.

90. Letter to Parents of All Students of Brown High School (form letter listing regulations to follow at desegregated schools), 17 August 1961, Eliza Paschall Papers, Box: 14; and Jenkins, pp. 54–58.

91. William Hartsfield, Letter to Mr. Burke Marshall, 30 July 1961, Herbert Jenkins Papers, Box: 5, Folder: 3.

92. George McMillican, "Atlanta's Peaceful Blow for Justice: With the Police on an Integration Job," *Life*, 51 (15 September 1961): 35–36.

93. Interviews with Bill Shipp and Celestine Sibley, conducted by Jed Dannenbaum and Kathleen Dowdey, Ralph McGill Papers.

94. One of the ten students selected won a scholarship to attend Spelman College. Only nine students transfer to new schools.

95. President John F. Kennedy, "Statement on Atlanta School Desegregation," Press Conference, 30 August 1961, printed in the *Atlanta Constitution*, 31 August 1961.

96. *New York Times*, 31 August 1961, editorial.

97. For examples of news coverage, see "Hope for Us All," *Reporter*, 25 (11 September 1961): 14; "Peaceful Integration: How Atlanta Did It," *U.S. News*, 51 (11 September 1961): 4; "Proud City," *Newsweek*, 58 (11 September 1961): 31–32; and "Southern Milestones," *Time*, 78 (11 September 1961).

98. Report of the Council Committee on School Desegregation, "Wanted: A Yardstick," pp. 2–3, Eliza Paschall Papers, School desegregation files.

99.   Eliza Paschall, Letter to Mr. John Oakes, 19 March 1962, Eliza Paschall Papers, Box: 2, Folder: 1.

100.   Reverend Sam Williams, Letter to Eliza Paschall, n.d., Eliza Paschall Papers, Box: 2, Folder: 1.

IV

The Battle for an Open City

On 1 February 1960 Ezell Blair, Jr., Franklin McCain, Joseph McNeil, and David Richmond, four African American students at North Carolina Agricultural and Technical College in Greensboro, violated the law by sitting down at the segregated lunch counter of the local Woolworth's. Due to southern tradition and segregation laws which prohibited African Americans and whites from eating together, African Americans could shop at the store, but could not eat at its segregated lunch counter. As the week continued, students from local black colleges, African American high schools, and a few white universities joined in the protest. Hoping to halt these demonstrations, local white business owners decided to close the lunch counters. They acted too late. African American churches, newspapers, and community leaders broadcast news of the protest throughout the African American community. Within weeks, similar sit-in demonstrations were rapidly spreading throughout the South. Between February and March 1960, sit-in demonstrations occurred in Alabama, Florida, Kentucky, Maryland, South Carolina, Tennessee, and Virginia.[1]

In early February 1960 Lonnie King, a Morehouse student, entered Yates and Milton's Drugstore, a local hangout for Atlanta University Center students. King was a native Atlantan who had grown up in a poor African American neighborhood in the West End of the city. Growing up, he faced the combined rigors of segregation and poverty. In the late 1950s, King had served in the navy largely to escape Atlanta and his poverty. Inside the drugstore, King encountered Julian Bond, a fellow student at Morehouse. Bond, who was four years younger, came from a different social and economic background. His father, Horace Mann Bond, was a prominent African American scholar who had served as the first black president of Lincoln University and later as Dean of Atlanta University's School of Education. While born in Nashville, Bond spent his childhood and teenage years on a black college campus in Pennsylvania. The campus provided a sheltered and self-contained environment. Bond, a gifted writer, had aspirations of being a poet. Before their meeting in Yates and Milton's Drugstore, King and Bond had only briefly spoken once.[2]

On that same day, the *Atlanta Daily World* gave coverage to the demonstrations in Greensboro. Inspired by these sit-ins, King wanted to instigate activities in Atlanta. While serving in the navy, King had informed a friend that he was going to return to Atlanta because "there's going to be a revolution in the South and I want to be there, be a part of it."[3] Because of Bond's reputation as an excellent writer, King wanted to involve him in the protest activities. While initially reluctant, Bond agreed to participate. King and Bond invited students to attend a meeting at the Sale Hall annex, a Morehouse campus building.[4]

About twenty students from the Atlanta University Center met that afternoon to discuss the racial situation in the city, the "revolution" in the South, and their role in the struggle. From this meeting, the organizational center of the student movement in Atlanta, the Committee on Appeal for Human Rights (COAHR), would eventually emerge. Similar to the demonstrations in North Carolina, the students approved of a plan to conduct sit-ins at local five-and-dimes in the city. In order to gain the approval and participation of their fellow students, COAHR members outlined their proposals before various student assemblies at the AUC schools. While preparations for the sit-ins were being made, students participated in workshops and seminars on the techniques of nonviolence. Student leaders required participants to take an oath of nonviolence.

In February student leaders informed Dr. Benjamin Mays, president of Morehouse College, of their plans to conduct demonstrations in downtown Atlanta. While sympathetic to their goals, he suggested that the students wait. The student presidents and two members from each of the six institutions met with the AUC Council of Presidents.[5] The six AUC presidents were concerned about racial unrest in the city, the safety of the students, and the impact that the demonstrations might have on the academic reputation and financial stability of the schools. The presidents asked the students to refrain from demonstrations and keep them informed of their plans. Student leaders agreed to meet with the Council on a regular basis. At one of these meetings in early March, a college president suggested that the students prepare a public statement of grievances before their demonstrations.[6] While some students felt that this suggestion was an attempt on the part of the presidents to delay their protests, they agreed to prepare the statement.[7]

Student leaders organized a committee to write the statement. Committee members included Julian Bond, Morris Dillard, Lonnie King,

Roslyn Pope, Herschelle Sullivan, and Carolyn Long. In preparing this statement, the students largely obtained the data from *A Second Look*. When this manifesto was completed, it received the approval of student assemblies and the Council of Presidents. Rufus Clement, the president of Atlanta University, obtained the funds to publish this document, "An Appeal for Human Rights," in the *Atlanta Daily World*, the *Atlanta Constitution*, and the *Atlanta Journal*. "An Appeal for Human Rights" received national attention. It was subsequently published in the *New York Times*.[8]

This statement was a dramatic and eloquent appeal for basic civil liberties. The purpose of the students' efforts was to "gain those rights which are inherently ours as members of the human race and as citizens of the United States." Student leaders pledged their "unqualified support" to those engaged in this cause. They expressed dissatisfaction with the "snail-like speed" at which racial injustices were being ameliorated. The students warned that they did not intend "to wait placidly for those rights which are already and morally ours to be meted out to us one at a time." They listed the "discriminatory conditions" faced by African Americans in Atlanta, "supposedly one of the most progressive cities in the South." The "Appeal" enumerated inequalities in education, employment, registration and voting, housing, public accommodations, and law enforcement. The students urged local authorities to solve these inequalities. They pledged to use "every legal and nonviolent means" to secure full citizenship rights.[9]

Though generally favorable, reaction to the "Appeal" was varied. Opponents of racial change questioned its authorship. Governor Vandiver argued that the "Appeal" "did not sound like it was written in this country." The statement "had the same overtones which are usually found in anti-American propaganda." Local newspapers, however, generally praised the document. A columnist for the *Atlanta Journal* found it to be "intelligent and most moving." Mayor Hartsfield believed that the "Appeal" expressed "the legitimate aspirations of young people throughout the nation and the entire world."[10]

"An Appeal for Human Rights" served as a plan for protest and political action in Atlanta. The purpose of this activity was broader than simple lunch counter desegregation. The student movement in Atlanta spearheaded a campaign by the city's African American community to combat inequalities in public accommodations, land use, and employment. The student's main goal was to "open" the city to all races. This campaign also questioned the goals and tactics of established African American leaders. The students wanted "freedom now."

Prior to the formation of COAHR, the participation of students in civil rights activities was limited. Students participated in community activities such as encouraging voter registration and teaching at citizenship schools. They attended university-sponsored conferences on the race question. Meetings between white and African American students occurred on these campuses. While they promoted African American leadership, racial pride, and community involvement, the colleges of the Atlanta University Center provided a desegregated, paternalistic, and protective environment. In dealing with the white community, these institutions, by necessity, maintained a low profile.

Due in a large measure to the *Brown* decision and the Montgomery Bus Boycott, signs of racial unrest began to appear on African American college campuses in Atlanta in the mid-1950s. According to a former Spelman professor, students were reluctant to confine themselves to their studies when racial change was occurring in the South.[11] In 1956 members of the Social Science Club at Spelman College decided to undertake action to affect racial change. In January 1957 members of this club attempted to sit in the "white only" section of the galleries in the State Capitol. The Speaker of the House ordered them to leave. Students periodically returned to sit in the galleries or picket the State Capitol. In January 1962 COAHR members formally adopted a program to desegregate the State Capitol. Due to these protests and the election of Georgia's first African American state senator, the galleries were desegregated in 1963.[12]

In 1959 members of the Social Science Club decided to challenge the library's policy of segregation. In Atlanta only three of the library's sixteen branches provided services for African Americans. Many African Americans were unable to get to these locations. The collections and resources of these libraries were not comparable to the "white only" branches. No state or city ordinances dictated segregated libraries. The Library Board of Trustees adopted a policy of social separation on the sole basis of local custom. It had the sole authority to change this policy.[13]

A.T. Walden and other African American leaders asked that all races be allowed to use the downtown Carnegie Library. The Library Board of Trustees refused to change its policy. It did commission, however, a bookmobile to serve inaccessible African American neighborhoods. The biracial American Veterans Commission and the Atlanta Council on Human Relations began an intense campaign to convince the Board to change its policy. The Council presented the Board with petitions requesting desegregation, and data about the inequalities in resources available to African American citizens, the patterns of library use, and library policies of other southern cities. The Board argued that it had been "generous" in its response to the needs of African American citizens. It felt that African American citizens did not utilize the provided services.[14]

While these negotiations were in progress, members of the Social Science Club, supported by students at Morehouse College, began their campaign to affect racial change. Students and faculty visited Carnegie Library whenever resources were not available at college or African American libraries. They were to accept whatever services the library offered.[15] The purpose of these visits was to make the Board aware that African Americans needed better facilities. Howard Zinn, a white professor of history and political science at Spelman and faculty sponsor of the Social Science Club, arranged a meeting with the director of library services. The director informed Zinn that the Board refused to desegregate the libraries due to the potential for racial conflict. Following this conversation, students increased their number of visits to the Carnegie Library.

Members of the Social Science Club decided to pursue legal action. Howard Zinn and Whitney Young, Dean of the Atlanta University School of Social Work and Executive Secretary of the Atlanta Council on Human Relations, undertook the duties of obtaining plaintiffs, money, and legal representation. Otis Moss, a young ministerial student, and Irene Dobbs Jackson, a professor of French at Spelman College and a daughter of John Wesley Dobbs, agreed to be plaintiffs. Faced with a possible lawsuit, demonstrations, and political pressure from Mayor Hartsfield (an ex-officio member of the Board), the Board agreed to change its policies. In May of 1959 the library was quietly desegregated. Fearing violence, the local newspapers refrained from publishing the story for five days. The libraries reported no disturbances due to desegregation.[16]

In early March 1960 students from the Atlanta-Morehouse-Spelman Players, a college drama company, obtained tickets for the matinee performance of *My Fair Lady* at the municipal auditorium. Their tickets were for the orchestra seats which were located in the "white only" section of the auditorium. The theatre manager requested the students to move. When they refused, he threatened to postpone the show. The students held their ground. When the manager called the mayor, Hartsfield calmly told him to begin the show.

Despite his support on this occasion for the students, the mayor was concerned about their activities. Immediately after the publication of "An Appeal for Human Rights," Hartsfield met with the students. He urged them to meet with the city's business leaders and members of the Board of Aldermen before beginning their protests. Later in a speech before the

Hungry Club, the mayor warned that student protests would harm businesses in the city. In a meeting with student leaders and the presidents of the Atlanta University Center, a group of white ministers also urged the students to meet with business leaders.[18]

Despite these appeals by traditional community leaders to wait, approximately two hundred students participated in sit-ins at local cafeterias and lunch counters on 15 March 1960. Originally, these demonstrations were to occur at private establishments. Student leaders, however, decided to demonstrate at eating facilities located on public property. Theoretically, on public property, the rights of the students would be guaranteed by the Fourteenth Amendment.[19] Students conducted demonstrations at City Hall, the State Capitol, two office buildings, the Fulton County Courthouse, two railroad stations, and the Greyhound and Trailways bus depots. Before conducting their protests, student leaders informed Benjamin Mays and Whitney Young of their plans. The students asked Howard Zinn to notify the press of their plans at the time of the demonstrations.[20] Atlanta police officers arrested approximately seventy-seven demonstrators.

After these initial demonstrations, African American students representing all six Atlanta University Center schools formally organized COAHR and selected a fifteen-member policymaking board. This Board elected Lonnie King of Morehouse College as chairman. The Committee issued a statement that it planned no further demonstrations and called for a discussion of the grievances listed in the "Appeal." Following the advice of Mayor Hartsfield and the group of white ministers, student leaders met with some of the city's leading businessmen. They urged the students to stop all demonstrations and criticized the content of the "Appeal." Shocked by the reaction of these business leaders, the students decided to continue their protests.[21]

When the students resumed their demonstrations in April, they targeted a local A&P grocery store. This establishment had a predominately African American clientele, but it did not hire African Americans above menial labor. The students attempted to negotiate with the store management. They had two meetings, but with very little results. The store management refused to change its hiring practices. It rejected the students as negotiators for the local community. Student leaders initiated a boycott of the store which eventually proved successful; the store hired African American clerks. The students frequently used this tactic. Changes in the employment practices of a local branch of a chain store often led to their adoption by the main corporation and other smaller neighborhood stores.[22]

To commemorate the sixth anniversary of the *Brown* decision, student leaders announced plans to march from the Atlanta University Complex (located on the west side of the downtown area) to a rally at the Wheat Street Baptist Church (located on the east side of the downtown area). They planned to stop at the State Capitol on their way to the rally. This announcement received coverage in the newspapers. Governor Vandiver authorized state troopers to "protect" the Capitol from the students. Because of the potential for conflict, the AUC presidents, Mayor Hartsfield, and Chief Jenkins urged the students to cancel or postpone the march. Nevertheless, on 17 May over 1500 students began marching from the Atlanta University Center Complex in the direction of the State Capitol. About two blocks from the Capitol, Chief Jenkins stopped the procession and warned the students to either divert the march or be arrested. Student leaders decided to proceed to the rally without stopping at the Capitol. Reverends William Holmes Borders and Martin Luther King, Jr. spoke at the rally.[23]

During the spring of 1960 the students' use of sit-ins, economic boycotts, and protest marches generated debate within the African American community as to the proper tactics to be used in the struggle for civil rights. Conservative leaders, mostly older businessmen and preachers, opposed on principle the use of economic boycotts and picket lines against privately owned businesses. They argued that the tactics of the student leaders heightened racial tensions, offered the potential for racial violence, and threatened the city's biracial coalition. Conservative leaders maintained that litigation, voting, and negotiations were the proper means to affect racial change.[24]

One of the most vocal proponents of these means was C.A. Scott. The editor of the *Daily World* was reluctant to publish "An Appeal for Human Rights." He asked for the full advertising rate to print the statement. The *World* editorially opposed the sit-ins. An editorial argued that the African American community should emphasize "removing segregation in education, more voting and political influence, equal consideration in the administration of justice at the state level, and improved economic opportunities than on places to eat."[25] The initial demonstrations, according to Scott, established the foundations for negotiations and litigation; no further protests were needed. Scott attempted to arrange meetings between students and store managers. Rather than allowing students and their advisors to determine targets, he called for the formation of a community organization to plan for future actions and conduct negotiations. Scott also refused to run the ads of COAHR and the *World* provided only limited coverage of student activities. Because the *World* was an important source of information within the African American community, the students had difficulty in relaying their message.[26]

Despite the opposition from some conservative black leaders like Scott, the students had many supporters within the African American community. Student leaders argued persuasively that very little progress had been made toward removing racial barriers, even after the *Brown* decision. While the students acknowledged that voting, negotiations, and litigation were important tools, they believed that pressure upon the white community was needed to affect immediate and revolutionary change in the South. Many members of ACCA were supporters and advisors to the student movement. Whitney Young, Carl Holman, Jesse Hill, LeRoy Johnson, and Clarence Coleman served in this capacity. Largely due to their advice, the students targeted businesses which had a large African American clientele. Members of ACCA served as important communication links between the students and conservative leaders. A small group of AUC faculty also embraced the student movement and served as advisors. These supporters included Howard Zinn, Robert Brisbane, Lionel Newsom, and Reverend Sam Williams. They advised the students as to targets, strategy, and how to mobilize support within the university complex and the community.[27]

White leaders were aware that dissension existed within the African American community. They appealed to those who favored negotiations and litigation. While praising the nonviolent character of the demonstrations, one newspaper noted that "old customs and traditions" were not changed by "battering rams and dramatics, but by time and attrition and with the help of good will."[28] Another newspaper editorial stated that Atlanta's citizens had "too much stake in the present and future of the city to besmirch it with violence or extreme action."[29] White leaders presented these types of argument to conservative African American leaders and organizations. Rather than dealing directly with the students, Mayor Hartsfield and business leaders attempted to engage conservative leaders into negotiations.

African American leaders made attempts to unify the community. At a public meeting organized to raise money for the students arrested in the demonstrations, Reverend Sam Williams, president of the local NAACP, pledged the organization's support for the students. Several leaders endorsed the concept of a committee to advise the students. In order to unite the various factions, conservative and liberal leaders met to discuss such a proposal. The participants prepared a statement endorsing the activities of the students and stressing the unity of the African American community. This statement, signed by officials of various civic organizations, appeared in city newspapers. In late May this meeting led to the formation of the Student-Adult Liaison Committee.[30]

The purpose of this committee was to serve as a bridge between the students and the larger African American and white communities. It thus served as a buffer for the students. Upon request, the committee also served in an advisory capacity. Members included business leaders, college presidents and faculty, ministers, lawyers, and students. Conservative and liberal factions were represented on the committee. Student leaders reluctantly agreed to the formation of the Student-Adult Liaison Committee. Many perceived the committee as an attempt on the part of established leaders to control the movement. Student leaders did not allow members of the committee to attend policy and strategy meetings of COAHR. They felt free to accept or reject suggestions made by community leaders.[31]

During the summer of 1960 a major goal of the students was to relay their message to the larger community. The leaders of COAHR prepared a program on the student movement which they performed before various civic and religious groups. They persuaded two radio stations which targeted the black community to schedule weekly shows on the activities of the movement. Students also began to print an information sheet which outlined their activities, goals, and strategies. They distributed copies of this sheet at African American churches.

Because the *Daily World* did not adequately cover their activities, the students decided that they needed a weekly newspaper which would support the movement. Student leaders asked Carl Holman to help them begin this venture.[32] In order to raise funds, they asked the Empire Real Estate Board, an association of African American realtors, to remove its advertising from the *Daily World* and place it exclusively in their newspaper. The Empire Real Estate Board had previously provided bail money for the students. William Calloway, a member of the association, challenged the organization to make a firm decision on whether to support the students or the *Daily World*.[33] The Empire Real Estate Board decided to remove their ads from the *Daily World*.[34] The Atlanta Life Insurance Company also decided to place ads in this new newspaper.

The first edition of the *Inquirer* appeared in late July. The newspaper's philosophical differences with the *Daily World* were clearly defined. The publisher credited the *Inquirer*'s existence "to a void that existed in the reporting of the news" within the African American community. A columnist for the *Inquirer* argued that the time for gradualism in the struggle for human rights had passed. The *Inquirer* supported economic boycotts, pickets, and other forms of nonviolent direct action. To encourage stores to change their discriminatory employment practices, it printed the names of establishments which had recently hired African American clerks and urged its readers to patronize these businesses. Similar to the *Daily World*, the *Inquirer* encouraged the development of African American businesses. The newspaper was also a vocal opponent of police brutality.[35]

Due to the departure of students during the summer break, the intensity of the demonstrations lessened. In an attempt to reach an agreement before the fall term, Lonnie King and student leaders met with Richard Rich. At this meeting, Rich directly linked the issues of lunch counter and school desegregation. After schools were desegregated, Rich promised that he would personally ask all store owners to end peacefully the segregation of their eating facilities. In exchange students had to halt all sit-ins and demonstrations. Rich and other business leaders felt that any situation which had the potential to create violence had to be avoided as not to disrupt the peaceful desegregation of the schools. Student leaders rejected Rich's proposals. They argued that lunch counter and school desegregation were two separate issues. The students asked for an immediate end to the segregation of eating facilities at Rich's. In late June a group of students attempted a sit-in at Rich's. Afterwards, the students called for a boycott of the store.[36]

The decision to target Rich's was controversial. Rich's was the first major store to extend credit to African Americans in Atlanta. Company policy instructed sales personnel to address African American customers as "Mr." and "Mrs." The store's water fountains were desegregated. While not in sales, managerial, or skilled positions, a number of African Americans worked at the store. Richard Rich was a respected community leader who had a record of supporting African American causes in the areas of housing and welfare. He was acquainted with several African American leaders.

The city's newspapers denounced the boycott. In a speech, Warren Cochrane, secretary of the ANVL and head of the Butler Street YMCA, criticized the tactics of the students and their concentration on Rich's. Rather than antagonize "friends" in the white community, Cochrane warned that the students should develop new ones.[37] The students realized that Rich's was the most effective possible target. If Rich's desegregated its eating facilities, other downtown stores would follow.[38] Rich's would be extremely vulnerable to a boycott because of its large African American clientele. Most of Atlanta's African American citizens carried the store's credit card.[39] However, student leaders decided to halt temporarily protests at the store. Lonnie King and Jesse Hill wrote to Rich requesting him to meet with the students. Believing that these meetings would be "fruitless," Rich refused to meet with them.[40]

In addition to Rich's, students conducted sit-ins at eating facilities located in the Capitol, City Hall, and the Fulton County Courthouse. They also began to stage kneel-ins at local churches. In early September, COAHR targeted a Colonial grocery store which had a large African American clientele. When the store manager refused to discuss his employment practices, the students established a picket line and urged African American patrons to boycott the store. The boycott was successful. The store hired an African American clerk and upgraded its other black employees. Due to a change in the employment practices at the Colonial store, smaller establishments in the neighborhood also agreed to hire African American clerks.[41]

During the summer and early fall of 1960, COAHR made preparations for large-scale demonstrations and a boycott of the downtown area. In order to influence the upcoming presidential election, student leaders scheduled the demonstrations for mid-October and planned to ask Martin Luther King, Jr. to participate. King's involvement would generate headlines and pressure the two presidential candidates, John Kennedy and Richard Nixon, to address civil rights issues. The decision generated some conflict within COAHR. Many students wanted to begin demonstrations in September fearing that the enthusiasm of the returning students would be gone by mid-October. Rejecting this argument, the Executive Committee of COAHR contacted King to ask him to participate in the demonstrations.[42]

Reverend King was extremely reluctant to participate in the demonstrations. In order to avoid offending established leaders and maintain unity within the black community, he had purposely limited his role during the spring sit-ins. He privately advised the students and spoke at a number of rallies. His participation in the October sit-ins would signify and be interpreted as a major commitment to the student movement in Atlanta. This action could thus alienate him from conservative leaders. Many conservative leaders, including his father, advised King not to participate in the sit-ins on the ground that they were student activities.

King was also concerned about the implications that his participation would have on national politics. Throughout the 1960 presidential campaign, he was under pressure from many of his aides and friends to endorse John Kennedy. King was determined to keep SCLC a nonpartisan organization and officially neutral in the presidential election. While King informed officials of the Kennedy campaign that he would not formally endorse either candidate, he suggested that he would issue a statement favorable to Kennedy if the candidate met with him in a southern city to discuss racial concerns. After intense negotiations between him and representatives of the Kennedy campaign, King agreed to meet with Kennedy in Miami. Kennedy was going to be in the city to address the national convention of the American Legion. While King was not particularly pleased with the choice of Miami because it was not a "true" southern city, he agreed, in part, because the dates of his trip would overlap those of the upcoming demonstrations. The meeting with Kennedy would provide a convenient excuse for him not to participate in the Atlanta demonstrations. During these discussions, officials of the Kennedy campaign warned King that public demonstrations would politically embarrass Kennedy and the Democratic Party. Kennedy eventually canceled this meeting because King insisted on inviting Nixon, who was also in Miami to address the convention, to a private meeting.[43]

On the eve of the demonstrations, Herschelle Sullivan phoned King and asked him for the final time to participate in the protests. King told her that he could not come because he was on probation for a minor traffic violation. That previous May, a DeKalb policeman had ticketed King for failing to exchange his Alabama's driving license for a Georgia license after returning to Atlanta. Judge Oscar Mitchell sentenced King to a twelve-month jail term, suspended, and a $25 fine. When Sullivan informed Lonnie King of Reverend King's decision, he made one last personal appeal. Lonnie, who was a member of Ebenezer Baptist Church, reminded King that he was the "spiritual leader of the movement" and a native Atlantan. King told Lonnie that he would meet him at Rich's.[44]

On 19 October students staged a sit-in at Rich's and seven other downtown department stores. The police arrested Reverend King and fifty-one demonstrators at Rich's for violating the state's anti-trespass law. The judge dropped charges against sixteen demonstrators.[45] Reverend King and the remaining thirty-five students refused bail. The following day, students resumed picketing in the downtown area. Police officers arrested approximately twenty-two students for attempting to eat at the Union News Restaurant at the Terminal Station. Student leaders promised to continue their demonstrations until all eating facilities were desegregated.[46]

Fearing that the situation was deteriorating, Hartsfield appealed to adult African American leaders for a sixty or ninety-day truce period. During this time, he promised to begin negotiations toward the desegregation of eating facilities at all downtown department stores if the African American students agreed to accept bail and refrain from further demonstrations. The students refused to leave jail unless all charges were dropped. As mayor,

Hartsfield could arrange to drop charges against those in city jails, but he had no jurisdiction over King and the students who were facing state charges. Because the mayor did not directly negotiate with them, student leaders rejected a truce period.

When this approach failed, Hartsfield invited black student and adult leaders to a meeting in the chamber at City Hall. While African American leaders privately met in the chamber to discuss who would be their spokesperson, Hartsfield returned to his office and noticed the large number of telegrams protesting the jailing of Reverend King. Morris Abram, a prominent Atlanta attorney and close friend, walked into the mayor's office. Earlier that morning, Harris Wofford, an advisor to the Kennedy campaign on racial matters and a personal friend of Reverend King, contacted Abram on his own initiative to have him speak with the mayor about releasing King. Abram and Hartsfield recognized the political implication that this particular incident could have on the presidential campaign. They believed that Kennedy should issue a statement of support and concern for King.

Abram phoned Harris Wofford from the mayor's office with this suggestion. Wofford told Abram not to invoke Kennedy's name in any manner until he got the senator's permission. Wofford personally feared that Kennedy's open support for King would lose the senator white votes in the South. After failing to make contact with Kennedy who was on the campaign trail, Wofford phoned Hartsfield's office to inform Abram that he could not contact Kennedy and, therefore, the mayor should not invoke the senator's name in any manner. After Hartsfield tried unsuccessfully to contact Kennedy, he returned to the council chamber to continue negotiations with the African American leaders.

This meeting resulted in an accord. The students agreed to suspend demonstrations for thirty days, and Mayor Hartsfield ordered the immediate release of students facing city charges. He indicated that he would urge merchants not to press charges and request state officials to release those in the Fulton County jail. The mayor agreed to serve as an intermediary in discussions between students and store owners. Despite Wofford's instructions and pleas, Hartsfield informed African American leaders that Kennedy had personally expressed his support for Reverend King and was aware of efforts to release him from jail.[47]

One of the participants involved in the negotiations was John Calhoun who was the director of the Nixon campaign in Atlanta's African American community. Like Hartsfield and Abram, he recognized the political implications of King's arrest. Immediately following the negotiations, he contacted Republican Party officials. Calhoun warned them that Nixon should make a statement of support for Reverend King. Ignoring this advice, the Nixon campaign refused to comment on King's arrest. While Nixon knew that he would lose some African American support, he believed that he would win enough white votes to offset this loss.[48] At this time, the Kennedy campaign also believed that a statement of support would hurt its candidate. Trying to offset Hartsfield's remarks to the African American leaders, it released a statement saying that the senator was simply trying to obtain information on King's arrest and that he hoped a satisfactory outcome would be achieved.

Officials released all of the participants in the demonstrations except Reverend King. Judge Oscar Mitchell issued a bench warrant ordering officials to keep King in jail until a hearing was held on whether his arrest at Rich's violated the terms of his probation in the May traffic case. The students accused Hartsfield of breaking the negotiated agreement. The mayor argued that he had no control over Judge Mitchell's actions. Supporters of Reverend King gathered at the Fulton County jail and later at the DeKalb County Courthouse. Judge Mitchell revoked King's probation and sentenced him to four months at hard labor on a state road gang. He denied a motion to release King on bond pending an appeal of both the current ruling and the original traffic sentence. That night, officials transported King to Reidsville, a remote maximum security prison.

Following King's arrival at Reidsville, Harris Wofford suggested to campaign officials that Kennedy should phone Corretta King and express his concern. He argued that a telephone call would be simpler and less controversial than a public statement. Senator Kennedy agreed to call her. Later, Robert Kennedy personally appealed to Judge Mitchell to release King. This personal attention apparently flattered the judge. Mitchell subsequently released King.

Word of Kennedy's intervention spread rapidly throughout the African American community. The Kennedy campaign distributed a pamphlet, "'No Comment' Nixon Versus a Candidate With a Heart, Senator Kennedy," within African American churches on the last Sunday before the presidential election. In order to minimize a possible backlash from white voters, it established a committee of African American ministers to officially sponsor the pamphlet which consisted of statements by the King family and African American preachers about Senator Kennedy's call to Coretta King. The pamphlet did not contain a statement from the senator or mention Robert Kennedy's conversation with Judge Mitchell. African Americans voted for Kennedy in large numbers on election day, particularly in the states of Illinois, Michigan, and South Carolina. These states were crucial to Kennedy's close victory over Nixon. Ironically, Nixon carried the African American precincts in Atlanta. This election, however, marked the end of Republican influence in Atlanta's black community. It would vote solidly Democratic in future national and local elections.[49]

During the thirty day truce period, Hartsfield made several attempts to reach a negotiated settlement. While many owners of small retail stores met with the mayor, a representative from Rich's did not attend the negotiation sessions. Instead, Rich tried unsuccessfully to convince conservative leaders to halt further demonstrations. One demonstration occurred during the truce period. Showing their support for COAHR, white students from Emory University, Georgia Tech, and Agnes Scott College demonstrated against segregation. On 22 November the mayor reported that no agreement had been reached, and he asked for another thirty-day truce. The students agreed to extend the truce for a period of three days.[50]

White and African American leaders made one last attempt to reach an agreement on Thanksgiving night. Cecil Alexander, chairman of the Citizens Advisory Committee on Urban Renewal and a respected businessman, gathered several African American businessmen, officers of the Student-Adult Liaison Committee, Lonnie King and other student leaders, Dr. Benjamin Mays, Reverend Martin Luther King, Jr. and Richard Rich in an informal meeting. African American leaders urged the immediate desegregation of lunch counters and restaurants. Rich insisted that schools and other public institutions should be desegregated before private businesses. He repeated his promise that he would urge other owners to open their facilities to all races after schools were desegregated. Rich also pledged to review his store's employment practices. In return, students had to immediately halt their demonstrations. The parties reached no agreement that night.[51]

The students resumed their demonstrations after Thanksgiving. The majority of store owners decided to close their eating facilities. To avoid conflict, many stores piled their counters with boxes, baskets, and holiday displays. Others roped their counters off or removed stools. Two drugstores attempted to serve "stand-up" style to white customers. Due to student "stand-ins," these stores eventually ceased this service. As stores closed down their segregated eating facilities, students began picketing around the downtown area.

The boycott was effective. Federal Reserve statistics for the week ending 3 December 1960 revealed that Atlanta department store sales were down by twelve percent. By mid-December Christmas sales in the city were down by sixteen percent, almost ten million dollars below normal.[52] On 30

November the YWCA desegregated its eating facilities. These "victories" were largely due to the organization and planning of these demonstrations. Student protestors were equipped with walkie-talkies and two-way radios to keep them in touch with the "central headquarters" or "those in the field." COAHR leaders divided the business district into five areas. Each district had an "area commander" to oversee activities and keep the "central headquarters" informed of developments. Student duties included "pickets," "sit-ins," and "sit-and-runs." When merchants closed lunch counters, those students assigned to sit-in went to jail if necessary. Those assigned to "sit-and-run" went to the next open counter in the city. Volunteer crews provided food and transportation for the protestors.[53]

Throughout the demonstrations, student leaders attempted to initiate meetings with white merchants. They sent letters expressing their desire to negotiate to the Retail Merchants Association, the Chamber of Commerce, and the Junior Chamber. These organizations refused to meet with the students. The Chamber of Commerce echoed the position of Richard Rich. The students maintained that lunch counter and school desegregation were two separate issues. Before halting demonstrations, students demanded a firm pledge from business owners to desegregate eating facilities. The owners refused to comply. A stalemate thus existed between the merchants and the students.

As the stalemate continued, support for the student movement within the African American community grew. African American citizens began to take a more active role in the demonstrations. Supporters of the movement returned their Rich's credit cards to the store or mailed them to the student headquarters.[54] In late November, adult leaders held a prayer meeting for the student movement at Herndon Stadium on the AUC campus. Following this meeting, approximately two thousand African American citizens marched in freezing rain through downtown Atlanta. They gathered for another prayer meeting at Plaza Park, located near the center of the city.

African American students also faced white resistance. They frequently faced taunts and jeers from white spectators. At a white-owned grocery store in a black neighborhood, students encountered a white mob carrying vials of a caustic solution and sharpened windshield wipers. A member of this mob threw a solution into Lonnie King's face which almost cost him his sight.[55] During a sit-in in November, a white merchant threatened a female student with a blackjack.[56] White spectators burned demonstrators with their cigarettes. On 26 November members of the Klan in full regalia marched in support of segregation while students picketed a store on the other side of the street. Mayor Hartsfield quipped that Atlanta was "the only city in the country where Negroes and the Klan can picket on the same street to music by the Salvation Army."[57] The Klan and Georgians Unwilling to Surrender (GUTS), a group organized by Lester Maddox, urged a boycott of any store that changed its segregation policy or employment practices due to student pressure. GUTS also advocated firing all African American employees if the demonstrations continued. Ironically, these groups claimed the credit for the drop in downtown retail sales.[58] To avoid violence between the students and the segregationist groups, police officers patrolled the downtown area and enforced picket regulations established by Chief Jenkins. To the credit of the police department and the nonviolent behavior of the students, the police department made no arrests in November, December, and January.[59]

Due to final exams and their involvement in other SNCC projects, students reduced their activities to picketing on weekends and occasional sit-ins during January 1961. In February, they resumed their activities with a new sense of mission. To commemorate the anniversary of the Greensboro sit-ins, approximately 400 students marched from the Atlanta University Center to downtown Atlanta. As they entered the downtown area, students peeled off from the main body and established picket lines around a six-block area. The following week, students conducted demonstrations at various eating facilities in the downtown area. By 10 February eighty students were in jail; they refused to post bond. Martin Luther King, Jr. spoke at a mass meeting to generate support for the students.

At a meeting of African American leaders, A.T. Walden, one of Atlanta's most conservative African American leaders, urged the students to negotiate. While Walden expressed support for the initial demonstrations and had served as an attorney for many of the students, he had concerns about the tactics of the students. Walden was a firm advocate of the use of negotiations and litigation to solve racial problems. While many students and younger leaders questioned Walden's support for the movement, they respected him. These leaders gave Walden permission to approach white leaders about seeking a solution to the racial situation in the city.[60]

Walden approached Robert Troutman, an attorney who had business connections with Richard Rich and had worked with Walden on a number of projects. Rather than concentrating on Rich's, Troutman suggested that African American leaders should negotiate with all the major downtown merchants. Troutman and Walden visited Ivan Allen, Jr., then Chamber of Commerce president. Allen agreed to arrange a meeting between leading merchants and African American leaders.[61] This meeting led to a series of negotiating sessions between African American leaders and downtown merchants.

In early March, Lonnie King and Herschelle Sullivan, the principal student leaders, attended one of the negotiating sessions. Fearful of attempts to "sell out the students," they asked for the immediate desegregation of the lunch counters.[62] Under pressure from those present, the student leaders agreed to a pledge that lunch counters and bathrooms would be open to all races after schools were desegregated. It was understood by these students that these facilities would be desegregated regardless of the outcome of the school situation. In exchange, the students agreed to halt their protests. All employees who had been laid off due to closed eating facilities would be rehired. Until the schools were officially desegregated, lunch counters would open on a segregated basis.

As announced to the public on 9 March 1961, the terms of the agreement were vague and open to interpretation. The terms of the agreement did not specifically state how and when the desegregation of the lunch counters would occur. In a "clarifying statement" issued by the Chamber of Commerce, lunch counter desegregation appeared to be directly linked to the outcome of school desegregation. Under this interpretation, the agreement was the same proposal that Richard Rich offered to the students in June 1960.[63]

The agreement thus provoked an outburst from the African American community. The original agreement, according to the students, did not directly link the issues of school and lunch counter desegregation. Lunch counters would be desegregated regardless of the outcome of the school situation. Because of their participation in the signing of the agreement, Lonnie King and Herschelle Sullivan resigned their positions. COAHR members, however, refused to accept their resignations. After much debate, student leaders agreed to refrain from picketing and sit-ins, but they decided to continue their boycott until facilities were desegregated.

In order to ease dissatisfaction within the community, the African American participants who negotiated the agreement circulated a statement clarifying the agreement. This statement was closer to the students' interpretation than the one issued by the Chamber of Commerce. Leaders of the Student-Adult Liaison Committee decided to sponsor a meeting at which the terms of the agreement could fully be explained. Over a thousand people attended the meeting at Warren Memorial Methodist Church. Students shouted down members of the "Old Guard" leadership who spoke in favor of the agreement. In a dramatic and emotional speech, Martin Luther King, Jr. spoke in favor of the agreement. He argued that the settlement was an extension of the principles of nonviolence. King called for the unity of the community in its battle against racial oppression. While dissatisfaction still existed and an unofficial boycott continued, the students decided to honor the agreement. The merchants who participated in the agreement desegregated their eating facilities in late September 1961.[64]

The movement to desegregate lunch counters revealed the ideological and generational differences that existed in Atlanta's African American community. These differences revolved around the proper tactics to use in ending segregation, the pace of racial change, and the perceived degree to which the white community resisted change. More importantly, younger African American leaders began to perceive the "Old Guard" leadership as an impediment to racial change. Student leaders believed that the established leadership had to be challenged in order to change the status quo. The differences between adult and younger leaders became apparent in the mayoral election of 1961.

William Hartsfield announced that he would not seek another term. The major candidates for office were State Representative M.M. "Muggsy" Smith, Ivan Allen, Jr., State Senator Charlie Brown, Fulton County Commissioner James Aldredge, and Lester Maddox. Of the candidates, Smith had the best record on race relations. As a state representative, he was an advocate of open schools and opposed the state's county unit system. Early in his career, Ivan Allen supported segregation policies and the county unit system. Recently, however, he had begun to moderate his racial views. During the sit-in negotiations, he impressed older African American leaders. Charlie Brown and James Aldredge attempted to avoid or defuse racial issues. Lester Maddox was an avowed segregationist who denounced the forced integration of the races.

The business community supported Allen. Despite Smith's record in race relations, the Atlanta Negro Voters League also endorsed Allen. Taking a large political gamble, Smith decided to align himself with the student movement. He accused the ANVL of betraying the students during the sit-in negotiations in order to advance its own interests. Because of his record on racial issues and this attack, Smith attracted the support of a large number of students and younger African American leaders. He chose Donald Hollowell, a young African American attorney, to run his campaign in the black community.[65]

Members of the ANVL attempted to counter Smith's attacks. William Holmes Borders argued that Smith's "vicious attack upon the integrity, honesty, and loyalty" of the League was "almost an unforgivable insult to the Negro citizenry of Atlanta."[66] In a statement, Walden attempted to address the complaints of students. Walden argued that "mature leadership often finds it necessary to take the middle approach to problems." Racial change "does not come suddenly." He assured the students that African American leaders have "always been in basic sympathy for which all Negroes, young and old, have stood for and have fought for years for their realization but maturity has told them that these things had to be accomplished step by step and not by violent changes."[67] ANVL leaders argued that disunity within the African American community would result in the election of Lester Maddox.

Some African Americans were uncomfortable with the League's insistence on unity. In a letter to A.T. Walden, Alfred "Tup" Holmes, a respected businessman, argued that the students "should be allowed the inherent right of vocally supporting their political preference without censure or pressure from the adult Negro community." The students felt that they were "duped once, and are extremely wary of the same thing happening again." He hoped that the League was "not degenerating into a vehicle for the political and financial furtherance of a select few."[68]

In the mayoral election, younger African Americans expressed their political independence by voting for Smith. Despite the students' defection, Allen defeated Smith by a two-to-one margin in the predominately African American districts. In the runoff, he faced Lester Maddox. While having a similar economic platform as Allen, Maddox opposed the massive integration of Atlanta's school system, favored the separation of the sexes in the schools to avoid miscegenation, and proposed the selling of municipal swimming pools in order to prevent desegregation. Allen accused Maddox of trying "to bring another Little Rock to Atlanta."[69] Allen received 64,311 votes to Maddox's 36,091. He won ninety-nine percent of the African American vote. Maddox won in the lower white income districts, many of which were beginning to experience racial transition.

Despite this apparent vote in confidence for the "Old Guard" leadership, the ANVL's political influence was severely weakened. The student movement in Atlanta directly challenged its leadership. In order to remain a credible and viable organization and maintain at least a pretense of unity within the African American community, the League realized that it had to involve younger leaders and more militant groups in its negotiations with the white community. In late 1962 it used this approach to solve a racial situation on the southwest side of the city.

In 1962 an African American physician attempted to purchase a home near Peyton Forrest, a white, posh neighborhood located in Southwest Atlanta. Rumors that the area was marked for racial transition created panic among whites in the community. The Southwest Citizens Association, an organization formed to achieve "residential stability," raised over $200,000 to purchase property from white owners who were threatening to place their homes on the African American market. Members of this organization argued that leaders from the north side were negotiating away the racial homogeneity of Southwest Atlanta in order to protect the property values on the north side of the city. They urged Allen to stop African American "encroachment."

In order to stop the panic, Allen wanted to rezone eight hundred acres of unused commercial land for low-to-middle income African American housing. This area, located north of Peyton Forest, had previously been used as a racial barrier. Allen also decided to erect a two-foot, ten-inch high steel and wood barrier at Peyton and Harlan Roads in Southwest Atlanta. This physical barrier was to serve as a dividing line between African Americans and whites in the area by blocking two roads that connected Collier Heights, an African American middle-class neighborhood, with Peyton Forrest.[70] The Southwest Citizens Association defended the barrier as a way to reduce racial tensions and argued that new land would be made available for African American housing. The erection of a barrier specifically designed to ensure residential segregation caused an uproar in the African American community. Reminiscent of the Berlin Wall, residents began to refer to it as the "Peyton Wall." Reverend Sam Williams, a political supporter of Allen, told the mayor that he didn't understand how "any decent white man can do what you have done."[71] Pictures of the "Peyton Wall" appeared in national publications diminishing Atlanta's reputation as a progressive city.[72]

In order to ease racial tensions produced by the barrier, Allen invited representatives of the Atlanta Negro Voters League, the Empire Real Estate Board, and the Southwest Citizens Association to a meeting at City Hall. African American leaders announced that they would be represented by a newly formed organization, the Citizens Committee for Better City Planning (CCBCP). The CCBCP was an umbrella organization consisting of such groups as the NAACP, ACCA, COAHR, ANVL, SNCC, and SCLC. Recognizing the changes occurring in the African American leadership, Dr. C. Miles Smith, co-chairman of the CCBCP and current president of the local NAACP, announced that "new blood" was "coming in."[73]

But members of CCBCP refused to participate in discussions until the wall was removed. The CCBCP also conducted demonstrations, protests, and a boycott of stores in Atlanta's West End. In January 1963 ACCA urged African American realtors not to agree to any negotiated settlements which would establish residential boundaries between white and African American citizens. African American leaders would now strive for integrated city neighborhoods. These positions were more militant than any taken by the ANVL in previous negotiations with white leaders. In an attempt to bypass the CCBCP, Mayor Allen and the Public Works Commission met privately with ANVL leaders in order to reach a settlement. But League officials informed the mayor that they supported the position of the CCBCP.[74]

In January 1963 the Board of Aldermen refused to remove the barrier. In March a Fulton County Superior Court judge ruled that the erection of barriers for the purpose of establishing a racial buffer or zone was unconstitutional. The ordinance creating the barrier was "unreasonable, arbitrary, and capricious." He ordered the immediate removal of the wall. Given a face-saving way out of the impasse, city officials promised not to erect physical barriers to further segregation. City officials and African American leaders agreed that informal settlements which established residential barriers were no longer workable.[75]

While students and younger leaders favored the use of nonviolent direct action, they realized that voting, litigation, and negotiations were necessary tools. In its battle against segregation, Atlanta's African American community used a combination of tactics. In May 1961 COAHR members filed a suit seeking the end of racial segregation and discrimination in the use of every public facility which was either owned, maintained, or subsidized by the city of Atlanta including parks, swimming pools, the municipal auditorium, and public buildings. As a result of this suit, a U.S. District Court in 1962 ruled that the ordinances requiring segregated parks and swimming pools were unconstitutional.[76]

After students began their protests, many businessmen chose to negotiate. In June 1961 COAHR members requested movie theatres to desegregate their facilities. The owners refused to negotiate with student leaders. On behalf of COAHR, representatives of the Atlanta Council on Human Relations, the NAACP, and the Young Adult Group of the Unitarian Church approached local owners of downtown and suburban movie theatres. After theatre owners failed to attend a prearranged meeting and refused to agree to attend another negotiating session, COAHR conducted demonstrations during the Thanksgiving and Christmas holidays. Over the next year, representatives of the theatre owners, the Atlanta Council on Human Relations, the Mayor's Office, the Atlanta police department, COAHR, SNCC, and NAACP met to discuss the situation.

In July 1963 theatre owners and student leaders agreed on a "memorandum of understanding." For a two-week period in July, eight suburban theatres agreed to accept up to six African American citizens per performance. If no incidents occurred during this period, the theatres would admit African Americans on a regular basis. If an incident occurred, owners could "resegregate" their theatres upon notifying the Atlanta Council of Human Relations of the reason. Owners of drive-ins feared that violence might erupt between white and African American customers at their concession stands. Since concession stands were more frequently used in the summer, drive-ins could wait until the fall to desegregate. During a two-week period in October, eleven suburban drive-ins agreed to admit up to six cars carrying African Americans per performance. During this period, owners could request African American patrons to limit their use of the concession stands and bathrooms to times when the movie was being shown and avoid use at the start of the feature and during intermission. The stated purpose of this provision was to avoid violence. After this period, African Americans would be accepted on a regular basis. The drive-ins had the same provision as to resegregation and informing the Atlanta Council on Human Relations. All parties agreed that no publicity would be given to the agreement. Church and civic associations were to inform their members. Mayor Allen and Chief Jenkins (as required by the terms) approved of the agreement. The theatres were quietly desegregated.[77]

The desegregation of Grady Hospital occurred through the use of demonstrations, negotiations, and litigation. In October 1961 COAHR and the NAACP requested the desegregation of all facilities, staff, teaching programs, and practices at the hospital. A biracial group of professional people advised and cooperated with the students. Dr. Roy C. Bell, an African American dentist who was greatly concerned about the health services provided for black citizens, and Eliza Paschall of the Atlanta Council on Human Relations headed this group. Beginning in November, students began to demonstrate at Grady Hospital and City Hall protesting segregated health facilities. They met with the Fulton County Commission and the Fulton-DeKalb Hospital Authority. As a result of the demonstrations and the meetings, Grady Hospital announced that it would accept applications from African Americans for intern positions. It also admitted an African American physician to its staff in February 1962. The hospital undertook no actions, however, regarding the desegregation of patients, facilities, or medical training programs.

While attempting to help an African American student gain entrance to the hospital's segregated emergency clinic, police officers arrested Dr. Bell and twenty-two students on charges of disorderly conduct and "disturbing the hospital's normal operation." After the arrests, eleven civil rights, professional, and human relations organizations urged the federal government to cut off funds to the hospital.[78] In June 1962 Dr. Bell filed a suit in federal court seeking the desegregation of all patient care facilities, staff, and student training programs at Grady. The suit also covered the desegregation of local and state medical societies. In 1963 Grady Hospital announced the appointment of its first African American intern. That same year the Northern District Dental Society removed "white" from its qualifications for membership. In 1964 an African American businessman became a board member of the Fulton-DeKalb Hospital Authority. As a result of the passage of the Civil Rights Act of 1964, Grady Hospital desegregated its emergency clinic and nursing school facilities. In 1965 a federal district court ordered Grady Hospital to end all discriminatory practices.

The desegregation of Atlanta's churches became a "cause celebre" due to the arrest of Ashton Jones, a sixty-seven year old minister. During the initial demonstrations in 1960-1961, students staged kneel-ins at local churches. Many students also attempted to attend segregated Sunday morning worship services. In the spring of 1963, COAHR began to challenge segregated worship services at Atlanta's First Baptist Church. It was the city's largest Protestant church, twelfth largest in the Southern Baptist Convention. The church's senior pastor, Reverend Roy McClain, had a national reputation. When kneel-ins began in the city, the church's board of deacons voted not to allow African Americans to enter the main sanctuary. The church followed the "practice" (not policy) of directing African Americans to an auxiliary auditorium.

In April and May 1963 students attempted to sit in the main sanctuary during worship services at First Baptist Church. Students claimed that they were physically manhandled and abused by hostile church ushers. On one occasion, a group of eight to ten men "protected" the door to the main sanctuary. In late June ushers denied Reverend Ashton Jones, two African American students, a black youngster, and a white girl entrance to the church's main sanctuary. As members of the congregation entered the church, Jones "preached" on the subject of worshiping a segregated God. He returned for the evening services and again preached to those who entered the church. When Jones attempted to enter the main sanctuary, ushers asked him to leave. When he refused, the ushers called the police, and officers arrested him on charges of disturbing public worship and disorderly conduct.

Prior to his arrest, Jones had participated in civil rights activities and peace protests throughout the region. In Atlanta he became involved in COAHR activities. In May 1963 police officers arrested Jones for violating the state anti-trespass law, and he spent twenty-two days in jail before being released on bail. For his activity at the First Baptist Church, the Fulton County Grand Jury convicted Jones of disturbing public worship, a misdemeanor in Georgia. Judge Durwood Pye imposed the maximum sentence of twelve months in public works, six months in jail, and a $1,000 fine. When attorneys for Jones filed a motion for a new trial, Judge Pye stayed the sentence and set bail at $20,000. Because he was unable to make bail, Jones was confined to jail. An unknown inmate attacked Jones, and, "for his own protection," prison officials placed the minister in a solitary cell. Protesting conditions in the jail and his own confinement, Jones went on a hunger strike.

The arrest of Jones outraged civil rights and human relations organizations. They began to raise funds for his bail. In August and September, Judge Pye refused to lower Jones' bail.[79] Letters urging Jones' release were sent to Governor Carl Sanders. Students began picketing outside the First Baptist Church every Sunday. Embarrassed by the attention caused by the arrest and demonstrations, First Baptist Church dropped its "practice" of segregation and Reverend McClain appealed for Jones' release. After the Georgia Supreme Court ordered a reduction in his bail, Judge Pye released Jones in March 1964. He had spent 188 days in jail.[80] While policy varied from church to church and denomination to denomination, religious institutions began to desegregate their services after the Jones' incident.

The student demonstrations, Peyton Wall, and the arrest of Ashton Jones diminished Atlanta's progressive image. In 1963 rumors spread that at least two national magazines nearly pulled positive articles on the city.[81] Officials feared that a bad reputation would economically hurt the city. Of prime concern was the city's tourist and convention business. Between 1950 and 1960, Atlanta's revenue from convention business rose from $16.6 million to $30 million. In April 1961 Walter Crawford, executive vice-president of the convention bureau, estimated that the city could no longer bid on twenty-five percent of national conventions and ten percent of southern conventions because these organizations did not restrict membership according to race. While Crawford argued that Atlanta had intensified its sales efforts toward the remaining market, segregation was financially hurting the city.[82] For this reason, Mayor Allen chose to become personally involved in negotiations over hotel and restaurant desegregation.

In accordance with the sit-in agreement, racial barriers fell at some eating facilities. The majority of restaurants and hotels, however, maintained a policy of segregation. Some variations in this policy existed.

A few hotels, at the request of city officials or the convention bureau, agreed to accept visiting African American dignitaries and black convention delegates. Some of the major downtown hotels and restaurants hosted "privately arranged" biracial luncheons and meetings. Hotels, however, maintained a firm policy of segregation in their eating facilities. Unlike rooms, these facilities were in public view. Because a large percentage of their revenues from eating facilities were dependent upon local patronage, owners claimed it was necessary to adhere to custom and tradition.

In the spring and summer of 1963, African American students conducted protests at segregated hotels and restaurants. In March students conducted a "lie-in" in the lobby of Grady Hotel. The following months, demonstrations occurred at the Ship Ahoy Restaurant, a S&W cafeteria, Leb's Restaurant, and Morrison's Cafeteria. Students also conducted demonstrations on the AUC campuses and at City Hall protesting segregated facilities. In each of these demonstrations, police officers arrested protestors. In July a spectator stabbed a fifteen-year-old demonstrator who was attempting to eat at a Morrison's Cafeteria.

These protests frequently drew angry white mobs and counterdemonstrators. In 1963 Lester Maddox, the founder of GUTS, organized the People's Association for Selective Shopping (PASS) in order to "restore and preserve constitutional government" and "protect the jobs and services of white people." Members of PASS pledged to "pass by" the products and services of merchants who integrated their establishments or "replaced" white workers with African Americans. PASS compiled a list of integrated establishments and distributed it to members. The organization enlisted volunteers to picket these businesses.[83]

In negotiations with African American leaders and Mayor Allen, owners of hotels and restaurants emphasized property rights. They maintained that a business owner had the right to sell his commodity or service to a client of his choosing. Privately, these owners feared that desegregation would harm their businesses by alienating white customers. In a conversation with Eliza Paschall, Walter Crawford noted that no establishment wanted to "take the first step." He felt that restaurant owners in the city were waiting to see if hotels first opened their eating facilities to African Americans.[84] In his memoirs, Allen noted that "hotel and restaurant associations would not even respond to the pragmatic argument that unless they opened up their doors to everyone, Atlanta's convention and tourist business—not to mention its favorable image—would plummet."[85]

In May 1963 the Atlanta Chamber of Commerce issued a "policy declaration" urging all businesses to desegregate in order to maintain a peaceful racial climate. Without fanfare or publicity, eighteen hotels and thirty restaurants agreed to desegregate in June. The Atlanta Council on Human Relations found, however, that many of these establishments resegregated. In a survey of hotels and restaurants conducted in August, the Council found that less than twelve restaurants (six in the downtown area) with "any reasonable degree of uncertainty" could be classified as being desegregated. Only five hotels (one in the downtown area) accepted all races on an unconditional basis. Of the thirty restaurants that desegregated in June, only twenty were still serving all races.[86]

As a number of hotels and restaurants began to change their racial policies, a haphazard pattern of segregation existed in the city. African American citizens did not know if a facility would be opened to them on a particular day. The Atlanta Council on Human Relations attempted to compile a list of desegregated facilities. The Council admitted, however, that changes in policy occurred daily. Many owners refused to publicly state or discuss their racial policies. To avoid being humiliated or embarrassed, the logical course for most African Americans was to assume that the facility was segregated. According to the Council, day-to-day changes in policy and the lack of public information perpetuated segregation.

In the midst of negotiations with restaurant and hotel owners, President John Kennedy asked Mayor Allen to testify before the Senate Committee on Commerce on behalf of a national civil rights act. By 1963 acts of African American civil disobedience had forced the Kennedy Administration to attempt to end discrimination and segregation through federal legislation. In April a massive civil rights demonstration in Birmingham, Alabama provoked national indignation when the city's police commissioner, Eugene "Bull" Connor, ordered officers to use police dogs, water hoses, and electric cattle prods on protesters. After federalized National Guardsmen forced the integration of the University of Alabama over the opposition of Governor George Wallace in June, President Kennedy in a televised address announced that he was sending to Congress an omnibus civil rights bill. The legislation contained a public accommodations section which would guarantee the rights of all Americans "to be served in facilities which are opened to the public—hotels, restaurants, theatres, retail stores, and similar establishments."[87]

The public accommodations section of the legislation outraged southern officials. They argued that this provision was an affront to private enterprise and the rights of businessmen. In Georgia Governor Carl Sanders, both state senators, and the entire congressional delegation condemned the proposal. In order for the bill to be credible and for reasons of political propaganda,

Kennedy realized that he needed to have at least one southern official speak on behalf of the bill before Congress. Due to the progress of civil rights in Atlanta and the mayor's past cooperation with the Kennedy administration, Ivan Allen, Jr. was a logical choice.

While Allen had made no public statement on the legislation, he was concerned that the voluntary desegregation of public facilities on the local level had "gone as far as it was going to go in the South and much of the rest of the nation."[88] Before going to Washington, Allen met with African American leaders. While they were pleased with his decision to testify, many leaders expressed concern that his testimony would harm his political career.[89] In his statement to the committee, Allen noted that desegregation in Atlanta had largely occurred on a voluntary basis. He argued, however, that failure to pass national legislation would result in "discrimination under the guise of private enterprise." Allen testified that if Congress failed to act, it would be endorsing "the right of private businesses to practice discrimination, and, in my opinion, would start the same old round of squabbles and demonstrations that we have had in the past."[90] While noting that Mayor Allen "has stood courageously for what he sincerely believes," the *Atlanta Constitution* refused to editorially support the civil rights bill (the newspaper endorsed the bill in January 1964).[91] Most of Allen's business peers also criticized his decision. His support for the desegregation of public accommodations thus had little influence in the short term on business owners.

Discouraged by the progress in Atlanta, over two hundred African American leaders representing eighty-two community, religious, civic, and civil rights organizations met in October to discuss the problems facing the African American community and consider the most effective approach to their solutions. From this meeting, the Summit Leadership Conference (SLC) emerged. These leaders elected a steering committee of fifteen members to guide this organization. One individual from each of the nine sponsoring organizations was placed on this committee with other members elected at-large. The nine sponsoring organizations were the NAACP, SNCC, SCLC, ACCA, COAHR, ANVL, the All Citizens Registration Committee, Operation Breadbasket, and the Gandhi Youth Society. The members elected Clarence Coleman and A.T. Walden as co-chairmen. The SLC thus represented an alliance between the "Old Guard" and emerging leaders. In its guidelines, the SLC stated that it did not want to upstage the authority, timetable, objectives, or methods of existing organizations. It wanted to establish communications between African American traditional and grass-roots leaders.[92]

Members charged the steering committee with the responsibility of designing a master plan for the total desegregation of Atlanta. This plan, *Action for Democracy*, addressed concerns in the areas of public accommodations, employment opportunities, housing, education, registration and voting, health and human services, political issues, and law enforcement. The plan presented more than thirty recommendations for city officials. These proposals included the desegregation of all public facilities; implementation of fair employment practices in private and municipal hiring; an open occupancy housing ordinance; a totally desegregated school system; neighborhood registration centers; the desegregation of services, staff, and training programs in all public health facilities; African American representation on municipal boards and agencies; and the desegregation of penal and correctional institutions. Following the announcement of this plan, SLC leaders called for the adoption of a local public accommodations ordinance.

In response to the formation of the SLC, the mayor appointed a coordinating committee to address the organization's recommendations. This committee consisted of eleven whites and one African American. The mayor appointed members from various segments of the community. The committee was divided into subcommittees to deal with each area addressed in *Action for Democracy*. Mayor Allen appointed Robert Troutman to serve as a liaison between the mayor, major employers in the city, and SLC leaders.

The strategy of the SLC was to encourage negotiations under pressure. Conservative leaders had the responsibility of negotiating with the white community. If negotiations failed, more militant organizations would conduct demonstrations. Between October and December 1963, the leadership of the SLC met with the Chamber of Commerce, the School Board, the Atlanta Housing Authority, the Fulton-DeKalb Hospital Authority, the Board of Family Services, and hotel and restaurant owners. In most instances, these bodies passed resolutions endorsing the basic objectives of the Summit, but undertook no action.[93]

Obviously, one reason for the passage of these resolutions was to create dissension between conservative and more militant African American leaders. The SLC threatened an economic boycott of the downtown area if racial problems were not addressed by mid-November. Immediately before the deadline, the Chamber of Commerce publicly urged businesses to desegregate. The SLC postponed its boycott. The Chamber's statement, however, was not enough for more militant organizations within the SLC. Independent of the Summit, COAHR, Operation Breadbasket, and SNCC staged demonstrations at Rich's demanding the store to hire more African American sales clerks and upgrade current black employees. Leaders threatened a Christmas boycott of the store. While the demonstrations ended due to the assassination of President Kennedy, Rich's agreed to hire additional black employees. Within the SLC, the success of this protest bolstered the argument for a more militant stance.

In December the SLC held a public rally, "Pilgrimage for Democracy," at Hurt Park in downtown Atlanta. Its purpose was to show public support, both white and African American, for the SLC's campaign to rid Atlanta of segregation. This "Pilgrimage for Democracy" attracted over two thousand citizens including members of the National States Rights Party which picketed the event. Speakers at the rally included James Forman of SNCC, Larry Fox of COAHR, Dr. C. Miles Smith of the NAACP, and Reverend Ralph David Abernathy of SCLC. All of these speakers argued that Atlanta was lagging behind other cities in the area of civil rights. They did not want to destroy the image of Atlanta, but instead make the image a reality.[94]

The main speaker at the rally was Martin Luther King, Jr. This event marked the first time that King had spoken in Atlanta at the invitation of all the civil rights organizations. While praising the city for its racial moderation, King argued that Atlanta had fallen "behind almost every major southern city in its progress toward desegregation." The city's image had "become a tranquilizing drug to lull us to sleep, and dull our sensitivity to the continued existence of segregation." Residents had to admit that they were "disappointed with Atlanta—disappointed with the failure of the political and economic power structures to be bold enough to take forthright action against discrimination, disappointed with the gulf between Atlanta's profession and practice." King argued that the "cancer of segregation can not be cured by the vaseline of gradualism, or the sedative tokenism." Atlanta's African American community had to adopt the means of nonviolent direct action to kill this cancer.[95]

Two days following the rally, SNCC, acting independently of the Summit, began sit-ins at a Toddle House Restaurant. Police officers arrested twenty-one students for violating the state's anti-trespass law. The students decided to stay in jail and accept no bail. Toddle House's parent company was Dobbs House, a national corporation based in Memphis, Tennessee. For this reason, SNCC conducted a national campaign around these arrests. SNCC leaders called for demonstrations at 222 Toddle House Restaurants in thirty states and Washington, D.C. and at another eighty-seven restaurants owned by Dobbs House. Locally, demonstrations also occurred at City Hall, Atlanta airport, Krystal's Restaurants, and eating facilities at the

Heart of Atlanta Motel and Holiday Inn. These demonstrations forced Dobbs House to enter into discussions with SNCC leaders. Negotiations resulted in the desegregation of Dobbs House and Toddle House Restaurants nationwide.[96]

By late December SLC realized that direct action would be necessary to accomplish the goals cited in *Action for Democracy*. Summit leaders asked Wyatt T. Walker, executive director of SCLC, to submit a plan for direct action in Atlanta. In early January, Walker presented this plan before the steering committee. Some conservative leaders were worried that the plan might provoke racial violence. SNCC, SCLC, COAHR, and some of the leaders of the NAACP favored Walker's plan. The SLC adopted a scale-downed version of this plan.[97]

Walker's plan assigned a certain responsibility to each organization. The SLC requested SNCC and COAHR to launch "a dignified, orderly, non-violent direct action campaign" against segregated restaurants. SNCC, in cooperation with the NAACP, was to pursue "legal and other actions" to improve the quality of African American education in the city.[98] In cooperation with the Atlanta Medical Board, the NAACP was to initiate litigation to desegregate Grady Hospital and other public health facilities. SLC leaders asked the NAACP and the ANVL to meet with the Atlanta Housing Authority in order to urge the passage of an open housing occupancy law. These organizations were also to discuss the possibility of a local public accommodations ordinance with the Board of Aldermen. The NAACP was also to conduct a direct action campaign against segregated hotels and begin a testing program of establishments that claimed to have an "open door policy."[99] The SLC asked SCLC and the All Citizens Registration Committee to launch a voter education and registration campaign. In the event that public accommodations and eating establishments were not desegregated by 25 January, all groups agreed to gather their forces behind a "legal and direct action" campaign to affect racial change in Atlanta.[100]

Racial conflict in the city increased throughout the first half of January 1964. "Playing hookey for freedom," approximately 150 high school students, under the guidance of SNCC, conducted a sit-in at Mayor Allen's office in order to protest the conditions of their schools. While no arrests were made, school officials suspended eighty-nine pupils. The following week, biracial groups of high school and college students were arrested at the eating facilities of the Heart of Atlanta Motel and Krystal's Restaurants. Following these arrests, student groups conducted a series of sit-ins at Krystal's Restaurants and Morrison's Cafeterias. On 18 January police officers arrested more than seventy-five demonstrators outside these restaurants.[101]

In an effort to ease racial tensions, Mayor Allen announced that fourteen hotels had agreed to desegregate their establishments. The accord was reached after a series of meetings between civic leaders, restaurant and motel operators, and Mayor Allen. Thirty-five hotel and over one hundred restaurant owners participated in these sessions.[102] Allen also promised to press for a local public accommodations ordinance. In order to deal with an increasing number of demonstrators, Chief Jenkins announced that owners of establishments would now have to obtain warrants before arrests were made. He also affirmed the right of students to engage in peaceful and legal demonstrations.

Despite pleas by city officials, the majority of hotel and restaurant owners refused to desegregate their establishments. In late January the Atlanta Restaurant Association in a statement published in the local newspapers presented "its side of the story." This statement emphasized property rights. The Association deplored the "ever increasing trend toward centralized control and regulation" of private businesses. It also criticized "the demonstrations of extremists who gathered in Atlanta and the coercive pressures of civic leaders designed to persuade them to change their ways."[103]

The Grand Dragon of the Klan offered a solution to the racial conflict in Atlanta. He urged the mayor to appoint a committee composed of African American "integrationists" and white "segregationists." The purpose of this committee would be to discuss racial problems in the city and find common areas of accord. Owners of businesses would decide whether to serve whites only, African Americans only, or whites and African Americans. The committee would publish a list of segregated and integrated institutions. An ordinance would require businesses to place a sign in their windows to signify this racial designation. Naturally, this solution was rejected.

Dissatisfied by the response of city officials and business leaders, John Lewis of SNCC announced an escalation of the demonstrations. In mid-January a subcommittee of the UN Commission on Discrimination Against Minorities met in the city. Student leaders planned protests at each place where the committee was scheduled to meet. When the committee met at the Atlanta University Center, students held a rally on the campus and marched downtown. Demonstrators blocked the area around Leb's, a popular New York-style deli. Some students entered the deli around three o'clock. The owner of Leb's requested his customers and employees to leave the building. He locked the bathroom doors and all entrances to the building. Throughout the afternoon and evening hours, African American students, members of the Klan, and angry white spectators gathered around the establishment as word leaked out that African American protesters were locked-in at Leb's. The police department sent reinforcements into the area, including one African American detail of about forty men. Demonstrators were not let out of Leb's by the owner until eleven o'clock. This incident resulted in only a few arrests, but the potential for racial violence existed.[105]

Following the sit-ins at Leb's, additional demonstrations occurred over a four-day period. Students demonstrated at a Peachtree Street motel, Leb's, Morrison's Cafeterias, and Krystal's Restaurants in downtown Atlanta. A soundtruck urging citizens to participate in the protests traveled throughout African American communities. At many of these establishments, students encountered jeering white mobs and Klan counterdemonstrations. During this period, police officers arrested over two hundred individuals and both sides cited numerous accounts of violence. Rumors circulated the city that the students left the interior of Leb's in shambles and relieved themselves on the floor of the restaurant. Policemen reported that the students shoved and kicked them. They also claimed that demonstrators damaged police and citizens' cars. Students alleged police brutality. News accounts of the demonstrations blamed the violence on the participation of SNCC members. Officials of SNCC charged that the actions of the police officers and white spectators provoked the violence.[106]

In response to the latest demonstrations, Allen urged the city's residents to help "work out a solution to a situation which threatens not only the good name, but beyond that the public safety of our city." At a meeting of white and African American leaders, Allen called for the adoption of a cooling-off period and a halt to demonstrations against restaurants. In return the mayor promised to use all the powers of the city government to guarantee racial harmony. He proposed to establish a civil rights section in the Mayor's Office and ask his coordinating committee to work with SLC in all areas of racial concern. The committee would make regular reports on the progress of race relations in the city to the mayor and SLC leaders. Allen repeated his support for a local public accommodations ordinance. Police Chief Jenkins again acknowledged the right of students to conduct legal demonstrations.[107]

In response the SLC noted that Allen did not specifically respond to the recommendations in *Action for Democracy*. Before accepting a cooling-off period, the SLC requested: (1) charges against all persons arrested in demonstrations sponsored by SNCC or SLC be dropped; (2) the mayor and the Chamber of Commerce arrange a meeting of restaurant owners with SLC officials to work out a plan of desegregation; (3) the same procedure be applied to motels and hotels; (4) the mayor and the Chamber of Commerce to publicly declare a need for a local public accommodations ordinance; (5) the Atlanta Housing Authority to declare an "open door policy" for federally supported housing; (6) the Fulton-DeKalb Hospital Authority to declare an end to racial segregation in all public health facilities; and (7) the mayor and the Chamber of Commerce to implement equal employment opportunities in municipal and private sectors. The SLC voiced its opposition to violent demonstrations and tactics which encouraged violence. It acknowledged, however, the right to protest within "the framework of American tradition and law."[108] While he promised to address these conditions, Mayor Allen refused to dismiss charges against those arrested. The SLC decided to sanction "limited" demonstrations until all proposals were met.

In their discussions with the mayor, SLC members presented a united front. Dissension within the SLC, however, existed. Protests which provoked violence by both demonstrators and police officers appalled conservative leaders. While the SLC had requested SNCC to conduct demonstrations, many were concerned about the intensity of the protests and the organization's independence. A.T. Walden, who was in failing health and had been recently appointed a "standby" judge for the municipal and traffic courts, expressed his displeasure by resigning as co-chairman of SLC. City leaders planted some seeds of dissension. In a statement to the press, Allen noted that "new" organizations "whose actions are alien to Atlanta's tradition of cooperation and understanding have come into being." These organizations "have exposed our city to the danger of infection, by the virus of violence that has paralyzed the progress of so many cities in our nation." In a speech, Chief Jenkins noted that James Forman, "who had taken charge of the Student Nonviolent Coordinating Committee," was uncooperative with the police department.[109] White leaders who had generally been supportive of the movement began to criticize its tactics.

These demonstrations, however, energized white college students in the area. Concerned about allegations of police brutality, white students from Emory University, Agnes Scott College, Georgia Tech University, Oglethorpe University, and Spelman College met in early February 1964 to discuss their participation in the movement. They decided to form an organization through which white students could participate. While maintaining a separate identity, the Georgia Students for Human Rights (GSHR) decided to cooperate with COAHR and other civil rights organizations in the Atlanta area. The GSHR invited two members of COAHR to sit on its steering committee. COAHR allowed two representatives of GSHR on its executive committee. Both organizations promised not to interfere with the activities of the other. While primarily an organization designed for white students, a number of GSHR members were African Americans. During February members participated in demonstrations against segregated restaurants. In March and April, GSHR cooperated with the All Citizens Registration Committee in a voter education and registration drive. GSHR membership eventually comprised representatives from seventeen Georgia colleges and universities.[110]

Demonstrations against segregated public facilities continued throughout the spring of 1964. On occasion African American professionals and elder leaders participated in the protests. In February white and African American ministers called for a special day of prayer for the city. The SLC sponsored an Easter boycott (food and medicine purchases only) of downtown Atlanta. Demonstrators still faced resistance from restaurant owners. At one place, a restaurant owner met demonstrators with electric cattle prods. Allegations of brutality from both sides continued. During this period, SLC offered proposals for settling racial problems by negotiations. In most instances, city officials were unresponsive to SLC requests. As final exams approached for many of the students and attention focused on the passage of a national civil rights act, participation in these demonstrations decreased.

In hopes of revitalizing the movement in Atlanta, the co-chairmen of SLC (Clarence Coleman and Sam Williams) issued a public statement entitled, "We've Got to Have Victories." The statement noted that city officials and government bodies were unresponsive to their requests. While SLC leaders received a "friendly and courteous reception," they argued that "courtesy cannot substitute for equal rights, nor friendliness for removal of racial barriers to live in freedom and dignity."[111] A major disappointment to the SLC was the failure of the Board of Aldermen to pass a local public accommodations ordinance. While Mayor Allen and the Chamber of Commerce had expressed their support for this proposal, questions arose as to its legality. After discussions between local and state officials, the Board of Aldermen tabled the measure.

In July President Lyndon Johnson signed the Civil Rights Act of 1964. The passage of this legislation, however, did not ensure its peaceful implementation on the local level. Prior to its passage, resistance to desegregation was strong. According to the Atlanta Council on Human Relations, only twenty eating facilities could be classified as desegregated. The Atlanta Restaurant Association was on record as being opposed to forced integration. With one or two exceptions, the city's business establishments, however, peacefully accepted this law. This acceptance was largely due to preparations taken by civic organizations and city officials as early as the winter of 1963.

In November 1963 more than six hundred women representing over one hundred civic and business organizations had formed Women for Progress (WFP) in order to show their support for desegregated commercial facilities. Members felt that Atlanta's "hard-won reputation for progress was threatened unless all segments of the community responded to the Chamber of Commerce's appeal for businesses to serve the public without regard to race, creed, or color."[112] In order to show its support, WFP presented a scroll to the Chamber which commended and expressed support for the Chamber's position on public accommodations. Members of WFP pledged to patronize desegregated establishments.

When city, business, and civic leaders began to meet informally in March 1964 to discuss the transition from a segregated to an "open" city, they turned to the example of WFP. They arranged a meeting with a former leader of WFP to determine if a new organization could be organized. The purpose of Partners for Progress (PFP) was to "encourage and support the extension of equal opportunity in business, government, and community affairs and to influence public opinion." "Partners" sent letters to owners and managers of restaurants encouraging them to desegregate their establishments. Members pledged to patronize desegregated establishments. They called upon businesses to inquire about their racial policies and attitudes toward the public accommodations bill. Partners distributed lists of desegregated facilities to its members and the public. They also wrote letters to members of the Fulton-DeKalb Hospital Authority, the Fulton County Commissioners, and Emory Medical School suggesting that racial segregation was inappropriate in public health facilities.[113]

In order to ensure the peaceful implementation of the Civil Rights Act in Atlanta, city officials adopted a program which included public statements supporting compliance and plans for testing establishments. After meeting with city officials and discussions among members, the board of directors of the Atlanta Restaurant Association issued a statement urging peaceful compliance with the Civil Rights Act. Partners and representatives of SLC agreed to test the compliance of establishments. Testing was to be done in small numbers. SLC members were to avoid restaurants which had a history of particularly strong resistance to desegregation attempts.[114]

Two legal suits involving the Civil Rights Act originated in Atlanta. The first case challenged the constitutionality of the public accommodations section of the Civil Rights Act. Immediately after its passage, the owner of the Heart of Atlanta Motel filed a suit in federal court contending that the Civil Rights Act exceeded the powers of Congress to regulate interstate commerce, violated the property rights of business owners, and subjugated owners to "involuntary servitude." In December 1964 the Supreme Court upheld the constitutionality of the public accommodations section of the Civil Rights Act. The decision was largely based on the right of Congress to regulate interstate commerce. The Heart of Atlanta Motel peacefully complied with this decision.[115]

In July 1964 three African Americans had filed suit against the Pickrick Restaurant for violating the public accommodations provision of the Civil Rights Act. Attorney General Robert Kennedy intervened in the case on the behalf of the plaintiffs. Pending a decision by the Supreme Court on whether the Civil Rights Act was unconstitutional, the Court in August 1964 enjoined the Pickrick Restaurant from refusing service to African American customers. Following this order Lester Maddox, on two occasions, refused to serve African American patrons. When District Court Judge Frank Hooper issued a citation of contempt, Maddox closed his establishment.

On the grounds of his restaurant, Maddox constructed a three-story tower dedicated to "free enterprise." Exhibits also included a copy of the Constitution in a casket and framed quotations of Daniel Webster, Lester Maddox, and a young Lyndon Johnson. Maddox sold "Pickrick drumsticks" (ax handles to warn off demonstrators), "Gold Water" (cans of carbonated drink), American flags, and bumper stickers promoting free enterprise. In September Maddox reopened the Pickrick under a new name, the Lester Maddox Cafeteria. He posted a sign announcing that integrationists (African Americans) and interstate travelers would not be served. When the constitutionality of the Civil Rights Act was upheld, the Court ordered Maddox to desegregate his establishment. In February 1965 a judge found Maddox guilty of civil contempt for refusing to serve African American customers. The Court ordered that future contempt charges against Maddox would result in a two hundred dollar fine per day from the date the original contempt order was entered (11 August 1964). Choosing not to desegregate, Maddox closed his establishment. The property was eventually sold to Georgia Tech University.

The transition from a closed to an open city was due to pressure from the African American community. Initiatives for racial change did not originate with public officials or the business community. As in most southern cities, this segment of the white community resisted racial change. Only when the inevitability of change became evident and segregation proved harmful to the city's economic growth and reputation did business and city leaders respond to pressures from the African American community. They either negotiated with African American leaders or complied with federal court decisions.

The battle for an open city altered African American leadership in the city. During this campaign, many younger African Americans perceived the "Old Guard" leadership as an impediment to racial change. While remnants of the "Old Guard" leadership remained, power shifted to younger African American professionals who supported students in their efforts. During the campaign for an open city, these professionals advised the students and served as communication links between the students and the "Old Guard" leadership. White businessmen began to view these younger leaders as spokespeople for the African American community. The changes in the city and the acknowledgement of new leaders became apparent in January 1965.

While not a major participant in local affairs, Martin Luther King, Jr. was the symbolic and inspirational leader of the student movement in Atlanta (as elsewhere in the nation). In 1964 King was awarded the Nobel Peace Prize. The question arose as to whether the city should honor King. Due to demonstrations against segregated public facilities, bitterness in the white community toward Dr. King existed.

In November 1964 African American leaders visited Ralph McGill. They proposed to have a biracial dinner honoring King. These leaders suggested that Ralph McGill, Rabbi Jacob Rothschild, Archbishop Paul Hallinan, and Dr. Benjamin Mays should co-chair the event. This committee discussed the plan with Mayor Allen who approved of the idea. When Allen approached business leaders, they rejected the proposal. Despite this opposition, Allen and a small group of civic and religious leaders continued to make preparations, in secret, for the dinner. In December the *New York Times* printed the first article about the planning of the dinner. The piece mentioned that a number of Atlanta's business leaders were invited to attend, but refused.

When Robert Woodruff of Coca-Cola announced his support of the dinner, opposition within the business community quickly died. Woodruff was concerned that the city's image would be damaged if Atlanta refused to honor Dr. King. At this time, Coca-Cola was beginning to market its product in the Third World.[117] The dinner was held at the Dinkler Hotel in downtown Atlanta. Almost every major business owner was present or represented. Over fifteen hundred African American and white leaders gathered to honor Reverend King. While some members of the Klan picketed the hotel, the event was a major success. At the end of the evening, everyone stood and sang, "We Shall Overcome." *Life* magazine characterized the dinner as "an emotional acceptance hereto unknown in the South." Atlanta, "once more," had "earned the reputation as the most progressive city in the South on race relations."[118]

Six months following the banquet, A.T. Walden died. For over thirty years, he was the voice of Atlanta's African American community. Few major decisions were made without his participation or knowledge. While his influence had declined prior to his death, he was well-respected. By this time, virtually all of Atlanta's African American leadership had moved to a more assertive stance largely due to the challenge from the student movement. His death and the end of legal segregation signified the passing of an era in the history of race relations in Atlanta.

Notes

1. Aldon Morris, *The Origins of the Civil Rights Movement: Black Communities Organizing for Change* (New York: The Free Press, 1984), pp. 197–199.

2. Interviews with Julian Bond and Lonnie King conducted by Jed Dannenbaum and Kathleen Dowdey, Ralph McGill Papers, Woodruff Library, Emory University, Atlanta, Georgia; John Neary, *Julian Bond: Black Rebel* (New York: William Morrow Company, 1971), pp. 43–73; Howell Raines, *My Soul is Rested: Movement Days in the Deep South Remembered* (New York: G.P. Putnam's Sons, 1977, reprint ed., New York: Penguin Books, 1987), pp. 83–84.

3. Raines, p. 83.

4. Interviews with Julian Bond and Lonnie King, Ralph McGill Papers; and Raines, p. 84.

5. Benjamin Mays, *Born to Rebel: An Autobiography* (New York: Scribner, 1971; reprint ed., Athens: University of Georgia Press, 1987), pp. 288–289.

6. In his autobiography, Benjamin Mays identified Albert Manley as being the college president who suggested a statement of grievances. In interviews, most students have identified Rufus Clement as making this suggestion.

7. Interviews with Lonnie King and Julian Bond, Ralph McGill Papers; and Raines, pp. 84–85.

8. Interview with Julian Bond, Ralph McGill Papers; and Nancy Weiss, *Whitney M. Young, Jr. and the Struggle for Civil Rights* (Princeton: Princeton University Press, 1989), pp. 65–66.

9. "An Appeal for Human Rights," *Atlanta Constitution and Atlanta Journal*, 9 March 1960.

10. *Atlanta Journal*, 9 March 1960 and *Atlanta Constitution*, 10 March 1960.

11. Interview with Howard Zinn conducted by Jed Dannenbaum and Kathleen Dowdey, Ralph McGill Papers.

12. Karen Vanlandingham, "In Pursuit of A Changing Dream: Spelman College Students and the Civil Rights Movement, 1955–1962" (Master's thesis, Emory University, 1983), p. 67; Howard Zinn, *The Southern Mystique* (New York: Alfred A. Knopf, 1964), pp. 115–117; and SNCC Press Release (re: project to desegregate State Capitol buildings), 1

February 1962, SNCC Papers, A=VIII=105, Woodruff Library, Atlanta University, Atlanta, Georgia.

13. "Library Fact Sheet," n.d., Frances Pauley Papers, Box: 6; Woodruff Library, Emory University, Atlanta, Georgia.

14. Whitney Young, Memorandum to the Executive Committee of the Atlanta Council on Human Relations (re: library desegregation), n.d., Southern Regional Council Papers, 4:134:293, Woodruff Library, Atlanta University, Atlanta, Georgia; Harold Martin and Franklin Garrett, *Atlanta and Environs: A Chronicle of Its People and Events: Years of Change and Challenge, 1940-1976*, Vol. III, (Atlanta: Atlanta Historical Society, 1987), p. 224; and Weiss, p. 68.

15. If African American libraries did not have the needed resources, the downtown library would send the desired material to an African American branch of the library. If immediate access was needed, a separate place for viewing was provided. At the beginning of the campaign, students were to accept these services without comment.

16. *Atlanta Daily World*, 27 May 1959; Zinn, *The Southern Mystique*, pp. 43–54; Vanlandingham, p. 68; and Howard Zinn, "A Case of Quiet Social Change," *Crisis*, (October 1959): 471–476.

17. J.L. Mosley, Memorandum to Herbert Jenkins, 10 March 1960, Herbert Jenkins Papers, Box: 5, Folder: 3, Atlanta History Center, Library and Archives, Atlanta, Georgia; Vanlandingham, pp. 74–75; and Zinn, *The Southern Mystique*, pp. 60–62.

18. David J. Garrow, *Bearing the Cross: Martin Luther King, Jr. and the Southern Christian Leadership Conference* (New York: William Morrow and Company, 1986), p. 131; and Jack Walker, *Sit-ins in Atlanta* (New York: McGraw Hill, 1964), pp. 8–10.

19. Interview with Julian Bond, Ralph McGill Papers; Vanlandingham, pp. 73–74; and Walker, p. 9.

20. Interview with Howard Zinn conducted by Jed Dannenbaum and Kathleen Dowdey, Ralph McGill Papers; Mays, p. 290; and Weiss, p. 67.

21. Mays, p. 291, and Walker, p. 10.

22. Mays, pp. 292, 294–296; Vanlandingham, pp. 75–76; and Walker, pp. 11–12.

23. Interview with Herbert Jenkins conducted by Jed Dannenbaum and Kathleen Dowdey, Ralph McGill Papers; Herbert Jenkins, *Keeping the Peace: A Police Chief Looks at His Job* (New York: Harper and Row, 1973), pp. 40–43; and Taylor Branch, *Parting the Waters: America During the King Years, 1954–63* (New York: Simon and Schuster, 1988), pp. 301–302.

24.   For a discussion of African American leadership and its role in the Atlanta sit-ins, see Jack Walker, "Protest and Negotiation: A Case Study of Negro Leadership in Atlanta," *Midwest Journal of Political Science*, 7 (May 1963): 99–124.

25.   *Atlanta Daily World*, 16 March 1960, editorial.

26.   Author's Interview with C.A. Scott, 20 February 1991; and Walker, *Sit-ins*, p. 11.

27.   Interview with Howard Zinn, Ralph McGill Papers; Walker, *Sit-ins*, pp. 10–11; and Weiss, p. 66.

28.   *Atlanta Journal*, 16 March 1960, editorial.

29.   *Atlanta Constitution*, 16 March 1960, editorial.

30.   Walker, *Sit-ins*, pp. 12–13; and *Atlanta Constitution*, 30 May 1960.

31.   Author's Interview with LeRoy Johnson, 13 November 1990; and interviews with Lonnie King and Julian Bond, Ralph McGill Papers.

32.   Interviews with Carl Holman and Julian Bond, Ralph McGill Papers; and Gloria Blackwell, "Black Controlled Media in Atlanta, 1960–1970: The Burden of the Message and Struggle for Survival," (Ph.D. dissertation, Emory University, 1973), p. 172.

33.   Author's Interview with William Calloway, 10 September 1991.

34.   By August of 1960 (one month later), the Empire Real Estate Board was placing ads in both newspapers.

35.   Alton Hornsby, Jr., "Georgia," in *The Black Press in the South, 1865–1979*, ed. Henry Suggs (Westport: Greenwood Press, 1983), pp. 138–141.

36.   Garrow, pp. 141–142; Raines, p. 88; and Walker, *Sit-ins,* pp. 14–15.

37.   Walker, *Sit-ins*, p. 15.

38.   Downtown merchants informed students that they would desegregate their establishments if Rich's "took the first step." Interview with Julian Bond, Ralph McGill Papers; and Raines, pp. 87–88.

39.   It was estimated that between seventy and ninety percent of Atlanta's African American population had a charge account at Rich's. According to Bond, African American citizens viewed a Rich's charge account as a "necessity, easy credit, and having pretty good credit terms." (Raines, p. 87).

40.   Richard Rich, Letter to Lonnie King, 10 August 1960; Jesse Hill, Letter to Richard Rich, 30 August 1960; and Richard Rich, Letter to Jesse Hill, 1 September 1960, Richard Rich Papers, Box: 37, Folder: 2, Woodruff Library, Emory University, Atlanta, Georgia.

41.   Walker, *Sit-ins* pp. 15–16; and Vanlandingham, pp. 77–87.

42.   Interview with Lonnie King, Ralph McGill Papers; and Raines, p. 89.

43.   Branch, pp. 345–349.

44.   Raines, pp. 89–90.

45.   The students were arrested in two groups. The first group included Dr. King and thirty-five African American students. They were charged with violating the state's anti-trespass law. The second group of protesters included Eric Ramsey, a white student. Ramsey, a member of the American Friends Service Committee, was attending a SNCC conference in Atlanta. The judge dropped all charges against Ramsey and his group. Ramsey believed that the judge's decision to drop the charges was due to his presence. Richard Ramsey, "Atlanta Report," 19 October 1960, Southern Regional Council Papers, 4:142:247.

46.   Vanlandingham, pp. 79–80; and Walker, *Sit-ins*, pp. 16–17.

47.   Branch, pp. 351–356; Garrow, pp. 145–146; and an interview with William Hartsfield conducted by Charles T. Morrissey for the John F. Kennedy Library (transcript), 6 January 1966, William B. Hartsfield Papers, Box: 31, Folder: 9, Woodruff Library, Emory University, Atlanta, Georgia.

48.   Raines, pp. 94–95.

49.   Numerous accounts of Kennedy's involvement in King's release and its effects on the 1960 presidential election have been written. See Branch, pp. 356–370; Carl M. Brauer, *John F. Kennedy and the Second Reconstruction* (New York: Columbia University Press, 1977), pp. 46–52; David Garrow, pp. 145–149; Herbert Parmet, *JFK: The Presidency of John F. Kennedy* (New York: Dial Press, 1983), pp. 54–56; and Raines, pp. 90–91, 95–96.

50.   *Student Voice*, November 1960, p. 4; and Walker, *Sit-ins*, pp. 17–18.

51.   Author's Interview with Cecil Alexander, 9 March 1991; and Walker, *Sit-ins*, pp. 18–19.

52.   While these figures also reflected a downward national trend for the season, they were significantly below most cities.

53.   Interview with Julian Bond, Ralph McGill Papers; and C. Eric Lincoln, "The Strategy of a Sit-in," *Reporter*, 24 (5 January 1961): 20–23.

54.   John W. Dobbs, Letter to Richard Rich, 16 September 1960, Richard Rich Papers, Box: 37, Folder: 2; and Raines, p. 88.

55. Interview with Lonnie King, Ralph McGill Papers; and Roger Williams, *The Bonds: An American Family* (New York: Athenaeum, 1971), p. 206.

56. Vanlandingham, p. 87.

57. Quoted in George B. Leonard, "The Second Battle of Atlanta," *Look* 25 (25 April 1961): 31.

58. *Southern School News*, January 1961, p. 1; Bruce Galphin, *The Riddle of Lester Maddox* (Atlanta: Camelot Publishing Company, 1968), pp. 49–52; and Walker, *Sit-ins*, p. 20.

59. Jenkins attributed no arrests during this period to the effectiveness of the police department and the cooperation of the community. Herbert Jenkins, address, "Understanding the Community: Community Change as It Affects Police-Community Relations (transcript)," Michigan State University, 23 May 1961, Herbert Jenkins Papers.

60. *Student Voice*, February 1961, p. 2; Walker, *Sit-ins*, pp. 20–23; and Vanlandingham, pp. 88–91.

61. Ivan Allen with Paul Hemphill, *Mayor: Notes on the Sixties* (New York: Simon and Schuster, 1971), pp. 37–40.

62. Lonnie King believed that an agreement between white merchants and conservative leaders had been reached before he and Herschelle Sullivan attended this session. Interview with Lonnie King, Ralph McGill Papers; and Raines, pp. 90–91.

63. *Atlanta Constitution*, 8 March 1961; and "The Atlanta Lunch Counter Desegregation Agreement of March 6, 1961," Eliza Paschall Papers, Box: 32; Woodruff Library, Emory University, Atlanta, Georgia.

64. Interviews with Lonnie King and Julian Bond, Ralph McGill Papers; Author's Interview with LeRoy Johnson; Allen with Hemphill, pp. 40–42; Lionel Newsom and William Gorden, "A Stormy Rally in Atlanta," *Today's Speech* 11 (April 1963): pp. 18–21; and Raines, p. 96.

65. *Atlanta Daily World*, 9 September 1961; Author's Interview with Donald Hollowell, 12 March 1991; Allen with Hemphill, pp. 43–63; Galphin, pp. 33–37; and Alton Hornsby, Jr., "The Negro in Atlanta Politics, 1961–1973," *Atlanta Historical Bulletin* 21 (Spring 1977): 9–11.

66. William Holmes Borders, Statement, 8 September 1961, A.T. Walden Papers, Files of the Atlanta Negro Voters League, Atlanta History Center, Library and Archives, Atlanta, Georgia.

67. A.T. Walden, Statement, 8 September 1961, A.T. Walden Papers, Files of the Atlanta Negro Voters League.

68. Alfred "Tup" Holmes, Letter to A.T. Walden, 6 September 1961, A.T. Walden Papers, Files of the Atlanta Negro Voters League.

69. Allen with Hemphill, p. 68.

70. Samuel L. Adams, "Blueprint for Segregation: A Survey of Atlanta Housing," *New South*, 22 (Spring 1967): 77; and Allen with Hemphill, pp. 70–72.

71. Allen with Hemphill, p. 72.

72. For examples of national press coverage, see "Atlanta Builds Racial Walls," *Business Week* (5 January 1963): 2; and "Divided City," *Time*, 81 (18 January 1963): 22. Pictures of the wall were published in magazines. National news shows covered the story.

73. Hornsby, p. 15.

74. SNCC Press Release, 22 December 1962, SNCC Papers, A=VIII=105; and Eliza Paschall, Letter to Mr. Ernest Lent, 22 January 1963, Eliza Paschall Papers, Box: 3.

75. Copy of Court Record, including order, re Peyton Road, in Eliza Paschall, *It Must Have Rained* (Atlanta: Emory University, 1975), pp. 58–60; and Executive Director, Council, "Report on Housing," in Paschall, p. 61.

76. By the date of this ruling, the municipal auditorium and most city office buildings were desegregated. *Atlanta Journal*, 20 May 1961; and *Atlanta Constitution*, 28 August 1962.

77. Memorandum of Understanding, 19 July 1963, Eliza Paschall Papers, Box: 3; Thomas McPherson, Jr., Letter to Mr. Ernest Lent 13 June 1963, Eliza Paschall Papers, Box: 3; and Janet Feagans, "Atlanta Theatre Desegregation: A Case of Prolonged Avoidance," *Journal of Human Relations*, 13 (June 1965): 208–215.

78. Grady Hospital was supported in part by taxes and federal funds. In 1960, for example, it received over $6 million in public funds. Memorandum from Atlanta Branch of the NAACP Requesting for Action to End Segregated Practices, Eliza Paschall Papers, NAACP files; Dr. Bell, Letter to the Fulton County Commissioners, n.d., Eliza Paschall Papers, Box: 19, Grady Hospital file; SNCC News Release, 14 February 1962, SNCC Papers, A=VIII=105; and SNCC News Release, March 1962, Eliza Paschall Papers, Box: 25.

79. Shortly after Ashton Jones was arrested, the National Council of Churches offered a $5,000.00 bail. A local insurance company was going to post bond as a surety. Judge Pye ordered the company to submit an affidavit showing the identity and amount of the collateral of the company. On grounds of confidentiality, the insurance company refused. Judge Pye ruled that the bond was defective. Pye justified the bail on the grounds that Jones had been arrested in twelve different cities (all charges stemming

from his participation in demonstrations). Howard Moore, Letter to the Atlanta Council on Human Relations in Paschall, p. 78.

80.   Rod Nave, "Report to the Church Study and Reference Committee on events concerning seating of the First Baptist Church, October 1963," in Paschall, pp. 72–76; "Report of October 22, 1963 on Ashton Jones in Fulton County Jail, Atlanta," in Paschall, pp. 76–78; and *Student Voice*, November, 1963.

81.   Due to demonstrations in the city, *Town and Country* magazine nearly pulled a positive article on how Atlanta solved its racial problems. The article ran in its February edition. Eugene Patterson, "A Mirror for Atlantans," *Atlanta Constitution*, 8 February 1963; and Allen with Hemphill, p. 72.

82.   Walter Crawford, Letter to Harry Boyte, 12 April 1961, Eliza Paschall Papers, Box: 1, Folder: 2.

83.   Eliza Paschall, Letter to Ernest Lent, 22 March 1963, Eliza Paschall Papers, Box: 3, Folder: 10; SNCC Press Release, 23 March 1963, SNCC Papers, A=VIII=105; SNCC Press Release, 29 July 1963, SNCC Papers, A=VIII=105; and Lester Maddox, Letter to 'friends' asking them to join PASS, July 1963, in Paschall, p. 65; and Martin and Garrett, pp. 367–369.

84.   Eliza Paschall, Letter to Ernest Lent, 22 December 1963, Eliza Paschall Papers, Box: 3; Folder: 10.

85.   Allen with Hemphill, p. 103.

86.   "Summary of Report on Public Accommodations," in Paschall, p. 94; and "Racial Desegregation in Atlanta, chronology, 1948–September 1963," in Paschall, p. 84.

87.   Parmet, p. 271.

88.   Allen with Hemphill, p. 107.

89.   Author's Interview with William Calloway, 10 September 1991; and Allen with Hemphill, pp. 109–110.

90.   Ivan Allen, Jr., "Statement before the Committee Regarding S1732 Bill to Eliminate Discrimination in Public Accommodations Affecting Interstate Commerce," 26 July 1963, Southern Regional Council Papers, 3:110:4.

91.   Allen with Hemphill, p. 114.

92.   Clarence Coleman, "Statement of Purpose of the Leadership Conference, October 1963," Paschall Papers, ASLC files; and Atlanta Council on Human Relations, *Atlanta: Protests and Progress, A Special Report* (Atlanta: April 1964), pp. 3–4.

93. Summit Leadership Conference, *Action for Democracy* (Atlanta: November, 1963); "Membership and Statement about Atlanta Coordinating Committee by Mayor Allen, November 27, 1963," in Paschall, p. 90; "Summary Report of Various Meetings of Public and Private Officials and Representatives of the Summit Leadership Conference," in Eliza Paschall, pp. 93–95; and Council on Human Relations, *Atlanta*, pp. 4–9.

94. *Student Voice*, 21 November 1963, p. 2; *Student Voice*, 16 December 1963; Atlanta Council on Human Relations, *Atlanta*, p. 8; and Adam Fairclough, *To Redeem the Soul of America: The Southern Christian Leadership Conference and Martin Luther King, Jr.* (Athens: University of Georgia Press, 1987), p. 175.

95. Martin Luther King, Jr., Address at the "Pilgrimage of Democracy," at Hurt Park in Atlanta, Georgia, 15 December 1963, transcript, Eliza Paschall Papers, Box: 24.

96. *Student Voice*, "Special Edition: Christmas in Jail," 23 December 1963; Mary King, *Freedom Song: A Personal Story of the 1960s Civil Rights Movement* (New York: William Morrow and Company, 1987), pp. 186–187.

97. Atlanta Council on Human Relations, *Atlanta*, p. 9; and Fairclough, p. 176.

98. Summit Leadership Conference, Memorandum to the Student Nonviolent Coordinating Committee, 16 January 1964, Eliza Paschall Papers, Box: 15, SLC files.

99. Summit Leadership Conference, Memorandum to Atlanta branch, National Association for the Advancement of Colored People, 16 January 1964, Eliza Paschall Papers, Box: 15, SLC files.

100. Summit Leadership Conference, Memorandum to Southern Christian Leadership Conference, 16 January 1964, Eliza Paschall Papers, Box: 15, SLC files.

101. SNCC Press Release, 10 January 1964, SNCC Papers, A=VIII=105; *Student Voice*, 20 January 1964; Martin and Garrett, p. 402; and Atlanta Council on Human Relations, *Atlanta*, pp. 9–15.

102. *Atlanta Constitution*, 11 January 1964; Atlanta Council on Human Relations, *Atlanta*, p. 13; and Martin and Garrett, p. 403.

103. *Atlanta Constitution*, 27 January 1964.

104. Martin and Garrett, p. 408.

105. Atlanta Council on Human Relations, *Atlanta*, pp. 17–18, 23–24; SNCC News Release: Atlanta Has Time—But Not Much, 10 February 1964, pp. 1–3, Eliza Paschall Papers, Box: 25, SNCC files; and Pat Watters, "Fruits of Tokenism," *Nation*, (17 February 1964): 162–165.

106.   "A Series of Affidavits by Students Concerning Events at Leb's Restaurant—January 26—and other Demonstrations," Eliza Paschall Papers, Box: 25, SNCC files; Atlanta Council on Human Relations, *Atlanta*, pp. 18–22; and *Student Voice*, 27 January 1964.

107.   Statement by Ivan Allen, Jr., Mayor, Citywide Meeting, 29 January 1964, in Paschall, pp. 96–97; Atlanta Council on Human Relations, *Atlanta*, pp. 24–28; and Martin and Garrett, p. 405.

108.   Summit Leadership Conference, Memorandum to Mayor Allen, 31 January 1964, in Paschall, pp. 97–98; and Atlanta Council on Human Relations, *Atlanta*, pp. 29–31.

109.   *Student Voice*, 3 February 1964; *Atlanta Journal and Constitution*, 29 January 1964; Atlanta Council on Human Relations, *Atlanta*, p. 1 (Jenkins' quote); and Fairclough, p. 176.

110.   Proposals for Atlanta for the White Southern Student Project, Eliza Paschall Papers, Box: 33; and "Georgia Students for Human Rights," Southern Regional Council Papers, 4:151:585.

111.   *Student Voice*, 11 February 1964; Atlanta Council on Human Relations, *Atlanta*, pp. 31–37; and SLC News Release: We've Got to Have Victories, 27 March 1964, Eliza Paschall Papers, Box: 15; SLC files.

112.   Woman for Progress, News Release, 13 November 1963, Eliza Paschall Papers, Box: 26, Women for Progress file; and "Scroll from Women for Progress to the Atlanta Chamber of Commerce," 13 November 1963, Southern Regional Council Papers, 1:45:1426.

113.   Partners for Progress, News Release, 17 March 1964, Southern Regional Council Papers, 1:45:1426; Grace Hamilton, Letter to Leslie Dunbar, 27 April 1964, Southern Regional Council Papers, 1:45:1426.

114.   Author's Interview with Cecil Alexander; Robert Woods and Cecil Alexander, Letter to Leslie Dunbar, 11 June 1964, Southern Regional Council Papers, 1:21:1; and Pat Watters, "The South Learns to Live With the Civil Rights Law," *Reporter*, 31 (13 August 1964): 44–46.

115.   *Heart of Atlanta Motel v. the United States and Robert Kennedy*, 22 July 1964, *Race Relations Law Reporter*, IX (1964), pp. 908–911.

116.   *George Willis et al. and Robert F. Kennedy v. the Pickrick Restaurant et al.*, 22 July 1964, *Race Relations Law Reporter*, IX (1964), pp. 911–918, 1434–1438; X (1965), pp. 353–358; M.G. Redding, Memorandum to Herbert Jenkins, 3 July 1964, Herbert Jenkins Papers, Box: 5, Folder: 3; Galphin, pp. 56–84; and Lester Maddox, *Speaking Out: The Autobiography of Lester Maddox* (New York: Doubleday and Company, 1975), pp. 54–70.

117. Ralph McGill, Letter to Rabbi Jacob Rothschild, Rabbi Jacob Rothschild Papers, Woodruff Library, Emory University, Atlanta, Georgia; Author's Interview with Cecil Alexander; Allen with Hemphill, pp. 96–100; Raines, pp. 411–413; Mays, pp. 273–274; and Janice Rothschild Blumberg, *One Voice: Rabbi Jacob Rothschild and the Troubled South* (Macon: Mercer University Press, 1985), pp. 169–171.

118. "Remarkable Dinner," *Life*, 58 (12 February 1965), pp. 4, 34.

V

The Forgotten Communities of Atlanta

In June 1963, a small group of students, the majority SNCC members, toured the neighborhoods of Southeast Atlanta for the first time. Previously, these students had participated in demonstrations protesting segregated facilities. They were searching for new areas in which to expand their struggle for civil rights. The living conditions of the residents in these communities appalled the students. They became dedicated to bringing racial and economic change to this area.

The neighborhoods on the south side of Atlanta were predominately African American. An estimated 60,000 African Americans resided in this area. In many of these communities, these students observed dilapidated housing, outdoor privies, unpaved and uncleaned streets, and vacant lots covered with trash. A poorly equipped library and medical clinic served the entire area. Neighborhood children and youth had limited access to parks, playgrounds, swimming pools, and other recreational facilities. South Atlanta had a large transient population. Unemployment in the area was high. Most families lived near or below the poverty level, and many residents were unable to read and write.[1]

A combination of demographic, socioeconomic, and racial factors contributed to the living conditions of African American residents in the slums of Southeast and Southwest Atlanta. Many middle-class white homeowners in Atlanta, anxious to escape the problems of inner-city neighborhoods, migrated to the city's periphery immediately following World War II. Highway construction, particularly north-south corridors, made migration easier. During the 1950s and 1960s, improving economic conditions and racial tensions stemming from housing shortages and the emerging Civil Rights Movement accelerated the pace of this "white flight." Between 1960 and 1970, the central city experienced a net loss of 60,000 white citizens, a twenty percent decline in Atlanta's white population.[2]

As white citizens left the city, Atlanta's black population grew. Residential segregation in the city increased. Between 1960 and 1970, Atlanta's African American population grew from thirty-eight to fifty-one percent. From 1950 to 1970, the number of census tracts in which African Americans constituted at least ninety percent of the population tripled. The communities of East Lake, Kirkwood, Watts Road, Reynoldstown, Almond Park, Mozley Park, Center Hill, and Cascade Heights experienced almost a total transition from white to African American occupancy.[3] Despite a small white middle-class countermovement to the process of neighborhood transition during the late 1960s and early 1970s, the inner-city neighborhoods became increasingly African American.[4]

Demographic changes were also occurring within the African American community. During the 1950s and 1960s, economic conditions improved for a large segment of the black community. In search of better housing, many middle-class African Americans moved from inner-city neighborhoods to formerly all-white communities and newly opened residential areas. At the same time, the mechanization of agriculture in the state displaced black (and white) Georgians while the lure of employment, civil treatment, and the city attracted them to Atlanta. Unskilled and regulated to the lowest paying jobs, many were forced to settle in the poorest sections of the city. Thus a two-tiered economic and residential black Atlanta emerged. While Atlanta had a sizable and growing African American middle-class, a large and growing segment of the black community was living near or below the poverty level.

These changes significantly affected the inner-city neighborhoods. As the racial characteristics and income levels of the residents changed, many commercial and industrial enterprises abandoned these areas. The resistance of white residents to the placement of public housing units in their communities and the changing racial and socioeconomic characteristics of Atlanta's neighborhoods led officials to locate these projects in South and West Atlanta. By 1968 eighty-three percent of the public housing units in Atlanta were located on the west side of the city in predominately African American communities.[5] As the economic vitality and political influence of these communities declined and many underwent transition from white to African American occupancy, the city paid less attention to these neighborhoods in terms of providing adequate municipal services. Living conditions in these communities deteriorated.

Ironically, the city's urban renewal program contributed to the deterioration of neighborhoods in South and West Atlanta. In 1968 the chairman of the Atlanta Housing Authority estimated that urban renewal projects in the city had dislocated 4950 families; ninety-five percent of which were African American. Over one-half lived below the poverty level.[6] While these projects removed dilapidated housing, most of the cleared land went to nonresidential uses such as highways, Atlanta Stadium, and the Civic Auditorium. The city provided Atlanta University, Georgia State, and Georgia Tech with some of this cleared area. Some parcels of land remained vacant. Only two projects went to the construction of significant public housing. During the period when most of the displacement and relocation occurred (1956–1966), public agencies and private companies built fewer than 2,000 low-cost public housing units.[7] Some of these dwelling units had higher rents than the demolished housing. Moreover, a time lag often existed between the clearing of land and the construction of needed housing. During this time period, many residents were forced to seek temporary, substandard housing. While Atlanta's leadership regarded the urban renewal program as critical to the city's economic growth and progress, it did not provide needed housing for its residents.

A 1963 report prepared by the Fulton County Department of Family and Children Services, "Appalachia in Atlanta," argued that the "bulldozing for renewal and highways" had pushed many "slum dwellers back to the fringes of the areas cleared, making their overcrowded conditions more crowded."[8] In order to meet their housing needs, these families crowded into discarded, single-family homes. Multi-dwelling units in these areas of the city increased. African American families paid exorbitant rents for this substandard housing. High population density and the overcrowding of families in single-dwelling units were contributing factors to substandard housing, family disorganization, and slum neighborhoods in Atlanta.

In addition to urban renewal, residential segregation and restrictions against open occupancy contributed to the slums of Southeast and West Atlanta.[9] These barriers created artificial shortages of residential land by limiting African American citizens to certain areas of the city and largely confining early African American residential expansion to areas along the fringes of slum neighborhoods. By 1969 African Americans occupied only twenty percent of the city's developed residential land. Overcrowding among African American citizens was nearly four times greater than among white residents.[10]

These conditions created economic and social barriers which were almost impossible to escape. Discrimination in employment and the lack of quality education hindered the possibility of advancement from these conditions. Local custom dictated that African Americans be subordinate to whites at their place of employment. Most of the city's African American residents worked as menial laborers, usually in the poorest paying occupations and at positions which paid less than those held by their white counterparts. In 1960 the average income of an African American family was approximately one-half that of a white family.

Education did not provide the means to escape these conditions. In 1960 the head of an African American family had an average of six years of schooling, whereas, the head of a white family had an average of eleven years. Due to segregation and the lack of adequate funding, the quality of education provided by most African American schools was poor. African American students also did not have access to adequate vocational and technical education. In the early 1960s, the curriculum at Carver High, an African American school, included training in the traditional African American occupations of laundering, dry cleaning, plastering, and shoe repair. At Smith-Hughes, a white vocational school, courses included machine shop, electronics, tool and die design, plumbing, and steam pipe fitting. Representatives of trade unions worked with trainees at Smith-Hughes. With the exception of an African American local of the Brotherhood of Painters, Paperhangers, and Decorators, trade unions did not participate in programs at Carver High.[11] Without economic and educational means, many African American residents were regulated to living conditions of the poorest quality.

In order to deal with these conditions, residents organized civic leagues to represent the interests of their particular neighborhoods. In South Atlanta, the communities of Pittsburgh, Peoplestown, Thomasville, Poole Creek, Georgia Avenue-Pryor Street, and Joyland-Highpoint organized civic leagues. Community leaders attempted to bring improvements to their neighborhoods through the use of letters, petitions, and personal visits to the mayor and various city officials. These leagues also sponsored and participated in voter registration drives.

As a result of the students' tour of Southeast Atlanta, the executive committee of SNCC appointed members to work in this area. The goals of this project were to develop local leadership and unite the area's civic leagues behind a program of racial and economic reform. SNCC members held a series of meetings with community leaders in order to develop a plan of action. Community leaders presented this program to residents of Southeast Atlanta in a series of mass meetings in July 1963. SNCC members organized and were present at each of these rallies. They served as background advisors to the neighborhood leaders and collected the data and information contained in this plan of racial change.[12]

Community leaders presented this program of change, *The City Must Provide, South Atlanta: The Forgotten Community*, to Mayor Allen after a demonstration at City Hall in August 1963. Over two hundred residents of Southeast Atlanta participated in this protest.[13] *The City Must Provide* was a list of grievances and inequalities that existed in the areas of health, recreational, and library facilities; city services (traffic control, public transportation, and garbage collection); housing; education; and employment. Demands included the construction of an additional medical clinic, recreational facilities, and public libraries in the area; mobile dental units; adequate bus service; better traffic control; street cleaning; increased garbage collection; enforcement of the city's building codes; and reform in the city's employment practices. Mayor Allen agreed to some of these demands. The city appointed more school crossing guards for the area, accelerated the construction of parks in Peoplestown, Joyland, and Poole Creek, employed African American drivers to operate garbage trucks, revamped the sewage systems of area neighborhoods, and made various traffic improvements.[14]

But SNCC workers believed that political and other nonviolent means were necessary to affect more changes in Southeast Atlanta. Following the demonstration at City Hall, members of SNCC and the civic leagues began to canvass the neighborhoods of Southeast Atlanta. Their main objectives were to increase participation in the activities of the civic leagues, develop youth councils, and register new voters. They were fairly successful. Between August and September 1963, membership in most of the leagues increased. SNCC formed three youth councils to work on problems that directly affected young adults in Atlanta. While only 150 residents registered to vote during this period, SNCC members believed that this number justified continued political activity in the area.[15]

SNCC members began to formulate plans for a massive registration drive in Southeast Atlanta. In addition to increasing registration, they believed that a campaign would politically activate residents in the area, lead to the development of new civic leagues, and increase participation in existing organizations. According to these plans, a team of volunteers would canvass a particular community each week to seek nonregistered citizens. They planned to organize car pools to transport residents to the Registrar's Office. Plans also included voter education. SNCC members wanted to establish citizenship schools and a community newspaper which would serve as a tool for political education. Their major goal was to register five thousand new voters by June of 1964. SNCC did not have the financial resources or manpower, however, to conduct a campaign of this scope. In

September SNCC representatives filed a proposal with the Voter Education Project (VEP). The proposal requested $3,365 to finance this campaign.[16]

The VEP was organized in early 1962 after a series of initial meetings in June 1961 between officials of the major civil rights organizations, the National Student Association, the Taconic Foundation, and the Field Foundation. The VEP's primary function was the allocation of funds to organizations involved in voter registration activities on the precinct and county levels. The Southern Regional Council supervised the VEP. Wiley Branton, an African American attorney, was director of this organization. Funding for the VEP was mainly by grants from the Taconic Foundation, the Field Foundation, and the Stern Family Fund.

In April 1962 representatives of the All Citizens Registration Committee met with Wiley Branton to discuss the availability of funds for a voter registration drive. Branton decided to invite representatives from all the civil rights groups working in Atlanta to discuss voter registration. The representatives agreed that the All Citizens Registration Committee was the proper organization to sponsor the drive. The VEP provided the All Citizens Registration Committee with a working grant of $2,000 to conduct the campaign.[17] During 1963, the All Citizens Registration Committee received over $11,395 from the VEP for voter registration activities in the Atlanta area.[18]

Initially an official of the VEP recommended the approval of SNCC's proposal to conduct a voter registration drive in Southeast Atlanta. Jesse Hill, chairman of the All Citizens Registration Committee, objected that an individual grant for voter registration in Southeast Atlanta would be through SNCC. Previously the civic leagues in this area had served as organizational units for drives sponsored by the All Citizens Registration Committee. Hill argued that the unity of the community and the cooperation of all organizations were needed for a successful voter registration drive. In a conversation with a VEP official, Fred Bennette, a member of SCLC who was working with the All Citizens Registration Committee, deplored "the notion that SNCC could do anything effective in Southeast Atlanta." He argued that a grant would "disrupt the program of the All Citizens Registration Committee."[19]

After meetings and discussions with representatives of SNCC, the All Citizens Registration Committee, and the civic leagues of Southeast Atlanta, the VEP denied SNCC's proposal. Instead, it approved a plan submitted by the All Citizens Registration Committee requesting $2,293 to conduct a "crash" December registration campaign throughout Fulton and DeKalb counties. In order to maintain unity, the proposal called for the employment of six to ten workers from SNCC. Various ministerial alliances cooperated by passing resolutions urging community participation in the drive. Reverend Martin Luther King, Sr. and Reverend J.A. Middleton were appointed co-chairmen of the campaign. They dedicated the drive as a memorial to President John F. Kennedy.[20]

This campaign failed to meet the expectations of its organizers. In a letter to Wiley Branton, Jesse Hill noted that the efforts to use field workers from SNCC did not materialize due to the "failure to secure a strong person to direct and coordinate the program."[21] In a report to SNCC's executive committee, a worker cited the lack of organization within the All Citizens Registration Committee as the reason for the campaign's disappointing results. According to this report, officials did not accept the suggestions or aid of student workers. Established leaders had "little understanding and no creative or attractive methods/means through which to get a significant number of people within the community to register." The report charged that the traditional leadership of the African American community was not "in touch with the people." With the exception of Summerhill (a community in Southeast Atlanta), the voter registration drive did not "touch the areas really needed such as the slums and rural areas of Atlanta."

The disagreements and rivalries between major civil rights organizations, civic leagues, and student groups impeded early attempts to improve conditions in Southeast Atlanta. A SNCC member noted in a report that a "constant struggle" existed between organizations over primarily "who is going to dictate to whom and who is going to guide the political conscience of the Southeast."[23] Factions developed within one civic league as to whom was going to obtain credit for getting community streets and sewage repaired. SNCC members encouraged Atlanta University students and residents of South and West Atlanta to become involved in neighborhood clean-up projects. While many students took part in efforts to improve Southeast Atlanta, they were reluctant to participate in projects directly sponsored by SNCC.[24]

Tensions began to grow between established and neighborhood leaders. A perception existed within these communities that established African American leaders and organizations did not address or care about their needs and desires. SNCC members noted that a sense of alienation existed between the leadership and the people. This alienation was due in a large measure to class divisions within the African American community. In addition to criticizing the mayor and local government for not providing needed services, *A City Must Provide* accused "wealthy Negro politicians" of ignoring their neighborhoods. According to this document, their communities were "represented by people who do not care for our needs." The report alleged that African American leaders were not concerned about the problems of the Southside because they did not live there. The city did not provide services for their neighborhoods because they were "Negro communities" and "not wealthy communities."[25]

Clearly, the perception existed among low-income residents that the benefits of the Civil Rights Movement were bypassing their communities. By the early 1960s, racial reforms had produced few direct tangible benefits for African Americans of lesser economic means. The housing agreements of the 1950s, for example, tended to benefit only those residents who had the economic resources to move. While important on a symbolic, humanitarian, and psychological basis, the desegregation of public accommodations meant little if the majority of African American residents could not afford their services. Despite the presence of a biracial coalition, many lower-income residents felt that their voices were not fully represented in the decision-making process.

White leaders encouraged class divisions by offering particular benefits to various segments of the African American community. Larger African American real estate, financial, construction, and educational institutions benefited from the city's urban renewal program and various municipal projects. Behind-the-scenes negotiations involved African American leaders of middle-to-upper income status. The inclusion of these leaders in the decision-making process lent them a degree of prestige and influence within the African American community. Arguably, these benefits advanced the interests of the total community. The perception, however, could be quite different. While "wealthy Negro politicians" received benefits from the white community, urban renewal projects dislocated poor African American families. Whether this perception was accurate, many black residents believed that only the interests of African American middle-class neighborhoods were being addressed in the decision-making process.

Despite this perception, established African American leaders did address many of the residents' concerns in the course of negotiations with white leaders. They pressed city officials for improved municipal services, more decent housing, and accelerated school desegregation. In particular, African American leaders began to address the issue of discrimination in employment. As in the case of education, African American leaders began to view merit employment as a means by which African Americans could escape the cycle of poverty and racism. Many leaders cited unemployment as the major problem facing Atlanta's African American community. In the late 1950s, leaders formed the General Citizens Committee on Employment and Economic Opportunity to address the issue of discrimination in hiring practices. This committee requested city officials to expand employment opportunities for African Americans by basing job considerations on merit rather than race.[26] Most civil rights and human relations organizations sponsored programs with the aim of increasing African American employment. In order to educate the public about this issue, the Atlanta Council on Human Relations and ACCA sponsored a 1963 survey of African American employment opportunities in Atlanta. In 1964 the SLC requested that construction and concession contracts for the new Atlanta Stadium forbid discrimination on the part of subcontractors and concessionaires.[27]

Gains were made in the area of municipal employment. In 1962 the city hired its first African American fireman. Mayor Allen recommended that all applicants for municipal jobs be maintained on a single civil service register. Previously, the city had maintained separate registers for white and African American applicants.[28] In early 1964 Mayor Allen appointed a biracial committee to study ways to increase job opportunities for African Americans. According to the findings of this committee, the city hired more African Americans than white citizens during the first half of that year. While the majority of these African American employees obtained menial positions (eighty percent), the city employed African Americans as brick masons, building mechanics, switchboard operators, clerk typists, waste collection drivers, pollution control operators, and supervisors for the first time.[29]

Believing that government had to provide a model for private industry, African American leaders mainly concentrated their reform efforts on municipal employment and industries which had government contracts. However, in the fall of 1962, several African American ministers active in SCLC's local affiliate decided to form an organization dedicated to work for employment opportunities in the private sector. The program of this organization was based on the techniques developed by a group of Philadelphia ministers led by Reverend Leon Sullivan. After consultation with Reverend Sullivan, these ministers launched Operation Breadbasket.

This organization sought to improve employment opportunities for African Americans at companies whose products and services were largely purchased by the African American community. Once Operation Breadbasket targeted a particular firm, members selected a negotiating committee to meet with company representatives. During the initial meeting, the negotiating committee would seek information about the establishment's employment practices and the working conditions of its

African American employees. At a second meeting, the committee would make specific requests for a certain number of African Americans to be employed or upgraded. If the committee felt that discriminatory working conditions existed at the plant, it suggested corrective measures. Operation Breadbasket indicated a time period in which the company would be expected to comply with its demands. If the firm refused to comply, Operation Breadbasket called for a boycott of the company. African American churches relayed the news of the boycott to the community.[30]

These tactics were effective. Between November 1962 and April 1963, seven bakeries negotiated agreements with Operation Breadbasket. After four months of negotiations and a "selective buying" campaign, Coca-Cola hired an additional twenty-two African American employees, desegregated all company facilities, and adopted a nondiscriminatory policy for future hiring of all personnel. Due to the initiatives of Operation Breadbasket, sixteen downtown department stores agreed to hire and upgrade African American employees. In 1964, representatives from this organization met with officials from Pepsi-Cola, Gordon Foods, Woolworth's, Rich's, Foremost Dairies, and Miss Georgia Dairies. Operation Breadbasket targeted the Atlanta automobile industry in 1965. Ford, General Motors, and Chrysler dealerships in the city began to hire African Americans as showroom salesmen, mechanics, and office help.[31]

Negotiations between municipal, business, and African American leaders occurred in the context of a new awareness of the problems of poverty and racism and the national debate over the proper role that government and business should perform in addressing these issues. In 1958 John Kenneth Galbraith, a Harvard economist, published *The Affluent Society*. In this influential work, Galbraith contrasted the private waste of American consumerism with the indifference toward public need. He argued that poverty could not simply be solved through an accelerated rate of economic growth. "Public efforts and public funds" were necessary to achieve civic equality. Galbraith's remedy included less private consumption and more public spending on schools, hospitals, slum clearance, and social services. He believed that programs such as national health care, subsidized housing, and the retraining and relocation of unemployed workers were necessary to relieve poverty and correct the "social imbalance" that existed in America.

In 1962 a series of articles written by Michael Harrington, a young socialist, were compiled and published as *The Other America: Poverty in the United States*. Appearing at a time when most politicians were praising the postwar achievements of the American economy, Harrington documented the prevalence of poverty among nonwhite minorities, children, the aged, migrant workers, the uneducated, urban dwellers, and women who headed households. These Americans were trapped in a "culture of poverty," the confining characteristics that he observed among disadvantaged groups. Michael Harrington warned that America was ignoring this large minority of poor citizens.

The positions of Galbraith and Harrington were outside mainstream economic and social thought. Most conservative economists were committed to a balanced federal budget; whereas, liberal economists generally argued for a stimulative fiscal policy. Few proposed the scope of federal programs that Galbraith or Harrington advocated. In their works, both scholars addressed the issue of civic equality. Because poverty was so prevalent among nonwhite minorities and disadvantaged whites, a federal anti-poverty program would have to alter traditional social and racial relationships, particularly in the South and urban areas. A "war on poverty" would have both economic and social dimensions.

While the Kennedy administration did not initially have a program to attack poverty, it proposed an increase in the level and coverage of the minimum wage, federal aid for education and housing, federally supported medical care, federal assistance for depressed areas, and a Manpower and Development Training Act. Despite the use of patronage, promises of local public works or military facilities, and an expressed reluctance to pursue national civil rights legislation, southern Democrats and northern Republicans joined forces to defeat or weaken many of these proposals.

Two areas in which the Kennedy Administration addressed the problems of poverty and racism were employment and housing. By executive order in March 1961, Kennedy established the President's Committee on Equal Employment Opportunity (PCEEO) to "ensure that Americans of all colors and beliefs will have access to employment within the government." President Kennedy designated Vice-President Lyndon Johnson as chairman of the committee. Other members included the Attorney General, the Chairman of the Civil Service Commission, as well as other government officials and private citizens. President Kennedy ordered the committee to conduct a survey of the government's employment practices. He gave PCEEO the authority to initiate investigations rather than wait for complaints of discrimination and terminate government contracts with private employers who persisted in discriminating against minorities. PCEEO established a solid record for addressing complaints of discrimination among government workers. It seldom used its authority, however, to terminate government contracts with private employers.

The most publicized program of PCEEO was Plans for Progress. Under this program, government contractors voluntarily agreed to review their employment practices and make specific improvements. This program was especially promoted by Robert Troutman, a member of the committee and an influential Atlanta attorney. Lockheed Aircraft in Marietta, Georgia signed the first Plans for Progress pledge. Within the next year, dozens of defense contractors, industrial firms, and labor unions signed pledges. Because of Troutman's participation and the voluntary nature of the program, Plans for Progress was heavily promoted in Atlanta's business community. Of the first fifty-two firms in the nation to sign Plans for Progress pledges, twenty-four were located in the Atlanta area.

The Plans for Progress program became a source of contention between PCEEO members who favored compulsory compliance and those who advocated the voluntary approach. A report prepared by the Southern Regional Council noted that only seven of the twenty-four Atlanta companies in the Plans for Progress program produced any evidence of compliance with their pledges. Only three firms (Lockheed, Western Electric, and Goodyear) demonstrated "a vigorous desire to create job opportunities." The report argued that these three companies were influenced more by complaints from local civil rights organizations than the voluntary pledge. The Southern Regional Council and other civil rights organizations called for required compliance with the pledges. While PCEEO continued to tout Plans for Progress, the program lost its momentum when Robert Troutman resigned from the committee in June 1962.[32]

Kennedy raised the issue of discrimination in housing during the 1960 presidential campaign. He criticized Eisenhower for not eliminating housing discrimination with a "stroke of the pen" and promised as president to issue an executive order prohibiting racial discrimination in federally assisted housing.

Discrimination in housing was public policy. Between 1935 and 1950, the underwriting manual of the Federal Housing Administration referred to "unharmonious racial or nationality groups" and advised appraisers to lower the rating of properties in mixed neighborhoods. The manual warned, "If a neighborhood is to retain stability, it is necessary that properties shall continue to be occupied by the same social and racial group."[33] In Atlanta, public housing units were rigidly segregated. Seven projects were designated for African Americans while four were designated for white citizens. They were located in areas occupied by the racial group for which the projects were built. One housing project was used as a physical boundary separating white and African American neighborhoods. City officials (particularly Mayor Hartsfield) and business leaders urged the Kennedy administration to delay any attempt to integrate public housing.[34]

Due to political, legal, and economic considerations, Kennedy delayed the order to integrate federally assisted housing until 1962. He also decided to issue the most narrow order possible. It was not retroactive and included only public housing and direct guaranteed federal loans.[35] The order had only a limited impact on racial patterns in Atlanta. Under Title VI of the Civil Rights Act of 1964, public housing officials in the city chose a "freedom of choice" tenant assignment policy (a person is offered the chance to live in any project he wants) rather than a "first come, first serve" policy (first vacant unit is assigned to the first person on the waiting list regardless of the location of the project or the race of that individual). The "freedom of choice" policy allowed only token integration to occur. As of December 1966, nine of the city's housing projects contained all African American citizens. The original African American projects were unaffected by the order. Three projects were integrated, but contained predominately white residents.[36]

After reading Michael Harrington's *Other America*, Kennedy realized that the problems of poverty demanded a broader legislative treatment. In late 1963 Kennedy asked the Council of Economic Advisors to begin a study of poverty and its remedies. Walter Heller, a principal economic advisor, drew up specific anti-poverty proposals. After Kennedy's assassination, he presented this program to Lyndon Johnson. In his first State of the Union message, Johnson declared an "unconditional war on poverty." In May of 1964 he incorporated this program into a conception of his own, the "Great Society." Unlike Kennedy's rather modest proposals to fight poverty, the programs of the Great Society constituted an expansion of the role of the federal government. In a speech at Ann Arbor, Michigan, Johnson explained that the "Great Society" rested "on abundance and liberty for all" and demanded "an end to poverty and racial injustice, to which we are fully committed in our time."

The battle against racial injustice was an important component in Johnson's conception of the "Great Society." In the first two years of his presidency, Congress passed two major civil rights acts. The 1964 Civil Rights Act forbade discrimination not only in public accommodations but also in employment. It authorized the federal government to withhold funds from public agencies that discriminated on the basis of race. The Voting Rights Act of 1965 removed any remaining barriers to the right to vote and empowered the federal government to register those whom the states refused to add to their voting lists. In September 1965 Johnson issued an executive order which established the policy of affirmative action. This order required contractors and institutions receiving federal assistance to make special efforts to employ nonwhites and women. A third Civil Rights Act in 1968 prohibited housing discrimination.

"Great Society" initiatives covered a broad range of programs. In the area of health care, Congress approved the Medicare program which provided federal funding for many of the medical costs of older Americans. It later extended this system to include welfare recipients of all ages through the Medicaid programs. Education was extremely important to a "Great Society." The Elementary and Secondary Education Act authorized over one billion dollars to be granted to local school districts to pay for new facilities or staff. The Higher Education Act provided federal assistance to colleges and universities. In the field of the Arts, the Johnson administration persuaded Congress to subsidize museums and offer fellowships and grants to artists, musicians, and scholars under the National Endowment for the Arts and the Humanities. Congress established the Corporation for Public Broadcasting to support public radio and television broadcasting. The president also responded to the needs of the environment. Congress set standards for water and air quality. Johnson also continued to add to the size and number of national parks and recreational facilities. In the area of housing, the Johnson administration established the Department of Housing and Urban Development. The Housing and Urban Development Act of 1965 provided federal funds for the construction of housing units and urban renewal.

The main component of Johnson's "Great Society" was the War on Poverty. In 1964 Congress passed the Economic Opportunity Act which provided funding for a wide variety of programs: a Job Corps for youths aged sixteen to twenty-one; a Head Start program which offered preschool education for poor children; the Volunteers in Service to American (VISTA), in effect a domestic Peace Corps; grants to farmers and low-income businessmen; loans to businesses willing to hire the chronic unemployed; work-study jobs for college students; and the Community Action Program (CAP). Johnson created an independent executive agency, the Office of Economic Opportunity (OEO), to coordinate the attack on poverty. The president appointed Sargent Shriver, Kennedy's brother-in-law and the former head of the Peace Corps, to lead the OEO.

The most controversial feature of the War on Poverty was CAP. This program involved the use of local development corporations to attack poverty by assembling and coordinating various local existing anti-poverty programs. In order to obtain federal funds, Congress required these programs to secure the "maximum feasible participation" of the poor in the planning and operation of the anti-poverty effort. Many local officials complained that these programs were not always under the supervision of City Hall or municipal welfare agencies. "Radical" organizations and individuals, according to these critics, could thus dominate CAPs. They noted that the Students For a Democratic Society operated experimental anti-poverty programs in many northern cities.[37] Professional social workers complained that the poor did not have the expertise to operate welfare and anti-poverty programs. These critics perceived the poor as being uneducated, irresponsible, and too divided by race. Local officials wanted to distribute the funds that were now coming from Washington.

In 1965 controversy arose when OEO withheld federal funds from five major cities on the grounds that their CAPs did not allow the poor "maximum feasible participation." Due to pressure from local officials and the Johnson administration, Congress eliminated the "maximum feasible participation" requirement. New enabling legislation set the representation of the poor on CAP boards to one-third of the membership. Local officials and community organizations each were allotted one-third. Congress also reduced anti-poverty appropriations to CAPs. These funds were redirected to less threatening programs such as Head Start and the Job Corps. While CAPs continued to operate, their budgets, like those of the majority of anti-poverty programs, were severely limited.[38]

The passage of "Great Society" legislation was keenly watched by city officials and business leaders in Atlanta. The city could not simultaneously finance highway construction, low-income housing, an urban renewal program, and assistance to the poor without state or federal funding. Due to a rural-dominated legislature and conflicts between state and municipal officials over racial issues, Atlanta could not appeal to the state for help in funding these expensive projects. Washington was the principal source of funds and assistance.

For this reason, Mayor Allen and a majority of business leaders favored "Great Society" legislation. In return for federal assistance, Atlanta had to comply at least nominally with regulations concerning minority participation in the planning, construction, and operation of these various projects. In 1964 Atlanta was one of the first cities in the nation to establish an anti-poverty program, Economic Opportunity Atlanta (EOA). City officials established this organization as an independent agency to serve the poor both inside and outside the city. While it was a conservative organization and certainly not a pioneer in "maximum feasible participation," its programs complied with federal guidelines. During his second term in office, Mayor Allen appointed a special liaison officer to facilitate communications between municipal and federal agencies. In 1967 the Atlanta Board of Aldermen passed an ordinance requiring equal opportunity employment clauses in city contracts. In May 1968 fifty-six prominent organizations sponsored a Metro Conference on Open Housing in order to prepare the city for provisions of a new federal housing law, to urge strict implementation of the law in Atlanta, and to create a positive racial climate. These actions signified at least an attempt on the part of the city to comply with federal regulations. In fiscal 1968, federal programs brought almost $60 million to Atlanta, a sum nearly equal to the total operating budget of the city.[39]

The debate over "Great Society" legislation, the efforts of the city to comply with federal regulations, and the end of legal segregation exposed the problems of poverty and racism that existed in Atlanta. In 1965 the Community Council of the Atlanta Area, a quasi-public agency for social planning, conducted a study detailing the deterioration of two neighborhoods adjacent to the newly constructed Atlanta stadium. City newspapers began to publicize slum conditions in Atlanta. In May 1965 a newspaper reported on health conditions in Blue Heaven, a slum neighborhood. A ten-part series, "Housing: People, Problems, and Profit," followed. These articles criticized slum landlords and the city's urban renewal program. Opponents of urban renewal cited instances of deterioration in neighborhoods adjacent to these projects, and the city's lack of interest in slum areas which did not have high redevelopment values.[40]

Poverty thus became an explosive political issue in Atlanta. Mayor Allen called for an "all-out" attack on the city's worst slum areas. With the end of legal segregation, African American leaders and civil rights organizations shifted their attention to the issue of poverty. The city's anti-poverty program became a target of attack. African American leaders cited the lack of minority participation in the city's anti-poverty effort and discrimination within the EOA. In April 1965 a petition demanded the immediate resignations of EOA directors and the installation of African Americans in policy-making positions.[41]

The war against poverty and racism in Atlanta, however, occurred not at the office of the EOA, but in the slum neighborhoods of the city. Small community organizations performed the most effective civil rights efforts. In 1965 attention focused on Vine City, a six-by-four block area in West Atlanta. Vine City was predominately an African American community of approximately fifteen hundred families. Due to a housing shortage in the area, many residents were crowded into single-family dwelling units. Home ownership in the area was extremely low; eighty percent of the families rented their housing. Most of these units were dilapidated. City services in the area were poor. Many streets were unpaved. A student at Morehouse College who lived in the area noted that the residents were largely unaware of the benefits of the 1964 Civil Rights Act and poverty assistance.

A group of students met at a local church to discuss ways to help the residents of Vine City. These students decided that they needed to mobilize the community. In order to better understand the problems of this neighborhood, a suggestion was made to interview the residents and elicit from them possible solutions to their plight. The students drew up a questionnaire and began a street-by-street, house-by-house survey of the area. Biracial teams of students conducted these interviews. A resident of the neighborhood went with each team to serve as a guide and help elicit responses. In addition to students from Atlanta University, representatives from the Georgia Students for Human Rights, the Southern Human Relations Branch of the National Student Association, and the Atlanta Council on Human Relations participated in the project.

In interviews with students, the residents of Vine City cited the lack of recreational facilities, police brutality, landlords who did not make repairs, exorbitant rents for substandard housing, unpaved streets, lack of cultural opportunities, and unemployment as the area's major problems. For the first project, students and neighborhood children cleared a vacant trash-covered lot for a playground. Residents formed the Vine City Improvement Association with the aim of improving conditions in housing, welfare, education, employment, and municipal services. This organization acquired a discarded house to use as a community center and library. It also conducted a survey of housing conditions in the area in order to educate the public and city officials about this enormous problem. In order to build community support, the Vine City Improvement Association mainly relied on neighborhood projects and contributions to finance its activities.[42]

In February 1965 Hector Black, "a Quaker activist," moved into the Vine City area. He was "interested in the Civil Rights Movement and wanted to participate in some way." He accepted a job with the Atlanta Quaker House supervising its tutorial program. Black had degrees in psychology and sociology from Harvard University. For a brief period of time, he participated in Quaker work projects in the slums of Cambridge, Bedford, and Boston. Shortly after World War II, as a member of the American Friends Service Committee, he helped to build playgrounds in Europe. Black hitchhiked from Europe to Israel where he worked on a kibbutz for six weeks. Later, he spent three months at the Catholic Worker on Chrystie Street in the New York Bowery Area. Immediately before moving to Atlanta, he lived in Paraguay and Farmington, Pennsylvania with the Society of Brothers, a religious group whose members shared common work and poverty.

Hector Black joined the Vine City Improvement Association. He became concerned that the leadership was too conservative and reluctant to bring about true reform. He quit and helped to form a new organization, the Vine City Council. The purpose of this organization was "the betterment and improvement of the total community of Vine City." It especially wanted to organize the poor. Unlike the Vine City Improvement Association, the Vine City Council often encouraged the use of direct action techniques. It organized rent strikes and picketed slumlords. While members of the Vine City Improvement Association made requests and applications for recreational facilities, the Council herded neighborhood children into the streets for traffic-snarling "play-ins."[42] In 1966 it politically challenged a popular incumbent African American state legislator (Grace Hamilton). Members petitioned the city for street paving. The Vine City Council was awarded a $4,700 grant to fight juvenile delinquency. In order to raise money for its activities and provide a model for African American financial independence, the Vine City Council operated a thrift shop where used clothing was sold.[44]

Most leaders within the Vine City Improvement Association viewed Black as an irresponsible troublemaker. Because of his popularity with members of the Council and poor African American residents, SNCC members sarcastically referred to Black as "white Jesus." In letters to an agent of the FBI, Police Chief Herbert Jenkins, and Paul Anthony of the Southern Regional Council, Ralph McGill also expressed "concerns" about Hector Black and the Vine City Council. Because of the approach of the 1966 primary, he feared that the Vine City Council was "going to try some confusion and division this summer."[45] McGill asked a reporter to check into Black's background. He was convinced that Black was "a bad one, and certainly Negroes in the area do not regard him as a Christian or Jesus."[46]

In late January 1966 a landlord evicted a woman from her home in the Markham Street area in West Atlanta. Having nowhere to go, she sought help from the Vine City Council. It raised the money to rent her another house, and SNCC members helped her to move. Residents in the area asked members of the Vine City Council and SNCC to attend a meeting to discuss the recent number of evictions in the area and the actions of their landlord. At the meeting, participants decided to picket his properties.

Before the demonstrations were to occur, an extreme cold snap hit the city. Statewide, it resulted in the deaths of eighteen people from cold and exposure. Instead of picketing, the protesters decided to canvass the area to see if residents had adequate heat. Members of SNCC and the Vine City Council decided to deliver blankets to those in need. The landlord encountered Black in one of his buildings and had him arrested and jailed for trespassing. He asserted that his tenants had complained about civil rights organizers. Black claimed that he was simply distributing blankets.[47]

This landlord owned most of the property in the Markham Street area as well as extensive slum properties in other areas of the city. He made profits on his investments by renting houses with five to six rooms to four, sometimes even five, families. He collected from $20 to $40 in monthly rents from each family. This landlord could thus collect up to $200 a month for a house that would normally rent for no more than $70 a month. His houses were often in need of repair and in direct violation of the city's housing codes. Serving also as banker, creditor, and employer, this landlord frequently cashed the checks of, provided employment for, and loaned money to his tenants. In this manner, he controlled his tenants. He warned them not to talk to civil rights workers or participate in their activities.[48]

After Black's arrest, the Vine City Council began to picket the landlord's properties and residence. Mrs. Benjamin Mays and Coretta King called a meeting at West Hunter Street Baptist Church to discuss the living conditions in the area. James Forman and Martin Luther King, Jr. visited the area. King described the living conditions as the worst he had ever seen. At a press conference, Julian Bond asked city officials to provide adequate heat, blankets, food, and medical care to residents who were undergoing hardships due to the weather. He also called for a program to force landlords to comply with the city's housing codes, public housing to be built before anyone was moved out of current housing, and the erection of temporary shelter in the area while facilities were being built or repaired.[49]

King's visit attracted the attention of the local media. City officials quickly responded to this publicity. Mayor Allen ordered building inspectors and clean-up crews into the area. Housing authorities condemned a number of homes. Allen assured residents that they would not be forced out of their homes and slumlords in violation of housing codes would be punished. If residents had to be relocated, city officials promised that aid and ample time to move would be provided. The mayor noted that existing vacancies within public housing units could be used by residents of the Markham Street area.

Residents regarded these assurances with skepticism, especially the offer of public housing. Many residents could not afford to move into public housing units or even pay rent for these facilities. Many were reluctant to leave their present community. The residents did not want public housing. They simply desired decent housing at affordable and fair rental rates. Activists regarded the mayor's offer as an attempt to block efforts to improve conditions in the Markham Street area.[50]

During his tour of the area, King asked residents if they would be willing to participate in a rent strike. A large group of residents in the area began a series of nightly meetings to discuss this possibility. Several families were already facing evictions. By the end of the week, these residents decided to participate in a rent strike. A local attorney, suggested by SNCC members, was retained. A delegation went to City Hall where they met with Mayor Allen and presented him with a petition calling for his public support of a rent strike. The mayor refused to support the strike. Representatives of SNCC and the Vine City Council discussed launching a citywide tenant movement to contest the power of landlords if municipal officials did not respond to their grievances. Residents in the area began legal proceedings against the landlord on the ground that his properties violated Atlanta's housing codes. After several legal maneuvers by both parties, the Court eventually upheld the eviction procedures. City officials offered to move striking residents into public housing units with rents and utilities free for the first month. The city also agreed to pay moving expenses. By the end of March, rent strikes on the west side of the city had ended.[51]

Community action was responsible for the limited changes that occurred in Vine City and the Markham Street area. The community center, the library, a grant to fight juvenile delinquency, and new playgrounds were due to the efforts of the Vine City Improvement Association and the Vine City Council. While the rent strike was unsuccessful, it publicized the area's terrible living conditions and forced city leaders to intervene to protect Atlanta's image. City officials failed, however, to undertake and sustain the actions necessary to improve living conditions in the area.

By participating in these activities, the residents of Vine City and the Markham Street area began to assert some control over public decisions which affected them. They believed that traditional political channels were closed. Voting, persuasion, and petitions had not led to a redress of their grievances. The refusal of the Georgia legislature to seat the district's duly elected representative, Julian Bond, confirmed their belief.

In the early 1960s, the small rural counties of Georgia wielded the political reins of the state legislature. Under the county unit system, the eight most populous counties were entitled to three representatives, the next thirty counties to two representatives, and the remaining counties to one. In 1961 the eight most populous counties which comprised forty-two percent of the state's population had twenty-four representatives in the house. The twenty-four smallest counties in the state which contained three percent of the state's population also had twenty-four representatives.

In April 1962 the Federal District Court found the county unit system to be unconstitutional (*Gary v. Sanders*). In May the Court ordered in *Toombs v. Fortson* that at least one house of the Georgia General Assembly must be reapportioned according to population by the beginning of the legislative session. The General Assembly complied with the decision by redrawing the state's fifty-four senatorial districts. Fulton County's senatorial districts rose from one to seven. In 1962 LeRoy Johnson, an African American attorney, defeated three white candidates for the Democratic nomination in the 38th district. By defeating an African American Republican nominee in the general election, he became the first African American to serve in the state senate since Reconstruction.

In June 1964 the Supreme Court handed down a series of decisions that dealt with the reapportionment of state legislatures. In cases from six different states, the Court ruled that representation in state legislatures must be based substantially on population. In *Reynolds v. Sims*, a case which originated in Alabama, the Court held that the Equal Protection Clause of the Fourteenth Amendment guaranteed to each citizen an equal weight in the election of state legislators. Within a period of two years, the composition of legislatures in several states changed as new constituency lines were drawn. Patterns of county and small-town domination of legislatures in several urban states ended. Following the Supreme Court's ruling in *Reynolds v. Sims*, the Georgia General Assembly reapportioned its lower house in 1965. This reapportionment created twelve additional house seats in the Atlanta area, several of which were located in predominately African American districts.

SNCC members urged Bond to run for one of the new seats. Since Bond's position as SNCC's director of communications had limited his participation in protest demonstrations, they thought that he could attract support from both liberal and moderate African Americans. Rather than organizing mass rallies and large political events, Bond spent most of his time speaking and listening to residents in his district. He supported an increase in the minimum wage, improved urban renewal and anti-poverty programs, the abolition of the death penalty, increased spending for education, and the repeal of the state's right-to-work law. While some members criticized his participation in the Democratic Party, SNCC's executive committee contributed funds to his campaign. In the Democratic primary, Bond easily defeated Harold Creecy, an African American minister. In the general election against Malcolm Dean, an Atlanta University administrator, Bond won eighty-two percent of the vote. Reapportionment resulted in the election of eight African American representatives; all were from newly created districts.[52]

Four days before the legislative session began, SNCC's executive committee issued a statement denouncing the United States' participation in the Vietnam War. It charged that the "United States government had been deceptive in its claims of concerns for the freedom of colored people in such countries as the Dominican Republic, the Congo, South Africa, Rhodesia, and in the United States itself." The statement argued that "Vietnamese are murdered because the United States is pursuing an aggressive policy in violation of international law." The United States was "no respecter of persons or law when such persons or law ran counter to its needs and desires." The statement suggested that participation in the Civil Rights Movement was a valid alternative to the draft. It urged "all Americans to seek this alternative, knowing full well that it may cost them their lives—as painfully as Vietnam."[53]

During his campaign, Bond did not address the issue of American participation in Vietnam. He had been on leave from SNCC since his campaign began and had not been involved in the drafting of the statement. Because of his association with SNCC, a reporter asked Bond to comment on the statement. Bond expressed support for the statement on the grounds that he was a pacifist and opposed to war. While he did not advocate the burning of draft cards, Bond expressed admiration for the courage of those who protested the war knowing that they faced possible legal consequences and community ostracism. He supported participation in the Civil Rights Movement as an alternative to military service.[54]

Reaction to Bond's statement was swift. The following day, three House members filed petitions with the House clerk to block the seating of Bond. One petition claimed that Bond "adheres to the enemies of the United States." Another charged him with advocating the violation of federal laws relating to military service. A third charged him with treason. Because his statements of opposition to the war proved that he was disloyal to his country, these petitions argued that Bond lacked the ability to support and uphold the state constitution. Anti-Bond petitioners maintained throughout the controversy that their opposition had nothing to do with race.[55]

During the weekend prior to the swearing-in ceremony of new legislators, Bond met with his supporters to discuss strategy. Some supporters wanted Bond to insist on being seated without any modifications of his views. Many wanted him to issue a statement explaining his position on the war. A few asked Bond to issue an apology for making the statements. Ralph Abernathy, a friend and SCLC official, told him "to just do something that you can live with." Rather than on the substance of his views concerning United States participation in the Vietnam War, Bond chose to argue his case on the grounds of free speech and the right of his constituents to have representation of their own choice.[56]

At the swearing-in ceremony, the Speaker of the Georgia House asked Bond to step aside while other state representatives took the oath of office. A hearing was held that afternoon before the House Rules Committee. Reverend Howard Creecy, Malcolm Dean, LeRoy Johnson, and Horace Ward, an African American state senator, testified on Bond's behalf. The Rules Committee voted twenty-three to three against seating Bond. The two African American members on the committee voted in favor of seating him.[57] The House approved the committee's recommendation that night by a vote of 184 to 12. Members of the Fulton County delegation (six whites, six African Americans) cast the dissenting votes. Two African American legislators did not vote.[58]

In a statement, Martin Luther King, Jr. noted that he found "it impossible to believe that the decision by 184 members of the state legislature to refuse to seat Mr. Bond did not have racial overtones." According to King, many of the legislators who supported the measure "were and are the very persons who have consistently defied the law of the land through their irresponsible acts and statements."[59] Four days after the legislative action, SCLC and SNCC recruited 1,000 protesters for a march on the State Capitol. A placard referred to the "ouster" of Bond as a "slap to the face of Negroes." The "white" General Assembly believed that it could "dictate whom we can choose to represent us." A poll by the *Inquirer* showed that while African Americans in Atlanta disagreed with Bond's opposition to the Vietnam War, they felt that he should be seated.

Bond's attorneys filed suit to regain his seat. Martin Luther King, Jr. and Mrs. Arel Keyes, two residents of Bond's district, joined as co-plaintiffs. The Federal Court had to determine whether the Georgia Constitution had been properly applied by the House and whether its provisions ran counter to the United States Constitution. The panel of three federal judges voted two to one to uphold the state's position. Griffin Bell and Lewis Morgan held that the Court should not intervene in a legislative matter. They argued that the House could determine the qualifications of its own members. In a dissenting opinion, Elbert Tuttle noted that Bond met the qualifications that were listed in the state constitution. The people had the right to choose their own representatives; therefore, Bond should be seated by the Georgia House. Bond filed an appeal with the Supreme Court.

In the months between the Federal and Supreme Court decisions, Bond ran in two special elections called by the General Assembly to fill the vacant seat. He won the first special election without any opposition. The House again refused to seat him. In September 1966 Bond ran and won a third time. Malcolm Dean, however, came within fifty votes of defeating him. In December 1966, the Supreme Court ruled unanimously in Bond's favor. When Bond took his oath of office in January 1967, many members walked out of the House Chamber in protest.[60]

Efforts of the Georgia legislature to bar a duly elected African American representative created grave concerns among a small group of SNCC members. This group attempted to mobilize residents of the district around Bond's ouster. They asked SCLC for help. SCLC offered this group the use of a print shop and helped to organize mass meetings at various churches in Bond's district. After discussing the impact of Bond's ouster on the African American community, this group decided that it should organize a project in Atlanta. Bill Ware, who had worked for SNCC in Mississippi and Alabama, became the head of this new project in the Vine City area.[61]

Members of the Atlanta Project staff wanted to organize a "political program" which would give African Americans control "over the public decisions which affected their lives." If this project failed, they warned that Atlanta would "succumb to the fate of northern ghettos: a welfare and patronage system will be established and the new voting powers of Negroes will work to the benefit of a small few." SNCC members noted that a "small established Negro leadership" was already working in Atlanta "to solidify still further its political control." Through canvassing, political workshops, block organization, and a community newspaper, members hoped to raise the issues of slum housing, inadequate medical care and education, low wages, job discrimination, welfare relief, and the Vietnam War with poor residents. Together they could find workable political solutions to these problems. Primary emphasis would be given to finding candidates of "Julian Bond's caliber and integrity." Atlanta was important because it was the "first city where Negroes had achieved a breakthrough in political representation."[62]

In order to organize the African American urban community, the staff of the Atlanta Project felt that it had to develop among the masses "an intense pride and self-respect that can only be gained when they see black people working together accomplishing worthwhile projects without the guidance and/or direction and control of non-Blacks."[63] For this reason, the Atlanta Project staff rejected the applications of white workers who wanted to participate in the project. At a SNCC meeting in March 1966, members of the Atlanta Project staff attacked the presence of whites in the organization. The position paper of the Atlanta Project staff argued that the development of a new black consciousness was the first step toward revolutionary struggle. The paper called for the exclusion of whites from SNCC as a necessary first step toward developing this sense of racial identity. As Clayborne Carson notes in his study of SNCC, the position paper of the Atlanta project staff was "actually the initial volley in a struggle among blacks over the control of SNCC and the future direction of black struggles."[64] In December 1966 SNCC officers passed a resolution excluding whites from the organization by a vote of nineteen for, eighteen against, and twenty-four abstaining.

In Atlanta this doctrine of racial separatism was expressed in the project's newspaper. The goals of this newspaper were to create racial pride and dignity; report the daily indignities inflicted upon African Americans; connect the worldwide, national, and local struggles of people of color; and inspire the participation of all African Americans in this struggle. The newspaper staff primarily directed its articles at the African American poor. In order to counteract the "white lies" of the "white press," staff members named this newspaper, *Nitty Gritty*. According to the first edition of the paper, "Nitty Gritty" meant "tell it like it is," "for real," and "down with it."[65]

In the Vine City area, the Atlanta staff worked on a variety of projects. In cooperation with the Vine City Council, members provided food and housing for poor residents, and helped to organize community protests during the Markham rent strike. Three SNCC members were arrested for trying to prevent the eviction of an African American family. In March 1966 the Atlanta staff picketed a local dry-cleaning establishment which had fired its African American employees and replaced them with white workers. The African American employees had also complained of hostile treatment, low wages, and long hours. Police officers arrested three members of the project for their participation in protests at the establishment. To the dismay and objections of the Atlanta staff, the African American employees reached a compromise with the company after only a week of demonstrations.[66]

In the summer of 1966 members of the Atlanta staff gathered at the 12th Army Corps and Induction Center for the Atlanta area. They protested the "drafting of Black men to fight in the racist illegal war in Vietnam." These demonstrations began shortly after Michael Simmons, a SNCC member, was drafted. Protesters carried placards saying, "The Viet Cong never called me Nigger." A placard portraying a lynching included the notation, "Did the Viet Cong do this?" Demonstrators drew the taunts of white passerbys and army personnel who threw lighted cigarettes from the headquarter's windows. On the second day of the protests, military personnel physically ejected demonstrators from the lobby of the center.

Chief Jenkins sent in policemen, white and African American, to secure the area. They arrested twelve demonstrators. Charges included disturbance, resisting arrest, assault and battery, and failure to obey an officer. One protester was bound over to the state and charged with insurrection which carried the death penalty in Georgia if found guilty. Jenkins placed twenty-five to thirty plainclothesmen, with arm bands designating them as police officers, across the front of the induction center. He stationed two African American officers at the immediate entrance to the building. Jenkins also sent African American policemen to patrol the area. At a rally held in Vine City, Bill Ware told the audience that African American officers represented "the white power structure and [Chief Jenkins] sent them down there to report on the activities of Black people." Ware claimed that African American officers were "white men with black skins." The Atlanta staff began a twenty-four hour vigil until the prisoners were released.[67]

While the militancy of the Atlanta project attracted some young African Americans, staff members were not able to build support for their activities in the Vine City area. SNCC members, for example, had difficulties in raising bail money for those jailed during the protests at the induction center. The doctrine of racial separatism and the issue of the Vietnam War did not appeal to the area's residents. In 1966 the staff's criticism of Hector Black as "white Jesus," damaged its relationship with the Vine City Council while conservative and moderate African American leaders criticized the project's disruptive tactics. Project members challenged the racial loyalty and authority of SNCC's national leadership. In 1967 Stokley Carmichael, SNCC's chairman, fired or suspended all members of the Atlanta Project staff for insubordination.[68]

City officials were wary of SNCC activities in the Vine City area. During the mid-1960s racial disturbances occurred in Harlem and Rochester, New York; Elizabeth and Jersey City, New Jersey; and

Philadelphia, Pennsylvania. In August 1965 the Watts riot in Los Angeles began when a highway patrolman stopped an apparently intoxicated African American man for speeding. In the summer of 1966 there were forty-three racial disturbances, all sparked by some minor incident between African American citizens and the police.[69] Taking note of these incidents, Allen began making preparations for any racial disturbances that might occur in Atlanta. He prepared a list of twenty-five leading African American ministers in the city. The mayor made a verbal agreement with them that this list would be distributed to the police, and, in a case of an emergency, officers would immediately transport the ministers to him. The mayor believed that these ministers would be able to reason with protesters. Allen also arranged with Governor Carl Sanders to obtain the help of the state highway patrol if necessary. Under these circumstances, the state patrol would be under the control of the municipal government.[70]

Despite the activity in Vine City, Atlanta's first major racial disturbance occurred in Summerhill, a community in Southeast Atlanta. Prior to World War II, white citizens in the area lived in fairly large houses on the main thoroughfares of the community. A number of African American residents lived in modest houses along back streets. After the war, white residents moved out of the area. The community underwent a transition from white to African American occupancy. By the early 1960s approximately ten thousand residents were crowded into 354 acres. Single-family homes were transformed into multi-dwelling units. The area began to attract rural migrants who were unemployed and had no skills. The dislocation of residents caused by the construction of Atlanta Stadium and expressways in the area made a heavily populated community more crowded.[71]

In 1965 the Atlanta Commission on Crime and Juvenile Delinquency, a twenty-one member blue-ribbon commission of white and African American civic leaders, identified Summerhill as one of the city's worst crime areas. The Community Council of the Atlanta Area released an interim report on social blight with special emphasis on the Summerhill community in February 1966. The report found that over one-half of the families lived near or below the poverty level; between a quarter and a third of the children lived with only one parent; the unemployment rate for African American men was extremely high; only eleven percent of the residents had finished high school; the infant mortality rate was twice that of the city; and a general attitude of despair, cynicism, and hopelessness prevailed in the community. To solve these problems, the report merely recommended that the city inform residents of the existing plans for the neighborhood and a "program of open dialogue" between the major community resource agencies and the low-income neighborhood be established.[72]

Residents of the Summerhill community discussed the possibility of rent strikes to protest housing conditions. This idea, however, was discarded. In October 1965, leaders of several neighborhood organizations, including representatives of Summerhill, appeared before the Citizens Advisory Committee on Urban Renewal. This delegation requested that housing conditions be improved, landlords be forced to comply with housing codes, regular meetings of the Advisory Committee be held in the evenings so residents could attend, special meetings be held in the communities of the city, and neighborhood advisory committees be appointed and consulted. Members of the Advisory Committee expressed sympathy with these demands and promised to improve communications with local leaders. When conditions did not improve, the residents of Summerhill participated in small street demonstrations during the early summer of 1966.[73]

In September 1966, while trying to escape arrest, an African American man was shot by a white police officer. Many witnesses believed that the use of gunfire was unnecessary. An angry crowd gathered at the scene of the shooting. The first contingent of police sent into the area were African American officers. They tried to disperse the crowd, but it kept regathering. Some residents suggested a demonstration to protest the shooting. They began making signs for a rally.

Upon hearing of the incident, Stokley Carmichael, SNCC's chairman, came to the neighborhood. Because of his advocacy of "Black Power" and African American self-determination, and his outspoken militant rhetoric, national and local white leaders, as well as a large portion of the popular media, perceived Carmichael as a "racial agitator" and "troublemaker." According to a reporter at a local radio station, Carmichael expressed support for the demonstration and promised to attend the rally that afternoon. Other SNCC members came to the area. Bill Ware and Bob Walton had sound equipment asking residents about the shooting. Police officers arrested both men when they refused to comply with an order to turn off the equipment.

The presence of policemen in their neighborhood and the arrests of residents angered the crowd. Bricks and bottles began to fly. A mob overturned and burned some police cars. As the crowd grew, the police called for reinforcements who arrived in riot helmets and carried rifles. Following Allen's orders, the police department radioed for two hundred state troopers and contacted the ministers on the list. In order to control the riot area, the police placed roadblocks at the area's main thoroughfares and intersections.

Accompanied by two police officers, Mayor Allen arrived at the scene. He began walking back-and-forth through the crowd urging residents to leave the area. Allen struggled to the roof of a police car which was parked in one of the area's intersections. When he tried to address the crowd, residents began to heckle him and rock the car. Allen lost his balance and fell into the arms of the police officers. Bottles and bricks once again began to fly. Once the mayor ordered the use of tear gas, the crowd began to disperse. Mayor Allen asked the ministers to talk to residents who were still in the area.[74] Martin Luther King, Sr. told Allen that "these people were not my people." They were "people who had moved in here out of South Georgia," and he could not "call them by their name."[75] Disturbances in the area were finished that night. Sixteen people were injured in the "riot;" the police arrested seventy-five individuals. Some cars were badly damaged, and a one-story frame building caught on fire. There was no looting or gunfire.

The day following the "riot," city officials and the press blamed SNCC for the racial disturbances that occurred in the Summerhill area. Mayor Allen stated that SNCC was directly responsible for the rioting. Police Chief Herbert Jenkins referred to the "present" SNCC as an organization consisting "mostly of criminals, hoodlums, and outlaws of all types."[76] Ralph McGill suggested that SNCC was "no longer a student movement or a civil rights organization." It was "openly, officially, committed to a destruction of existing society."[77] Eugene Patterson, publisher of the *Atlanta Constitution*, argued that SNCC was "betrayed by roughnecks who turned it away from nonviolence."[78] An assistant to the mayor noted that Allen had "the guts to call a spade a spade, not blame the trouble on economics or any sociological business." This aide thought Allen's handling of the situation would "kill Black Power and SNCC."

Allen received support from established African American leaders. Soon after the racial disturbances, the mayor attended a meeting of the Summit Leadership Conference and urged it to adopt a statement condemning SNCC. While mentioning the economic problems in the area and not directly attacking SNCC, the Summit Leadership Conference issued a statement condemning "those who would initiate disorder and disrupt the city's peaceful racial climate."[80] Reverend Sam Williams argued that violence was "not the way to rectify the wrongs done Negro people for centuries." Reverend Otis Smith claimed that "our main concern here is Stokley Carmichael."[81] African American workers in an anti-poverty program near the Summerhill area were instrumental in forming "Good Neighborhood Clubs." Members pledged to maintain law and order. A group of residents in the Vine City area burned a table which SNCC had set up to collect bail money for those arrested at the induction center.[82] Shortly after the disturbances, Julian Bond resigned from SNCC for personal reasons.[83] The press publicized these reactions to illustrate that SNCC did not have the support of the city's African American community.

The racial disturbances in the Summerhill area captured the attention of the national media. Articles were generally favorable of Mayor Allen's handling of the situation and condemned SNCC's advocacy of "Black Power." The *New York Times* referred to the disturbance as an "induced riot involving a few susceptible Negroes." They had been "whipped to a frenzy, reportedly by the so-called Student Nonviolent Coordinating Committee, espouser of the separatist and inflammatory slogan, Black Power."[84] *Time* magazine referred to the riot as a "peculiar and perverse triumph for Stokley Carmichael."[85] Basing their information on police reports and local accounts, most articles quoted Carmichael as saying, "We're going to tear this place up," a statement that he vigorously denied making.

A statement of support for SNCC came from the Atlanta Council on Human Relations. This statement warned that the incident was "another in a long series of warnings that poverty and segregation breed conditions which cannot be solved through the personal courage of the mayor or the competence of the police to handle race riots, neither of which has been the question." The Atlanta Council on Human Relations noted that neither "outside agitators" nor SNCC were directly responsible for the rioting in the Summerhill Community.[86] In a letter to Mayor Allen, the professional staffs of fourteen human relations agencies warned him that it "would be tragic indeed if a community consensus were to be argued against certain individuals and organizations and thus become a mere substitute for a more constructive response to the conditions which brought it about."[87] Both statements warned that the city should focus on inadequate housing, overcrowded schools, the lack of recreational facilities and municipal services, minimal enforcement of the city's housing codes, and unemployment.

SNCC members argued that attacks by city officials and the press were part of an organized campaign to discredit their organization. Following the disturbances, Carmichael canvassed the Summerhill community denying that he had caused the conflict. City officials obtained warrants for the arrest of Carmichael on charges of inciting to riot and disorderly conduct. While Carmichael was later convicted on these charges in a lower court, his conviction and those of other SNCC members on rioting charges were overturned on appeal.[88]

The arrest of SNCC members did not end the violence in Atlanta. Four days following the disturbance in Summerhill, a white motorist shot two African American youths as they walked up Boulevard Avenue in Northeast Atlanta. A police officer who arrived at the scene was struck by a flying object, apparently thrown from a crowd of onlookers. This crowd grew angry when the officer, who had been only slightly injured, was taken to the hospital before the two youths.[89] Because a nearby private institution would not accept the black youths, a second ambulance transported them to a public hospital located much further away from the scene of the shooting. One of the youths died before he received medical treatment.

A crowd gathered in the Boulevard area. Police Chief Jenkins sent in officers to secure the area. Angry residents responded with bottles and bricks. Hosea Williams and other SCLC workers came to the area in order to calm the crowd. Instead, police officers arrested them for failure to "move on." The following day, a peaceful protest march turned violent when demonstrators burned down four white-owned businesses. Until this incident, the crowd's anger in both areas had been only directed at the presence of police officers. Throughout the night and into the early morning hours, rioters threw bricks, bottles, and fire bombs at policemen and businesses. After three nights of violence, the police were eventually able to secure the area.[90]

In an analysis of these racial disturbances, an employee of the Atlanta Council on Human Relations noted that the majority of those involved in the violence were between the ages of sixteen and twenty-five. According to one civil rights worker, the vast majority had not previously participated in civil rights activities. Rather, this age group had "largely been unaffected (positively) by the civil rights developments of the past decade." They were cynical about society. According to this report, these individuals felt that legitimate channels of communication were closed to them. Through acts of racial violence, these participants could voice their displeasure and frustrations over the slum conditions in their neighborhoods.[91]

Racial violence caused grave concerns among religious, civic, and political leaders. Due to these racial disturbances, the Atlanta Episcopal Diocese established a neighborhood center, Emmaus House, in the Summerhill community. Reverend Austin Ford was chosen to head the center. Prior to his appointment, Ford was the rector of a parish in an upper middle-class white suburb for twelve years. Despite this position, he was extremely active in human relations causes. He was a member of the

Georgia Council on Human Relations, signed the Atlanta Manifesto, participated in the Selma March, became a vocal critic of the Vietnam War, and urged his congregation to become involved in helping the residents of slum neighborhoods. He resigned from his parish in March 1967 and moved into the center on Capitol Avenue.

Emmaus House provided traditional services such as tutorials, day-care, recreational programs for children, the distribution of food and clothing to the needy, adult education classes, and religious programs. Under Ford's leadership, the center also sponsored several controversial programs. Reverend Ford established a Poverty Rights Office in order to help residents reach the proper governmental and private agencies where relief would be made available. The Poverty Rights Office published a monthly periodical, "Poor People's Magazine," to inform welfare families of available resources and their rights. It established an emergency fund from which members could borrow. When residents complained of high prices at the corner grocery store, the center helped residents to organize a cooperative. In 1969 Reverend Ford organized Tenants United for Fairness (TUFF) to improve living conditions in public housing projects. TUFF requested a ninety dollar maximum rent, the election of tenant associations by residents, and the removal of unnecessary regulations placed upon tenants. Emmaus House also began to monitor closely programs which affected the Summerhill Community such as Model Cities.[92]

While the city had already begun to address the problems of racism and poverty, acts of racial violence created a sense of urgency among local officials. Mayor Allen was eager to demonstrate his concern for slum areas. In November 1966, the mayor called for a conference of civic, business, and public officials to discuss the city's need for low-income housing. At this conference, Allen established a five-year goal of 17,000 new low- and moderate-income housing units. He also ordered a crash program of 9,800 units to be built within two years. To achieve these goals, the mayor appointed a Housing Resources Committee to assist and stimulate the private development of low-income housing and recommend needed changes in existing programs.[93]

Mayor Allen also expressed interest in a new federal program, Model Cities, which directed government funds toward upgrading employment, housing, education, and health in target neighborhoods. The Allen administration quickly worked to have Atlanta selected as one of the first recipients of Model City funding. Community leaders in Summerhill and Mechanicsville urged the mayor to include their neighborhoods in the designated Atlanta Model Cities Area. Because of the recent disturbances, Allen was receptive to their request.

The city designated roughly 3,000 acres as a Model Cities Area. It contained approximately ten percent of Atlanta's population. Sixty percent of the residents in the area were African Americans. Four African American communities (Summerhill, Mechanicsville, Peoplestown, and Pittsburgh) and two white neighborhoods (Grant Park and Adair Park) were located in the target area. Approximately $78 million was to be spent to upgrade these neighborhoods. Of this amount, approximately $23.9 million was to be spent for social programs; $44 million for physical development; $5 million for employment; $4.7 million for administration; and $431,000 for citizen participation. The Model Cities program was a coordinated attack on all phases of urban blight. These programs included job training, day-care centers, pre-school programs, hot breakfasts for children, and scholarships for college students. The main priority, however, was housing.[94]

Despite the successes of several of its social programs, Model Cities failed to meet the high expectations of residents. Conflicts immediately arose as to the extent of minority and neighborhood participation in the planning of projects. Community leaders demanded representation in all phases of the program. Several African American leaders expressed concern that residential desegregation was not an integral part of the Model Cities program. Many advocated that federal funds be withheld until the city adopted an open occupancy law. Residents expressed fear that neighborhoods would be cleared without adequate rehabilitation.

The Model Cities program failed to meet its goal of increasing the area's housing supply by 2,000 units. While a substantial number of housing units were constructed and rehabilitated, neighborhoods in the Model Cities program actually lost dwelling units due to the demolition of substandard housing. Between 1965 and 1974 the Model Cities Area experienced a twenty percent decline in housing units. Residents were forced to leave the area. Between 1968 and 1974, the area's population declined by thirty-one percent.[95] Reverend Ford, a critic of the program, estimated that the population of Summerhill declined from 50,000 to 30,000 during this period.[96] While the Model Cities program demolished substandard housing in the community, few housing units were built to accommodate the area's residents. In many instances, cleared land remained vacant.

In addition to promises of municipal and federal aid to improve living conditions, racial violence accelerated the passage of an ordinance establishing a biracial commission to promote better understanding between the races. This idea actually had a long history in Atlanta. In 1960 the

Fulton County Grand Jury and the Southern Regional Council recommended the formation of a biracial committee to discuss racial problems in the city. Mayor Hartsfield rejected this proposal on the grounds that a committee would be "impractical in a city as large as Atlanta" and "the type of people who would make an effective committee which would be respected in the community will not at this juncture, give their service."[97] Mayor Allen also initially rejected the formation of a biracial commission. In testimony before the Senate Commerce Committee, Allen noted that the city had not "appointed a huge general biracial committee which too often merely becomes a burial place for unsolved problems." Each time the city faced a problem, the mayor explained that the involved participants worked out a solution.[98]

In July 1966 the idea of a biracial commission was revived when Benny T. Smith and other African American leaders called for a meeting to discuss the problems prevailing in South Atlanta. Smith was a resident of the area and chairman of the Metropolitan Atlanta Grass-Roots Council, an umbrella organization consisting of several low-income neighborhood groups and civic leagues. In addition to residents in the area, Vice-Mayor Sam Massell, six aldermen, five state legislators, Police Chief Herbert Jenkins, and an Atlanta school board member attended the meeting. Participants passed a resolution requesting the mayor and Board of Aldermen "to establish a human relations office with direct responsibilities to aid in resolving problems that are prevailing in the city."[99]

In August the Board of Aldermen passed a resolution establishing an ad hoc committee to visit the slum areas of the city and study the feasibility of forming a Community Relations Commission. Mayor Allen convened this committee three days after the Summerhill disturbance. Members took a bus tour of Blue Heaven, Vine City, Mechanicsville, Summerhill, Cabbage Town, and other slum areas of the city. The committee decided that a Community Relations Commission was necessary to address these problems. After studying information gathered from the Civil Rights Commission and biracial committees in other cities, the ad hoc committee presented a draft of a proposed ordinance to the Board of Aldermen which was passed in November 1966.[100]

According to the city ordinance, the purposes of the Community Relations Commission included the fostering of "mutual understanding, tolerance, and respect among all economic, social, religious, and ethnic groups in the city," the preparation of educational programs and studies in the field of human relations, the investigation of discriminatory practices, the mediation of controversies involving human relations, and the submission of an annual report to the mayor and the Board of Aldermen. Upon request, other city agencies and departments were required to provide their services to the Commission. The Community Relations Commission had the power to investigate and hold hearings, but no power of enforcement.[101]

Due to uncertainty about the exact activities that fell under the nebulous category of human relations and the vague mandate outlined in the ordinance, confusion arose as to the proper role of the Commission. Many city officials argued that the functions of the Commission were limited to those listed in the ordinance. Vice-Mayor Sam Massell urged the Commission to broaden its scope by directly addressing community issues. Mayor Allen perceived the Commission mainly as an agency where citizens could bring their complaints. Many felt that the Commission should be used as a fact-finding agency and a link between residents and city agencies. Some argued that the Commission should be used as an advocate for the poor.[102]

Because of these differences in opinions, the choice of an executive director for the Commission was an extremely important decision. To a large extent, the executive director would determine the role of the newly created Commission. The only requirement listed in the ordinance was that the chosen person must have experience in intergroup and interracial relations. Seventeen candidates applied for the position. In January 1967 Mayor Allen and the Board of Aldermen named Eliza Paschall as the Commission's first executive director.

This choice was controversial. Prior to her appointment, Eliza Paschall had served as the president of the League of Women Voters, a board member of the Georgia Council of Human Relations, and the executive director of the Atlanta Council on Human Relations for six years. During the 1960s she was an active participant in demonstrations and negotiations that led to the desegregation of public facilities in Atlanta. Eliza Paschall was an outspoken advocate for human rights. Even among her supporters, she had a reputation, however, for being extremely headstrong and inflexible. Many had criticized her for being unwilling to make any type of compromise on issues. City officials were undoubtedly aware of this potential problem. Her popularity within the African American community and among poor residents most likely overrode this concern. By appointing Eliza Paschall as executive director, city officials were making a symbolic gesture to these residents.

As executive director, Eliza Paschall initiated the town hall meeting. From March to September, the Community Relations Commission held ten of these public hearings in slum neighborhoods. Before each meeting, the Commission constructed a profile of the neighborhood listing boundaries, developmental programs, zoning classifications, racial patterns, political representation, housing conditions, neighborhood organizations, municipal services, and relief programs. At these meetings, the Commission gave residents the opportunity to air their grievances. These complaints ranged from police brutality to lack of recreational facilities to inadequate garbage and sewage disposal. Following these meetings members of the Commission passed these complaints to the appropriate municipal agency for study and action. The Commission pressured these agencies until a solution to the problem was reached.[103]

In June Mayor Allen requested the Community Relations Commission to investigate racial disturbances in Dixie Hills, a lower middle-class African American community located southwest of the central business district. The arrests of an African American man and his sister and their charges of police brutality triggered racial disturbances in the area. Over a two-day period, several rock-throwing and gunfire incidents between police officers and residents occurred. Police officers arrested a "visiting" Stokley Carmichael for "failure to move on." African American leaders held mass meetings to protest police brutality and the large number of officers patrolling the community. Conservative leaders circulated a petition requesting SNCC members to leave the area, and Senator LeRoy Johnson formed "youth patrols" to calm residents. Violence occurred when a youth allegedly threw a Molotov Cocktail at a police officer. Several policemen fired their weapons into a crowd at an apartment complex. The results were one dead and three wounded, including a nine-year-old boy.[104]

As in the case of the Summerhill disturbances, local press accounts centered on the presence of Stokley Carmichael and SNCC members in the area. In a hearing held by the Community Relations Commission, residents cited other reasons for the disturbances. These reasons included police brutality, bad treatment by local white merchants, inadequate municipal services, the lack of recreational facilities, and substandard living conditions. One resident argued that "the disturbances would come about sooner or later, mainly because our kids are on the street."[105] Immediately following these hearings, the YMCA arranged to take seventy youngsters from this area to the recently opened Six Flags over Georgia Amusement Park. Another relief agency supplied three hundred tickets to the Atlanta Braves baseball game. The city brought in equipment to construct a playground and assist in a neighborhood clean-up campaign.[106]

In June the Community Relations Commission also participated in efforts to desegregate Wren's Nest, the home of Joel Chandler Harris. This tourist attraction did not admit African American citizens on the ground that the staff could not "handle any other additional traffic on the premises."[107] Because a private association operated Wren's Nest, the attraction was not covered by the provisions of the 1964 Civil Rights Act. African American leaders picketed the attraction. Eliza Paschall felt that the Commission should align itself with the demonstrators. Without consulting other members, she participated in the picketing. Meanwhile, other Commission members were negotiating behind-the-scenes with representatives from Wren's Nest. Eliza Paschall's actions gave these representatives an excuse to break off negotiations with the Commission. Wren's Nest did not admit African Americans until September 1968.[108]

The Community Relations Commission was somewhat more successful in resolving differences between the Summit Leadership Conference and the Atlanta Board of Education. During the spring and summer of 1967, many residents voiced concerns over conditions in African American schools, particularly the problem of overcrowding. In July rumors reached the Commission that African American high schools would operate on double sessions. According to an independent study conducted by Eliza Paschall, this policy would mean that over fifty percent of the city's African American high school students would receive a half-day's education. The Commission sent telegrams to the Board of Education requesting a meeting to discuss the situation. Superintendent Letson and Board members refused to meet privately with the Commission. The Board Chairman referred to the efforts by the Commission as outside interference in school affairs.[109]

In September a group of African American residents led by Hosea Williams disrupted a meeting of the Board of Education. This group, the Freedom Coalition, demanded an end to double sessions in three schools on the west side of the city and the appointment of more African Americans to administrative positions in the school system.[110] They began to picket the Board of Education building. A few nights after the Board meeting, approximately one thousand African Americans met at Moriah Baptist Church. Dr. Martin Luther King, Jr. informed the audience that citizens had to organize nonviolent demonstrations to solve problems in the fields of education, housing, and jobs.

In order to calm the situation, the Atlanta Summit Leadership Conference presented twelve written requests to the Board. Six of these requests were for factual and statistical information pertaining to African American students. The other requests included the end of double sessions by transporting excess students to predominately white schools, the appointment of African Americans to high administrative positions, the assignment of African American principals to schools where black students comprised over sixty percent of the school's enrollment, the establishment of a biracial committee to study textbooks in order to eliminate any racial basis that existed in educational materials, the deposit of a portion of school funds in African American owned banks, and more effective distribution of textbooks to African American schools. If their demands were not met, they threatened to close schools and mount an effort to recall school board members.[111]

The Community Relations Commission and the Chamber of Commerce assisted in working out a compromise. The Board of Education agreed to end double sessions by supplying the African American schools with portable metal air-conditioned classrooms. An African American area superintendent was to be promoted to the status of assistant superintendent. The Board promised to appoint an African American to his former position. With respect to the placement of African American principals and personnel to head central administrative departments, the Board stated that the selection and promotion of employees would be made without regard to race.[112] It had no objections to the other requests.

This compromise did not please all leaders. It divided the leadership of the Summit Leadership Conference. More militant leaders denounced the compromise and urged a school boycott. More than fifty organizations eventually withdrew from the Summit and formed the Metropolitan Atlanta Summit Leadership Congress (MASLC). Most of these groups were neighborhood, low-income, and "militant" organizations. A major goal of this new organization was to develop "the Summit into what it originally was set-up to be." According to MASLC leaders the "reorganization of the Atlanta Summit Leadership Conference" was "the only way to prevent individuals from continuing to use the Summit for personal purposes."[113] This division eventually led to the demise of both organizations by separating established leaders from neighborhood and grass-roots leaders.

City officials and some Commission members began to criticize Eliza Paschall. In January 1968, a member of the Commission's executive committee informed her that she might not be reappointed executive director. Some Commission members and city aldermen disagreed with Eliza Paschall's perception of the Commission as an outspoken advocate for civil rights and the poor. Many criticized her unwillingness to compromise on issues. They felt that she could best serve from outside City Hall. Unsubstantial rumors arose that she had somehow mishandled Commission funds. Actually the city comptroller and the executive committee, not Eliza Paschall, controlled all funds. Some conservative members of the Board of Aldermen indicated that they might vote against the funding of the Commission if Eliza Paschall remained as executive director.

When the press reported rumors of Eliza Paschall's impending dismissal, African American leaders and organizations rallied to her defense. Organizations such as the NAACP, the Grass-Roots Council, Operation Breadbasket, the All Citizens Registration Committee, SCLC, the Fulton County Citizens Democratic Club, and ACCA urged the retention of Eliza Paschall as executive director. Julian Bond and LeRoy Johnson spoke against her dismissal. They argued that she represented the interests of the African American community and the poor on the Commission.

A proposal to dismiss Eliza Paschall was brought quickly before the Commission. Her supporters objected that her status as executive director had not been discussed at a prior meeting. Nevertheless, ten members of the Commission voted for her dismissal; five for retention. With one exception, all white members voted for dismissal. Four African Americans voted for retention. Reverend Sam Williams, who was presiding at the meeting, did not vote. African American members expressed outrage at the decision. The Commission refused to state the actual reasons for her dismissal.[114]

Because the vote was divided along racial lines, many believed that the dismissal of Eliza Paschall would lead to the demise of the Community Relations Commission. Members worked quickly to dispel this notion. In particular, the Commission reaffirmed its support for the total desegregation of Atlanta's public school system. The Commission, for example, conducted a town hall meeting to give Better Schools Atlanta an opportunity to publicize its report about conditions in Atlanta's schools.

Early in 1968 the Public Issues Committee of the Unitarian Universalist Congregation established an educational subcommittee to investigate the school situation in Atlanta. This committee eventually evolved into a larger organization known as Better Schools Atlanta. The goals of this organization were to alert the community to the extent of educational problems in the city and develop a climate in which these issues could be addressed. The report of Better Schools Atlanta was primarily an analysis of published and unpublished statistical data prepared by the Atlanta public school system. This data revealed several inequalities in schools. The report noted that ninety-two percent of African American elementary students attended all-black schools; sixty-five percent of schools were still segregated, all-black or all-white; African American elementary students attended larger classes, and had fewer textbooks and special education programs than white pupils; the student-teacher ratio was much higher in African American schools than white schools; African American elementary schools had a lower proportionate value of building, furniture and equipment, and smaller school sites than white schools; and eighth-grade pupils in African American schools were four years behind pupils in white schools. The report recommended meaningful desegregation, the correction of inequalities, and greater communication between the Atlanta School Board and the African American community.[115]

At a meeting in February 1969, Superintendent John Letson defended the actions of the School Board. Using a slide and lecture presentation, he argued that African American schools received more in the ways of funds over the last few years than white schools. He detailed the achievements of the school system in terms of construction, education, and school desegregation. The difference in the educational level of white and African American students, according to Letson, was the cultural deprivation of African American children. While no solutions were reached, the meeting publicized the conditions in Atlanta's public schools and the communication gap that existed between school officials and African American and poor families.[116]

The Community Relations Commission offered temporary solutions to problems that affected minority and low-income neighborhoods. By performing the functions of a grievance committee, a fact-finding agency, and a mediator, the Commission gained the confidence of low-income residents and demonstrated the city's concerns about providing services to low-income areas. In this manner, the Commission helped to abate racial tensions in the city. It did not, however, offer solutions or initiate programs that met the long-term problems of minority and low-income residents.

The inability or unwillingness of municipal officials or agencies to address these problems forced community leaders and organizations to deal with racial issues. One of these issues was racial transition. Due to the deterioration of living conditions in many African American neighborhoods and the desire for better housing, many middle-class African American families moved to formerly all-white neighborhoods. In 1967 neighborhood organizations in Vine City criticized middle-class leaders for leaving rather than fighting for better housing conditions and schools. In the past, racial transition often led to violence between white and African American residents. Many argued that the transition from white to African American occupancy merely extended slum areas. Community leaders realized that new solutions to this problem were needed.

Throughout the 1960s, neighborhoods in Southwest Atlanta were undergoing racial transition. In 1967 residents in Cascade Heights, a community in Southwest Atlanta, formed Southwest Atlantans for Progress (SWAP) to deal with this issue. While Cascade Heights was still predominately a white community, African American residents were beginning to move into the area. The goal of SWAP was to maintain Cascade Heights as an integrated community. SWAP sponsored public forums in which white and African American residents were encouraged to express their fears, animosities, and anxieties. Members believed that harmonious race relations could be achieved through discussions between white and African American residents and a sense of communal pride. The main argument presented to white residents was that the African Americans who were moving into the area had the same social, economic, and educational status. According to SWAP leaders, Cascade Heights would still be regarded as a middle-class neighborhood.

SWAP members faced several obstacles in trying to maintain an integrated community. As African Americans moved into the area, white residents began to receive phone calls and letters from real estate agents wanting to assist them in the sale of their homes. Some realtors informed residents that their neighborhood was now in "transition." "For Sale" signs began to dot Southwest Atlanta. In an attempt to halt panic selling, SWAP members convinced the Board of Aldermen to pass an ordinance regulating the use of "for sale" signs. Members also successfully lobbied state and local officials for the passage of an open occupancy law. Federal laws prohibiting housing discrimination were enacted in 1968.[117]

Efforts by SWAP to maintain an integrated community were unsuccessful. By 1969 most of the transitional areas in Southwest Atlanta were predominately African American. SWAP's example, however, inspired the formation of several small groups in white neighborhoods across the city. The activities of these organizations ranged from informing residents on the provisions of federal open housing laws to urging white residents to accept African Americans as neighbors. Without active help from municipal agencies and officials, most of these efforts, like that of SWAP, were unsuccessful.[118]

Racial issues and tensions were temporarily set aside when Martin Luther King, Jr. was assassinated in Memphis in April 1968. While riots occurred in Baltimore, Chicago, Washington, D.C., and elsewhere in the nation, Atlanta was peaceful. City officials had anticipated violence in some form. A march by students from Atlanta University, however, was peaceful and orderly.

A survey measuring the reactions of Atlantans to the death of Martin Luther King, Jr. found the dominant response of African Americans to be emotional, yet immediately hopeful. Of those African American respondents who said that their racial attitudes had been changed by the death of Reverend King (forty percent), twenty-eight percent stated that their attitudes were "better." The majority of African American respondents believed that the racial attitudes of whites would be "better" as a result of King's assassination; that discrimination and inequality would be ameliorated through nonviolence; and that the upcoming Poor People's March on Washington would benefit the poor. The survey noted that an unanimity in response existed among African Americans that was not present among white responses.

The majority of white Atlantans reacted differently to the assassination of King, and they also had different expectations about the course of race relations in the United States. Approximately eighty-four percent of white respondents stated that the death of King had no effects upon their racial attitudes. Less than one-third believed that King's assassination would improve the racial attitudes of other white citizens. In general, white respondents did not believe that the philosophy of nonviolence would prevail, and that the Poor People's March on Washington would be ineffective. Respondents from a higher socioeconomic status tended to be more positive in their racial attitudes and their expectations about the course of race relations.[119] Undoubtedly, the shock of Reverend King's assassination and the riots and racial disturbances that were occurring across the nation influenced the responses of both white and African American residents.

Hope was all many residents in low-income neighborhoods had. The quality of residential life in the slum areas of the city did not improve during the 1960s. Municipal and federal programs had only a limited impact. Several reasons accounted for this lack of success. City officials failed, for example, to initiate and maintain the actions and programs necessary for neighborhood redevelopment. Overt conflict pressured the Allen administration to undertake many municipal programs. When this pressure was not maintained over a period of time, city leaders lost interest. The main priorities of Atlanta's urban renewal program were economic growth and the revitalization of the downtown business district, not poverty and neighborhood redevelopment. City officials continued to stress economic growth as the solution to poverty. Due to the Vietnam War and a conservative backlash against the Great Society programs, federal funding for projects such as Model Cities was curtailed. African American leaders and organizations failed to develop a cohesive strategy to attack poverty in the city. Rivalries and competition between neighborhood and human relations organizations prevented the formation of a united front. For these reasons and others, the slum areas of the city remained forgotten communities.

Notes

1.   Judy Welborn, "The South Atlanta Project - SNCC, 1963," SNCC Papers, A=XV=47, Woodruff Library, Atlanta University, Atlanta, Georgia.

2.   Research Atlanta, *Which Way Atlanta?* (Atlanta: Research Atlanta, Inc., 1973), pp. 9–11, 16.

3.   Donald S. Bradley, "Back to the City," in *Urban Atlanta: Redefining the Role of the City*, ed. Andrew Marshall Hamer (Atlanta: Georgia State University Press, 1980), p. 115.

4.   During the late 1960s and early 1970s, white middle-class income families began moving into a string of communities extending east from the central business district to the city limits. These communities included Ansley Park, Morningside, Midtown, Virginia-Highlands, Inman Park, Candler Park, and Grant Park.

5.   Georgia State Advisory Committee to the U.S. Commission on Civil Rights, *Toward Equal Opportunity in Housing in Atlanta, Georgia* (Washington: Government Printing Office, 1968), p. 8.

6.   Ibid., p. 6.

7.   Leon S. Eplan, address, "Background Remarks before the Metropolitan Atlanta Conference on Equality of Opportunity in Housing," 29 May 1968, transcript, p. 5, Southern Regional Council Papers, 9:201:19, Woodruff Library, Atlanta University, Atlanta, Georgia.

8.   Quoted in "Atlanta Housing, A Program to Achieve Equal Opportunity in Atlanta, Section II and III," Southern Regional Council Papers, 3:111:402.

9.   While Atlanta had no laws enforcing residential segregation, it was maintained through custom and agreements between white and African American leaders.

10.   James W. Harris, "This is Our Home: It is Not for Sale," (Senior thesis, Princeton University, 1971), p. 37.

11.   Smith-Hughes was desegregated in 1963. Atlanta Committee for Cooperative Action and Greater Atlanta Council on Human Relations, "The Negro and Employment Opportunities in the South: Atlanta," (Atlanta, 1963), pp. 2–3.

12.   Welborn, "The South Atlanta Project - SNCC, 1963."

13. SNCC staff, "South Atlanta Project - Critical Analysis," 18 August 1963, SNCC Papers, A=XV=47; and *Atlanta Inquirer*, 10 August 1963.

14. Southeast Atlanta Civic Council, *The City Must Provide, South Atlanta: The Forgotten Community*, (Atlanta, Georgia, 1963), SNCC Papers, A=XV=47; and Debbie Amis, "Report from SE Atlanta," October 1963, SNCC Papers, A=XV=48.

15. Amis, "Report from SE Atlanta;" SNCC staff, "A Proposal for a Voter Education Project - Southeast Atlanta," 1 September 1963, SNCC Papers, A=XV=48.

16. SNCC staff, "A Proposal for a Voter Education Project - Southeast Atlanta;" and Vernon E. Jordan, Jr., Memorandum to Leslie W. Dunbar, 18 September 1964, p. 5, Grace Towns Hamilton Papers, Box: 10, Folder: 4, Woodruff Library, Atlanta University, Atlanta, Georgia.

17. Jordan, Memorandum, p. 1.

18. Ibid., p. 7.

19. Jack Minnis, Memorandum to Wiley Branton, 12 September 1963, Southern Regional Council Papers, 6:179:203; and Jack Minnis, Memorandum to Wiley Branton, 11 October 1963, Southern Regional Council Papers, 6:179:203.

20. Jordan, Memorandum, pp. 5–7.

21. Jesse Hill, Letter to Wiley Branton, 17 December 1963, Southern Regional Council Papers, 6:179:203.

22. Debbie Amis, "Atlanta," 16 December 1963, SNCC Papers, A=XV=42.

23. Ibid.

24. Amis, "Report from SE Atlanta."

25. Southeast Atlanta Civic Council, p. 1.

26. Jesse Hill, Letter to Mayor William Hartsfield, 27 May 1959, Eliza Paschall Papers, GCEEO file, Box: 17, Woodruff Library, Emory University, Atlanta, Georgia.

27. The Atlanta Board of Aldermen denied this request. Summit Leadership Conference, Letter to Mayor Allen, Vice-Mayor Sam Massell, and the Board of Aldermen, 4 April 1964, Eliza Paschall Papers, SLC file, Box: 15.

28. Carl Sutherland, Letter to Eliza Paschall, 4 December 1962, Eliza Paschall Papers, Box: 2; and Ivan Allen, Jr. with Paul Hemphill, *Mayor: Notes on the Sixties* (New York: Simon and Schuster, 1971), pp. 84–85.

29.   Alton Hornsby, "Blacks in Atlanta Politics, 1961–1973," *Atlanta Historical Bulletin*, XXI (Spring, 1977): 17–18.

30.   Georgia Council on Human Relations, "Opening the Door to Employment," Southern Regional Council Papers, 3:112:103, pp. 3–5; Ralph Abernathy, *And the Walls Came Tumbling Down: An Autobiography* (New York: Harper and Row, 1989), pp. 401–405; and David Garrow, *Bearing the Cross: Martin Luther King, Jr. and the Southern Christian Leadership Conference* (New York: William Morrow and Company, 1986), p. 223.

31.   Ralph Abernathy, Letters to "Ministers:" 12 September 1963, 27 March 1963, 4 April 1963, 10 October 1963, 21 November 1963, 21 January 1964, and 25 August 1964, Eliza Paschall Papers, "Negro Ministers of Atlanta" File, Box: 22; *Atlanta Inquirer*, 30 October 1965; and Garrow, p. 223.

32.   Carl M. Brauer, *John F. Kennedy and the Second Reconstruction* (New York: Columbia University Press, 1977), pp. 79–84, 147–151, 214–216; and Pat Watters, *The South and the Nation* (New York: Pantheon, 1969); pp. 142–143.

33.   After the Supreme Court ruled that restrictive covenants were legally unenforceable (1948), the Federal Housing Administration removed these statements from the manual in 1950. Quoted in John Hope Franklin, *From Slavery to Freedom: A History of Negro Americans*, fifth ed. (New York: Alfred A. Knopf, 1980), p. 478.

34.   Greater Atlanta Council on Human Relations, "The Public Housing Program in Atlanta," 19 March 1959, Southern Regional Council Papers, 4:143:296.

35.   Brauer, pp. 202–211.

36.   In July 1967 federal officials requested local housing authorities to assign tenants on the basis of "first come, first serve." Georgia State Advisory Committee to U.S. Commission on Civil Rights, pp. 8–10, 28.

37.   In the summer of 1963, Students for a Democratic Society organized the Economic Reach and Action Program (ERAP) in order to mobilize poor whites around issues that affected them and provide these citizens with the means to express their grievances. They began projects in eight northern and border cities. While the original purpose of ERAP was to work primarily with white residents, many of these projects were located in African American slum neighborhoods. Critics of CAPs argued that

these types of "radical" programs and organizations could receive federal funding and capture control of the anti-poverty effort in these cities. ERAP projects were funded through a $7,500 working grant from the United Automobile Workers and private donations.

38. For a discussion of Johnson's Great Society program, see John Morton Blum, *Years of Discord: American Politics and Society, 1961–1974* (New York: Norton and Company, 1991), pp. 162–187, 267–270; Vaughn Davis Bornet, *The Presidency of Lyndon Johnson* (Lawrence: University of Kansas Press, 1983), pp. 101–103, 249–250, 341–342; Barbara Jordan and Elspeth D. Rostow, eds., *The Great Society: A Twenty Year Critique* (Austin: The University of Texas, 1986); and James T. Patterson, *America's Struggle Against Poverty, 1900–1985* (Cambridge: Harvard University Press, 1986), pp. 126–170.

39. Allen with Hemphill, pp. 150–152; and Clarence Stone, *Regime Politics: Governing Atlanta, 1946–1988* (Lawrence: University of Kansas Press, 1989), pp. 67–68.

40. *Atlanta Constitution*, 25 July – 3 August 1965.

41. The governing board of the EOA was mainly composed of white "progressive" business and social leaders who had close ties to the white leadership of the city. The petition was rejected by EOA leaders who defended the agency's program and employment practices.

42. *Atlanta Constitution*, 1 June 1965; *Atlanta Inquirer*, 19 June 1965; Eliza Paschall, Letter to the Director of Public Relations, H.G. Hastings Seed Company, Eliza Paschall Papers, Vine City Project file, Box: 26; Minutes from meeting of 26 March 1965 of Vine City Improvement Association, Eliza Paschall Papers, "Notes 197–212" file, Box: 34; Greater Atlanta Council on Human Relations, "Report on Vine City Project," 25 April 1965, Eliza Paschall Papers, "Notes 197–212" file, Box: 34; Southern Regional Council, "A City-Slum People and Problems: A Special Report on an Attempt to Build a Community Organization Around Local Self-Interest Issues in a Southern City," Eliza Paschall Papers, SRC file, Box: 24; and Vine City Project, "Vine City: An Experiment in Self-Help," leaflet, Eliza Paschall Papers, "Notes 197–212" file, Box: 34.

43. Following this "play-in," the city built two new playgrounds in the area. Municipal officials denied that this construction was due to the protest.

44. Hector Black, Letter to Eliza Paschall, 18 September 1966, Eliza Paschall Papers, Vine City Project file, Box: 26; Hector Black, Letter to Reverend Jones of the Vine City Improvement Association, Southern Regional Council Papers, 1:64:1989; Vine City Improvement Association, "Statement Distributed at a meeting on July 11, 1966 at Cosmopolitan AME Church," Southern Regional Council Papers, 1:64:1989; Southern Regional Council, "A City-Slum People and Problems," p. 16; "Hector Black, White Power in Black Atlanta," *Look*, (13 December 1966): 137–140; and "White Jesus, Hector Black, Vine City, and SNCC," *Newsweek*, (25 June 1966): 29.

45. McGill was concerned that funds and personnel from the Voter Education Project and the Southern Regional Council were being used by Helen Hunt who was running for a seat in the state legislature currently held by Grace Hamilton. The Vine City Council supported Helen Hunt; McGill was a friend and supporter of Grace Hamilton. McGill heard from residents in the community that young African Americans were being "given spiked punch, unlabeled cigarettes, and taught to turn over automobiles" by members of the Vine City Council. All of these allegations were false. Ralph McGill, Letter to Mr. Charles Hardin (copies of this letter were sent to Police Chief Herbert Jenkins and Jack Tarver), 6 July 1966, Ralph McGill Papers, File: 1, Box: 71, Woodruff Library, Emory University, Atlanta, Georgia; Ralph McGill, Letter to Paul Anthony 6 July 1966, Ralph McGill Papers, File: 1, Box: 71; and Paul Anthony, Letter to Ralph McGill, 7 July 1966, Ralph McGill Papers, File: 1, Box: 71.

46. Ralph McGill, Memorandum to Bill Shipp, 7 July 1965, Ralph McGill Papers, File: 1, Box: 71.

47. Hector Black was found innocent of trespassing charges in February 1966. Atlanta Project staff, "Atlanta Project Proposal to the New York Office," 22 January 1966, SNCC Papers, A=XV=45, pp. 13–15; and Clarence Stone, *Economic Growth and Neighborhood Discontent: System Bias in the Urban Renewal Program of Atlanta* (Chapel Hill: UNC Press, 1976), pp. 121–122.

48. Atlanta Project staff, "Background of the Atlanta Project," SNCC Papers, A=XV=42, pp. 4–5.

49. Atlanta Project staff, "Day-to-Day Account of Events in the Markham Area During the Past Week," 7 February 1966, SNCC Papers, A=XV=41; SNCC Press Release, 31 January 1966, SNCC Papers, A=XV=41; and Stone, *Economic*, pp. 123–125.

50.   Atlanta Project staff, "Atlanta Project Proposal to the New York City Office," p. 14; and Stone, *Economic*, p. 122.

51.   Atlanta Project staff, "Atlanta Project Proposal to the New York Office," pp. 15–25; SNCC News Release, 9 February 1965, SNCC Papers, A=VII=105; *Atlanta Constitution*, 5 February 1966; and "Movement on Markham Street," *Nitty Gritty*, 23 February 1966, p. 3.

52.   Clayborne Carson, *In Struggle: SNCC and the Black Awakening of the 1960s* (Cambridge: Harvard University Press, 1981), pp. 166–168; Sharon Mullis, "The Public Career of Grace Towns Hamilton: A Citizen too Busy to Hate" (Ph.D. dissertation, Emory University, 1976), pp. 224–228; John Neary, *Julian Bond: Black Rebel* (New York: William Morrow, 1971), pp. 77–87; and Roger Williams, *The Bonds: An American Family* (New York: Athenaeum, 1971), pp. 216–218.

53.   Quoted in Carson, *In Struggle*, p. 188.

54.   ACLU of Georgia Newsletter, January 1966, p. 1; and Neary, p. 102.

55.   SNCC staff, "Julian Bond Fact Sheet," January 1966, SNCC Papers, A=VIII=173; and Neary, p. 102.

56.   This strategy meeting occurred at the home of Senator LeRoy Johnson. Those present included Julian Bond, Ivanhoe Donaldson, Charles Cobb, James Forman, Donald L. Hollowell, Dr. Samuel DuBois Cook; and Howard Moore. Author's Interview with LeRoy Johnson, 13 November 1990; James Forman, "Report in regards to his meeting with eight Negro representatives from the state of Georgia, and Senators Ward and Johnson," 10 January 1966, SNCC Papers, A=VIII=173; Neary, pp. 105–107; and Williams, pp. 224–225.

57.   The Georgia House Rules Committee was expanded to include two of the newly elected African American representatives.

58.   One of the two African American legislators claimed that his automatic vote recorder did not function. ACLU of Georgia Newsletter, p. 2; Neary, pp. 108–124; and Williams, pp. 227–229.

59.   Martin Luther King, Jr., Statement in support of Julian Bond, 12 January 1966, SNCC Papers, A=VIII=173.

60.   "Negroes Support Bond Seat, but Oppose SNCC Vietnam View," *Atlanta Inquirer*, 15 January 1967; "U.S. Court Upholds House on Bond, Cites Right to Bar Him in 2–1 Ruling," *Atlanta Constitution*, 11 February 1966; "High Court Issues Rebuff to Ga. In Bond Case," *Atlanta Inquirer*,

19 November 1966; "Bond is Seated," *Atlanta Constitution*, 6 December 1966; Neary, pp. 125–147; and Williams, pp. 230–232.

61.   Atlanta Project staff, "Proposal to the New York Office," pp. 1–4; and Carson, pp. 192–193.

62.   Atlanta Project staff, "Prospectus for an Atlanta Project," SNCC Papers, A=XV=45.

63.   Atlanta Project staff, "The *Nitty Gritty* - The Reasons Why," SNCC Papers, A=XV=42.

64.   Carson, pp. 193–200.

65.   Atlanta Project staff, "The *Nitty Gritty* - The Reasons Why;" and *Nitty Gritty*, 23 February 1963, p. 1.

66.   Atlanta Project staff, "Proposal to the New York Office," pp. 13–25; and Atlanta Project staff, "Chronology of the One-Hour Valet Movement," SNCC Papers, A=XV=45.

67.   Atlanta Project staff, "Atlanta's Black Paper," 25 August 1966; and Carson, p. 239.

68.   Carson, pp. 238–241.

69.   Mary Frances Berry, *Black Resistance, White Law: A History of Constitutional Racism in America* (Englewood Cliffs: Prentice Hall, 1971), pp. 211, 213.

70.   Allen with Hemphill, pp. 181–182.

71.   Allen with Hemphill, pp. 179–180; and Chet Fuller, "Black Belt: The Abandoned South," part 5, *Atlanta Constitution*, 20 November 1986, p. 10a.

72.   Community Council of the Atlanta Area, "Interim Report Number 1: Social Blight and Its Causes," (Atlanta, February 1966).

73.   Stone, *Economic*, pp. 117, 119–121.

74.   Atlanta Project staff, "Atlanta: A Special Report," September 1966, SNCC Papers, A=XV=42, pp. 1–2; Lawrence Goldman, "The Atlanta Demonstrations: An Analysis," Eliza Paschall Papers, "Notes 323–329" File, Box: 34; *The Southern Patriot*, October 1966; and Allen with Hemphill, pp. 182–191.

75.   Author's Interview with Ivan Allen, Jr., 7 November 1990; and Allen with Hemphill, p. 191.

76.   Quoted in Goldman, p. 7.

77.   *Atlanta Constitution*, 8 September 1966, p. 1.

78.   Ibid., p. 4.

79. Quoted in Paul Good, "Out to Get SNCC: A Tale of Two Cities," *Nation* (21 November 1966): 538.

80. Carson, p. 226.

81. Atlanta Project staff, "Uncle Toms and Dr. Thomas' Statements about the Riot and about SNCC and Stokley Carmichael," September 1966, SNCC Papers A=XV=40.

82. Goldman, p. 16.

83. Bond stated that his resignation was due to his inability to financially support his family on SNCC's salary. He claimed that his resignation was not due to the racial disturbances or any disagreement with SNCC policies.

84. Quoted in Good, p. 537.

85. "Stokley's Spark," *Time*, (16 September 1966): 37.

86. Atlanta Council on Human Relations, Statement on the Disburbances, 9 September 1966, in Eliza Paschall, *It Must Have Rained* (Atlanta: Emory University, 1975), pp. 158–160; and *Atlanta Daily World*, 11 September 1966.

87. The letter was signed by representatives of the Southern Regional Council, Anti-Defamation of B'nai B'rith, NAACP, American Friends Service Committee, National Conference of Christians and Jews, United Presbyterian Church USA, Episcopal Society for Cultural and Racial Unity, American Jewish Committee, Anti-Poverty Task Force, Citizens Crusade Against Poverty, SCLC, Southern Student Organizing Committee, Georgia Council on Human Relations, and Georgia ACLU. The staffs of intergroup relations agencies in Atlanta, Letter to Mayor Ivan Allen, Jr., 9 September 1966, Southern Regional Council Papers, 1:4:80.

88. Atlanta Project staff, "Atlanta," p. 7; *Atlanta Daily World*, 10 September 1966; and Carson, p. 226.

89. The driver of the first ambulance said that he did not see the wounded youths. The white motorist who shot the youths was quickly apprehended.

90. Atlanta Project staff, "Atlanta," p. 9; Goldman, pp. 16–22; *Atlanta Daily World*, 14 September 1966; and *Atlanta Inquirer*, 17 September 1966.

91. Otis Cochran, "Confidential Report No. 1," 21 April 1967, Eliza Paschall Papers, HRC files, Box: 11.

92. Author's Interview with Reverend Austin Ford, 3 December 1990.

93.   Author's Interview with Cecil Alexander, 9 March 1991; and Stone, *Economic*, pp. 127–129.

94.   *Atlanta Constitution*, 18 August 1974.

95.   *Atlanta Constitution*, 18 August 1974; Georgia State Advisory Committee to the U.S. Commission on Civil Rights, pp. 11–13; and Stone, *Economic*, pp. 131–132.

96.   Author's Interview with Reverend Austin Ford.

97.   William Hartsfield, Letter to Harold Fleming, 7 June 1960, Southern Regional Council Papers, 1:33:1158; and *Southern School News*, June 1960, p. 16.

98.   Ivan Allen, Jr., "Statement before the Committee Regarding S1732 Bill to Eliminate Discrimination in Public Accommodations Affecting Interstate Commerce," p. 7, 26 July 1963, Southern Regional Council Papers, 3:110:4.

99.   Author's Interview with Sam Massell, 3 December 1990; Author's Interview with Benny T. Smith, 12 December 1990; Eliza Paschall, address, "History of CRC's Establishment," Hungry Club, 1 November 1967, Eliza Paschall Papers, Community Relations Commission file, Box: 11; and Anne Rivers Siddons, "The Seeds of Sanity," *Atlanta Magazine*, (July 1967): 55–56.

100.   "Background on the Establishment of the Community Relations Commission," 30 November 1966, Eliza Paschall Papers, note files, Box: 34; and William Boone, "The Atlanta Community Relations Commission" (Ph.D. dissertation, Atlanta University, 1969), pp. 13–15.

101.   1966 Ordinance to establish the Community Relations Commission, 8 November 1966 (approved), Eliza Paschall Papers, Community Relations Commission file, Box: 11.

102.   Author's Interviews with Allen, Massell, and Smith; and Boone, pp. 19–20.

103.   Helen Bullard, "Report of the Program Committee," 20 January 1967, Eliza Paschall Papers, Community Relations Commission file, Box: 11; *Atlanta Daily World*, 28 January 1967; Boone, pp. 37–38; and Siddons, pp. 56–57, 104.

104.   Author's Interview with LeRoy Johnson; Community Relations Commission, "Report on Dixie Hills," Eliza Paschall Papers, Community Relations Commission file, Box: 11; *Atlanta Constitution*, 20 June 1967; Fred Crawford, *Civil Aggression and Urban Disorders* (Atlanta: Emory

University, 1967), pp. 11–13, chronology; and James Holloway, "The Paradigm of Dixie Hills," *New South*, (Summer 1967): 75–81.

105. "Minutes of the Community Relations Commission Hearing in Dixie Hills Area," 23 June 1967, Eliza Paschall Papers, Community Relations Community file, Box: 11.

106. Crawford, chronology.

107. Eliza Paschall, Letter to *New York Times Magazine*, 6 October, 1968, Eliza Paschall Papers, "Correspondence 1963–1968 file, Box: 28.

108. *Atlanta Inquirer*, 1 July 1967; *Atlanta Constitution*, 1 July 1967; *Atlanta Inquirer*, 23 November 1968; and Boone, pp. 46–47.

109. "Report by the Community Relations Commission," 4 October 1967, Eliza Paschall Papers, Community Relations Commission file, Box: 11; and Boone, pp. 70–71.

110. The Atlanta Freedom Coalition was an umbrella organization formed specifically to address problems in African American schools. Members of this coalition included SCLC, NAACP, Operation Breadbasket, the Summit Leadership Conference, and other local and neighborhood organizations. "Press Release of the Atlanta Freedom Coalition," 26 September 1967, Eliza Paschall Papers, Box: 14.

111. *Atlanta Journal*, 16 November 1967; National Education Association, National Commission on Professional Rights and Responsibilities, *Central Issues Influencing School-Community Relations in Atlanta, Georgia* (NEA, 1969), p. 23; and Joseph Baird, "Atlanta Negroes Rock the Boat," *Reporter*, (14 December 1967): 33–34.

112. National Education Association, National Commission on Professional Rights and Responsibilities, p. 24.

113. Metropolitan Atlanta Summit Leadership Congress, "First Annual Meeting of the Atlanta Metropolitan Summit Leadership Congress," (Atlanta: MASLC, 1969); and Metropolitan Atlanta Summit Leadership Congress Press Release, 22 April 1968, Eliza Paschall Papers, MASLC file, Box 22.

114. Boone, pp. 107–114.

115. Better Schools Atlanta Press Release, 9 October 1968, Southern Regional Council Papers, 1:39:1329; Deposition of Robert Truve for the *Calhoun v. Cook* case, 25 April 1969, Southern Regional Council Papers, 1:5:99; and National Education Association, National Commission on Professional Rights and Responsibilities, p. 25.

116. National Education Association, National Commission on Professional Rights and Responsibilities, pp. 25–27; and Boone, p. 68.

117. Author's Interview with Xernona Clayton, 14 December 1990; Xernona Clayton with Hal Gulliver, *I've Been Marching All the Time: An Autobiography* (Atlanta: Longstreet Press, 1991), pp. 142–145; Georgia State Advisory Commission to U.S. Commission on Civil Rights, p. 22; and Claudia Turner, "Changing Residential Patterns in Southwest Atlanta from 1960 to 1970," (Master's thesis, Atlanta University, 1970), pp. 11, 24.

118. Harris, pp. 44–47.

119. Fred R. Crawford, Norman R. Crawford, and Leah Dabbs, *A Report of Certain Reactions by the Atlanta Public to the Death of Martin Luther King, Jr.* (Atlanta: Emory University, 1969).

VI

The Transition from White to African American Political Power in Atlanta

In 1969 Ivan Allen, Jr. announced that he would not seek a third term as mayor and would not formally endorse any candidate to succeed him. After this announcement, a delegation of African American leaders including Martin Luther King, Sr., Reverend Sam Williams, Jesse Hill, and Senator LeRoy Johnson met with the mayor. These leaders expressed their interest in maintaining a political alliance between the African American community and the business-civic leadership of the city. The delegation requested Allen to serve as a liaison between the two groups.[1]

This coalition, however, was not the same one that elected Allen in 1961 and 1965. The internal dynamics of the alliance had changed. During the 1960s, the center of political power shifted from the business-civic leadership toward the African American community. In 1965 Q.V. Williamson, an African American realtor, became the city's first black alderman since Reconstruction. Although white registration was slightly larger in his district, Horace Ward, an African American attorney, defeated the white president of the Board of Education in the Democratic primary and a white Republican opponent in the general election to become the second African American elected to the state senate. Following reapportionment, eight African Americans in the Atlanta area won seats in the state house. This shift in political power was basically due to an increase in Atlanta's black population and voter registration. By 1969 African Americans comprised forty-nine percent of Atlanta's population and forty-one percent of the city's registered voters.[2] African American leaders anticipated gaining seats on the Board of Aldermen and Board of Education in the upcoming municipal elections.

The voice of Atlanta's African American community began to be heard on several issues facing the city. Fearing that the expansion of the city would dilute the voting strength of the black community, African American legislators successfully blocked the passage of annexation legislation. African American leaders, parents, and neighborhood organizations began to place enormous pressure on the Board of Education to negotiate a settlement to the school desegregation suit. While unsuccessful in achieving all of their goals, the city's garbage collectors, most of whom were African American, went on strike in 1968 to protest low wages and poor working conditions. In 1969 African American firemen protested the department's discriminatory employment practices. The African American community now had the political power to place many of these concerns upon the city's political agenda.

The delegation of African American leaders that approached Allen wanted the black community to have a greater voice in selecting the coalition's mayoral candidate. Learning that white business support was beginning to consolidate around the anticipated candidacy of Rodney Cook, a white alderman and state representative, this informal group arranged a second meeting with Allen. The leaders informed the mayor that they would not support Cook under any circumstances. Allen urged the leaders to discuss Cook's potential candidacy with business leaders, but the delegation remained adamant in its position.[3]

Following these meetings, African American leaders began to discuss the possibility of a black candidate for mayor. They drew encouragement from the strong showing that Tom Bradley, an African American ex-policeman and councilman, made against incumbent Sam Yorty in the Los Angeles mayoral primary. Even though only a relatively small percentage of Los Angeles' population was African American, Bradley won the primary with forty-two percent of the vote (In a bitter runoff, Sam Yorty soundly defeated Tom Bradley).[4] In order for an African American candidate to win in Atlanta, he would have to win the overwhelming support of the African American community and be moderate enough on racial issues to win the support of white voters.

The three most frequently mentioned names as possible African American candidates for mayor were LeRoy Johnson, Maynard Jackson, and Vernon Jordan, Jr. Each candidate had strengths and weaknesses. Since 1962 LeRoy Johnson had served in the state senate. As an active member of the Atlanta Negro Voters League, the Fulton County Citizens Democratic Club, ACCA, the Summit Leadership Conference, and other local groups and organizations, he was an established African American leader. His moderate stances on racial issues would win support from the white community. He was hesitant, however, to enter a contest in which he thought that no African American candidate had a chance of winning.[5] Many younger and more militant African American leaders distrusted Johnson. Among these leaders, he had a reputation as a "political wheeler dealer" who would compromise on issues in order to enhance his own status.

Maynard Jackson, an African American attorney, was a descendant of two prominent middle-class families in Atlanta. His maternal grandfather was John Wesley Dobbs. His father, Maynard Holbrook Jackson, Sr., served as pastor of Friendship Baptist Church. Several of his family members were prominent educators at leading African American schools. His aunt was the opera singer Mattiwilda Dobbs. Shocked by the assassinations of Martin Luther King, Jr. and Robert Kennedy in 1968, he announced his candidacy for the United States Senate seat occupied by Herman Talmadge. While losing to Talmadge by a three-to-one margin, he carried the city of Atlanta by six thousand votes.[6] Many conservative leaders believed that Jackson, only thirty-one, was too politically ambitious and inexperienced to run for mayor. They felt that he was not deferential to the black community's traditional leadership. Before making political decisions such as running for the senate, he failed to consult with established leaders. In March 1969 Jackson announced that he was going to run for vice-mayor.

Many leaders cited Vernon Jordan, Jr., an African American attorney, as a possible candidate who could unite the various factions within the African American community and win support from white voters. Between 1961 and 1963, Jordan served as field director for the state NAACP branch. In 1965 he succeeded Wiley Branton as director of the Voter Education Project. He was considered a "rising star" within the community. While respected among African American and white leaders, he was less known to the mass public. Early in 1969 rumors circulated that Jordan was considering a bid for vice-mayor or a seat on the Board of Aldermen. Even many of his supporters, however, questioned whether Jordan had the desire to enter the political arena.[7]

Most African American leaders believed that a black candidate could not win under any circumstances, particularly if two African American candidates ran and split the African American vote. Many also believed that white citizens would not vote for both a black mayor and vice-mayor. Since Jackson was running for vice-mayor, most leaders felt that an African American should not run for mayor. For these reasons, Johnson, potentially the strongest African American candidate, was hesitant to run. Only one African American leader, Horace Tate, expressed a desire and willingness to make a mayoral bid. Tate, an educator, was a member of the Atlanta

Board of Education and executive secretary of the Georgia Teachers and Education Association (GTEA), a predominately African American teachers' organization. In early April, Johnson held a series of meetings with African American leaders in order to gauge their reactions to a black candidate. During this period, he met with Tate. Johnson thought that an understanding had been reached between leaders that no African American would run for mayor.[8] Following his meeting with Johnson, however, Tate announced his candidacy.

Members of the business-civic leadership were also discussing potential candidates for mayor. An early favorite was Charles Weltner, the former United States Congressman. In 1966 Weltner withdrew from his re-election bid rather than support Lester Maddox, the party's gubernatorial candidate.[9] Early in 1969, Weltner announced that he would not run for mayor. Other possible candidates mentioned were John Wilson, the incoming president of the Chamber of Commerce; Henry Bowden, the city attorney; and Rawson Haverty, a prominent businessman.[10]

Eventually, business support began to consolidate around Rodney Cook, a city alderman and state legislator. Cook, a Republican, believed that the Republican Party could increase its southern membership by appealing to African American voters. As an alderman and state legislator, Cook attacked the problems of low-income housing and slum clearance, and addressed other matters of importance to African American citizens. In 1962 he was one of the few aldermen to vote against the Peyton Wall barrier.

Prior to 1969, Cook generally won the support of the African American community. In his bids for alderman and state representative, Cook won nearly half of the votes cast by African American citizens. In his 1965 re-election bid to the Board of Aldermen, he won almost ninety percent of the African American vote. However, in his 1968 re-election bid to the state legislature, he won only thirty percent of the black vote. Local commentators and Cook argued that this poor showing was due to his party affiliation. In this presidential election year, Richard Nixon and Spiro Agnew headed the national ticket. Atlanta's African American community voted overwhelmingly for Hubert Humphrey, the Democratic nominee. By this time, Cook had also parted with the African American community on several key issues. During the mid-1960s, Cook introduced legislation to annex Sandy Springs, a white middle-class community. Many African American leaders viewed this legislation as an attempt to dilute the influence of the African American vote in Atlanta. In 1968 he opposed the selection of Jesse Hill to the State Highway Board. Cook also voted against the creation of a new, predominately African American ninth ward in the city. African American leaders criticized these actions.[11]

In addition to Cook, Sam Massell entered the race for mayor. For eight years, Massell had served as the city's vice-mayor. During this time, he had a record of consistently supporting measures favored by the African American community and labor. He developed close ties with African American and labor leaders. For this reason and possibly due to prejudice against his Jewish heritage, many business leaders distrusted Massell. While he claimed the mantle of past administrations, he did not have the support of the business-civic leadership.

Everett Millican, an alderman and former state legislator, entered the race as the "law-and-order candidate." He attacked the city's high crime rate and Atlanta's growing "hippie" colony. Concerned about municipal spending on social and redevelopment programs, Millican stressed financial stability. Because of his long ties to the business community, Millican expected its endorsement. When this support did not materialize, he began to criticize the business-civic leadership. His main base of support was the white, lower-class neighborhoods on the south side of the city. He did extremely well, however, in other white sections of Atlanta. Millican did not actively campaign in the African American community.[12]

With four major candidates in the race, no one expected a majority of the votes in the general election. Since a runoff was almost inevitable, the goal of each candidate was to obtain enough votes to avoid elimination. Whoever forged the most effective coalition would win. Since African Americans comprised forty-one percent of the city's registered voters, African American support, as in the past, would be crucial in determining the outcome of the election.

Sam Massell and Horace Tate especially needed that African American support. The Massell campaign distributed literature suggesting that an African American candidate could not be elected mayor; a vote for Tate was thus a wasted ballot and would lead to the election of conservative Everett Millican. Even though the mayoral election was a nonpartisan contest, Massell portrayed himself as a liberal Democrat while campaigning in the African American community. He constantly reminded his African American audiences that Cook was a member of the Republican Party.[13]

Horace Tate had to win overwhelming support from the African American community. Because Sam Massell had some support within the white community, a split in the black vote would work to his advantage. Tate had to alleviate fears that an African American candidate could not win. He largely confined his activities to the African American community.

His campaign headquarters was located in the Georgia Teachers and Education Building in an African American residential neighborhood. Tate's campaign largely depended upon the financial support of African American businessmen.

The contest between Massell and Tate divided the leadership of the African American community. Younger and more militant leaders supported Tate. He won the endorsements of the Metropolitan Atlanta Summit Leadership Congress (MASLC), SCLC, and small neighborhood organizations. Several well-known African American leaders delayed their endorsements until only days before the election. Local leaders who were also actively involved in the national movement for civil rights such as Coretta Scott King, Reverend Ralph Abernathy, and Julian Bond endorsed Horace Tate while local established leaders generally supported Massell, who won the backing of the Summit Leadership Conference and the *Inquirer*. Established leaders questioned whether an African American candidate could win. An extremely small number of conservative leaders backed Cook.[14]

While he campaigned in the African American community, Cook received little backing. His main base of support was white, middle-to-upper income neighborhoods. He also received considerable support in low-income areas of the city and won the endorsements of the local white dailies. Within the white community, Massell formed an effective coalition comprising Jewish residents, liberals, and union members. Tate had almost no support within the white community.

In the general election, Massell won thirty-one percent of the total votes cast. Cook finished second with twenty-seven percent of the vote. Tate drew twenty-three percent of the vote, while Millican garnered nearly nineteen percent. Four minor candidates received less than one percent of the total vote. The African American vote was almost evenly divided between Tate (forty-nine percent) and Massell (forty-four percent). The majority of the remaining African American votes went to Cook. The white vote was divided between Cook (forty-five percent), Millican (thirty-one percent), and Massell (twenty-two percent). Tate received less than two percent of the white vote. The split in the African American vote virtually eliminated Tate, and Massell and Cook advanced to the runoff.[15]

Following the general election, Mayor Allen called the low voter turnout (forty-seven percent) a "disgrace." He asked civic and business groups to participate in an effort to increase voter turnout in the runoff by organizing a telephone campaign and offering transportation to the polls. Massell called this suggestion a veiled request for white citizens to come out and vote against him. Actually, business leaders had long been pressing Allen to endorse Cook. While Allen privately supported Cook, he did not want to become personally involved in the selection of his successor. His chance to help Cook came when questions arose as to the use of a police officer who had been specifically requested by the Massell campaign to protect the candidate. Harold Massell, the candidate's brother, was soliciting campaign funds from night club and strip joint owners in the presence of this officer, a former vice-squad captain who was known by most people in the Atlanta entertainment business. The officer believed that the Massell campaign was using his name and reputation in soliciting funds. Allen asked Massell to withdraw from the race. Supporters of Massell charged Allen with anti-Semitism. Members of the Cook campaign feared that Allen's charges would create sympathy for Massell, particularly among African American voters.[16]

In the runoff, Massell won by capturing fifty-five percent of the vote. Despite Tate's endorsement of Cook, most of his supporters backed Massell. Ninety-three percent of the African American vote went to Massell. Most of Millican's support shifted to Cook. Seventy-three percent of the white vote went to Cook.[17]

The 1969 mayoral election represented a dramatic break with the past. The previous political coalition of African Americans, northside whites, and the business-civic leadership was shattered. Massell forged a new coalition consisting of African Americans, Jewish residents, and labor. Several factors led to the formation of this new coalition. African Americans were not willing to support the candidate backed by the business-civic leadership. Instead of having the usual choice between the candidate endorsed by the business community and another candidate whose racial views were unacceptable, African Americans had several alternatives. They could support an African American, a white liberal, or a white moderate candidate. In this instance, most chose to support the white liberal candidate. Due to the size of the city's black electorate, Massell needed only a few white votes to win. Labor and Jewish residents provided the margin of victory for Massell. Still, the success of this new coalition depended upon the support of the African American community.

In addition to the mayoral race, other political contests were significant. In the race for vice-mayor, Maynard Jackson soundly defeated Milton Farris, a white alderman, by capturing fifty-eight percent of the vote in the general election. Jackson won ninety-eight percent of the African American vote and twenty-eight percent of the white vote. Recognizing the growing political influence of the African American community in municipal affairs, many businessmen supported Jackson over Farris, who was one of their peers. On the north side of the city, Jackson won, for example, nearly one-third of the vote.[18] In the aldermanic races, four additional African Americans were elected; African American representation on the eighteen-member board increased from one to five members. Two African Americans were elected to the Board of Education. Because one African American incumbent did not seek another term, African American representation on the nine-member board increased from two to three seats.

While African Americans comprised nearly fifty percent of the city's population, they occupied only one-third of the elective offices in Atlanta. Less than one-third of the aldermen and only one-third of the school board members were African Americans. The impact of the black community on the decision-making process in Atlanta remained limited. Because of increased representation, African American leaders expected, however, to have a larger voice in municipal affairs under the Massell administration.

During the campaign, Massell pledged that African Americans would have an active role in his administration. Once in office, he assigned at least one African American to each aldermanic committee and appointed African Americans as chairmen of the powerful Finance and Police committees. Atlanta had a weak mayor-form of government in which aldermanic committees monitored the operations of the heads of the various city departments. Since Massell appointed relatively small committees (averaging three to five members) and the vice-mayor was a permanent voting member of each committee, these assignments gave African American aldermen considerable political leverage and a voice in city affairs.[19]

African American aldermen began a campaign to end racial discrimination within city departments. The vice-mayor called upon city department heads to "prove that they are not discriminating against employees or face firing."[20]

In late 1969 African American firemen charged the city with job discrimination. Following these charges, the Community Relations Commission conducted an examination of the department. The Commission found that discriminatory conditions existed and that the "Mental Ability Test" given to all applicants was unfair to African Americans due to the inferiority of black schools. The Commission's report recommended that all applicants who had a tenth grade education be exempted from the test. The study also recommended expanding the all-white Fireman Interview Panel to include an African American, requiring a human relations course for all workers, desegregating the Atlanta Firemen's Recreation Club, advertising for firemen in African American newspapers, hiring an African American recruiter, and assigning at least two African American firemen to each shift (instead of the practice of assigning a single African American to an all-white shift). While the fire department changed some of its practices, the modifications were more superficial than fundamental. The African American chairman of the Board of Firemasters, an aldermanic committee, sent a memorandum to the Chief of the Fire Department requesting him to immediately end all discriminatory practices and double the number of African American firemen in the department.[21]

In March 1970 an African American alderman on the Water Department Committee learned of segregated locker room facilities at the Atlanta Water Works Maintenance and Division Centers. The Water Department Superintendent maintained that workers voluntarily chose to associate along racial lines. The alderman, along with the help of Vice-Mayor Jackson, forced the immediate desegregation of these facilities. They also requested the Community Relations Commission to conduct an investigation of the department's employment practices and working conditions.[22]

In addition to ending discrimination in city departments, African American aldermen wanted to ensure that the African American community receive a more equitable share of benefits and services from the municipal government. Committee chairmen and the vice-mayor undertook efforts to ensure that city contracts were awarded to African American firms and that all contractors were equal opportunity employers. Although many white contractors began to accuse Vice-Mayor Jackson of reverse racism, less than one percent of the city contracts in most years were awarded to African American firms.[23]

In June 1970 the Community Relations Commission conducted a study of the city's minority hiring practices. The Commission's findings indicated that seventy percent of the city's minority work force were laborers or service workers as compared to fourteen percent of the white municipal work force. Only five of the twenty-eight city departments had minorities in top-level positions. The Commission recommended that the city accelerate the recruitment of minorities, create a position (Assistant Deputy · Personnel Director) to work closely with the department heads and the Mayor's Office to achieve equal employment opportunities, set specific goals for the employment and promotion of minorities within each department, establish a comprehensive career development program, and keep records of minority promotions. At the urging of the African American aldermen and Vice-Mayor Jackson, Massell endorsed the report and established a fifty percent goal for African American employment in city government by 1975. The mayor asked department heads to submit a plan for achieving this percentage. While this goal was not reached and the bulk of African American employees continued to be laborers and service workers, modest gains, particularly in the top-level job categories, were made during the Massell administration.[24]

Ironically, the first major strain in the relations between African American leaders and the mayor stemmed from a labor dispute between municipal employees and the city. In January 1970 the Board of Aldermen passed a two-step 8.5% pay raise for municipal employees. In late February the local of the American Federation of State, County, and Municipal Employees (AFSCME) requested a $2.5 million across-the-board, one-step pay raise. The Board of Aldermen turned down this request. Massell argued that the city could not financially afford the raise. In March approximately 2,500 sanitation workers walked out on their jobs. These workers, predominately African American, were the city's lowest paid workers and had in the past few years received only minimal salary increases. Officials of AFSCME, most of whom were white, agreed to negotiate for the employees.[25]

In negotiations with union representatives, the mayor took a firm position. After five hours of mediation had failed to produce a settlement, Massell fired the striking employees. While he continued to meet with representatives of the union, Massell maintained throughout the negotiations that the striking workers were no longer municipal employees. The city hired additional workers to operate the garbage trucks. The few garbage trucks that rolled through Atlanta during the strike were under police protection. Throughout the strike, Massell attempted to divide the workers from their "union bosses." The mayor consistently expressed sympathy for the workers who had "apparently been made a tool by a small band of power-seeking union bosses."[26]

As the strike continued, many African American leaders such as Reverend Hosea Williams, Reverend Joseph Boone of MASLC, and Lonnie King voiced their support for the striking workers. Reverend Ralph Abernathy stated that SCLC would concentrate its resources on the city in order "to gain equality and justice for Atlanta's striking employees."[27] In early April Boone, Williams, and Abernathy organized rallies and marches in downtown Atlanta in support of the striking workers. Protest leaders called for a boycott of major Atlanta businesses and threatened to "shut-off" the central business district if the demands of the striking employees were not met. Leaders who were active in the Civil Rights Movement compared their efforts to those of Dr. King in Memphis during its 1968 sanitation workers' strike. Representatives of the Memphis local came to Atlanta to offer support for the striking workers.[28] In mid-April Vice-Mayor Jackson split with the mayor by stating that the wages of the striking employees were a "disgrace before God" and that the strikers' demands on the city were fair.[29] The vice-mayor suggested that the dispute be settled by arbitration. Many conservative members on the Board of Aldermen wanted to strip Jackson of his aldermanic powers. Mayor Massell, however, thwarted this attempt.[30]

Many city officials accused the striking workers of trying to turn the conflict into a "full-fledged civil rights matter." An editorial in the *Atlanta Constitution* argued that the strike was "an economic issue over workers' demands for higher wages and the city's ability to pay such wages." Because the majority of the striking workers were African Americans, "irresponsible voices" were attempting to create a racial crisis.[31] This position also had support within the African American community. Both Reverend Martin Luther King, Sr. and LeRoy Johnson characterized this strike as a labor dispute rather than a civil rights issue.[32] The *Daily World* urged employees to return to work while negotiations continued.[33]

A group of African American leaders including LeRoy Johnson, Bishop E.L. Hickman, Reverend Martin Luther King, Sr., Jesse Hill, Reverend Sam Williams, John Middleton, and Benjamin Mays began to work behind-the-scenes to achieve a settlement between the city and striking workers. Their primary objective was to tone down the militancy of the strike while trying to find common ground between the two parties.[34] After intense negotiations between the city and union officials, a settlement was eventually reached. City officials agreed to a one-step pay raise which varied according to job description. In most cases, this raise would actually be less than five dollars a week. The proposal also included a promise by the city personnel board to examine 550 positions in twelve classifications with the aim of seeing if these job duties warranted reclassification and thereby raises. The city agreed to reinstate workers, but without back pay for the period of the strike. While city officials refused to drop charges against those arrested during the protests, they promised not to press the cases in court. An agreement was also reached as to the amount of overtime pay employees would earn for collecting the excess garbage. Hosea Williams and younger African American leaders lambasted the terms of the settlement as being too favorable to the city.[35]

The mayor's actions during the garbage strike alienated many younger African American leaders. At a SCLC rally at Morehouse College, the audience heckled the mayor from the platform[36] Massell retained, however, the support of most established leaders by maintaining his commitment to African American participation in municipal affairs and voicing his concerns for racial justice. In addition to his aldermanic assignments, he appointed the city's first African American department heads. Massell upgraded African American employees in the Mayor's Office. African Americans received appointments to several advisory boards and commissions. Massell increased the membership of and broaden the mandate of the Community Relations Commission.

Many questioned the mayor's commitment, however, when he reassigned aldermanic committees in January 1971. Four important committees—finance, ordinance, legislative planning and development, and zoning—did not have African American members.[37] Because of this "purge," Reverend Ralph Abernathy argued that Massell had "not kept faith with his supporters." Leaders of MASLC called for Massell's resignation. They accused the mayor of catering to the white community and attempting to halt the efforts of African American aldermen to end discrimination in municipal departments. While he did not state specific reasons for his reassignments, Massell replied that the "abilities of aldermen to get along with their colleagues, department heads, and the Mayor's Office, as well as the aldermen's wishes" were factors in his decision.[38]

In a speech before the Hungry Club in October 1971, Massell warned a large and predominately African American audience that "an all consuming preoccupation with black power would ruin Atlanta." He asked African Americans to stop their opposition to programs that they feared would dilute African American political strength. The mayor accused some African American leaders of "political blindness" over the mass exodus of Atlanta's affluent white population. White flight was "lessening the city's economic base at the same time that an influx of blacks is increasing the need for expensive government services." To halt the flow of whites from Atlanta, Massell suggested that African Americans had to "think white" and "work to make the city more attractive as an inducement for them to stay."[39]

Massell found some support within the African American community for his speech. While he found the tone and rhetoric of the speech insulting, Alderman Ira Jackson expressed support for the content of the speech. Benjamin Mays, who was currently president of the school board, expressed his approval of the address. Mays was becoming increasingly concerned about the effects of white flight on the city's public school system. The *Atlanta Daily World* termed the speech "challenging" and praised the mayor for his "leadership, know-how and courage." But the reaction of the majority of African American leaders to the speech was outrage. Alderman Henry Dodson called the address an "insult to the city." Many argued that the speech bordered on open racism. Massell, according to these critics, was implying that the African American community was responsible for the flight of white citizens to the suburbs and the city's dwindling tax base. Alderman Marvin Arrington suggested that Massell was now "shifting over to the white power structure for help in his next mayoral campaign."[40]

Despite the negative reaction of many African Americans to the address, the speech was a recognition of the growing political power of Atlanta's African American community. In his address, Massell asked for African American support of programs favored by the business-civic leadership such as annexation and a rapid public transit system. The passage of these programs depended upon the support of the African American community. Rather than simply informing African American leaders of its plans and expecting support, the white community realized that it had to bargain with the African American community to determine the specifics of policy initiatives. The political relationship between the two groups had changed.

Two months following his address to the Hungry Club, Massell announced that he would have legislation introduced in the upcoming General Assembly that would expand the city limits by incorporating the areas immediately north and south of Atlanta. The annexation proposal included the predominately white communities of Sandy Springs to the north and College Park to the south. Approximately 50,000 persons would be added to the city's population. The new racial composition of the city would roughly be fifty-seven percent white and forty-three percent African American. Massell insisted that his plan was not racially or politically motivated. The purpose of this legislation, according to Massell, was to supplement the city's diminishing tax base.[41]

Annexation was a major area of disagreement between white and African American leaders. The business-civic leadership publicly promoted annexation as a means to expand the city's tax base and eliminate the duplication of costly municipal services. Because of their economic resources, the most desirable targets for annexation were white residential and commercial areas located north of the city. African American leaders realized that the addition of a few white voters to the city through annexation or consolidation would dilute the political power of the African American community. African American political power would undoubtedly be challenged in an enlarged city. During the 1940s and 1950s,

Hartsfield and members of the business-civic leadership privately promoted annexation as a means by which whites could remain in political control of the city. In 1952 the city annexed eighty-one square miles and added 100,000 people, predominately white. The city's African American population was reduced from thirty-five to thirty percent of the total. Lacking the political means to block this annexation and wishing to maintain amicable relations with the business-civic leadership, African American leaders endorsed the annexation proposal and worked for its adoption.[42]

One of the first major disputes over annexation occurred in the mid-1960s when the state legislature passed an act allowing Atlanta to annex Sandy Springs, a white middle-to-upper class community located north of the city. The annexation of Sandy Springs would change the racial composition of the city to forty-six percent African American and fifty-four percent white. To counter the proposed influx of white voters, Senator LeRoy Johnson successfully amended the proposal to include the annexation of Boulder Park, a predominately African American area. Under the provisions of the legislation, residents of these areas had to approve of the annexation. Residents of Sandy Springs overwhelmingly voted to reject annexation; whereas, citizens of Boulder Park voted for the proposal. The annexation of Sandy Springs was successfully defeated.[43]

Prospects for the passage of Massell's proposal appeared favorable. Despite the opposition of several African American legislators, the measure passed the Georgia House of Representatives. Unlike the earlier measure to annex Sandy Springs and Boulder Park, this legislation did not require a referendum. Local commentators and politicians believed that the measure had an excellent chance of passing the senate without being amended. The annexation proposal died, however, when Lester Maddox, currently the presiding officer, refused to call the measure from the senate calendar.[44]

In addition to annexation, a long-range objective of the business community was the construction of a practical, large-scale rapid transit system. This initiative was one of the items contained in the Atlanta Chamber of Commerce's "Six Point Program" of 1961. In 1964 voters amended the state constitution so that the public transit system could be built. The General Assembly passed the necessary enabling legislation establishing the Metropolitan Atlanta Rapid Transit Authority (MARTA). A blue-ribbon MARTA board, representing Atlanta and the surrounding counties, was appointed. Atlanta's four representatives, including the board's only African American member, were business executives. Richard Rich was elected chairman of the MARTA board.

In conjunction with the Regional Metropolitan Planning Commission, the MARTA board drew up a referendum to finance the project. The federal government was to fund two-thirds of the billion dollar system while the local share of one-third was to be financed by an ad valorem property tax. In 1968 the voters soundly defeated the measure. All of the suburban counties participating in the project as well as the city voted against the measure. Strong opposition existed in Atlanta's African American community. African American residents in nearby DeKalb County also voted against the measure in large numbers.[45]

In 1967 the Summit Leadership Conference had warned the MARTA board that it would oppose a transit system that failed to serve the poor neighborhoods of the city. African American leaders argued that MARTA had to be more than a transit system for white suburbanites working in the city. At one point in the discussions, a consultant to the MARTA board suggested a north-south railway and an east-west busline. Due to the residential patterns in the city, this proposal would have resulted in a white rail system and an African American bus line. Of course, this idea was unacceptable to African American leaders. Concerns also existed about the lack of African American participation in the planning of MARTA and whether contracts would be awarded to African American firms. The 1968 MARTA referendum did not address these issues.[46]

After the defeat of the first referendum, the MARTA board realized that it had to involve the public in the decision-making process. Participation on the part of the public in the drafting of the first referendum was almost nonexistent. In particular, the supporters of MARTA realized that they had to make a special effort to win the approval of the African American community. Immediately after the defeat of the referendum, Mayor Allen appointed Jesse Hill, a vocal critic of the measure, to the MARTA board. Hill urged the employment of a Community Relations Director to promote MARTA within African American communities. Since this individual would work specifically with black leaders, the MARTA board appointed an African American to fill this position.[47.]

The MARTA board also wanted local officials to become more involved in the drafting of a new referendum. During his mayoral campaign, Massell voiced his support for an effective public transportation system. Upon entering office, he participated in the shaping of a new referendum and undertook a high visibility role in promoting its passage in 1971.

Sam Massell played a major role in drafting a new proposal for the financing of MARTA. Many believed that white suburbanites rejected the initial plan because of its reliance on the property tax for funding. The mayor and many African American leaders preferred a local income tax to finance the system. Massell and the counsel for MARTA reached a compromise. MARTA would be financed through a one percent sales tax for the first ten years of its existence and a subsidized bus fare of fifteen cents for the first seven years. The agreement on the subsidized bus fare was a nonbinding statement of intent, but MARTA officials honored it as if it was a binding policy. MARTA agreed to buy the privately owned Atlanta Transit Company and improve and expand its service both in poor communities of the city and in the suburbs.[48]

Discussions were also taking place between the MARTA board and a group of African American leaders, the Atlanta Coalition on Current Community Affairs, headed by LeRoy Johnson and Vice-Mayor Maynard Jackson.[49] This organization agreed to support the change from financing by a property tax to a sales tax if the MARTA board promised to honor its guarantee of a subsidized fifteen cent fare for the first seven years of its operation. The MARTA board also agreed to establish affirmative action programs for hiring employees and awarding contracts. Of particular importance to African American leaders was a symbolic gesture on the part of MARTA that it would serve poor African American neighborhoods. The MARTA board agreed to construct a spur off its western rail line ("Proctor Creek") to serve the Perry Homes housing project.[50]

The Atlanta Coalition on Community Affairs endorsed the new proposal. Coalition members warned, however, that "every contract between the agency, local governments, and contractors, will be challenged in the courts and in the political arena" if these promises were not kept.[51] The revised MARTA plan was narrowly approved by voters in DeKalb and Fulton counties, but overwhelmingly rejected in Gwinnett and Clayton counties. Approximately fifty-four percent of African Americans voted in favor of MARTA. Some African American organizations opposed MARTA on the ground that it was a transportation system to serve suburban whites. Many white suburban opponents characterized MARTA as a plot to scatter African Americans throughout the metropolitan area.[52]

The passage of the 1971 referendum was a joint effort by white and African American leaders. The business-civic leadership realized that it needed the support of the African American community on major policy issues. This coalition was not, however, that of the 1940s, 1950s, and 1960s. While the coalition remained intact, significant concessions were made to the African American community due to its increased electoral power.

These political changes were reflected in the effort to revise the Atlanta city charter. In 1971 State Representative Grace Hamilton sponsored legislation to revise the city's charter. According to the provisions of the state constitution, the General Assembly had the responsibility of determining the substance of the charter as well as the procedures through which one would be adopted or amended. Since measures which applied only to a particular country had to be approved by members of that county's delegations in the house and senate, any new charter would need the backing of Fulton County's African American representatives. The legislature appointed a thirty-member commission with the responsibility of revising the charter. Four members were appointed by Sam Massell; nine (one from each ward) by the Board of Aldermen; two by the Board of Education; and the remaining fifteen by the Fulton and DeKalb legislative delegations. Legislation required that at least eight members of the state legislature and seven private citizens serve on the commission. All members were citizens of Atlanta. A special effort was made to ensure that the commission had significant African American representation. The vice-chairman of the commission and ten of the thirty members were African American.[53]

The Atlanta Charter Commission discussed issues such as the size and procedure of electing members to the Board of Aldermen and the Board of Education, the separation of powers between the executive and legislative branches of municipal government, the redistricting of the city, and the restructuring of the city's administrative apparatus. Because of the growing political power of Atlanta's African American community, the Commission's decisions would have many racial as well as political implications. These discussions and decisions occurred with the knowledge that the next mayor, who would have the responsibility for reconstructing the city's administrative apparatus, would probably be an African American.

A major issue faced by the Atlanta Charter Commission was whether to retain the aldermanic council in its present form. At this time, the Board of Aldermen consisted of eighteen members who were elected at-large. One proposal before the Commission suggested ward rather than citywide elections. While African American leaders were divided over the issue, citywide elections would theoretically benefit Atlanta's African American community due to its voting majority. Proponents of the at-large system such as Lonnie King and C.A. Scott argued that ward politics "would enable the election of persons who might be racists."[54] Reverend Ralph Abernathy, who favored ward elections, referred to the present system as being "inefficient and unresponsive" to the needs of African American citizens.[55] The Commission eventually reached a compromise on this issue. Under the new charter, twelve councilmen would be chosen from single-member districts and the other six would run at-large but for designated districts. African Americans had sizable majorities in seven of the twelve designated districts and a slight majority in the eighth. Four districts had a white majority. It was commonly assumed that voters would elect members of their own race to be their councilmen.

Commission members also debated the proper size of the city council. At one point, the Atlanta Charter Commission suggested reducing the council from eighteen to twelve members. Eight members of the council were to be elected on the basis of single-member districts and the remaining four at-large. The majority of African American leaders rejected this proposal. Representatives of the local branch of the NAACP urged the Charter Commission to retain the present size of the council. They argued that "to reduce the number would reduce the base of representation and thereby reduce the influence of Negro voters."[56] Most African American leaders viewed the proposal as a blatant attempt to reduce African American participation in the decision-making process. The Commission dropped this proposal and recommended retaining the present size of the council.[57]

These same issues and arguments arose as to the Board of Education. The present board consisted of nine members who were elected at-large. The Atlanta Charter Commission recommended a nine-member board with six members to be elected from single-member districts and three chosen at-large.

Due to the possibility of the election of an African American mayor, there was intense discussion as to the powers of that office. Under the old charter, Atlanta had a weak-mayor form of government in which aldermanic committees supervised the daily operations of city departments. Because of the presence of mayors such as James Key, William Hartsfield, and Ivan Allen, local commentators sarcastically referred to Atlanta as having a weak-mayor form of government with a strong mayor. Power was more evenly balanced during Massell's tenure. African American aldermen used their power to end discrimination in city departments and Vice-Mayor Jackson undertook a more active role in city affairs than his predecessors. The Charter Commission wanted to establish a strict separation of powers between the executive and legislative branches. Under the new charter, the supervision of the city departments became a function of the Mayor's Office. The mayor lost, however, the right to appoint councilmanic committees, and he was limited to two consecutive terms in office.

Interestingly, the Charter Commission recommended converting the largely ceremonial post of vice-mayor into the much more powerful position of president of the council. The duties of this new position included appointing all councilmanic committees, presiding over council meetings, and supervising the council's staff. He would serve as the mediator between the city council and the mayor. A powerful individual in this position would be able to block the initiatives of the mayor. With these assigned powers, the president of the council was the second most important official in Atlanta's municipal government.

Clearly two major aims of the Charter Commission were to balance racially and politically the government and alleviate white fears of black political control. The Charter Commission reached important compromises on such issues as the size and procedure for electing new members to the council. Ward elections, for example, assured that various white viewpoints would be represented.   African American leaders successfully fought against proposals which they perceived as reducing the political influence of black voters. The separation of powers between the legislative and executive branches and the creation of the president of the council position were proposed by the Commission in part to alleviate white fears that African Americans would control all of the city's formal political structures. The Charter Commission did not, however, directly address highly emotional issues such as new sources of revenue for the city and the meaningful desegregation of the public school system[58]

School desegregation was a contentious issue between white and African American leaders. After the initial nine students desegregated Atlanta public schools in 1961, the process moved slowly. In 1962 the number of African American pupils increased only to forty-four as the tenth grade was included. Attorneys for the African American plaintiffs asked for a decree which would accelerate the original twelve year plan for desegregation by five years; re-assign all teachers, principals, and other professional personnel on the basis of qualifications and needs without regard to race by September 1963; desegregate school-sponsored extracurricular activities; and replace the freedom of choice plan by the establishment of zone lines for each school without regard to race.

The District Court refused to amend the Atlanta plan. It also ruled that the assignment of school personnel should be delayed until further progress had been made in the desegregation of students. The Fifth Circuit Court of Appeals upheld this ruling in a two-to-one decision. Writing for the majority, Judge Griffin Bell argued that the Atlanta School Board had acted in the "utmost good faith throughout this litigation." The Circuit Court of

Appeals did stipulate, however, against the discriminatory use of test scores and personality interviews as a basis for approval of African American applications for transfer.

Anticipating an appeal to the Supreme Court, School Superintendent John Letson announced new criteria for transfer: the choice of the pupil or parent, the availability of facilities, and the proximity of the school to the residence. In May 1964 the Supreme Court remanded the case to the District Court for a re-examination of school policies concerning the assignment and transfer of students. In April 1965 the District Court ruled that the rate of desegregation in the Atlanta public school system was inadequate. It amended the original school plan to include kindergarten and first grade during school year 1965–1966 and to move upward at the rate of two grades per year thereafter. All grades would be desegregated by the 1967–1968 school year. The Board of Education announced its willingness to proceed on this basis. In June 1965 it voted to end the grade-a-year plan and make the freedom of choice plan applicable to all grades. Despite this change in procedure, only 20,000 students out of more than 100,000 attended desegregated schools in the 1969–1970 school year.[59]

Two issues complicated the desegregation process in Atlanta, overcrowding in African American schools and resegregation. During the first year of court-ordered desegregation, Atlanta's African American high schools had an overcapacity enrollment of more than 3,000 students. The four desegregated schools and the all-white schools had enough available space to handle this excess. African American leaders urged school authorities to relieve the overcrowding of black schools by dispersing these students to available spaces in white high schools. Officials argued that they were bound by the provisions of the Atlanta plan. They chose to deal with overcrowding in other ways.[60]

In 1964 the Board of Education assigned, for example, African American eighth grade students from several high schools to a renovated building which had once served as a vocational school (the old Smith-Hughes building). Even though white students lived in the vicinity of this building, they were not assigned to this "new" school. African American parents and civil rights organizations protested that to base an enrollment at a particular school on race was to further entrench segregation. The Board gave assurances that this reassignment would only be a temporary measure until a replacement school could be built. Four years later, the school was still in operation.[61]

The Board also suggested portable classrooms, the conversion of white schools into African American schools, the building of new facilities, and the transfer of African American students from extremely overcrowded schools to less overcrowded schools as a means to handle this problem.[62] The local branch of the NAACP attacked these solutions as expensive ways to maintain segregation. Black parents viewed the unwillingness of the School Board to utilize desegregation as a means of relieving overcrowding as a breach of good faith on the part of school officials.

An almost impossible problem for school officials and African American leaders to solve was school resegregation. With the exodus of whites from the city, the process of resegregation accompanied that of desegregation. Between 1962 and 1965, two formerly all-white schools became predominately African American. One elementary school went from an all-white to a predominately African American enrollment within the first year that the Atlanta Plan was extended to include elementary schools. In January 1965 Kirkwood Elementary School, previously all-white, changed to a predominately African American school. Before admitting African American students to Kirkwood, Superintendent Letson sent a letter to white parents notifying them of the impending action and informing them that their children could transfer to other schools. White personnel at Kirkwood were also allowed to transfer.[63] Other city schools began to resegregate as white citizens left the city. By 1970 white enrollment in Atlanta schools was only a little more than half of its 1963 peak. Between 1964 and 1970 school enrollment shifted from an equal division between white and African American students to a two-to-one African American majority.[64] As white enrollment continued to decline, fewer and fewer students were available to provide racially mixed schools.

The issues of resegregation and overcrowding created a sense of distrust between school officials and the African American community. A 1969 report prepared by the National Education Association (NEA) on school-community relations in Atlanta noted that a "communication gap" existed between school officials and the African American community. According to the report, the current "polarization of the black and white communities" created a situation that was "potentially explosive." The NEA report was critical of the Atlanta School Board. It argued that the present Board did not "provide adequate representation of the interests of Atlanta's communities." The Board exhibited "a lack of commitment to the cause of a racially integrated school system."[65]

In 1968 the United States Supreme Court ruled in *Green v. New Kent County, Virginia* that if freedom of choice plans did not achieve effective desegregation, other plans had to be formulated to eliminate segregation. Atlanta's freedom of choice plan was ineffective. In 1970 the Board of

Education abolished its freedom of choice plan and proposed a majority-to-minority transfer program which allowed students to move from a school where their race was in the majority to one in which they would be in the minority. The District Court required the school system to provide free transportation for students participating in the program. The Board of Education also proposed new zoning in order to create a larger number of integrated schools. The District Court appointed a biracial committee to advise the Board of further means to achieve desegregation. Lyndon Wade, executive director of the Atlanta Urban League, headed this committee.

The Atlanta Board of Education was also under a court order to desegregate school faculty by March 1970. In January of that year, the District Court held that racial proportions among teachers at each school had to represent the same racial composition of the system as a whole (currently fifty-seven percent African American and forty-three percent white). Through a lottery, approximately 1,600 teachers (800 white and 800 African American) were transferred to satisfy the court order.[66]

In April 1971 the Supreme Court ruled in *Swann v. Charlotte-Mecklenburg* that busing was a legitimate tool for achieving desegregation. The Fifth Circuit Court of Appeals ordered the District Court to implement a plan for the desegregation of Atlanta schools in compliance with the *Swann* decision. Attorneys for the Legal Defense and Education Fund (known as the Inc. Fund) asked Dr. Michael Stolee of the School of Education at the University of Miami (Florida) to design a plan for Atlanta. Dr. Stolee had previously designed busing plans for a number of school districts in the region. The Stolee plan called for cross-town busing of approximately 30,000 children among sixty-four elementary schools and most of the city's high schools. Each school would have a black student population of at least fifty-six percent. Due to the decline in white enrollment, most schools would be fifty to eighty percent African American.

In June of the following year, attorneys for the American Civil Liberties Union (ACLU) filed suit in District Court requesting either a metro-wide desegregation plan or the consolidation of the nine public school systems in the Atlanta metropolitan area (Atlanta, Buford, Decatur, Marietta, Fulton, DeKalb, Clayton, Cobb, and Gwinnett). Later that month, the Inc. Fund filed a motion to consolidate the existing school cases with the ACLU suit. The District Court decided to postpone hearing litigation in this suit until the Supreme Court ruled in a similar case.[67]

At the beginning of the 1972–1973 school year, the Board of Education implemented its majority-to-minority transfer program. Approximately 2,000 of 7,000 African American students participated. Critics of the program charged that the School Board did not actively promote this program in the African American community. The staff at Emmaus House began a program to assist African American parents in securing majority-to-minority transfers and facilitating the children's integration in predominately white schools. Reverend Ford surveyed the African American parents in the vicinity of Emmaus House and found them to be enthusiastic about the majority-to-minority program. Emmaus House eventually provided transportation so that over 700 African American students from South Atlanta could attend white schools on the north side of the city. Reverend Ford enlisted white suburban volunteers trained by Literacy Action to help tutor the students.

Having recruited the most visible bloc of African American students participating in the majority-to-minority transfer program, Reverend Ford and Emmaus House came under attack. School officials claimed that they were not informed about the students, and the schools lacked adequate facilities and programs to handle the excess students. Officials also cited inaccuracies in the transfer applications. Many white teachers and parents complained that the African American students were far below the academic level of white children of the same age. Despite these objections, the schools were required to accept these students. The Cathedral of St. Philip's governing body named a committee to investigate the programs of Emmaus House, since the Atlanta Diocese of the Episcopal Church contributed over one-third of Emmaus House's operating budget. Reverend Ford denied the accusations leveled against him, the students, and the busing program. He maintained that the Board of Education, not human relations and civil rights organizations, should have coordinated the transfers and provided adequate transportation. Bishop Sims pledged his full support of Reverend Ford and Emmaus House.[68]

Despite the implementation of the majority-to-minority transfer program and the rezoning of some school districts, approximately 106 of the 153 schools were totally or virtually segregated. In October 1972, the Circuit Court of Appeals ruled that the existing Atlanta plan was not in compliance with court decisions and gave the Board of Education six weeks to submit another plan for immediate desegregation.

Following this decision, members of the Atlanta Action Forum met to discuss the desegregation crisis. White and African American leaders organized the Action Forum in 1971 in order to provide a setting where they could informally and privately meet to discuss the major issues facing the city. This organization was based on the principle that problems could best be solved through frank and open discussion between leaders rather than public confrontation. Members of the Action Forum were predominately the chief executive officers of major businesses.[69] They met once a month with no presiding officer and no recorded minutes. Before becoming actively involved in the school situation, Forum members played an active role in the passage of the MARTA referendum.[70]

U.S. Circuit Court Judge Griffin Bell was a guest speaker at this Forum meeting. While he was not currently sitting in the Atlanta school desegregation case, Judge Bell could not specifically discuss the details of the litigation. He did obtain clearance, however, from the Chief Judge of the Circuit Court to discuss the legal precedents established by other school desegregation cases. After discussing these cases, Bell urged Forum members to try to negotiate an out-of-court settlement. He warned his audience that the federal courts would not likely permit any further delay in submitting a plan for the immediate desegregation of Atlanta's schools.

Following this meeting, negotiations began between African American leaders and members of the Board of Education. While various individuals participated in these meetings, the main negotiators were William VanLandingham, Lyndon Wade, and Lonnie King. Their importance to the negotiations was due in part to their ability to muster support for a plan from various segments of the community. VanLandingham, a member of the School Board and executive vice-president of Citizens and Southern Bank, believed that he could persuade a majority of board members to support a reasonable desegregation plan. Three fellow businessmen served on the Board. Because of his prominence in the community, VanLandingham could generate support from business leaders. Lyndon Wade, executive director of the Atlanta Urban League, was respected by both African American and white leaders. He was an established African American leader. Because of his previous civil rights activities and business connections, Lonnie King, president of the Atlanta branch of the NAACP, could muster support for a reasonable plan from civil rights leaders, African American businessmen, and the business-civic leadership. For a school desegregation plan to be successful, it needed the approval of these various groups in Atlanta.

King and Wade had experience in dealing with the school desegregation issue. King was a former employee of the Department of Health, Education, and Welfare's Office of Civil Rights. He formulated Title VI school desegregation plans for various southern cities and towns. His current position as president of the Atlanta NAACP placed him in the middle of the controversy. As Executive Director of the Atlanta Urban

League and chairman of the court-appointed advisory committee, Wade had long struggled with the issues of school desegregation in the city.

The main goal of white leaders was the negotiation of a settlement that did not include massive busing. Business leaders believed that busing would simply accelerate white flight. They warned that the exodus of white citizens from Atlanta would result in an all-black, insolvent city surrounded by white suburbs. Many believed that court-ordered busing would also exacerbate racial tensions in the city. Busing was currently a very emotional issue. Business leaders were aware that busing in other cities had led to incidents of racial violence. Finally, as parents, many simply did not want their children bused to predominately African American schools.

To the surprise of white negotiators, African American leaders also expressed opposition to large-scale busing. Like their white counterparts, many believed that busing would accelerate white flight and increase enrollment in private schools. In particular, Benjamin Mays, president of the School Board and a vocal critic of large-scale busing, feared that white flight would lead to an all-black, insolvent public school system. Leaders questioned whether busing could integrate a public school system that was already seventy-seven percent African American. Lawyers for the plaintiffs informed King that massive busing was needed in order to reach a reasonable level of school desegregation.[71]

Many African American organizations in the city also opposed busing. In particular, African American PTAs took strong anti-busing stands. The predominately black City-Wide PTA Council passed a resolution condemning busing. Reverend O.L. Blackshear, African American pastor of the Mount Pleasant Baptist Church, organized residents on the south side of Atlanta against busing. African American parents at Price and Douglass High Schools voted to intervene in the class action suit for the purpose of opposing busing. The Quality Education Council was specifically organized by African American parents to intervene in the desegregation case in order to dispute the original plaintiffs' claim that they represented the interests of all black parents in Atlanta.[72]

In general, African American opponents of busing in Atlanta argued that educational reform, not desegregation, was the main priority of black parents. Desegregation and the busing of students would not guarantee a quality education for their children. African American parents wanted their children in improved neighborhood schools. A white public school system had ignored conditions at African American schools. Parents believed that the educational needs and personal safety of their children could best be served under the control of African American educators and school administrators. They were asking for community control over their schools. African American residents appeared willing to yield on the question of busing in return for black administrative control of the public school system.[73]

The Inc. Fund attorneys who represented the African American plaintiffs objected to this "deal."[74] They favored a plan which would require massive busing in order to redistribute students in each school in accordance with the racial composition of the city as a whole. In November, James Nabritt, II, one of the Inc. Fund attorneys handling the desegregation case, informed the Atlanta Board of Education that the Inc. Fund would have to approve of any negotiated settlement to the case.

Lonnie King recognized that a negotiated settlement with the Board of Education would be impossible as long as the plaintiffs' attorneys had a veto over any proposed plan. The Atlanta NAACP fired Nabritt as its counsel in the case and hired another attorney to represent its interests. In order to become a party to the case instead of his present legal standing as "friend to the court," King acquired power of attorney from eight of the original nine plaintiffs. He acquired these powers on an individual basis rather than as a representative of the Atlanta NAACP. King was now in position to influence the outcome of the case.

With this authority, King continued his negotiations with the Board of Education. They reached an agreement in late November 1972. This settlement called for the reassignment of about 4,000 students, the closing of four elementary schools, the pairing and rezoning of existing schools, and the creation of between nine and twelve middle schools. The plan called for racial parity among the school system's top administrative positions. The superintendent of schools would be an African American.[75]

At a hearing before the Fifth Circuit Court of Appeals, Inc. Fund attorneys opposed the negotiated settlement. James Nabritt argued that nearly two-thirds of the city's elementary school children would remain in predominately black schools under the terms of the compromise. Another Fund attorney criticized the plan as the trading of "the constitutional rights of Negro pupils for the constitutional rights of Negro administrators."[76] They urged the rejection of the compromise settlement and the acceptance of the Stolee plan. Attorneys for King and the Board of Education argued that the compromise would advance the integration of schools in the city. The Court of Appeals remanded the case to the District Court and ordered it to determine which of the two African American legal factions represented the interests of the African American plaintiffs. In December African American leaders and officials of the Inc. Fund met for over three hours. The participants agreed to work together to formulate a new compromise. Despite this appearance of unity, the differences between the two factions remained.[77]

While negotiations between African American leaders and the School Board were in progress, one potential obstacle was removed. Superintendent John Letson's contract expired in 1972. Letson had presided over school desegregation in Atlanta since its inception. Early in his tenure, segregationists denounced him for his role in the desegregation process. Later, Letson became the focus of African American criticism. Black leaders accused Letson of trying to delay integration and not being responsive to the legitimate grievances of the African American community. They called for Letson's resignation several times during his tenure. Because of this lack of support, Letson could not have effectively served another term as superintendent.

His support among members of the board had also eroded. Private discussions as to Superintendent Letson's future occurred between Dr. Mays and school board members. An understanding was reached. The Board of Education offered Letson a four-year contract. Letson promptly announced his desire not to remain for more than two years. The Board established a search committee to find a successor.

While this search committee stated that race, creed, and residence would be irrelevant factors in its decision, most assumed that the new superintendent would be African American. Negotiations between the Board of Education and African American leaders were currently headed in this direction. The search committee held its early meetings behind closed doors. Neighborhood and ad hoc citizen groups complained about the lack of public participation in the selection of the new superintendent. The search committee narrowed its list down to two main candidates, Dr. Alonzo Crim and Johnnie Jones. Crim was superintendent of schools in Compton, California; Jones was an area superintendent in the Miami-Dade County school system. Both candidates thus had experience in administrating racially and ethnically diverse school systems.

The Board of Education and citizens at public hearings interviewed each candidate. Alonzo Crim was the unanimous recommendation of the search committee and the Board. By this time, a compromise had been reached between the School Board and the plaintiffs in the desegregation case. Letson agreed to relinquish his position as superintendent.[78]

The African American plaintiffs and the School Board reached a negotiated settlement in February 1973. This plan addressed three main areas: student reassignment, staff and administrative desegregation, and the school system's majority-to-minority transfer program. Under this settlement, the number of students in desegregated schools would increase from 27,239 to 37,065. Approximately 59,000 pupils would remain in segregated schools. The number of desegregated schools would increase from forty-seven to sixty-four, and the other eighty-three schools would be predominately African American. Each school would have at least a thirty percent black enrollment.[79]

The most controversial and publicized component of this settlement was administrative and staff desegregation. The plan specified that thirty-five top administrative positions, including the school superintendent, be designated for African Americans. Future hirings to these particular positions, however, would be on a nondiscriminatory basis. The racial balance of the staff at each school was to be within ten percent of the system's racial composition. The settlement thus affected the one-time transfer of 200 staff members at twenty-seven schools.

The negotiated settlement called for the busing of some 4,800 pupils. Because some 2,000 students were already participating in the majority-to-minority transfer program, the plan would involve the busing of only 2,800 pupils.[80] The Board of Education agreed to provide additional funds and staff for its majority-to-minority transfer program and promised to actively recruit students of both races to participate in the program. Several African American schools agreed to establish magnet programs in the arts and sciences in order to attract white students.

The negotiated settlement included other means to increase desegregation. The Board agreed to redraw the school attendance zones of eighteen schools providing for an African American student population of twenty-seven to thirty-five percent at each school. Nine schools were to be closed and their students reassigned in order to achieve a more equitable racial balance. Two previously all-black schools were desegregated. The plan also called for the pairing of schools if applicable. Pairing involved the combining of attendance zones of two nearby schools which had majority enrollments of the opposite race. When schools were paired, all students of certain grades would go to one school, while the pupils of other grades went to the other institution.[81]

The compromise was much closer to proposals offered by the Board of Education then those of the NAACP and the Inc. Fund. The last proposal submitted by the NAACP (January 1973) would have resulted in a seventy percent increase in the number of students attending desegregated schools, a ninety-one percent increase in the number of desegregated schools, and the busing of 18,000 students. The counterproposal of the Board of

Education (February 1973) offered a thirty-three percent increase in the number of students attending desegregated schools, a twenty-one percent increase in the number of desegregated schools, and no busing. The negotiated settlement called for a thirty-eight percent increase in the number of students attending desegregated schools, a thirty-six percent increase in the number of desegregated schools, and the busing of some 2,800 pupils.[82]

Administrative desegregation was not included under the original court order. It was the critical key, however, to this new settlement by serving as the main bargaining chip between the two parties. White leaders were willing to give African Americans a decisive role in the administration of the school system in exchange for no massive busing. Believing that cross-town busing would not achieve acceptable levels of integration, desegregated schools would not necessarily guarantee quality education, and an African American school administration would be more sympathetic to black interests, African American leaders were willing to agree to this exchange.

Initially, the negotiated settlement received little criticism. The Atlanta Chamber of Commerce passed a resolution in support of the compromise. The *Atlanta Constitution* and other local newspapers editorially praised the settlement. With the exception of Reverend Ralph Abernathy, most local African American leaders approved the plan. Congressman Andrew Young expressed his support and promised to help obtain federal funds to affray any additional costs that might arise from the plan. In an article in the *New York Times*, Roy Wilkins, the executive secretary of the national NAACP, was quoted as arguing that the "achievement of a quality education for black children is a more important goal than putting blacks and whites in classrooms together."[83]

This article correctly noted that Wilkins' apparent statement of support for the Atlanta settlement was a major departure from the NAACP's national policy. In 1971 the NAACP's Minneapolis Convention unanimously passed a resolution calling for "NAACP units in every part of the country to achieve the basis set forth in the Charlotte-Mecklenburg, North Carolina School case."[84] The *Times* article argued that the Atlanta plan accepted the "minimum of integrated classrooms in exchange for a maximum of integrated administrative positions," a clear contradiction of previous NAACP policy (Ironically, while this article was viewed as being critical of the Atlanta settlement, the *New York Times* editorially praised the plan).[85]

Largely due to this article, the Atlanta settlement began to receive national news coverage. While the settlement received editorial praise, the media, in most instances, portrayed the compromise simply as a trade-off—no busing in exchange for administrative jobs. Many civil rights leaders began to pressure Roy Wilkins and Jack Greensberg, executive director of the Inc. Fund, to denounce the Atlanta settlement. These leaders argued that the Atlanta compromise would undermine school desegregation cases in other cities. Currently, litigation was pending in Boston, Benton Harbor, Brooklyn, Dayton, Detroit, Grand Rapids, Hartford, Indianapolis, Kalamazoo, and San Francisco.[86]

Wilkins' eventual decision to oppose the Atlanta settlement was likely due to his concern over the progress of civil rights during the Nixon administration and his belief that the opposition to busing was an attempt to halt further school integration. Wilkins believed that the Nixon administration was attempting to turn back the progress on civil rights that was made during the presidencies of John Kennedy and Lyndon Johnson.[87] This belief had some legitimacy. Nixon's 1968 presidential campaign with its emphasis on law and order and racist overtones appealed to those conservative voters who were uncomfortable with the Great Society programs and the advancement of civil rights. Early in his administration, Nixon attempted to enhance his status in the white South. In his inaugural address, the president stated that he would not ask for further civil rights legislation. In 1970 Attorney General John Mitchell testified against the renewal of the Civil Rights Act of 1965.[88]

When Abe Fortas resigned as an associate justice on the Supreme Court, Nixon nominated Clement Haynsworth, a native southerner and judicial conservative who had sided with segregationists in two cases. After Haynsworth's rejection by the Senate, he nominated G. Harrold Carswell of Georgia, another judicial conservative who had questionable credentials to sit on the Supreme Court. After both his nominees were rejected, Nixon argued that "the real issue of their rejection was their philosophy of strict construction of the Constitution—a philosophy which I share—and the fact that they had the misfortune of being born in the South."[89] Wilkins considered the nominations of Carswell and Haynsworth to be an "affront to the legal profession and Black Americans." Wilkins realized that Nixon was attempting to mold the Supreme Court's decisions on civil rights and busing.[90]

Early in the Nixon administration, the Justice Department joined officials in Mississippi in arguing against the integration of state school districts on the ground that it would be an educational setback for the children, both white and African American. In interviews, Nixon argued that the federal government should make every attempt to eliminate de jure segregation, but de facto segregation could not and should not be rectified through the courts. He opposed court-ordered busing to achieve racial balance in the schools. In his 1968 presidential campaign, he had pledged not to curtail federal funds to schools opposing integration through busing. While the Nixon administration enforced the *Green* and *Swann* decisions, it did simply what the courts required.[91]

By opposing busing, Nixon hoped to appeal not only to white southerners but to those northerners who also faced "the threat" of busing. In 1972 busing became a heated issue in the presidential election. Largely due to his opposition to busing, Governor George Wallace of Alabama won the Florida and Michigan Democratic primaries. While the Nixon campaign realized that Wallace could not win the Democratic presidential nomination, officials believed that Wallace could possibly attract enough votes on the strength of the anti-busing sentiment to deny Nixon's re-election if he chose to run again as an independent. In March, following the Florida primary, Nixon called on Congress to impose a "moratorium" on federal courts to prevent them from ordering any new busing to achieve racial balance. Stressing his support for neighborhood schools, Nixon also called for legislation which would direct $2.5 million in federal aid for the education of children in central cities. He argued that children would not have to be bused to the suburbs to obtain a better education.[92]

Many civil rights leaders, including Wilkins, recognized that this action was a clever ploy to halt integration. Nixon reaffirmed his opposition to segregation while, at the same time, rejecting one of the most effective ways to bring about its end. Wilkins argued that the Nixon administration opposed "busing in such a way that beclouded the whole issue, splitting the country just when the civil rights law needed full backing from the White House."[93] He thus regarded Nixon's support for neighborhood control of schools as a ploy to halt busing and further integration. He could not possibly support any plan which substituted neighborhood control for busing, even if it was negotiated in good faith.

In early March 1973, representatives of the national NAACP and the Inc. Fund disavowed Atlanta's negotiated settlement. National NAACP leaders argued that the compromise was an abandonment of integration in exchange for administrative jobs. They maintained that black politicians in Atlanta were seeking to preserve their own interests at the expense of African American children. Roy Wilkins and Bishop Steven G. Spottswood, chairman of the NAACP board, ordered the Atlanta branch to reverse its position on the settlement or face the suspension of its charter. Despite this warning, the executive committee of the Atlanta branch unanimously voted to continue backing the settlement. Wilkins suspended all of the NAACP officers and executive committee members. The Inc. Fund filed a brief opposing the negotiated settlement and urging the reconsideration of the Stolee plan. The District Court, however, approved of the implementation of the negotiated settlement.[94]

The 1973 school settlement, the new city charter, and the successful passage of the MARTA referendum demonstrated that biracial cooperation was still deeply embedded in Atlanta politics. In these particular instances, each party depended to a great extent upon the support of the other in pursuing its policy objectives. These cases also illustrated the changing political relationship between white and African American leaders. The white business-civic leadership was forced to bargain with African American leaders in order to determine the specifics of various policy initiatives.

By the early 1970s African American leaders were beginning to occupy positions of power within the city. African Americans served on the city council, the school board, various municipal commissions, and the boards of major white businesses. Many became members of Atlanta's leading business, social, and charitable institutions. Several factors accounted for this shift in black-white political relations. The Civil Rights Movement of the 1960s opened the way for greater participation in the decision-making process. In response to black demands for greater equality in incomes and better neighborhood facilities and schools, the business-civic leadership responded by providing economic and political opportunities for select segments of the African American community. Business leaders realized that African American support was needed for important policy initiatives. Racial cooperation facilitated the integration of the city's business community. The Chamber of Commerce, for example, began to encourage African American businesses to participate in its activities. Major firms in the city such as Coca-Cola and Delta Airlines added African Americans to their executive boards.

Greater participation on the part of African American leaders in the decision-making process did not necessarily entail benefits for all segments of the African American community. Black officials tended to represent the interests of Atlanta's growing African American middle class. Black officeholders appeared, for example, to be more concerned with assuring that African American businesses receive their fair share of city contracts than promoting less discriminatory hiring practices within white firms. A constant criticism of African American leaders was that they compromised the interests of poorer African Americans in order to obtain political and economic patronage for the black middle class. According to many critics, the values of these leaders tended to resemble those of white leaders as they rose in the city's leadership structure. In response to these critics, African American leaders argued that a more equitable share of city contracts and administrative posts benefitted the entire community.

Like their white counterparts, African American leaders urged the use of quiet negotiations to solve racial tensions rather than public confrontation. In April 1973 Reverend Ralph Abernathy and Hosea Williams conducted demonstrations at Rich's protesting the store's discriminatory employment practices and the working conditions of its African American employees.[95] Rich's denied any discriminatory treatment of its black employees. Approximately 350 workers went on strike. The confrontation became extremely personal. At a graduate business luncheon at Emory University, Richard Rich referred to Hosea Williams as a "charlatan, a drunkard, and an extortionist."[96] Williams filed a libel and slander suit against Rich, and protestors picketed Rich's residence. With the aid of the Community Relations Commission, a settlement to the strike was eventually reached. A number of African American leaders publicly criticized the tactics of Hosea Williams and the strikers. Jesse Hill, a member of Rich's executive board, contended that he had already been negotiating with Rich's management. He argued that quiet discussions would have resulted in greater concessions than the public protest achieved.[97]

By 1973 African American leaders were confident that a black candidate could be elected in the upcoming mayoral election. African Americans comprised over fifty percent of the city's population, and it was obvious that a sizable African American electorate would allow blacks to control the city's formal political structures. Thirty-eight African Americans were currently serving as mayors of southern cities; approximately seventeen of these cities had an African American population of greater than fifty percent. This observation offered hope to leaders in Atlanta that white and African American citizens could work together to ensure the election of qualified candidates without racist appeals being made.

In order to ensure that the African American vote would not be divided, African American leaders attempted to keep the number of black candidates to a minimum. Only two candidates, Vice-Mayor Jackson and Senator LeRoy Johnson, made serious bids for the position. Reverend William Stafford, pastor of the Free For All Baptist Church, was briefly in the contest, but later withdrew in favor of Jackson. Despite his tenure as vice-mayor, Jackson was not the first choice of established African American leaders. As in 1969, most established leaders favored Senator LeRoy Johnson, the senior African American officeholder in the city. The vice-mayor was able, however, to obtain the support of Jesse Hill, who later became his campaign manager.

In the spring of 1973, Jan Douglass, an assistant professor in the Atlanta University School of Social Work, called a meeting of AUC faculty and students to discuss the upcoming mayoral primary. The participants believed that the election provided an opportunity for AUC students to increase their activity in community affairs and help elect Atlanta's first African American mayor. They decided to organize the university complex behind a single candidate. AUC students and younger faculty formed the University Movement for Black Unity (UMBU).

In order to develop a consensus around a single candidate, UMBU decided to hold a mock campus election. They conducted a voter registration drive among AUC faculty and students. Members agreed to organize the community on behalf of the selected candidate.

The mock election received widespread attention. Atlanta's white and African American newspapers covered the event. The African American candidates actively campaigned on the college campuses, and student supporters distributed literature. On the eve of the election, the candidates participated in a debate. In addition to those of Maynard Jackson and LeRoy Johnson, the names of Reverend W.J. Stafford, Alderman Ira Jackson (no relation to the vice-mayor), and Horace Tate appeared on the ballot. Approximately forty-seven percent of the student body voted. Maynard Jackson received eighty-four percent of the vote. Johnson finished second with eleven percent of the ballots cast.

In a press release, Johnson charged that the results of the election had been "rigged." UMBU issued a statement denying the accusation and calling Johnson's remarks an insult to the integrity of the organization and the student body of the Atlanta University Center. The statement noted that supporters of Senator Johnson aided in the organization of the mock election and representatives of his campaign signed the election's tally sheet.

UMBU sponsored a voter registration drive during the first week of May at the AUC. It recruited student volunteers to distribute literature, canvass neighborhoods, and perform other campaign-related activities on behalf of Maynard Jackson. Several UMBU members obtained important staff positions in the Jackson campaign. Due to the publicity surrounding the event and the efforts of the UMBU, the mock election was a major boost for the Jackson campaign. The vice-mayor began to emerge as the consensus "African American candidate."[98]

Atlanta's white business leadership was more divided in its choice than the African American community. Despite his support of several business-backed initiatives during his first term, Massell was unpopular with members of the business-civic leadership. As in 1969, considerable support for Charles Weltner, the former Congressman, existed. Harold Dye, a former state administrator, had some support from residents on the north side of the city. During the campaign, Dye would emerge as the spokesperson for conservative groups in Atlanta. In order to maintain access to City Hall, many businessmen argued that the business-civic leadership should endorse one of the African American candidates. LeRoy Johnson, as did Maynard Jackson, had some support within the business community. As Jackson began to build momentum within the African American community, many white leaders began to seriously consider Jackson for mayor.[99]

Missing from this field of major candidates was a spokesperson for the extreme right. Since 1946, the business-civic leadership had argued that it was a buffer between the city's African American population and race-baiting politicians on the local and state level. With a growing African American electorate inside the city and the political empowering of African Americans on the state and national level, the business-civic leadership was no longer needed as a buffer. The African American community was free to vote for a black candidate.

During the campaign, the major candidates generally avoided the race issue and concentrated on the problems facing the city. Both African American candidates realized that an appeal to race consciousness would cost them support in the white community. Jackson and Johnson stressed their interest in continuing amicable relations with the business community. In a speech devoted to race relations, Jackson pledged an end to hostility between the races and stated his opposition to "reverse racism."[100] The vice-mayor maintained, however, that he was totally committed to seeking parity for African Americans. Both African American candidates had to be "black enough" for African American voters while at the same time win support within the white community.

Sam Massell ran on the accomplishments of his first term. In many respects, his record was quite good. He worked closely with the business community on several issues, including the passage of the MARTA referendum and the building of Atlanta's indoor coliseum, the Omni, on the western periphery of the city. Massell increased the number of African American municipal employees and appointed the city's first African American department heads. He named an African American as director of personnel and created an Office of Affirmative Action within that department. The membership and duties of the Community Relations Commission increased during Massell's tenure. Massell supported the political career of Andrew Young by selecting him to chair the Community Relations Commission and aiding his 1972 election to Congress from a district that was predominately white.

Massell also managed, however, to alienate almost every major group in the city. Friction developed between Massell and business leaders when he replaced Rawson Haverty, the popular businessman chairing the MARTA board, with John Wright, the president of the Atlanta Labor Council. Massell argued that organized labor needed representation on the MARTA board. The mayor's handling of the garbage strike, his "purging" of African American aldermen from major committees in 1971, the "think white" speech, and his annexation proposals dismayed many African American leaders. Many believed that the mayor's actions were motivated by his desire to capture the support of white voters. Labor officials were disappointed by Massell's handling of the garbage strike and his support of several business initiatives. In 1969 labor was an important component of Massell's winning coalition; however, in 1973 the Atlanta Labor Council endorsed Jackson.

The editorial positions of the city's major newspapers illustrated the changing political relationships and divisions that existed. The major white dailies divided their support. The *Atlanta Constitution*, generally supportive of the business-civic leadership, backed LeRoy Johnson. The more conservative *Atlanta Journal* endorsed Charles Weltner. Among the city's African American newspapers, the conservative *Atlanta Daily World* expressed its support for Sam Massell. The *World* praised Massell's record, courage, and independence. For these reasons, the newspaper argued that the African American community owed him a second term in office. Publisher C.A. Scott feared that the election of an African American candidate would accelerate white flight to the suburbs. While acknowledging the progress made by African Americans during Sam Massell's administration, the *Inquirer* and *Atlanta Voice* argued that the negative aspects of his administration outweighed the positive. Both newspapers endorsed Jackson.

In the general election, Jackson received forty-seven percent of the vote, while his closest competitor, Massell, had only twenty percent. Charles Weltner received nineteen percent of the vote and Johnson had a disappointing four percent (Harold Dye received nine percent of the ballots cast). While the race issue was muted in the mayoral campaign, voters cast their ballots along racial lines. The African American candidates received approximately eighty-four percent of the black vote. The top three white candidates received roughly seventy-nine percent of the white vote. Jackson received only six percent of the white vote. Because Jackson did not receive a majority of the votes cast, a runoff between the two leading candidates was required.[101]

During the period between the general election and the runoff, the tone of the campaign changed. Race became an issue in the campaign. By adopting the slogan "Atlanta's too Young to Die," the Massell campaign implied that the city would not economically prosper if an African American was elected mayor. In particular, Sam Massell, a realtor before becoming actively involved in politics, predicted that property values in the city would decline. The Atlanta Real Estate Board took out a full-page ad in the *Journal-Constitution* endorsing Massell. Another ad on Massell's behalf warned white voters that "It's Cheaper to Vote Than to Move." While these tactics were obviously designed to attract conservative white voters, they were more successful in driving white moderates into Jackson's camp. The city's major newspapers as well as many white businessmen criticized Massell's campaign tactics. With the exception of the *Daily World*, all of the city's newspapers endorsed Jackson.[102]

In the runoff, Jackson received fifty-nine percent of the ballots cast. He received ninety-five percent of the vote in the predominately African American districts and seventeen percent of the white vote. Massell garnered five percent of the African American vote and eighty-two percent of the white vote. African American citizens were determined to elect a black candidate. The African American voter turnout increased from fifty-five percent in the general election to sixty-seven percent in the runoff (white voter turnout increased from forty-five to fifty-five percent). The split in the white vote and Massell's unpopularity also contributed to his defeat.[103]

An equally important contest was the campaign for city council president. Wade Mitchell, a white banker and former alderman, and Wyche Fowler, a white attorney and alderman, announced their candidacies. A rumor circulated the city that a political deal between white and African American leaders had been reached. According to the rumor, a group of influential white businessmen agreed to back Maynard Jackson in the mayor's race in exchange for African American support for Mitchell in the council presidency race. Mitchell and Jackson denied the story. Shortly before the race's filing deadline, Hosea Williams entered the contest in order to "bust the deal."[104] Robert Hunter, an African American rector, also announced his intention to run. While this rumor was unverifiable, African American leaders did not encourage or recruit an African American candidate to run for the post, and no prominent African American politician filed as a candidate. Most leaders did not believe that African American candidates could win both offices.

In the general election, Wyche Fowler won thirty-one percent of the vote. His closest competitor was Hosea Williams with twenty-nine percent of the ballots cast. Despite the opposition of African American leaders to his candidacy, Williams received fifty-five percent of the African American vote. He received little support within the white community. In the runoff, Wyche Fowler received sixty-four percent of the votes cast. He won with over eighty-five percent of the white vote and thirty-four percent of the African American vote.[105]

The 1973 elections represented a break with the past. The new city council was evenly divided between nine whites and nine African American members. The newly elected school board consisted of five African Americans and four whites. Atlanta had an African American mayor and a white city council president. City leaders engaged in a self-congratulatory rhetoric about a racially balanced government. Political reality was somewhat different.

The business-civic leadership was electorally reduced to the junior partner in the biracial coalition. The municipal elections of 1973 gave African Americans nominal control of the city's formal political structure. African American citizens undoubtedly expected the new government to redress their grievances. White business leaders were apprehensive about changes that a majority African American government would bring. For the city of Atlanta, this was a new situation. New norms of racial and political behavior had to be established for a city with a majority black government, but dominated economically by white business interests. The Jackson administration faced a unique challenge.

Notes

1. Ivan Allen Jr. with Paul Hemphill, *Mayor: Notes on the Sixties* (New York: Simon and Schuster, 1971), pp. 220–222.

2. Charles Rook, *The Atlanta Elections of 1969* (Atlanta: Voter Education Project, 1970), p. 2.

3. Allen, pp. 220–222.

4. Tom Bradley was elected mayor of Los Angeles in 1973. After serving twenty years in this position, he declined to run for another term in 1993. *Atlanta Constitution*, 31 May 1973; *New York Times*, 28 May 1969; and Alton Hornsby, Jr., "The Negro in Atlanta Politics, 1961–1973," *Atlanta Historical Bulletin*, XII (Spring, 1971): 21–22.

5. Author's Interview with LeRoy Johnson, 13 November 1990.

6. Duncan R. Jamieson, "Maynard Jackson's 1973 Election as Mayor," *The Midwest Quarterly*, 18 (1976): 10.

7. After leaving his position as director of the Voter Education Project, Vernon Jordan was an attorney with the Office of Economic Opportunity in Atlanta (1969), Executive Director of the United Negro College Fund (1970–1972), Executive Director of the National Urban League (1972–1981), and co-chairman of President-elect Bill Clinton's transition team (1992–1993). Hornsby, p. 23.

8. Author's Interview with LeRoy Johnson.

9. In 1966 state Democratic candidates were asked to sign a Democratic loyalty oath to support the party's gubernatorial candidate, Lester Maddox. Because he could not support Lester Maddox with good conscience, Weltner withdrew from his re-election bid to the Fifth Congressional District seat. Many viewed this action as a sign of strength; others viewed this action as a sign of weakness.

10. Allen with Hemphill, pp. 223–224.

11. Author's Interview with LeRoy Johnson; Numan Bartley, "Atlanta Elections and Georgia Political Trends," *New South*, (Winter 1970): 22–23, 25–26; and Reece Cleghorn, "Shooting an Elephant: 1969 Mayoral Elections," *Nation*, 210 (30 March 1970): 358–361.

12. Allen with Hemphill, p. 223; Bartley, pp. 22–25; and Rook, pp. 3–4.

13. In an interview with this author, LeRoy Johnson stated that Cook's defeat was largely due to his party affiliation. Campaign posters used in the African American community told voters to "Vote Democratic October 21st, Elect Sam Massell Mayor."

14. Bartley, p. 23.

15. Based on the numbers, a united African American community would have given Tate enough votes to at least reach the runoff. For a complete breakdown of this vote in the mayoral contest by race and class, see Bartley, p. 24 and Rooks, pp. 6–18.

16. Allen with Hemphill, pp. 226–234; and Rooks, pp. 25–26.

17. For a complete breakdown of the vote in the runoff by race and class, see Rooks, pp. 19–24.

18. Allen with Hemphill, p. 234. For a complete breakdown of the vote in the vice-mayor's race by race and class, see Rooks, pp. 34–60.

19. While Sam Massell was an ex-officio member of all aldermanic committees, he normally did not attend meetings. Jackson was actively involved in city affairs. Mack H. Jones, "Black Political Empowerment in Atlanta: Myth and Reality," *Annals of the American Academy of Political Science*, 439 (September 1978): 100.

20. Quoted in Jones, p. 100.

21. *Atlanta Constitution*, 9 August 1969; *Atlanta Constitution*, 30 December 1969, p. 3; Jones, p. 101; and Rosa Marie Wells, "Samuel Woodrow Williams, Catalyst for Black Atlantans, 1946–1970" (Master's thesis, Atlanta University, 1975).

22. *Atlanta Constitution*, 17 March 1970, p. 3; and Jones, p. 101.

23. "Can Atlanta Succeed Where America Has Failed? An Exclusive Interview with Maynard Jackson," *Atlanta Magazine*, (June 1975): 40–41.

24. Author's Interview with Sam Massell, 3 December 1990; Jones, pp. 101–102; and Wells, pp. 44–47.

25. *Atlanta Constitution*, 23–25 March 1970.

26. *Atlanta Constitution*, 26 March 1970.

27. *Atlanta Constitution*, 28 March 1970.

28. *Atlanta Constitution*, 1–15 April 1970.

29. *Atlanta Constitution*, 17 April 1970.

30. Jamieson, p. 17.

31. *Atlanta Constitution*, 23 April 1970, editorial.

32. *Atlanta Constitution*, 26 March 1970.

33. *Atlanta Daily World*, 29 March 1970.

34. Author's Interviews with LeRoy Johnson and Sam Massell; *Atlanta Constitution*, 26 March 1970; and *Atlanta Constitution*, 23 April 1970.

35. In an interview with the author, Sam Massell stated that he viewed the garbage strike as a labor dispute between striking municipal employees

and the city. He did not regard the strike as a civil rights issue. He maintained that the city could not afford a large one-step pay raise.

36.   Hornsby, p. 28.

37.   Jones, p. 102.

38.   Scholars have portrayed this incident as an attempt on the part of Massell to broaden his political base within the white community. In an interview with the author, Massell still maintains that his reassignments were not politically or racially motivated. The municipal elections were not until 1973 (two years away). Quotes are from the *Atlanta Constitution*, 6 January 1971.

39.   Sam Massell, address, 6 October 1971, Hungry Club, Atlanta, Georgia.

40.   *Atlanta Constitution*, 7 October 1971; and *Atlanta Daily World*, 7 October 1971.

41.   Author's Interview with Sam Massell; Peter Eisinger, *The Politics of Racial Displacement: Racial and Ethnic Transition in Three American Cities* (New York: Academic Press, 1980), p. 139; Hornsby, p. 29; and Jones, p. 102.

42.   Bradley R. Rice, "The Battle of Buckhead: The Plan of Improvement and Atlanta's Last Big Annexation," *Atlanta Historical Journal*, 25 (1981): 18.

43.   Author's Interview with LeRoy Johnson.

44.   Author's Interview with Sam Massell; and Hornsby, pp. 29–30.

45.   Jones, p. 103; and Clarence Stone, *Regime Politics: Governing Atlanta, 1946–1988* (Lawrence: University of Kansas Press, 1989), pp. 98–99.

46.   Author's Interview with LeRoy Johnson.

47.   Jones, p. 103; and Stone, p. 101.

48.   Author's Interview with Sam Massell.

49.   Other members of the Atlanta Coalition on Community Affairs included Reverend Andrew Young; Johnny Johnson (Model Cities Director); Lyndon Wade (Executive Secretary of the Atlanta Urban League and MARTA board secretary); John Cox (Butler Street YMCA Director); John Calhoun (former president of the Atlanta NAACP and EOA consultant); and Reverend J.C. Ward.

50.   Author's Interview with LeRoy Johnson; Ben Brown, "Black Coalition Bargains, Supports MARTA," *Southern Journal*, 2 (Winter, 1972): 8; Jones, p. 103; and Stone, p. 103.

51.   *Atlanta Constitution*, 9 September 1971.

52.   *Atlanta Constitution*, 11 November 1971.

53. "Atlanta Charter Commission Fact Sheet," Grace Hamilton Papers, Box: 44, Folder: 1, Atlanta History Center, Library and Archives, Atlanta, Georgia; and "Roster of Atlanta Charter Commission," Grace Hamilton Papers, Box: 43, Folder: 3.

54. Sherman Burge, C.A. Scott, and Lonnie King, Letter to Charter Commission Members, 13 November 1972, Grace Hamilton Papers, Box: 43, Folder: 11.

55. Reverend Ralph Abernathy, Statement made to the Atlanta Charter Commission, 19 September 1972, Grace Hamilton Papers, Box: 47, Folder: 11.

56. Burge, Scott, and King, Letter to Charter Commission Members.

57. The first draft of the new city charter called for a twelve-member city council.

58. Jones, p. 104.

59. A chronology of the Atlanta school desegregation case listing "court action" and "extent of desegregation in Atlanta school system" can be found in Research Atlanta, *School Desegregation in Metro-Atlanta, 1954–1973* (Atlanta: Research Atlanta, 1973), pp. 13–22.

60. National Education Association, National Commission on Professional Rights and Responsibilities, *Central Issues Influencing School-Community Relations in Atlanta, Georgia* (NEA, 1969), p. 19.

61. Council on Human Relations of Greater Atlanta, Memorandum to the Summit Leadership Conference, 19 June 1964, Eliza Paschall Papers, Box: 5, Woodruff Library, Emory University, Atlanta, Georgia; Petition to the Atlanta Board of Education From GACHR, 4 September 1964, Eliza Paschall Papers, Box: 5; *Southern School News*, August 1963, p. 18; and *Southern School News*, August 1964, p. 2.

62. National Education Association, National Commission on Professional Rights and Responsibilities, pp. 19–20.

63. National Education Association, National Commission on Professional Rights and Responsibilities, p. 22; and Susan McGrath, "Great Expectations: The History of School Desegregation in Atlanta and Boston, 1954–1990" (Ph.D. dissertation, Emory University, 1992), pp. 319–320.

64. Stone, p. 103.

65. National Education Association, National Commission on Professional Rights and Responsibilities, pp. 10, 50.

66. Barbara L. Jackson "Desegregation: Atlanta Style," *Theory into Practice*, 17 (1): p. 46; and Research Atlanta, pp. 18–19.

67. The Supreme Court rejected the concept of one consolidated school district. These cases were eventually settled on an individual basis.

Jane A. Hansen, "Blacks Traded Busing for Power in 1973 'Atlanta Compromise,' Divided We Stand: The Resegregation of Our Public Schools, part 5," *Atlanta Journal*, p. 9a; McGrath, pp. 323–324, 332; and Research Atlanta, pp. 19, 21.

68. Author's Interview with Reverend Austin Ford, 3 December 1990; *Atlanta Constitution*, 2 September 1972; and "Busing to Buckhead," *Atlanta Journal and Constitution Magazine*, 29 October 1972, pp. 8–9, 12, 15.

69. The African American membership was more diverse due to differences in the leadership structure of the two communities. Prominent African American educators and civil rights leaders were also invited to participate. Stone, p. 97.

70. Author's Interview with William Calloway, 10 September 1991; *Atlanta Journal and Constitution*, 19 June 1988, pp. 1b, 5b; and Stone, p. 97.

71. Dr. Benjamin Mays, Statement, Minutes, Education Subcommittee of the Atlanta Charter Commission, 5 October 1971, Grace Hamilton Papers, Box: 44, Folder: 5 (re: the effects of white flight and massive busing on the Atlanta public school system); Joel L. Fleishman, "The Real Against the Ideal—Making the Solution to Fit the Problem: The Atlanta Public School Agreement of 1973," in *Roundtable Justice: Case Studies in Conflict Resolution, Reports to the Ford Foundation*, ed. by Robert B. Goldmann, (Boulder: Westview Press, 1980), pp. 130–136; and Stone, pp. 103–104.

72. Fleishman, pp. 148, 154, 157–158.

73. For an excellent discussion of the concept of community control, see Susan McGrath, "Great Expectations: The History of School Desegregation in Atlanta and Boston, 1954–1990."

74. James Nabritt, Elizabeth Rinskopf, and Howard Moore, attorneys for the Inc. Fund, insisted on adherence to the NAACP's policy on busing. See McGrath, pp. 335–340.

75. Fleishman, pp. 140–144.

76. Ibid., p. 166.

77. Ibid., p. 146.

78. Bruce Galphin, "The Education of Dr. Crim," *Atlanta Magazine*, (November 1974): 130–131.

79. Schools which had a twenty percent African American population and had stabilized at this level for a number of years were to be excluded from the thirty percent goal.

80. Busing figures were dependent upon the public school system's total enrollment and the effectiveness of the majority-to-minority transfer program. It was estimated that the school system needed to bus roughly 4,800 to reach the goal of having all schools with an African American enrollment of at least thirty percent.

81. For details of the negotiated settlement, see Jackson, pp. 48–49; Research Atlanta, "An Analysis of the Compromise Desegregation Plan," 4 March 1973, Grace Hamilton Papers, Box: 74, Folder: 8; and Stone, p. 104.

82. Research Atlanta, p. 7; and Fleishman, p. 162.

83. *New York Times*, 25 February 1973.

84. Buell G. Gallagher, "Integrated Schools in the Black Cities?," *The Journal of Negro Education*, XLIII (3/Summer 1973): 36–37.

85. *New York Times*, 25 February 1973.

86. Fleishman, p. 164; and Gallagher, p. 73.

87. For a discussion of Wilkins' view of the Nixon Administration, see Roy Wilkins with Tom Matthews, *Standing Fast: The Autobiography of Roy Wilkins* (New York: Viking Press, 1992), pp. 332–333.

88. John Morton Blum, *Years of Discord: American Politics and Society, 1961–1974* (New York: W.W. Norton and Company, 1991), pp. 332–333.

89. Blum, pp. 337–339; and Stephen E. Ambrose, *Nixon: The Triumph of a Politician, 1962–1972* (New York: Simon and Schuster, 1989), pp. 296, 301, 315–317, 330–331, 337–338.

90. Wilkins with Matthews, p. 333.

91. Blum, pp. 334–335; and McGrath, p. 316.

92. Congress did not pass a moratorium on busing. Ambrose, pp. 522–524.

93. Wilkins, *Standing Fast*, p. 333.

94. Fleishman, pp. 164–166; Hansen, p. 9a; McGrath, pp. 343–344, 353–354; and Stone, p. 105.

95. The striking employees demanded: an "across-the-board" one dollar wage increase for associate and superior level employees; improved sick leave, hospitalization, and insurance benefits; a Management-Employees Review Board for the purpose of settling labor disputes; job promotion and/or job transfer be based on service and merit without regard to race, sex, or creed; that the top management at all Rich's stores reflect the approximate racial composition of the city in which the store is located; the store be closed on 15 January in honor of Dr. King's birthday; that Rich's utilized African American banks, construction firms, retailers,

manufacturers, and media; that Rich's locate stores in predominately African American neighborhoods; and that Rich's make annual contributions to nonprofit civil rights and human relations organizations such as SCLC. "We are not Shopping at Rich's," *The People's Crusader*, 6 April 1973, XI (6), p. 6; and Rich's Inc., Memorandum to Reverend Hosea Williams, 10 April 1973, Richard Rich Papers, Box: 25, Folder: 5, Woodruff Library, Emory University, Atlanta, Georgia.

96.   *Atlanta Constitution*, 20 April 1974; and Richard Rich, statement, 20 April 1973, Richard Rich Papers, Box: 27, Folder: 5.

97.   Basically, the settlement allowed striking employees to return to work. Rich's management made no major concessions to the workers. Richard Rich, Letter to employees, 30 May 1973, Richard Rich Papers, Box: 27, Folder: 5.

98.   Robert A. Holmes, "The University and Politics in Atlanta: A Case Study of the Atlanta University Center," *Atlanta Historical Journal*, XXI (Spring 1977): 58–63.

99.   Stone, p. 81.

100.   Jamieson, p. 16.

101.   Jones, p. 107.

102.   Jamieson, p. 18; Jones, p. 107; and Stone, p. 80.

103.   Jones, pp. 107–108.

104.   *Atlanta Constitution*, 28 August 1973; and *Atlanta Voice*, 30 June 1973.

105.   Irene Hill, "Black Political Behavior in Georgia: An Analysis of the Politics of Exchange, 1908–1973 (Master's thesis, Atlanta University, 1980), p. 100; Jamieson, pp. 18–19; and Jones, p. 108.

VII

The Jackson Years

In January 1974 Maynard Jackson was inaugurated Atlanta's first African American mayor. The Atlanta Symphony Orchestra, Mattiwilda Dobbs, and students from Morehouse college entertained the predominately African American audience at the inaugural ceremony. In his rather lofty address, Jackson spoke of "love" rather than policy or politics. He defined "love" as the willingness to embrace the goals of "strong economic growth and prosperity for all," "giving the youth a voice in our government," "concern for the welfare of all our citizens," "a balanced diet for all of our children," and the "absence of racism and sexism." He called upon Atlantans to turn away from the "Old South" and build a new city based on love.[1] While ex-Mayor Sam Massell and Governor Jimmy Carter were present, few members of the business-civic leadership attended the inauguration. In the succeeding weeks, most white leaders were silent about their feelings toward the new mayor.

The enthusiasm displayed by African American leaders and the reserve of the business-civic leadership during Jackson's inauguration reflected the attitudes of their respective communities. African American citizens expected the new government to address their grievances. To these citizens, Jackson's election symbolized a new politics which offered hope to all who had previously been excluded. His election also generated intense racial pride. For the first six months of Jackson's tenure, individuals besieged City Hall with telephone calls desiring to speak to the African American mayor. Jackson established "People's Day" whereby anyone could meet with the mayor for five minutes without an appointment.[2] He felt the burden of becoming the mayor "not just of Atlanta, but the black people of Georgia and even some neighboring states."[3]

African American interest in the city of Atlanta and the new mayor was reflected in and partly generated by a number of articles in national publications which praised the state of race relations in the city. A 1971 article in *Ebony* magazine referred to Atlanta as the "black Mecca of the South." Atlanta was a "promising, yet uncertain emerging giant that dangles before America the possibility of peaceful—and profitable—racial co-existence."[4] A 1974 article in the *New York Times Magazine* proclaimed Atlanta as the "Capital of Black-is-Bountiful."[5] Both articles profiled Atlanta's growing African American middle-class and black enterprise. They discussed the biracial cooperation that existed between white and African American leaders. Both articles correctly noted that a number of young African American professionals were moving to the city. They downplayed, however, the fact that over two-thirds of the Atlantans living below the poverty level were African Americans. With the exception of the Atlanta Life Insurance Company and the Citizens Trust Bank, the majority of black enterprises in Atlanta were small businesses with ten or less employees. After reading the article in *Ebony* magazine, Walter Huntley, a master's degree candidate in urban affairs, moved to Atlanta because he "just wanted to see what it was like." Huntley later worked for the Jackson administration as an expert in taxation and finance.

In marked contrast with the reactions of African American residents, white leaders were anxious and apprehensive about the new administration. Part of this uncertainty was due to their role as the new "political minority." They feared that a majority black government would mean white subordination.

The apprehension of white leaders was also due in part to the personality and political agenda of the new mayor. Jackson was a relatively young politician. With the exception of the fact that he was the grandson of John Wesley Dobbs, the mayor had few links to the biracial coalition of the 1940s, 1950s, and 1960s. He was not beholden to established African American leaders. In fact, many conservative leaders considered Jackson to be a political maverick. If they viewed Jackson as urbane, articulate, intelligent, and charismatic, they also considered him to be "touchy" and "arrogant."[7]

White leaders believed that Jackson had other concerns and constituencies which sometimes took priority over the well-being of the city. After being elected vice-mayor, Jackson reportedly told a journalist that he intended to be a spokesperson for African American interests.[8] As vice-mayor, he pressed officials to end racial discrimination in city departments and award municipal contracts to African American firms. During the 1970 garbage strike, the vice-mayor supported the striking city employees. To many white leaders, these activities suggested that Jackson was absorbed in "black politics," not "city politics." Many white businessmen wondered if Jackson, as mayor, would continue to place the interests of the black community above those of the city and the business community.[9]

In the early 1970s, the Atlanta Chamber of Commerce began a concerted effort to attract career and honorary consulates and international trade offices and tourism bureaus to the downtown area. Its goal was for Atlanta to become an international city. The Chamber adopted the advertising slogan, "Atlanta: The World's Next Great City." For the program to be successful, the business community desired a mayor who was completely devoted to this goal and placed what it perceived to be the interests of the city above all other concerns and constituencies. Business leaders doubted that Jackson could make this commitment. They believed that Jackson was a man caught between two constituencies with opposite interests, the white business community on one hand and the African American community on the other.

Jackson's support of Atlanta's neighborhood movement also concerned many white leaders. In the 1960s, the state highway department proposed two major expressways: Interstate 485, which would have a main artery through Northeast Atlanta, and the Stone Mountain Tollway, which would connect the city with her eastern suburbs. The Atlanta Chamber of Commerce and Central Atlanta Progress (CAP), the city's two main business organizations, endorsed the proposal, but many of the communities in the path of the proposed expressways were affluent white intown neighborhoods. Community organizations arose in opposition to the state highway department's proposal. These independent citizen groups formed an umbrella organization, the Atlanta Coalition on the Transportation Crisis, in order to raise funds for a legal challenge to the proposed expressways and promote a program of political action. This organization gained the support of Governor Jimmy Carter, Congressman Andrew Young, and other state and local officials. The proposal to build these planned expressways was eventually scrapped.

After achieving this victory, neighborhood organizations added other issues to their political agendas. These issues included the development of local neighborhood shopping facilities, the construction of an effective transportation system (as an alternative to the proposed expressways), and a new city charter which would give neighborhoods a greater voice in municipal affairs, crime prevention, and enforced zoning regulations. Neighborhood leaders formed a political organization, the Citywide League of Neighborhoods, in order to promote these concerns. This organization interviewed candidates, made endorsements, and channeled its resources behind "pro-neighborhood candidates." The neighborhood movement became a viable political force.

Jackson supported the neighborhood movement. As vice-mayor, he cast an important tie-breaking vote against city support for Interstate 485. In his 1973 mayoral bid, Jackson ran on a pro-neighborhood platform. He opposed the construction of interstate highways which would bisect neighborhoods and displace residents. He supported the improvement and expansion of MARTA to meet the city's transportation needs. The vice-mayor proposed the creation of a comprehensive system of bicycle-walking trails. Jackson attacked the urban development programs of past administrations. He argued that the city should allocate more funds for neighborhood redevelopment. The vice-mayor believed that enhanced inner-city communities would attract people to downtown Atlanta.[10] As a result of the 1973 municipal elections, the neighborhood movement could claim the mayor, the president of the council, and one-third of the city council members as sympathetic to its causes. The neighborhood movement challenged the hegemony of the business-civic leadership and added a new element to Atlanta's political environment.[11]

Throughout his mayoral campaign, Jackson spoke of the need for political inclusion. He rejected the tradition of "slavish, unquestioning adherence to downtown dicta."[12] Jackson consistently maintained that he wanted to bring the grass roots to the political bargaining table. He argued that the inclusion of neighborhood leaders, the poor, women, and other minorities in the decision-making process would not threaten the interests of the white business or African American communities. For a municipal leadership which had sought to limit citizen participation in the decision-making process, this suggestion was a revolutionary idea.

White anxiety about the new administration was first publicly expressed in the city's newspapers. Three months following Jackson's inauguration, an article appeared in the *Atlanta Constitution* raising speculation as to whether an African American administration and the increased influence of the neighborhood movement would limit the business community's access to City Hall. In this article, several business leaders expressed their frustrations at being unable to directly communicate with the mayor. Their "greatest fear" was that Jackson would lean toward the "immediate demands of the little people rather than the interests of the business community." One downtown developer stated that he was hesitant to invest more money into Atlanta until he understood Jackson's motives.[13]

After becoming mayor, Jackson requested Dan Sweat, executive director of CAP, to compose a detailed statement of the organization's assessments of business conditions in Atlanta, including any complaints or grievances which CAP had against his administration. He promised to correct any problems that might exist in the relationship between the Mayor's Office and the business community.[14]

In late August 1974 the executive committee of CAP held a meeting in which the relationship between the business community and the Jackson administration was the primary topic. The original purpose of this meeting was to "determine whether or not rumors of an impending exodus of business from the city are true." The executive committee found "no discernible trend to indicate any business movement from the downtown area to warrant major concern." CAP decided, however, to offer a set of fourteen proposals to the mayor that it believed would ensure the continued economic growth of the city. The concerns of CAP members included crime in the downtown area, traffic congestion, the lack of parking facilities, a poor pedestrian environment, a lack of funds and commitment to downtown development projects, a growing racial imbalance among the city's labor force, and a perceived racial split in the city's leadership. Two main worries expressed by CAP were the mayor's "inaccessibility" to the members of the business community and a breakdown of close government-business cooperation. The committee noted that some members of the business community perceived the Jackson administration to be anti-white. Some businesses had "moved and more are considering moving for other than economic or management reasons." CAP members expressed fears that more businesses would relocate if these conditions were not addressed by the new administration.[15]

Harold Brockey, CAP's president, voiced these concerns in a letter to Maynard Jackson and City Council President Wyche Fowler. The local newspapers portrayed the "Brockey letter" as a highly critical and personal attack on the mayor by members of the business establishment. National publications such as the *New York Times*, *Business Week*, *Chicago Sun-Times*, and *LA Times* covered the story. Following the lead of the local newspapers, these publications reported that a serious rift existed between Atlanta's black majority government and the white business community. The mayor and CAP representatives denied that any problems existed in their relationship. Dan Sweat stated that the letter was "in no way intended as a warning or an ultimatum." CAP members were simply communicating "some of the problems or possible problems of the city." Jackson received the letter "in good faith." He stated that he did not view the letter as "a threat, as a condemnation, or as a prediction that Atlanta is failing." Members of CAP and the mayor agreed that the letter, in fact, represented the commitment of the business community to the continued economic well-being of the city.[16]

A few days following the Brockey letter, Mayor Jackson and some eight hundred businessmen participated in a forum at the Atlanta Memorial Arts Center. The original purpose of this meeting was to discuss issues facing the city. During the meeting, many business leaders criticized the mayor and African American leaders for their opposition to annexation and several downtown improvement projects. Many charged that black leaders were "selfish" in wanting to maintain political control at the expense of the well-being of the city. Former Mayor Ivan Allen warned that "black and white racism" threatened the economic progress of the city. He urged business leaders and city officials to rise "above petty racism" and cooperate with each other. Mayor Jackson pledged closer cooperation with business leaders.[17]

In order to ensure closer cooperation, Jackson promised to increase his accessibility to members of the business community. He removed all responsibility for scheduling local appointments from his administrative staff and placed it directly under his own supervision. The mayor scheduled meetings with CAP, the Atlanta Chamber of Commerce, and the Action Forum to discuss any grievances that might exist. Jackson also began a "Breakfast with the Mayor Program" and later "Pound Cake Summits" wherein members of the business community could discuss their differences with his administration.[18]

The Brockey letter damaged relations between the local white newspapers and African American leaders. The Atlanta Coalition on Current Community Affairs called the newspapers' coverage of the incident "inflammatory, vicious, and biased." At a press conference, Julian Bond, speaking for the Coalition, charged that the two Atlanta newspapers had "consistently attacked the mayor of the city, viciously and blatantly, creating widespread fear among the citizens of Atlanta."[19] African American leaders criticized the white dailies for not accurately presenting their views. Another criticism was that the newspapers often featured articles accusing black officials of misconduct without adequate supporting evidence. Many black leaders believed that the newspapers were more diligent in their search for any type of misconduct on the part of African American officials than white leaders. In May 1973, the *Atlanta Voice*, one of the city's most liberal black newspapers, had charged the white dailies of harassing African American officials.[20]

Ironically, the criticism of African American leaders was mainly directed at the *Atlanta Constitution*. Of the major white dailies, the

Constitution was generally more supportive of the policies of the business-civic leadership than the more conservative *Atlanta Journal*. Many considered Jack Tarver, Vice-President of Cox Enterprises Inc. which owned the *Atlanta Journal* and *Atlanta Constitution*, to be a member of the city's leadership structure. He was a close friend of Ivan Allen and several members of the business community. He was not, however, personally close to Maynard Jackson. While the *Constitution* was generally favorable in its editorial assessments of the Jackson administration, the tone of its newspaper articles was more critical than that of the *Journal*. Early in his term, Jackson considered the *Journal* to be more "objective," "fairer," and "professional" in the coverage of his administration even though, editorially, it was more critical of his policies.[22]

Relations between African American leaders and the local press further deteriorated when the *Atlanta Constitution* ran a seven-part series entitled "A City in Crisis." The seven installments cited such problems as white flight, a high crime rate, improprieties on the part of city officials, racial polarization, and the lack of experienced leadership. Much of the blame for these problems was placed upon the Jackson administration. The first installment of the series noted that the mayor had "come to symbolize to many white businessmen the troubles in Atlanta."[23]

As in the case of the Brockey letter, national publications covered this story. A columnist for the *New Republic* noted that "wither Atlanta stories have replaced Hank Aaron's home run record as the newspaper's principal occupation." The city had moved from a period of "unrelieved boosterism" to one of "contemplation."[24] An article in *Time* magazine noted that "blacks and whites are not getting along as well as they used to and Mayor Jackson is getting the blame." *Time* magazine referred to "A City in Crisis" as "an all-out attack on the mayor" by members of the business community.[25]

Believing that too much publicity about white anxiety or a breakdown in business-government cooperation would damage the city's image and discourage outside investment, officials of the Chamber of Commerce and CAP denounced "A City in Crisis" as being overstated and misleading. CAP members privately assured outside investors that Atlanta had a harmonious racial climate. Many businessmen tried to explain the series as a personal conflict between Jack Tarver and the mayor.[26]

"A City in Crisis" was not, however, simply the result of a conflict between two individuals. The sentiments expressed in the articles were quite similar to those communicated in the Brockey letter and various forums (the news media, business meetings, and informal conversations). Clearly, businessmen participated in the preparation of the articles. They felt compelled, however, to later denounce the series because it also reflected negatively on the city's image. African American leaders were aware of the anxiety that existed in the white business community. While understanding these fears, most resented and deplored these sentiments.

Despite the tensions that existed between white business leaders and the Jackson administration, both parties realized that they needed the support of each other. The white business community needed a sympathetic city government in order to accommodate its plans for Atlanta's continued economic growth and development. Members of the business community were in the process of building or formulating plans for luxury hotels, a sports complex, a second airport, and MARTA. With the cooperation and encouragement of Maynard Jackson, a consortium of CAP members, called Park Central Communities, was planning to undertake a $250 million housing development of a vacant urban renewal tract in the downtown area.[27] The white business community could not abandon the central business district; it had too much financially and emotionally invested in the city. The city government needed the economic investment of the white business community in order to maintain existing municipal services. Like other cities across the nation, Atlanta was beginning to experience financial difficulties due to the national recession and a slowdown in its growth.

In order to alleviate white fears about African American political control, Jackson balanced his appointments between whites and African Americans. He appointed five whites and four African Americans to head city departments. Almost every commission, task force, and committee was racially balanced with white and African American co-chairpersons. The mayor appointed a white coordinator to act as an intermediary between the black administration and the predominately white state legislature. Jackson also chose a white individual to be the city's chief administrative officer. He generally won praise from business leaders for his efforts to create a biracial government.

Policy differences between the business-civic leadership and the Jackson administration were more difficult to resolve. During Jackson's term in office, African American and white leaders debated such issues as urban renewal, affirmative action, annexation, and the restructuring of various municipal agencies. On some of these issues, business leaders eventually recognized the need to cooperate with the mayor. While they did not always agree with the Jackson administration, they learned to accept many of its policies. Due to the economic resources of the business community and the long tradition of biracial cooperation, Jackson was forced inevitably to compromise on certain issues. As these conflicts were resolved, the two parties established new norms of behavior. By the end of the 1970s, the Jackson administration and the business community had resolved many of their conflicts.

One of the main areas of disagreement between the business community and the Jackson administration was urban renewal. The main priority of the business community had always been the revitalization of the central business district. The cornerstone of Jackson's urban renewal program was neighborhood redevelopment. Revitalizing housing as well as the construction of new homes in inner-city neighborhoods were major goals of Jackson's program. Jackson also sought the protection of residential areas from other forms of land use.

In order to call attention to the need for increased redevelopment in African American neighborhoods, Jackson moved into Bankhead Courts, a low-income housing project, for a weekend. Even though the project was only four years old, residents were already complaining of mice, rats, and roaches. The units also had inadequate sewage and heating systems. Following an inspection of living conditions at the project, the mayor judged the units "unfit for human habitation." Jackson called for increased federal assistance for urban housing programs and suggested that local government officials follow his example of spending time in the projects in order to become better aware of the conditions in public housing facilities and inner-city communities.[29]

Two weeks following this stay at Bankhead Courts, Jackson visited East Lake Meadows, another low-income housing project. Accompanying the mayor were representatives of the Atlanta Housing Authority, the Commissioner of the Department of Community and Human Development, and a representative of the East Lake Meadows Tenant Association. The mayor used this opportunity to announce that the city had received one million dollars in special development funds that would be used to improve sewage conditions at Bankhead Courts and construct a community center at East Lake Meadows.

Early in 1975 the city requested $18.7 million in community development funds. Jackson indicated that these federal funds would be used to revitalize deteriorating neighborhoods. The City Council designated fifty-one neighborhoods (thirty-eight predominately African American) as a community development impact area. Programs in housing and neighborhood economic development were to be concentrated in eighteen neighborhoods; fifteen of which were African American. Public works were planned in sixteen neighborhoods; eleven of which were predominately

African American communities. The City Council and federal authorities approved of these plans.

Many business leaders, however, were extremely critical of the proposal. Officials of CAP sent a letter to a city councilman expressing dissatisfaction that none of the projects to be funded by the grants were located in the central business district. CAP argued that new downtown parking facilities, traffic improvements, and other public works projects in the downtown area would be more beneficial to the city's interests than neighborhood improvements. The letter charged that Davey Gibson, the African American Community and Human Development Commissioner, monopolized the decision-making process in regard to how the federal funds were to be spent.[31] Due to this complaint, Jackson and the City Council were more careful thereafter in allocating some funds to downtown projects when the city received or raised funds for urban development.[32]

In addition to his concentration on neighborhood redevelopment, Jackson wanted to give communities a greater voice in the planning of urban renewal projects. The City Council passed an ordinance dividing Atlanta into twenty-four neighborhood planning units, known as NPUs. Each NPU consisted of a cluster of neighborhoods. The intent of the ordinance was to bring representatives from more than one hundred neighborhoods into contact with each other. The ordinance required that all planning and zoning proposals be referred to the affected NPU in order that comments and reactions could be gauged before the city acted. Officials agreed to an on-going process of developing one-, five-, and fifteen-year plans so that NPUs could determine their situation in the city's overall plan of development.

In order to provide the NPUs with a more formal and effective voice in city government, Jackson created a Division of Neighborhood Planning under the supervision of Leon Eplan, Commissioner of Budget and Planning. Eplan, a former realtor and prominent planner, had previously criticized past urban renewal projects because of their massive dislocation of city residents. The commissioner was sympathetic to the new form of city planning.

Realizing the growing political power of the neighborhood movement, members of CAP and the Chamber of Commerce attempted to initiate contacts with the Citywide League of Neighborhoods. The Chamber of Commerce established a liaison program called Outreach. CAP initiated a program to finance home ownership and redevelopment projects in previously red-lined neighborhoods. These efforts to reconcile differences between the business community and neighborhood organizations failed, however, when CAP revived a proposal to build an expressway through Northeast Atlanta.[33]

While Jackson remained sympathetic toward the neighborhood movement, his support for the NPU system and community planning weakened. Jackson eventually reduced the neighborhood planning staff. Despite his own popular mandate, the mayor realized that he needed the cooperation of the business community. The city's business community was a highly cohesive force which controlled economic and political resources. These resources were needed to facilitate a wide variety of city projects. In addition to its links to city government, the business community had strong ties to Atlanta's leading charitable and social institutions. It was thus a formidable adversary.

While successful in the early 1970s, the Atlanta neighborhood movement could not sustain its efforts. It was unable to build a true citywide coalition. Atlanta's neighborhoods were divided by race, class, and geography. The neighborhood movement discovered that it had to build its constituency on an issue-by-issue basis. Most community organizations had to fight their own political battles. Though there were some successes, most contests with the business community ended in defeat.[34]

One of the projects being considered by the business community was either the expansion of existing facilities at Hartsfield International Airport or the construction of a second municipal airport. Most businessmen favored the latter. Controversy arose as to the possible site of a second airport. Delta and Eastern Airlines favored a site in Paulding County in the northern portion of the Atlanta metropolitan area. Representatives of the airlines argued that this region of the metropolitan area was experiencing the greatest economic growth. The Jackson administration favored a site in Henry County, located southeast of the city. The mayor argued that the Henry County site was closer to the central business district and less expensive.[35] Both sides tried to downplay the racial component of this controversy but the Paulding County site was located in a predominately white area while an African American community was located near the proposed Henry County site. An airport would be an economic bonanza for either county, particularly for the African American residents of Henry County.

The controversy over the site became intense. In August 1974 Delta Airlines announced that it would ask the General Assembly to create a state authority over Atlanta airport facilities. This action would divest the city from any authority over site selection. A second option mentioned was the rerouting of their lines to other southern cities if Mayor Jackson persisted in his demands for the Henry County site.[36] These threats, however, soon became mute points. Early in 1975 the Atlanta Regional Commission, a planning agency for the metropolitan region, suggested that the city should place its emphasis on seeking more efficient use of existing airport facilities. The Commission found that cost benefit problems associated with operating two major airports in the same metropolitan area were too high. In April the City Council voted to expand facilities at Hartsfield International Airport.

Jackson used airport expansion as a means to establish and publicize his affirmative action program. Late in 1974, the mayor expressed his concern to members of the city's aviation department that no African American companies were involved in projects at the airport.[38] After the City Council approved airport expansion, Jackson indicated that Atlanta should establish a goal of having twenty to twenty-five percent of the contracts awarded to minority-owned firms. He suggested that white businesses receiving contracts should form partnerships or joint ventures with minority-owned firms.[39]

Joint ventures were arrangements in which two companies temporarily merged their resources, submitted a bid, and shared contract work and profits on the basis of a negotiated settlement. The purpose of joint ventures was to allow a small-to-middling size company to bid and work on construction projects. Jackson's proposal required white businesses to form partnerships with local minority-owned firms in order to be awarded a city contract. Small African American firms, which could not effectively compete with large white companies on their own, had the opportunity to work on and reap the benefits from airport expansion. While joint ventures were commonly used in the building trades, they had not been previously utilized or required to increase minority participation on a municipal project.

One month following the Council's approval of airport expansion, Jackson announced that the drawing of initial plans for the project would have to be delayed in order to give the contracting firms additional time to find minority partners. In particular, Atlanta Airport Engineers, one of the major firms contracted for the project, sought to be exempted from the joint venture provision, because it could not find a local "qualified" minority-owned business. Jackson indicated that the company could form a partnership with a minority-owned business that was located outside the state. The *Atlanta Constitution* charged that the Jackson administration was pressuring Atlanta Airport Engineers to form a joint venture with Polytech, a Cleveland-based firm which had an office in Atlanta. Jackson's former law partner represented Polytech. The mayor denied that he was pressuring Atlanta Airport Engineers.[40]

"Unnecessary and ridiculous" delays and misconduct on the part of city officials and white firms were two major criticisms of the joint venture provision. The architectural firm of Stevens and Wilkerson, a major contractor on the project, laid off one-third of its workers and switched from a five- to a four-day work week. The company charged that these actions were due to the delay in implementing plans for the airport.[41] The two airlines, which were underwriting the construction costs for the expansion, alleged that the delays were increasing the costs of the project.[42]

The *Atlanta Constitution* charged that individuals and companies associated with Jackson's mayoral bid were receiving lucrative city contracts. In response to these accusations, Jackson noted that "most of the black community and substantial portions of the white community would be blocked from doing business with the city" if past associations with him or his campaign disqualified companies from bidding on municipal projects.[43] Local newspapers also claimed that many of the joint ventures were "frauds" and "shadow corporations" in which African American businesses were only nominally associated with white-owned firms in order that white firms could retain their contracts with the city.[44]

Business leaders argued that joint ventures were unfair to white contractors. Many claimed that Jackson's proposal violated public bidding provisions in the city charter that stated the city should award contracts to perform services on the basis of the lowest bid. The Fulton County Grand Jury issued a presentation stating that to award contracts on any other basis than low bid would harm the city's reputation for "fair and honest dealing."[45] Ten months following this presentation, a Fulton County Superior Court Judge and the Atlanta Bar Association urged the Grand Jury to investigate possible reverse discrimination by city and county governments in awarding contracts. Following an investigation, the Fulton County Grand Jury found no evidence that the city and county governments were guilty of reverse discrimination in the awarding of contracts.[46]

Controversy also surrounded Emma Darnell, the African American commissioner of administrative services under Mayor Jackson. In this position, she supervised the awarding of city contracts. Commissioner Darnell was a strong, assertive individual who strongly adhered to the affirmative action provision. She warned all firms that if they did not meet the city's minority participation goals, the Mayor's Office would cancel their contracts. In part because of her race and gender, business leaders found Emma Darnell to be "difficult," "contentious" and "arrogant."[47]

Mayor Jackson defended joint ventures as a "matter of what's right." Commissioner Darnell argued that the provision was made necessary by previous policy which discriminated against minority-owned firms.[48] The mayor did not have, however, the total support of the African American leadership on this particular issue. Many conservative leaders were afraid of the aggressiveness of the policy. They were concerned that a white backlash might develop against the black community.[49]

New guidelines for the bidding of contracts were set forth in the Finley ordinance which passed late in Jackson's first term. This ordinance established the post of the city contract compliance officer who had the responsibility of scheduling minority employment goals for firms planning to bid on municipal projects. This legislation called for thirty-five percent of city contracts to go to minority-owned firms either through contracts, sub-contracts, or joint ventures. Businesses that did not meet the city's goals or have an acceptable plan for compliance were declared ineligible to bid.[50]

Despite the criticisms directed at joint ventures, the business community accepted provisions relating to minority contracting. Few firms withdrew from bidding on municipal projects due to the city's affirmative action program. Of some three thousand firms that did regular business with the government, only thirty companies were declared ineligible to bid on city projects in 1978.[51] While many businessmen argued that the joint venture proposal went beyond the requirements established by the federal government, Jackson's actions to promote minority employment opportunities actually paralleled those on the national level. The business-civic leadership had already agreed to minority participation in the construction of MARTA and other municipal projects.

Jackson also made some concessions to the business community. City officials agreed to alter affirmative action provisions when Hertz and Avis car rentals threatened to move their operations outside the airport if they were required to form joint ventures. The car rental companies agreed to buy some of their products from African American companies rather than form minority partnerships. Similar concessions were made to other national and local firms. While not directly due to the complaints from businessmen, Mayor Jackson pressured Emma Darnell to resign and the Department of Administrative Services was abolished.[52] Her departure somewhat eased tensions between the Jackson administration and the business community over joint ventures.

The expansion at Hartsfield International Airport opened on schedule in September 1980 and within the allotted budget. All phases of the airport project involved minority participation. The city estimated that seventy-one of the two hundred firms involved in the construction were minority-owned firms and handled contracts totaling $87 million. The project employed more than eight hundred African Americans out of a peak labor force of eighteen hundred.[53] When Jackson became mayor, less than one percent of the municipal contracts went to minority-owned firms. By 1981 African American companies were awarded around twenty-five percent of the city's contracts.[54]

Jackson's affirmative action programs extended beyond minority contracting. He initiated extensive recruitment efforts to find minority job candidates. The mayor also changed municipal employment procedures by imposing a residency requirement on all appointed city personnel (eventually extended to include policemen and firemen) and placing less emphasis on standardized written exams. The imposition of the residency requirement increased the chances of an African American job candidate because the city could no longer draw upon a predominately white metropolitan labor force. Minorities often charged that standardized tests were discriminatory.[55] Between 1973 and 1977, the percentage of African American municipal employees increased from forty-one to fifty-one percent.[56] The mayor also aided the establishment of affirmative action programs at local banks. Jackson warned local financial institutions that he would deposit city funds in banks at Birmingham if Atlanta banks were unwilling to name minorities and women to their boards and develop effective affirmative action programs.[57]

Differences over the city's urban renewal and affirmative action programs were not the only policy conflicts that existed between white leaders and the Jackson administration. In the mid-1970s annexation became a divisive issue. In 1975 the Georgia General Assembly appointed study committees to examine the issues of annexation and "metropolitanization." The upcoming 1976 legislative session was expected to address the issue of metropolitan reform. Political figures and organizations began to formulate various proposals addressing this issue.

Three issues served as major barriers to the passage of annexation legislation: the impact of metropolitan reform on black voting strength, the status of existing municipalities, and the consolidation of area school systems. Most African American leaders opposed annexation and metropolitanization on the grounds that these processes would dilute black political power. Leaders warned that any proposal would have to strictly adhere to the Voting Rights Act of 1965 which forbade governmental boundary changes expressly designed to dilute the voting strength of minorities. African American state legislators had been effective in blocking annexation measures.

The presence of small municipalities to the east and south of the city obstructed Atlanta's expansion in these directions. Various proposals suggested the annexation of these cities by Atlanta or the consolidation of these municipalities into one or two cities. Annexation and metropolitanization thus threatened small municipal governments in the area. Representatives of Roswell, Alpharetta, East Point, and College Park expressed concerns about being annexed or "politically dominated" by Atlanta. White Fulton County Commissioners "Shag" Cates and Charlie Brown stated their opposition to any annexation measure which would result in the abolition of an existing municipality without a popular referendum.[58]

White parents outside Atlanta were concerned that metropolitanization would result in the consolidation of area school systems. This fear was particularly expressed by residents in Fulton County. While Atlanta schools were eighty-five percent African American, the enrollment of Fulton County schools was eighty-seven percent white.[59] Parents feared that the 1973 Atlanta School Compromise would be applied to all schools if Atlanta and Fulton County were consolidated. They did not want their children to attend predominately African American schools.

By the mid-1970s, white leaders were beginning to view metropolitanization as the solution to the area's problems of financing and coordinating services. Research Atlanta, a private consulting firm, was conducting a study on the possible effects of a merger between the city and Fulton County.[60] Commissioner Cates suggested the consolidation of Atlanta and the unincorporated areas of Fulton County. While refusing to endorse any specific proposal, the Chamber of Commerce, CAP, and the League of Women Voters supported the process of metropolitanization to varying degrees.[61]

Carl Sanders, a former Georgia governor, suggested one of the more ambitious plans for metropolitan reform. Sanders, an attorney in Atlanta, proposed the formation of a five-county government (Clayton, Cobb, DeKalb, Fulton, and Gwinnett counties). The "Greater Atlanta Federation" would be governed by a thirty-member council and an appointed chief executive. This body would administer police services, mass transit, highways and expressways, and public utilities for the entire metropolitan region. Under this federation, fifteen to twenty community units would be empowered to deal with local issues. These units would administer the local school systems, sanitation services, parks and small recreational facilities, libraries, local construction projects, and social services. This plan would reduce the black voting population to only twenty-one percent of the electorate.[62]

While Mayor Jackson did not endorse a specific proposal, he indicated his desire to annex the Fulton Industrial District, an industrial site located west of the city. Jackson noted that the annexation of this area would solve the financial problems of the central business district. The Mayor's Office released a report showing that Atlanta would receive an annual net gain of $835,000 in taxes from the Fulton Industrial District by 1985.[63] Areas in the proximity of the site would receive a "special services district status" which would allow them to contract services from the city without being formally annexed. The addition of this territory would not require the abolition of any existing municipalities in the area. Since the site contained little residential property, the annexation of the Fulton Industrial District would not change the racial composition of the electorate.

All the plans being discussed by white leaders at this time would have the effect of reducing the African American electorate in the reconstituted city to less than fifty percent. At a press conference in August 1975, Julian Bond announced his opposition to any annexation proposal that would fatally weaken black political power. He noted that the whole question of annexation stemmed "from the displeasure across the state with black men exercising power." Bond indicated that he could support the annexation of the Fulton Industrial District, because its addition would not change the racial composition of the electorate.[64] In an interview, Mayor Jackson noted that he could personally accept a reduction in the African American voting population to forty-five percent, providing that the Fulton Industrial District was included in the annexation proposal. He did not believe that he could "sell a greater dilution."[65]

In an October 1975 speech before the Hungry Club, Jackson requested the General Assembly to delay any drastic reorganization of the city government for a three-year period so that all issues could be examined in detail. While the mayor did not endorse a specific proposal, Jackson noted that any plan would have to result in the improvement of municipal services, the area's economic development, and citizen participation. It would also have to reduce the overlapping of city and county services and their costs. The mayor recommended that no metropolitan reform should occur without a referendum or the approval of the involved governing bodies. Jackson also warned that "particular attention must be given to assuring that black voters will retain a strong role in local politics." Any proposal, according to Jackson, would have to adhere to the Voting Rights Act of 1965.[66]

In early January 1976, the mayor switched from his position that the state should proceed slowly on metropolitan reform. At a press conference, Jackson stated that it was now a "strategic necessity" for the Mayor's Office and the City Council to devise a new annexation proposal or "forcefully endorse" an existing one. Businesses were "worried about the uncertainty that issue is causing." Jackson urged the state legislature to "settle this issue one way or the other." Until a broad consensus was reached on a plan, the mayor warned that the issue would pose a deterrent to industry desiring to locate in the region.[67]

Jackson's haste was also due in part to the introduction of legislation which was harmful to the city's interests. One bill called for the incorporation of Sandy Springs. The second piece of legislation would prevent any municipality from annexing the Fulton Industrial District. These bills would block Atlanta's expansion to the north and west. The presence of municipalities to the east and south already obstructed Atlanta's expansion in these directions. If both bills passed, the city would have difficulty in utilizing annexation as a means to expand its tax base.

The Jackson administration also opposed legislation introduced by State Representative Ben Brown, chairman of the legislative Black Caucus. Brown proposed the consolidation of Atlanta with the unincorporated areas of Fulton County. Existing municipalities would remain intact. They would have the option of contracting services from or joining the new metropolitan government. His proposal called for the merger of the city and county school systems. Mayor Jackson opposed the proposal on the ground that the costs of city services would increase under Brown's plan.[68] Many of Brown's African American colleagues opposed the legislation because it would dilute black voting strength. According to data provided by the League of Women Voters, the consolidation of Atlanta and the unincorporated areas of Fulton County would reduce the African American electorate to forty-three percent of the total voting population.[69]

Among the city's proposals to the General Assembly was a measure which would allow municipalities to annex contiguous areas that received three or more city services. Julian Bond introduced the legislation in the General Assembly. The bill would not affect existing municipalities or change the racial composition of the electorate. This legislation would allow Atlanta to annex the Fulton Industrial District.[70]

Representatives from districts inside Atlanta's city limits blocked the measure to incorporate Sandy Springs. The bill to prevent municipalities from annexing the Fulton Industrial District also failed to pass. Little support existed in the state house or senate for annexation or government reorganization measures in regard to Atlanta. A poll of members in the state senate found that only twelve senators supported any annexation measure. A survey of the house members found that a majority of representatives would not favor any annexation measure or consolidation plan without a referendum.[71]

While annexation proposals were brought before the General Assembly in the late 1970s and 1980s, no significant annexation or metropolitan reform legislation passed the legislature. The opposition of the African American community and white suburbanites as well as the general lack of interest in this issue muted the drive for metropolitan reform in Atlanta. Many white businessmen believed that Atlanta's African American leaders could eventually be convinced to support annexation if its importance to the city was stressed. They found, however, that white suburban opposition to metropolitanization was almost impossible to overcome.[72] Annexation became less of a divisive issue between the African American and white communities because the chances for metropolitan reform were slim.

One of the most publicized conflicts between the white business community and the Jackson administration was the mayor's attempts to reform the police department. Police-community relations was a sensitive issue in Atlanta. Generally, white Atlantans were worried about the city's high crime rate, particularly black crime. They were wary of attempts to control the behavior of police officers in the performance of their duties. African American citizens were concerned about the police department's apparent indifference toward black-on-black crime and police brutality.

Relations between the police department and the African American community deteriorated during the early 1970s. In 1972 Sam Massell appointed Lieutenant John Inman as police chief to replace the retiring Herbert Jenkins. Among African Americans, Inman earned a reputation as a "racist." Between 1973 and July 1974, police officers in the line of duty killed twenty-three African Americans.[73] In most of these cases, African American leaders questioned the officer's use of force. Chief Inman strongly backed his officers. African American leaders believed that Inman was too inclined to condone the use of force by his officers.

Black leaders also questioned the police department's employment practices. Only twenty-three percent of the city's police officers were African American.[74] In 1973 the city personnel board recommended that two-thirds of all new police officers hired be African American until this racial balance was corrected. Chief Inman announced that he would defy this recommendation. While this action enraged black leaders, the city's white newspapers and councilmen backed Inman's decision.[75]

In his 1973 mayoral campaign, Jackson had criticized the operations of the Atlanta police department. After his election, the mayor decided to dismiss Inman and name a white senior police officer as acting police chief. In defiance, Inman brought members of Atlanta's SWAT squad to keep the white officer out of his office. Inman, who had six years remaining on his contract, filed suit. The Court upheld his contract and enjoined the mayor from removing Inman and appointing an acting chief.

Under authority granted him in the city charter, Mayor Jackson decided to implement his government reorganization plan which called for the establishment of a public safety department. The commissioner of public safety (commonly referred to as the "superchief") would supervise police, fire, and civil defense operations. The head of the division of police services (formerly the police chief) would be subordinate to the commissioner of public safety. Chief Inman filed suit charging that the charter's provision which authorized this action was unconstitutional.

The court eventually upheld Jackson's authority to establish and appoint a commissioner of public safety. It also held that the mayor could not be prevented from exercising his power of direction and supervision over city employees. Since Chief Inman's contract did not expire until 1980, Jackson was forced to appoint him to head the division of police services. This appointment, however, removed Inman from actual command of the police department.[76]

Jackson appointed Reginald Eaves, his chief administrative assistant and a former college classmate, to the position of the commissioner of public safety. This choice was extremely controversial. While Eaves had worked briefly in the corrections system, he had no police experience. Businessmen and the local media criticized the choice and accused the mayor of "cronyism." The City Council, however, approved the nomination by a twelve-to-six vote. Three white and all nine African American councilmen supported Eaves.[77]

In the following months, a number of articles appeared in local dailies charging Eaves with misconduct. One article alleged that one of the commissioner's relatives had been given special treatment in obtaining a government-funded job. Another article reported that Eaves' personal secretary had a criminal record.[78] In February 1975, four "leading members of Atlanta's business community" met with the commissioner. They warned Eaves that his personal image was damaging the city's reputation. The businessmen reminded him that Police Chief Jenkins' reputation had been beneficial to the city and they urged Eaves to improve his image.[79] Downtown businessmen began to press Jackson for the commissioner's resignation, a position endorsed by Wyche Fowler, the president of the city council.[80] At one point, it appeared that the mayor would succumb to the pressure. But in part to Eaves' popularity in the African American community, Jackson decided to defend him. In April 1975 the mayor reappointed Eaves as the public safety commissioner.[91]

Despite the complaints and allegations that were brought against him, Eaves was successful in initiating several changes in the police and fire departments. He established affirmative action guidelines for police and fire department recruitment and promotion. Between 1974 (when Eaves was appointed) and 1976, the percentage of African Americans on the police force increased from approximately twenty-one percent to thirty-five percent.[82] Unlike Inman, Eaves did not condone the use of unnecessary force. Complaints about police brutality declined during Eaves' tenure. The commissioner, to a large extent, restored the black confidence that was lost during Inman's tenure.

Ironically, these changes led indirectly to both Eaves' downfall and his eventual political resurrection. In March 1978, Eaves was accused of providing answers to questions on promotion exams to selected African American policemen. Due to this exam-cheating scandal, Mayor Jackson felt that he had to dismiss Eaves from office. During an emotional speech broadcast by local television stations, Eaves denied knowledge of any incidents of cheating, but the City Council refused his appeal. Largely due to the goodwill that he developed in the African American community while director of public safety, Eaves was subsequently elected to the Fulton County Commission.[83]

During the mid-1970s, city council deliberations reflected the tensions that existed between the business-civic leadership and the mayor. On important issues, African American aldermen tended to vote as a bloc. While neighborhood issues and political ideologies were important determinants in council voting, most members believed that the positions taken by their colleagues were mainly due to racial considerations. In December 1975, ten councilmen, seven white and three African Americans, "admitted" to a reporter that the council was "threatened by serious racial dissent." White Councilwoman Panke Bradley noted that "there has always been a racial split and our attempts to get through it are less and less successful." Black council members charged that their white colleagues were responsible for the dissension; white members blamed their African American counterparts. A white councilman charged that Mayor Jackson "has hinted at racism as a motive whenever I disagree with him on an idea." Jackson denied this accusation.[84]

In March 1977 Jackson had an opportunity to show many of his white critics that his loyalties rested with the well-being of Atlanta when city workers, represented by the American Federation of State, County and Municipal Employees (AFSCME), went on strike. Garbage workers had registered complaints concerning wages and benefits with the Jackson administration since 1975. They desired a $500 salary increase and improved benefits. Because of the local's support of his mayoral bid, members believed that Jackson would be sympathetic to their demands. Instead the mayor assumed the position taken by his two immediate predecessors claiming that sufficient city revenues were not available at the present time to meet the workers' demands.[86]

Conflict between AFSCME and the Jackson administration began in February 1977. The city docked the paychecks of garbage workers for failing to make residential pick-ups during two days of severe cold weather in January. While not part of a formal agreement, three previous administrators had not required garbage workers to make pick-ups when temperatures were below freezing. Workers decided not to report to their jobs for a day in order to protest the docking of their pay. AFSCME leaders urged workers to remain off their jobs and restate their demands for better wages and improved benefits.[87]

While expressing sympathy for the workers' demands, Jackson restated his position that no funds were available in the 1977 general budget. He called the workers' refusal to return to their jobs an "illegal strike." Three days later, the mayor issued a statement indicating that all workers who did not report to work the upcoming week would be fired. After this deadline passed with no terminations, AFSCME escalated its wage demand by requesting a fifty cent per hour increase (instead of a flat $500 raise) during 1977. The union claimed that the city had $28 million in discretionary funds from which it could finance the workers' demands. Jackson denied that these funds existed.

In order to pressure the mayor, AFSCME's parent international union began a $60,000 national advertising campaign. It sponsored ads in national magazines which portrayed Atlanta as an anti-union city with a nonprogressive mayor.[88] AFSCME leaders argued that Jackson's refusal to accommodate workers was a betrayal of his concern for social justice. They warned that the strike would threaten the city's economic growth unless the workers' demands were met. Mayor Jackson countered with the charge that the strike in Atlanta was the first stage of an AFSCME strategy over the next three or four years aimed primarily at discrediting African American mayors and the cities which they governed. AFSCME denied this charge.[89]

Jackson threatened to fire all workers who had not reported back to their jobs by April. He also announced the establishment of an emergency collection system which would operate on a biweekly basis. On the second of April, Jackson announced that one thousand one garbage workers had been fired and the city would begin to hire replacements. The workers who had returned to their jobs along with the replacements began regular biweekly pick-ups.

AFSCME decided to call off its strike. It began negotiations with the Jackson administration in order to find the means by which fired strikers could return to their jobs. When hired, the replacement workers were promised permanent jobs. The Jackson administration decided to use CETA (Comprehensive Employment Training Act) funds as a means of providing limited benefits to fired workers. It promised to return former workers to garbage collection crews as soon as vacancies occurred, and the mayor pledged to seek wage increases for sanitation workers in the next year's operating budget (Jackson honored this pledge).[90]

Despite their support of striking workers during the Allen and Massell administrations, most black leaders and organizations backed the mayor's handling of the strike. At a press conference, Martin Luther King, Sr. announced that he supported the mayor and that Jackson should "fire the hell out of the striking workers."[91] The local branches of the NAACP and the Urban League also supported the mayor's position. The business-civic leadership strongly backed the handling of the strike. In fact, the labor dispute was an important milestone in the relations between the mayor and the business community. To many, Jackson, for the first time, had placed the interests of the city and the business community over those of the African American community. In his handling of the strike, conservative whites concluded that Jackson had acted like the mayor of Atlanta.

Jackson's handling of the strike placed him in a favorable position in the upcoming 1977 mayoral election. Six weeks after the strike ended, a poll revealed that Jackson had a sixty percent favorable rating. In each of the major racial and socio-economic groupings, the mayor's favorable rating was greater than fifty percent.[92] His closest white competitor in the polls was former Georgia Governor Carl Sanders. In one poll, Jackson led Sanders by twenty-one percentage points. After these poll figures were released, Sanders and Ivan Allen, III, president of the Atlanta Chamber of Commerce and son of the former mayor, announced that they would not make mayoral bids. There were no clandestine efforts by the business-civic leadership to produce a candidate. Due to the city's racial demographics and the lack of an identifiable candidate, no opposition from the business community developed; no serious business candidate emerged to challenge Jackson. The business community realistically accepted Jackson's re-election.

Jackson announced his plans to run for re-election in late June 1977. Six other candidates entered the race. Representing the conservative elements in the city were Harold Dye and Milton Farris. Both candidates basically ran on a law-and-order platform. Vince Egan, a candidate running on the Socialist Workers Party ticket, argued that the city should attend to the social needs of its citizens rather than business priorities. Rayanna Childers and Ernest Moschella were write-in candidates. Emma Darnell, who had previously served as Jackson's commissioner of administrative services, announced her candidacy. She accused the mayor of "selling out" to corporate interests. Miss Darnell cited her firing and the handling of the sanitation workers' strike as proof that Jackson had abandoned his commitment to social justice. AFSCME endorsed Emma Darnell, while the Atlanta Labor Council, which had endorsed Jackson in 1973, decided not to formally support any candidate in the mayoral contest. In the general election, Maynard Jackson won sixty-three percent of the vote. Harold Dye was a distant second with seventeen percent of the vote. The racial composition of the school board and the city council remained unchanged.[93]

By 1977 most of the major disagreements between the Jackson administration and the business community had been settled. While Jackson was still sympathetic to the neighborhood movement, his ties to the business-civic leadership were growing stronger. While complaints about the program continued, the business community learned to accept affirmative action and minority partnerships. The opposition of white suburbanites and lack of interest by state legislators largely muted disagreements over metropolitan reform. Jackson's handling of the 1977 garbage strike lessened white business fears that the mayor would place the interests of the African American community above those of the city. The cooperation between the business-civic leadership and the Jackson administration grew during his second term. While earlier tensions had not completely disappeared, the biracial coalition had largely been restored by the end of Jackson's second term.

One reason for its restoration was simple need by both parties. The business-civic leadership had too much financially and emotionally invested in the city to completely disengage itself from the municipal government. While the business-civic leadership criticized the Jackson administration, it never threatened to abandon the city. On the contrary, it repeatedly asserted the need for greater cooperation between business and government.

Likewise, Jackson realized that he needed to cooperate with the business community in order to attract and maintain investment capital. The business community controlled many of the key economic and political resources needed to facilitate a wide range of municipal projects. If Jackson intended to pursue an aggressive economic agenda, he would need the cooperation of the business community. Despite his popular mandate as mayor and the backing of the neighborhood movement, Jackson had to reach some form of accommodation with the business-civic leadership.

While some business leaders complained about their lack of access to the mayor, Jackson tried to maintain open lines of communication with the business community. He periodically met with business leaders. These meetings provided an opportunity for them to discuss any problems or grievances. In order to attract more outside investment to the city, the mayor frequently traveled with representatives from the Chamber of Commerce. These actions led to greater cooperation and trust between the mayor and the business-civic leadership.

The cooperation between the Jackson administration and the business-civic leadership was especially evident when Atlanta was devastated by the murders of twenty-eight African American children. Due to the age, race, and economic status (most were from poor, single-parent households) of the victims, racial tensions in the city were intense. Rumors circulated the city that the murders were part of a racial plot or vendetta against African Americans. National news publications justly described Atlanta as a "city of fear." A black leadership coalition formed to combat community fragmentation denounced the "circus-like" atmosphere generated by the national publicity. It criticized national black leaders who were trying to use the crisis as a means to draw attention to the problem of racism that existed in the United States. African American leaders in Atlanta tried to dispel rumors that the murders were part of a racial plot or conspiracy.[94]

In the midst of this crisis, a boiler exploded at a day-care center at Bowen Homes, a predominately African American housing project, killing four children and a teacher. CAP quickly raised money for the construction of a new day-care center. While the explosion was unrelated to the murders, Jackson cited this action as a sign of biracial concern for the African American children in the city. The Atlanta Chamber of Commerce launched a $150,000 advertising campaign, "Let's Pull Together, Atlanta," in order to improve the city's image and lift the spirits of its citizens in the wake of this terrible tragedy. The mayor initiated a campaign to raise reward money and federal funds to cover the cost of the city's investigation of the murders.[95] The business-civic leadership praised Jackson for his effective handling of the crisis. The cooperation between the mayor and the business-civic leadership was instrumental in maintaining racial calm during a highly emotional crisis.[96]

The cooperation that emerged during the crisis between white and African American leaders did not extend to the 1981 mayoral election. Under the provisions of the city charter, Jackson could not run for another term. Three major candidates representing different constituencies emerged—Andrew Young, Reginald Eaves, and Sidney Marcus. Andrew Young had been one of King's top aides in the SCLC, chairman of the city's Community Relations Commission, a United States Congressman from the Atlanta area, and more recently United States Ambassador to the United Nations under the Carter Administration. Eaves was still a member of the Fulton County Commission. Marcus was a popular white state legislator who was extremely active in civic affairs. He had close personal ties to both business and neighborhood leaders.

The business-civic leadership strongly backed Marcus, who also won the endorsement of the *Atlanta Constitution*. While the business community supported Marcus, many business leaders were impressed with Young who made economic growth a major cornerstone of his platform. Young suggested that Atlanta could become a headquarters for trade with Third World countries, an idea which strongly appealed to the white business community. Young won the support of the traditional African American leadership in the city. Eaves appealed to those voters who were dissatisfied with "politics as usual" and the city's traditional leadership.

In the general election, Young won forty-one percent of the ballots cast; Marcus was a close second with thirty-nine percent of the vote. During the runoff campaign, both candidates were responsive to voters of both races and avoided making racist appeals. Reginald Eaves threw his support behind Young. In the runoff, Young easily defeated Marcus with fifty-five percent of the vote. Voting followed racial lines. Local commentators attributed the small number of racial crossover votes to the presence of two extremely well-qualified candidates (the assumption being that the voter will most likely cast his ballot for the candidate of his race). The ability of Andrew Young, however, to defeat a popular and well-financed white business candidate underscored to many white businessmen and politicians the political dominance of the black community in Atlanta.

Andrew Young and other black leaders, however, were not ones to gloat over the election of another African American mayor. Immediately following the election, Young was espousing the traditional phrases of "racial peace and harmony" and "the city too busy to hate." He pledged his cooperation to the business community. Shortly after his inauguration as mayor, Young held a series of meetings with businessmen, most of whom supported Marcus. Young appeared willing to cooperate with the business community and heal any rifts that existed between white and African American leaders. The governing coalition would enter the 1980s a united front.

Notes

1. *Atlanta Constitution*, 8 January 1974.

2. Henry Hampton and Stephen Fayer, *Voices of Freedom: An Oral History of the Civil Rights Movement From the 1950s Through the 1980s* (New York: Bantam Books, 1990), pp. 626–627.

3. Hampton and Fayer, p. 629.

4. Phyl Garland, "Atlanta, Black Mecca of the South," *Ebony* 10 (August 1970): 152–157.

5. Peter Ross Range, "Making It in Atlanta: Capital of Black-is-Bountiful," *New York Times Magazine* (7 April 1974): 21–29, 68–78.

6. Hampton and Fayer, pp. 622–623.

7. Peter K. Eisinger, *The Politics of Displacement: Racial and Ethnic Transition in Three American Cities* (New York: Academic Press, 1980), p. 80.

8. "Can Atlanta Succeed Where America Has Failed? An Exclusive Interview with Maynard Jackson," *Atlanta Magazine* (15 June 1975): 40.

9. Eisinger, p. 81.

10. Duncan R. Jamieson, "Maynard Jackson's 1973 Election as Mayor," *The Midwest Quarterly*, (18 October 1976): 14.

11. For a discussion of the neighborhood movement, see Clarence N. Stone, *Regime Politics: Governing Atlanta, 1946–1988* (Lawrence: University of Kansas Press, 1989), pp. 82–84.

12. Quoted in Stone, p. 87.

13. *Atlanta Constitution*, 7 April 1974.

14. "Can Atlanta Succeed Where America Has Failed?" p. 110.

15. *Atlanta Constitution*, 21 September 1974.

16. *Atlanta Constitution*, 21 September 1974; and "Can Atlanta Succeed Where America Has Failed?" p. 110.

17. *Atlanta Constitution*, 26 September 1974.

18. Jacob E. Butler, "Racial Conflict and Polarization as a Constraint on Black Mayoral Leadership in Urban Policy: An Analysis of Public Finance and Urban Development in Atlanta During the Mayoral Tenure of Maynard Jackson, 1973–1977" (Ph.D. dissertation, Atlanta University, 1979), p. 137.

19. *Atlanta Constitution*, 22 September 1974.

20. Mack Jones, "Black Political Empowerment in Atlanta: Myth and Reality," *Annals of the American Academy of Political Science* 439 (September 1978): 113.

21. Eisinger, pp. 96–97.

22. "Can Atlanta Succeed Where America Has Failed?" p. 110.

23. *Atlanta Constitution*, 23 March 1975.

24. Milton Viost, "Black Mayor, White Power Structure," *New Republic* 172 (7 June 1975): 9.

25. "Mayor, Learning on the Job," *Time* 105 (21 April 1975): 33.

26. Jackson believed that Reg Murphy, editor of the *Atlanta Constitution*, was responsible for the tone of the articles toward his administration. Stone, p. 90.

27. Jamieson, p. 13; and Stone, p. 80.

28. Jones, p. 110.

29. Butler, p. 130; and Hampton and Fayer, p. 628.

30. *Atlanta Constitution* 18 October 1974; and Butler, p. 131.

31. As head of the Department of Community and Human Development, Davey Gibson oversaw Atlanta's urban renewal program. He was a frequent target of the business community. Butler, p. 185.

32. Stone, pp. 86–87.

33. Austin Scott, "Mayor Shifts Atlanta Power," *Washington Post*, 6 July 1977, p. A1; and Stone, pp. 91–92.

34. Stone, pp. 131–132.

35. *Atlanta Constitution*, 14 September 1974.

36. Butler, pp. 188–189.

37. *Atlanta Constitution*, 5 April 1975.

38. Butler, p. 193.

39. Joint ventures were only suggestions. They were not required if a company could meet the minority participation goals through contracts or subcontractors. Most firms could not meet the city's goals unless they formed joint ventures. Jackson suggested the twenty-five percent minority participation goal to the architectural and engineering firms involved in the project. Construction firms could meet municipal requirements using a twenty percent to minority-owned firms and five percent to small firms formula. *Atlanta Constitution*, 9 August 1975.

40. Atlanta Airport Engineers did not form a joint venture with Polytech. They formed a minority partnership with a firm based in New York.

41. *Atlanta Constitution*, 8 August 1975.

42. Ibid.

43. *Atlanta Constitution*, 20 August 1975.

44. A series of articles appearing in the March 1980 edition of the *Atlanta Journal* alleged that fifty-five percent of the contracts awarded to

minority firms had been misused or were "in question." According to these articles, contracts were awarded to "white-front" firms, black businesses that failed, and conduit companies for white firms.

45.   *Atlanta Constitution*, 1 November 1975; and Jones, p. 113.

46.   Jones, p. 113.

47.   Norman Shavin and Bruce Galphin, *Atlanta: Triumph of a People* (Atlanta: Capricorn, Inc., 1982), p. 315.

48.   *Atlanta Constitution*, 3 August 1975.

49.   Hampton and Fayer, p. 633.

50.   Eisinger, p. 164.

51.   Ibid.

52.   Emma Darnell accused a subordinate of insubordination and incompetence. When the mayor refused to fire this individual, Commissioner Darnell filed federal discrimination charges against Jackson. The mayor asked for her resignation. Emma Darnell and her supporters charged that the real reason for her dismissal was her unpopularity with the business community due to her enforcement of the affirmative action provisions in city contracts.

53.   "Airport that Maynard Built: Blacks Reap Bonanza at World's Biggest Airport," *Ebony* 36 (December 1980): 53, 60.

54.   Bradley R. Rice, "If Dixie were Atlanta," in *Sunbelt Cities: Politics and Growth Since World War II*, ed. Richard M. Bernard and Bradley R. Rice (Austin: University of Texas Press, 1983), p. 51.

55.   Eisinger, p. 163.

56.   Jones, p. 116.

57.   Stone, pp. 87–89.

58.   Butler, p. 162.

59.   *Atlanta Constitution*, 8 August 1975.

60.   Research Atlanta was conducting the study for the Commerce Club. Eisinger, pp. 138–139.

61.   *Atlanta Constitution*, 27 August 1975; and Eisinger, pp. 138–139.

62.   *Atlanta Constitution*, 25 August 1975.

63.   Butler, p. 163.

64.   *Atlanta Constitution*, 23 August 1975.

65.   "Can Atlanta Succeed Where America Has Failed?" p. 41.

66.   *Atlanta Constitution*, 2 October 1975.

67.   *Atlanta Constitution*, 7 January 1976.

68.   *Atlanta Constitution*, 14 January 1976.

69.   Eisinger, p. 139.

70.   Butler, p. 22.

71. *Atlanta Constitution*, 24 January 1976.

72. Eisinger, pp. 140–141.

73. Jones, p. 109.

74. Ibid.

75. Jones, p. 110.

76. Jones, p. 111; and Stone, p. 88.

77. Eisinger, p. 88.

78. *Atlanta Constitution*, 16 June 1975.

79. *Atlanta Constitution*, 14 February 1975.

80. Eisinger, p. 88.

81. *Atlanta Constitution*, 17 April 1975.

82. Jones, pp. 115–116.

83. Stone, p. 88.

84. Eisinger, p. 89.

85. *Atlanta Constitution*, 17 December 1975.

86. Butler, pp. 279–282; and Hampton and Fayer, p. 264.

87. *Atlanta Constitution*, 4–9 February 1977.

88. Butler, pp. 282–283.

89. Jones, p. 115.

90. Ken Bode, "Crying Wulf," *New Republic* 177 (2 July 1977) : 15–16.

91. *Atlanta Constitution*, 2 April 1977.

92. Butler, pp. 285–286.

93. Quoted in Jones, p. 115.

94. Favorable ratings among the main racial and socio-economic groupings: 84 percent middle and upper class African Americans; 61 percent middle and upper class whites; 64 percent lower income African Americans; and 54 percent lower income whites, Butler, p. 305.

95. *Atlanta Constitution*, 5 October 1977.

96. "City of Fear," *Time*, 117 (2 March 1981): 31.

97. Vice-President George Bush announced the creation of a federal task force to aid in the investigation in early February 1981. In March President Reagan announced that $979,000 would be given to the city for programs dealing with social and mental problems arising from the murders.

98. Stone, p. 107.

Conclusion

By all appearances, the interracial coalition that governed Atlanta from 1949 to 1981 was extremely successful. Under its leadership, Atlanta grew from an "overgrown country town" to an international city. For most of this period, Atlanta, as a whole, economically prospered. One of the main reasons for the city's economic success was the political coalition that developed between the white business-civic leadership and African American leaders. With African American political support, the business community of Atlanta was free to pursue a program of economic growth and downtown redevelopment. In return, the business-civic leadership provided a congenial racial climate under which the African American community could feel secure and prosper. The business community allotted a share of the benefits that resulted from the city's economic growth to Atlanta's growing African American middle class in order to ensure the black community's continuing support. These benefits not only solidified the relationship between the coalition partners, but also gave African American leaders a personal and financial stake in the city's well-being.

White business leaders realized that a reputation for good race relations would attract outside investment and provide favorable national press for the city. Representatives of Atlanta boasted of the use of negotiations to solve racial problems; the city's African American colleges, businesses, and middle-class neighborhoods; an atmosphere of racial peace and harmony; and a leadership dedicated to economic and social progress. The maintenance of this reputation was often used as a justification for racial reform in the city. This economic justification was often combined with an appeal to civic pride. Municipal officials portrayed Atlanta as a New South city that would be a model and set the standards for race relations in the region.

The national media perpetuated this image of racial progress. For most of this period, journalists used the absence of overt racial conflict as the primary standard to assess the state of race relations in a particular location. In contrasting the racial situation in Atlanta with that of other southern cities, race relations in Atlanta seemed ideal. The only racial incident that even began to resemble a "riot" in Atlanta occurred in the Dixie Hills community in June 1967. While some journalists began to question the "myth of Atlanta" during the late 1960s, the general image of Atlanta as portrayed by the media was one of "a city 'too busy to hate,' ready to set aside the uglier aspects of a bad social system and move on to newer ways."[1]

Whether this portrayal was accurate, it was a belief to which many subscribed. Atlantans, both white and African American, shared a sense of pride in the accomplishments and racial progress that had been made. Many African American leaders were enticed with the image of Atlanta as a New South city and the so-called "Cradle of the Civil Rights Movement." Senator LeRoy Johnson believed that there was no other "city in the nation where a Negro has more opportunity to achieve his ambitions."[2] While acknowledging that more racial reform was needed, other African American leaders voiced this same sentiment.

But the majority of African American residents experienced social and economic realities that contradicted Atlanta's image. While Atlanta's African American community had a developed middle and upper class, most black citizens lived in poverty areas and slums. A two-tiered social and economic black Atlanta existed. In 1966 Roger Williams described the living conditions of these two "Negro Atlantas." One community consisted of areas where "the houses are large, well-tended, and set off from the streets by rolling lawns and carefully placed shrubbery." The other "Negro Atlanta" consisted of areas where "houses are broken down shacks, sitting right on the teeming, dirty street with no lawn and little shrubbery."[3] African American residents of lesser economic means hoped and expected that the Civil Rights Movement and African American political dominance would initiate reforms that would propel their neighborhoods into the economic mainstream.

One of the major accomplishments of the Civil Rights Movement in Atlanta was African American participation in the political process. Due to their efforts during the Civil Rights Movement in Atlanta and the changing racial demographics of the city, African Americans won their place in the city's leadership structure. While the white business community initially resisted this development, it gradually learned to accept the growing political power of the African American community. White business leaders discovered that they needed the political support of the African American community in order to pursue their program of economic growth for the city.

Since 1981 the African American community has increased its political strength. In that year, more African Americans were elected to the City Council than whites. By 1984 African Americans held more than forty-five elective positions. Atlanta had an African American mayor, four African American state representatives, three African American county commissioners, thirteen African American council members, nine African American judges, and six African American school board representatives. In 1986 John Lewis, a veteran civil rights leader and one of the original founders of SNCC, became the second African American to represent Georgia's Fifth Congressional District in the United States Congress.[4]

The political gains made by Atlanta's African American community have not yet fully been translated into tangible benefits for African Americans of lesser economic means. The policies enacted by the governing coalition have generally favored the interests of the upper economic strata of both communities. In particular, the coalition has benefited only a small portion of Atlanta's African American community. For example, the business-civic leadership exhibited strong support for private African American housing during the 1950s, but showed a lack of enthusiasm for needed public housing. The main priorities of the governing coalition have remained economic growth and downtown revitalization rather than poverty and neighborhood redevelopment.

A sizable portion of Atlanta's African American population continues to be poor, unemployed, ill-housed, and trapped in deteriorating neighborhoods with little means of escape. In 1980 one in four African American households fell below the poverty level. African American residents were more than three times more likely to be poor than white residents of the city. Due to the loss of industrial jobs in the inner-city and Atlanta's movement toward white-collar economy, employment prospects for African Americans were bleak during the 1970s and early 1980s. In 1986 the African American unemployment rate was over eight percent as compared to three percent for white residents. African American residents were more than three times more likely than white citizens to be unemployed. The out-migration of affluent white and African American residents has continued to erode the city's tax base. Business disinvestment has followed the out-migration of middle-income residents resulting in the deterioration of many inner-city communities.[5]

In an interview, Ethel Mae Matthews, president of the Atlanta chapter of the National Welfare Rights Organization, noted that the city was "an excellent place to live for some black people. . . . But not for all black people, its not an excellent place to live."[6] For a majority of African

American citizens a wide gap existed between the progressive image of Atlanta as promoted by the business-civic leadership of the city and the daily realities that they faced. In order for this gap to diminish, the interracial coalition must face the challenge of propelling its large African American underclass into the economic mainstream.

Notes

1. Reece Cleghorn, "The Death of the Myth," *Atlanta Magazine* (December 1968): 24.
2. Roger Williams, "The Negro in Atlanta," *Atlanta Magazine* (June 1966): 25.
3. Ibid.
4. Robert Bullard and E. Kiki Thomas, "Atlanta: Mecca of the Southeast," in *In Search of the New South: The Black Urban Experience in the 1970s and 1980s*, ed. By Robert Bullard (Tuscaloosa: University of Alabama Press, 1989), pp. 94–95.
5. Bullard and Thomas, pp. 85–92, 96.
6. Henry Hampton and Stephen Fayer, eds. *Voices of Freedom: An Oral History of the Civil Rights Movement from the 1950s Through the 1980s* (New York: Bantam Books, 1990), p. 623.

Bibliography

SELECTED BOOKS AND PAMPHLETS

Abernathy, Ralph D. *And the Walls Came Tumbling Down: An Autobiography.* New York: Harper and Row, 1989.

Alexander, T.M., Sr. *Beyond the Timberline: The Trials and Triumphs of a Black Entrepreneur.* Edgewood, Maryland: M.E. Duncan and Company, 1992.

Allen, Ivan, Jr. with Paul Hemphill. *Mayor: Notes on the Sixties.* New York: Simon and Schuster, 1971.

Ambrose, Stephen E. *Nixon: The Triumph of a Politician 1962–1972.* New York: Simon and Schuster, 1987.

Atlanta Committee for Cooperative Action. *A Second Look: The Negro Citizen in Atlanta.* Atlanta: The Atlanta Committee for Cooperative Action, 1960.

Atlanta Council on Human Relations. *Atlanta: Protests and Progress, A Special Report.* Atlanta: Atlanta Council on Human Relations, April 1964.

Atlanta Metropolitan Planning Commission. *Up Ahead: A Regional Land Use Plan for Metropolitan Atlanta.* Atlanta: Atlanta Metropolitan Planning Commission, 1952.

Bacote, Clarence. *The Story of Atlanta University: A Century of Service 1865–1965.* Atlanta: Atlanta University, 1969.

Bartley, Numan V. *The Creation of Modern Georgia.* Athens: University of Georgia Press, 1990.

————. *From Thurmond to Wallace: Political Tendencies in Georgia 1946–1969.* Baltimore: Johns Hopkins Press, 1970.

————. *The Rise of Massive Resistance: Race and Politics in the South During the 1950s.* Baton Rouge: Louisiana State University Press, 1969.

Bartley, Numan V. and Hugh D. Graham. *Southern Politics and the Second Reconstruction.* Baltimore: John Hopkins Press, 1975.

Beardslee, William R. *The Way Out Must Lead In: Life Histories in the Civil Rights Movement.* Atlanta: Center for Research in Social Change, Emory University, 1977.

Berry, Mary Francis. *Black Resistance, White Law: A History of Constitutional Racism in the United States.* Englewood Cliffs: Prentice-Hall, 1971.

Black, Earle and Merle Black. *Politics and Society in the South.* Cambridge: Harvard University Press, 1987.

Bloom, Jack. *Race, Class, and the Civil Rights Movement.* Bloomington: Indiana University Press, 1987.

Blumberg, Janice Rothschild. *One Voice: Rabbi Jacob Rothschild and the Troubled South.* Macon: Mercer University Press, 1985.

Bond, Julian. *A Time to Speak, A Time to Act: The Movement in Politics.* New York: Harper and Row, 1972.

Bornet, Vaughn Davis. *The Presidency of Lyndon Johnson.* Lawrence: University of Kansas Press, 1983.

Branch, Taylor. *Parting the Waters: America During the King Years 1954–1963.* New York: Simon and Schuster, 1981.

Brauer, Carl M. *John F. Kennedy and the Second Reconstruction.* New York: Columbia University Press, 1977.

Brisbane, Robert H. *Black Activism: Racial Revolution in the United States 1954–1970*. Valley Forge: Judson Press, 1974.

Button, James. *Blacks and Social Change: Impact of the Civil Rights Movement in Southern Communities*. Princeton: Princeton University Press, 1989.

Calloway, W.L. *The 'Sweet Auburn Avenue' Business History 1908–1988*. Atlanta: Central Atlanta Progress, 1988.

Carson, Clayborne. *In Struggle: SNCC and the Black Awakening in America*. Cambridge: Harvard University Press, 1981.

Chafe, William. *Civilities and Civil Rights: Greensboro, North Carolina and the Black Struggle for Freedom*. New York: Oxford University Press, 1985.

Clayton, Xernona with Hal Gulliver. *I've Been Marching All the Time*. Atlanta: Longstreet Press, 1991.

Colburn, David. *Racial Change and Community Crisis: St. Augustine, Florida 1877–1980*. New York: Columbia University Press, 1985.

Coleman, Kenneth, ed. *A History of Georgia*. Athens: University of Georgia Press, 1977.

Conyers, James. *Black Youth in a Southern City*. Atlanta: Southern Regional Council, 1968.

Crain, Robert. *The Politics of School Desegregation: Comparative Case Studies of Community Structure and Policy Making*. Chicago: Aldine Press, 1968.

Crawford, Fred. *Civil Aggression and Urban Disorders*. Atlanta: Center for Research in Social Change, Emory University, 1967.

Crawford, Fred, Norman R. Crawford, and Leah Dabbs. *A Report of Certain Reactions by the Atlanta Public to the Death of Martin Luther King, Jr.* Atlanta: Center for Research in Social Change, Emory University, 1969.

Eisinger, Peter K. *The Politics of Displacement: Racial and Ethnic Transition in Three American Cities*. New York: Academic Press, 1980.

English, James W. *The Prophet of Wheat Street: The Story of William Holmes Borders*. Elgin, Illinois: David C. Cooke Publishing, 1973.

Fairclough, Adam. *To Redeem the Soul of America: The Southern Christian Leadership Conference and Martin Luther King, Jr.* Athens: University of Georgia Press, 1987.

Franklin, John Hope. *From Slavery to Freedom: A History of Negro America*, fifth edition. New York: Alfred A. Knopf, 1980.

Frazier, E. Franklin. *The Black Bourgeoisie*. New York: The Free Press, 1957.

Galphin, Bruce. *The Riddle of Lester Maddox*. Atlanta: Camelot Publishing Company, 1968.

Garrett, Franklin M. *Atlanta and Environs: A Chronicle of Its People and Events*. 3 Vols. New York: Lewis Historical Publishing Company, Inc., 1954.

Garrow, David. *Bearing the Cross: Martin Luther King, Jr. and the Southern Christian Leadership Conference*. New York: William Morrow and Company, 1986.

Garrow, David, ed. *Atlanta, Georgia 1960–1961: Sit-ins and Student Activism*. New York: Carlson Publishing Company, 1989.

Gates, Robbins L. *The Making of Massive Resistance: Virginia's Politics of Public School Desegregation 1954–1956*. Chapel Hill: University of North Carolina Press, 1962.

Goodwyn, Lawrence. *The Populist Movement: A Short History of the Agrarian Revolt in America*. New York: Oxford University Press, 1968.

Grant, Donald L. *The Way It Was In the South: The Black Experience In Georgia*. ed. Jonathan Grant. New Jersey: A Birch Lane Press Book, 1992.

Grantham, Dewey W. *Hoke Smith and the Politics of the New South*. Baton Rouge: Louisiana State Press, 1958.

————. *The South in Modern America: A Region at Odds*. New York: HarperCollins, 1994.

Hall, Kermit L., ed. *The Oxford Companion to the Supreme Court of the United States*. New York: Oxford University Press, 1992.

Hamer, Andrew Marshall, ed. *Urban Atlanta: Redefining the Role of the City*. Atlanta: Georgia State University Press, 1980.

Hampton, Henry and Stephen Fayer, eds. *Voices of Freedom: An Oral History of the Civil Rights Movement from the 1950s Through the 1980s*. New York: Bantam Books, 1990.

Henderson, Alexa Benson. *Atlanta Life Insurance Company: Guardian of Black Economic Dignity*. Tuscaloosa: University of Alabama Press, 1990.

Henderson, Harold P. and Gary L. Roberts, eds. *Georgia Governors in an Age of Change: From Ellis Arnall to George Busbee*. Athens: University of Georgia Press, 1988.

Hunter, Floyd. *Community Power Structure*. Chapel Hill: University of North Carolina Press, 1953.

————. *Community Power Succession: Atlanta Policy Makers Revisited*. Chapel Hill: University of North Carolina Press, 1980.

Hunter-Gault, Charlayne. *In My Place*. New York: Farrar Straus Giroux, 1992.

Hutcheson, John D. *Racial Attitudes in Atlanta*. Atlanta: Center for Research and Social Change, Emory University, 1973.

Inger, Morton. *Politics and Reality in an American City: The New Orleans School Crisis of 1960*. New York: Center for Urban Education, 1969.

Jacoway, Elizabeth and David R. Colburn, eds. *Southern Businessmen and Desegregation*. Baton Rouge: Louisiana State University Press, 1982.

Jenkins, Herbert. *Forty Years on the Force: 1932–1972*. Atlanta: Center for Research in Social Change, Emory University, 1973.

————. *Keeping the Peace: A Police Chief Looks at His Job*. New York: Harper and Row, 1970.

Jennings, M.K. *Community Influentials: The Elites of Atlanta*. Glencove: Free Press, 1964.

Jordan, Barbara and Elspeth D. Rostow, eds. *The Great Society: A Twenty Year Critique*. Austin: University of Texas Press, 1986.

Key, V.O. *Southern Politics in State and Nation*. New York: Alfred A. Knopf, 1949.

King, Martin Luther, Sr. with Clayton Riley. *Daddy King: An Autobiography*. New York: William Morrow and Company, 1980.

King, Mary. *Freedom Song: A Personal Story of the 1960s Civil Rights Movement*. New York: William Morrow and Company, 1987.

Kluger, Richard. *Simple Justice: The History of Brown v. Board of Education and Black America's Struggle for Equality*. New York: Alfred A. Knopf, 1976; reprint ed. New York: Random House, 1977.

Kousser, J. Morgan. *The Shaping of Southern Politics: Suffrage Restriction and the Establishment of the One-Party South, 1880–1910*. New Haven: Yale University Press, 1974.

Kuhn, Clifford, Harlon Joyce, and Bernard West. *Living Atlanta: An Oral History of the City 1914–1948*. Athens: University of Georgia Press, 1990.

Lawson, Stephen F. *Black Ballots: Voting Rights in the South 1944–1969*. New York: Columbia University Press, 1976.

————. *In Pursuit of Power: Southern Blacks and Electoral Politics 1965–1982*. New York: Columbia University Press, 1985.

Lewis, David L. *King: A Critical Biography*. New York: Praeger, 1970.

McGill, Ralph. *The South and the Southerner*. Boston: Little Brown and Company, 1963.

Maddox, Lester. *Speaking Out: The Autobiography of Lester Maddox*. New York: Doubleday, 1975.

Marble, Manning. *Race, Reform, and Rebellion: The Second Reconstruction in Black America*. Jackson: University of Mississippi Press, 1984.

Martin, Harold. *William Berry Hartsfield: Mayor of Atlanta*. Athens: University of Georgia Press, 1978.

Mathews, Donald R. and Prothro, James W. *Negroes and the New Southern Politics*. New York: Harcourt, Brace, and World, 1966.

Mays, Benjamin E. *Born to Rebel: An Autobiography*. New York: Scribner, 1971; reprint ed., Athens: University of Georgia Press, 1987.

Morris, Aldon. *The Origins of the Civil Rights Movement: Black Communities Organizing for Change*. New York: Free Press, 1984.

Muse, Benjamin. *Virginia's Massive Resistance*. Bloomington: Indiana University Press, 1961.

National Education Association, National Education Committee on Professional Rights and Responsibilities. *Central Issues Influencing School-Community Relations in Atlanta, Georgia*. Washington: National Education Association, 1968.

Neary, John. *Julian Bond: Black Rebel*. New York: William Morrow and Company, 1971.

Norrell, Robert J. *Reaping the Whirlwind: The Civil Rights Movement in Tuskegee*. New York: Alfred A. Knopf, 1985.

Oates, Stephen. *Let the Triumph Sound: The Life and Times of Martin Luther King, Jr.* New York: Harper and Row, 1972.

Organizations Assisting Schools in September. *Background Atlanta: A Handbook for Reporters Covering the Desegregation of Schools.* Atlanta: OASIS, 1961.

Parmet, Herbert S. *JFK: The Presidency of John F. Kennedy.* New York: Dial Press, 1983.

Paschall, Eliza. *It Must Have Rained.* Atlanta: Center for Research in Social Change, Emory University, 1975.

Patterson, James T. *America's Struggle Against Poverty 1900–1985.* Cambridge: Harvard University Press, 1986.

Raines, Howell. *My Soul is Rested: Movement Days in the Deep South Remembered.* New York: G.P. Putnam's Sons, 1977.

The Report of The General Assembly Committee on Schools. Atlanta, Georgia, 28 April 1960.

Research Atlanta. *Atlanta School Compromise Plan.* Atlanta: Research Atlanta, 1973.

————. *School Desegregation in Atlanta 1954–1973.* Atlanta: Research Atlanta, 1973.

————. *Which Way Atlanta?* Atlanta: Research Atlanta, 1973.

Rooks, Charles. *The Atlanta Elections of 1969.* Atlanta: Voter Education Project, 1970.

Rose, Thomas and John Greenya. *Black Leaders: Then and Now.* Garrett Park: Garrett Park Press, 1984.

Rouse, Jacqueline. *Lugenia Burns Hope: Black Southern Reformer.* Athens: University of Georgia Press, 1989.

Schutze, John. *The Accommodation: The Politics of Race in an American City.* New Jersey: Citadel Press, 1986.

Shavin, Norman and Bruce Galphin. *Atlanta: Triumph of a People.* Atlanta: Capricorn, Inc., 1985.

Smith, David. *Inequality in an American City: Atlanta, Georgia 1960–1970.* London: Department of Geography, Queen Mary College, University of London, 1981.

Smith, Bob. *They Closed Their Schools: Prince Edward County, Virginia 1951–1965.* Chapel Hill: University of North Carolina Press, 1965.

Spritzer, Lorraine. *The Belle of Ashby Street: Helen Douglas Mankin and Georgia Politics.* Athens: University of Georgia Press, 1982.

Southeast Atlanta Civic Council. *The City Must Provide, South Atlanta: The Forgotten Community.* Atlanta: Southeast Atlanta Civic Council, 1963.

Stone, Clarence N. *Economic Growth and Neighborhood Discontent: System Bias in the Urban Renewal Program of Atlanta.* Chapel Hill: University of North Carolina Press, 1976.

------. *Regime Politics: Governing Atlanta 1946–1988.* Lawrence: University of Kansas Press, 1989.

Suggs, Henry, ed. *The Black Press in the South 1865–1979.* Westport: Greenwood Press, 1983.

Summit Leadership Conference. *Action For Democracy: Recommendations from the Citywide Leadership Conference of October 19, 1963.* Atlanta: Summit Leadership Conference, 1963.

Taeuber, Karl E. and Alema F. Taueber. *Negroes in Cities: Residential Segregation and Neighborhood Change.* Chicago: Aldine Publishing, 1965.

Tindall, George Brown. *The Disruption of the Solid South.* New York: W.W. Norton Company, 1972.

————. *The Emergence of the New South 1913–1945.* Baton Rouge: Louisiana State Press, 1964.

Trillin, Calvin. *An Education in Georgia: Charlayne Hunter, Hamilton Holmes, and the Integration of the University of Georgia.* New York: Viking Press, 1964.

United States Commission on Civil Rights. *Hearings Before the United States Commission on Civil Rights: Housing, Atlanta, Georgia, 10 April 1959.* Washington: Government Printing Office, 1959.

Walker, Jack. *Sit-ins in Atlanta.* New York: McGraw Hill, 1964.

Weiss, Nancy. *Farewell to the Party of Lincoln: Black Politics in the Age of FDR.* Princeton: Princeton University Press, 1983.

————. *Whitney Young, Jr. and the Struggle for Civil Rights.* Princeton: Princeton University Press, 1989.

Weltner, Charles. *Southerner.* Philadelphia: J.B. Lippincott, 1966.

Wilkins, Roy with Tom Matthews. *Standing Fast: The Autobiography of Roy Wilkins.* New York: Viking Press, 1992.

Williams, Roger. *The Bonds: An American Family.* New York: Athenaeum, 1971.

Williamson, Joel. *The Crucible of Race: Black/White Relations in the American South Since Emancipation.* New York: Oxford University Press, 1984.

Woodward, C. Vann. *The Origins of the New South, 1877–1913.* Baton Rouge: Louisiana State Press, 1951.

————. *The Strange Career of Jim Crow.* New York: Oxford University Press, 1965.

Zinn, Howard. *The Southern Mystique.* New York: Alfred A. Knopf, 1964.

SELECTED ARTICLES AND ESSAYS

Abney, F. Glen and John D. Hutcheson. "Race, Representation, and Trust: Changes in Attitudes After the Election of a Black Mayor." *Public Opinion Quarterly* (Spring 1981): 91–100.

Adams, Samuel L. "Blueprint for Segregation: A Survey of Atlanta Housing." *New South* 22 (Spring 1967): 73–84.

Alexander, Robert J. "Negro Business in Atlanta." *Southern Economic Journal* 17 (4/1951): 451–464.

Bacote, C.A. "The Negro in Atlanta Politics." *Phylon* XVI (4/1955): 333–350.

Baird, Joseph. "Atlanta Negroes Rock the Boat." *Reporter* (14 December 1967): 32–34.

Bartley, Numan V. "Atlanta Elections and Georgia Political Trends." *New South* (Winter 1970): 22–30.

Bayor, Ronald H. "Roads to Racial Segregation: Atlanta in the Twentieth Century" *Journal of Urban History* 15 (November 1988): 3–21.

———. "Race and City Services: The Shaping of Atlanta's Police and Fire Departments." *Atlanta History* 36 (3/Fall 1992): 19–35.

Bullard, Robert and E. Kiki Thomas. "Atlanta: Mecca of the Southeast," in *In Search of the New South: The Black Urban Experience in the 1970s and 1980s* ed. by Robert Bullard. Tuscaloosa: University of Alabama Press, 1989, pp. 75–97.

Bullock, Charles S. and Bruce A. Campbell, "Racist or Racial Voting in the 1981 Municipal Elections." *Urban Affairs Quarterly* 20 (2/December 1984): 149–164.

Burman, Stephen. "The Illusion of Progress: Race and Politics in Atlanta." *Ethnic and Racial Studies* 2 (4/October 1979): 441–454.

"Can Atlanta Succeed Where America Has Failed?—An Exclusive Interview with Mayor Maynard Jackson." *Atlanta Magazine* (June 1975): 40–41, 106–112.

Cater, Douglas. "Atlanta: Smart Politics and Good Race Relations." *Reporter* (11 July 1957): 18–21.

Coffin, Alex. "Number Two Tries Harder." *Atlanta Magazine* (June 1971): 42–43, 68–73.

Cleghorn, Reece. "Allen of Atlanta Collides with Black Power and Racism." *New York Times Magazine* (16 October 1966): 32–33, 134–140.

Driskell, Curtis. "The Force of 'Forward Atlanta'." *Atlanta Magazine* (August 1963): 37–40.

Dudley, J. Wayne. "'Hate' Organizations of the 1940s: The Columbians Inc." *Phylon* XLII (3/September 1981): 262–274.

Elliott, Jeffrey. "The Civil Rights Movement Reexamined: An Interview with Julian Bond." *Negro Historical Bulletin* 39 (6/1976): 606–610.

Feagans, Janet. "Atlanta Theatre Segregation: A Case of Prolonged Avoidance." *Journal of Human Relations* 13 (2/1965): 208–218.

Fleishman, Joel L. "The Real Against the Ideal—Making the Solution Fit the Problem: The Atlanta Public School Agreement of 1973," in *Roundtable Justice: Case Studies in Conflict Resolution*, ed. by Robert S. Goldmann. Boulder, Colorado: Westview Press, pp. 129–180.

Gallagher, Buell G. "Integrated Schools in the Black Cities?" *The Journal of Negro Education* XIII (3/Summer 1973): 336–350.

Galphin, Bruce. "The Education of Dr. Crim." *Atlanta Magazine* (November 1974): 63–64, 130–132, 134–136, 138.

———. "Racial Coverage in Atlanta: Once Over Lightly." *Atlanta Journalism Review* (July/August 1971): 8, 27–30.

Garofalo, Charles. "The Atlanta Spirit: A Study in Urban Ideology." *South Atlantic Quarterly*, 74 (1/1975): 34–44.

Garland, Phyl. "Atlanta: Black Mecca of the South." *Ebony* (August 1971): 152–157.

"Hector Black, White Power in Black Atlanta." *Look* (13 December 1966): 137–140.

Hein, Virginia. "The Image of 'A City Too Busy': Atlanta in the 1960s." *Phylon* XXXIII (2/1972): 205–221.

Holloway, James. "The Paradigm of Dixie Hills." *New South* (Summer 1967): 75–81.

Holmes, Robert. "The University and Politics in Atlanta: A Case Study of the Atlanta University Center." *Atlanta Historical Journal* (Spring 1981): 49–66.

Hornsby, Alton. "The Negro in Atlanta Politics, 1961–1973." *Atlanta Historical Bulletin* XXI (Spring 1973): 7–33.

Jackson, Barbara. "Desegregation: Atlanta Style." *Theory Into Practice* 17 (1/1973): 43–53.

Jamieson, Duncan. "Maynard Jackson's 1973 Election as Mayor." *Midwest Quarterly* 18 (1/1976): 7–26.

Jennings, M. Kent and Harmon Zeigler. "Class, Party, and Race in Four Types of Elections: The Case of Atlanta." *Journal of Politics* 28 (2/1966): 391–407.

Jones, Mack H. "Black Political Empowerment in Atlanta: Myth and Reality." *Annals of the American Academy of Political and Social Science* 439 (September 1978): 90–117.

Leonard, George B. "The Second Battle of Atlanta." *Look* (4 April 1961): 31–42.

Lincoln, C. Eric. "The Strategy of a Sit-in." *Reporter* (5 January 1961): 20–23.

McCain, Ray. "Speaking on School Desegregation by Atlanta Ministers." *Southern Speech Journal* 29 (3/64): 256–262.

Martin, Charles H. "White Supremacy and Black Workers: Georgia's 'Black Shirts' Combat the Great Depression." *Labor History* 18 (3/1977): 366–381.

Martin, William C. "Atlanta: Political Transfer and Succession in a Southern Metropolis." *Journal of Intergroup Relations* 4 (3/1975): 22–32.

Meier, August and David Lewis. "History of the Negro Upper Class in Atlanta, Georgia 1890–1958." *Journal of Negro Education* 28 (Spring 1959): 128–139.

Moore, John Hammond. "Communists and Fascists in a Southern City." *South Atlantic Quarterly* 67 (3/Summer 1968): 437–454.

Newsom, Lionel and William Gorden. "A Stormy Rally in Atlanta." *Today's Speech* 11 (4/1963): 18–21.

Petrof, John. "The Effect of the Student Boycott Upon the Purchasing Habits of Negro Families in Atlanta, Georgia." *Phylon* 24 (3/1963): 266–270.

Powledge, Fred. "Profiles: A New Politics in Atlanta." *New Yorker* (31 December 1973): 28–40.

Ravitch, Diane. "The 'White Flight' Controversy." *The Public Interest* 51 (Spring 1978): 135–149.

Range, Peter Ross. "Making It in Atlanta: Capital of Black-is-Bountiful." *New York Times Magazine* (7 April 1974): 28–29, 68–78.

Rice, Bradley. "The Battle of Buckhead: The Plan of Improvement and Atlanta's Last Big Annexation." *Atlanta Historical Journal* XXV (Winter 1981): 5–22.

Ross, Edyth. "Black Heritage in Social Welfare: A Case Study of Atlanta." *Phylon* XXXVII (4/1976): 297–307.

Shankman, Arnold. "A Temple is Bombed—Atlanta 1958." *American Jewish Archives* 23 (2/1971): 125–153.

Siddons, Anne Rivers. "The Seeds of Sanity." *Atlanta Magazine* (July 1967): 55–57, 104.

Sitton, Claude. "Atlanta Example: Good Sense and Dignity." *New York Times Magazine* (6 May 1962): 22, 123, 128.

Thompson, Robert A., Hylan Lewis and Davis McEntire. "Atlanta and Birmingham: A Comparative Study in Negro Housing," in *Housing and Minority Groups*, ed. by Nathan Glazer and Davis McEntire. Berkeley: University of California, 1960, pp. 14–42.

Stone, Clarence N. "Preemptive Power: Floyd Hunter's 'Community Power Structure' Reconsidered." *American Journal of Political Science* 32 (February 1988): 82–104.

Trillin, Calvin. "'Atlanta Settlement'." *New Yorker* 17 (March 1973): 101–105.

Vowels, Robert. "Atlanta Negro Business and the New Black Bourgeoisie." *Atlanta Historical Bulletin* 21 (Spring 1977): 48–66.

Walker, Grace. "How Women Won the Quiet Battle of Atlanta." *Good Housekeeping* (May 1961): 76–77, 194–207.

Walker, Jack. "The Functions of Disunity: Negro Leadership in a Southern City." *Journal of Negro Education* 23 (Summer 1963): 227–236.

———. "Negro Voting in Atlanta Georgia, 1953–1961." *Phylon* XXIV (Winter 1963): 379–387.

———. "Protest and Negotiation: A Case Study of Negro Leadership in Atlanta, Georgia." *Midwest Journal of Political Science* VII (2/May 1963): 99–124.

White, Dana F. "The Black Sides of Atlanta: A Geography of Expansion and Containment, 1870–1970." *The Atlanta Historical Journal* XXVI (2/3 Summer/Fall 1982): 199–225.

Williams, Roger. "The Negro in Atlanta." *Atlanta Magazine* (June 1966): 471–476.

DISSERTATIONS AND THESES

Blackwell, Gloria. "Black-Controlled Media in Atlanta, 1960–1970: The Burden of the Message and the Struggle for Survival." Ph.D. dissertation, Emory University, 1973.

Bolster, Paul. "Civil Rights Movements in Twentieth Century Georgia." Ph.D. dissertation, University of Georgia, 1972.

Boone, William H. "The Atlanta Community Relations Commission." Ph.D. dissertation, Atlanta University, 1969.

Butler, Jacob. "Racial Conflict and Polarization as a Constraint on Black Mayoral Leadership in Urban Policy: An Analysis of Public Finance and Urban Development During the Mayoral Tenure of Mayor Jackson, 1973–1977." Ph.D. dissertation, Atlanta University, 1979.

Calhoun, John. "Some Contributions of Negro Leaders to the Progress of Atlanta." M.A. thesis, Atlanta University, 1968.

Corley, Robert. "The Quest for Racial Harmony: Race Relations in Birmingham, Alabama, 1947–1963." Ph.D. dissertation, University of Virginia, 1979.

Deaton, Thomas. "Atlanta During the Progressive Era." Ph.D. dissertation, University of Georgia, 1969.

Fleming, Douglas. "Atlanta, the Depression, and the New Deal." Ph.D. dissertation, Emory University, 1984.

Fort, Vincent. "The Atlanta Sit-in Movement, 1960–1961: An Oral Study." M.A. thesis, Atlanta University, 1980.

Frick, Mary Louise. "Influences on Negro Political Participation in Atlanta, Georgia." M.A. thesis, Georgia State University, 1967.

Garofalo, Charles. "Business Ideas in Atlanta, 1916–1935." Ph.D. dissertation, Emory University, 1972.

———. "A Study of the Interracial Coalition in Atlanta Politics." M.A. thesis, Emory University, 1970.

Gibson, Elizabeth. "Eliza K. Paschall and the Southern Civil Rights Movement: From Dedication to Disillusionment." M.A. thesis, Emory University, 1983.

Hill, Irene. "Black Political Behavior in Atlanta, Georgia: An Analysis of the Politics of Exchange, 1908–1973." M.A. thesis, Atlanta University, 1980.

Harris, James W. "This is Our Home: It is Not For Sale." Senior thesis, Princeton University, 1971.

Huie, Henry Mark. "Factors Influencing the Desegregation Process in the Atlanta School System, 1954–1967." Ed.D. dissertation, University of Georgia, 1967.

Klopper, Ruth. "The Atlanta Elections, 1969: Alliances in Transition." M.A. thesis, Atlanta University, 1971.

McGrath, Susan M. "Great Expectations: The History of School Desegregation in Atlanta and Boston, 1954–1990." Ph.D. dissertation, Emory University, 1992.

Matthews, John. "Studies in Race Relations in Georgia." Ph.D. dissertation, Duke University, 1970.

Porter, Michael. "Black Atlanta: An Interdisciplinary Study of Blacks on the East Side of Atlanta, 1890–1930." Ph.D. dissertation, Emory University, 1974.

Rosenzweig, Charles. "The Issue of Employing Black Policemen in Atlanta, Georgia." M.A. thesis, Emory University, 1970.

Sloan, Vetta Marie, "Some Aspects of the Atlanta Urban League's Campaign for a Negro Hospital, 1947–1952." M.A. thesis, Atlanta University, 1977.

Suber, Michael. "The Internal Black Politics of Atlanta, Georgia, 1944–1968: An Analytic Study of Leadership Roles and Organizational Thrusts." Ph.D. dissertation, Atlanta University, 1975.

Turner, Claudia. "Changing Residential Patterns in Southwest Atlanta from 1960 to 1970." M.A. thesis, Atlanta University, 1970.

Vanlandingham, Karen. "In Pursuit of a Changing Dream: Spelman College Students and the Civil Rights Movement, 1955–1962." M.A. thesis, Emory University, 1983.

Wells, Rosa Marie. "Samuel Woodrow Williams: Catalyst for Black Atlantans, 1946–1970." M.A. thesis, Atlanta University, 1975.

Zaring, Russell. "The Resegregation of a Neighborhood: The Resegregation of Southwest Atlanta in the 1960s." Honors paper, Emory University, 1976.

NEWSPAPERS

Atlanta Constitution

Atlanta Daily World

Atlanta Inquirer

Atlanta Journal

Atlanta Journal-Atlanta Constitution (Sunday)

Clippings File, Southern Regional Council, Atlanta, Georgia

The New York Times

The Washington Post

INTERVIEWS

Alexander, Cecil. Interview with author. Atlanta, Georgia, 9 March 1991.

Alexander, Cecil. Interview with Jed Dannenbaum and Kathleen Dowdey. Ralph McGill Papers, Woodruff Library, Emory University, Atlanta, Georgia.

Allen, Ivan, Jr. Interview with author. Atlanta, Georgia, 7 November 1990.

Allen, Ivan, Jr. Interview with Thomas H. Baker. Atlanta, Georgia, 15 May 1969, Lyndon Baines Johnson Oral History Collection, Lyndon Baines Johnson Presidential Library, Austin, Texas.

Bond, Julian. Interview with Jed Dannenbaum and Kathleen Dowdey. Ralph McGill Papers.

Calloway, William. Interview with author. Atlanta, Georgia, 10 September 1991.

Clayton, Xernona. Interview with author. Atlanta, Georgia, 14 December 1990.

Clayton, Xernona. Interview with Jed Dannenbaum and Kathleen Dowdey. Ralph McGill Papers.

Fleming, Harold. Interview with Jed Dannenbaum and Kathleen Dowdey. Ralph McGill Papers.

Ford, Austin. Interview with author. Atlanta, Georgia, 3 December 1990.

Grigsby, Lucy. Interview with Jed Dannenbaum and Kathleen Dowdey. Ralph McGill Papers.

Hartsfield, William B. Interview with Charles T. Morrisey. Atlanta, Georgia, 6 January 1966. William Hartsfield Papers, Woodruff Library, Emory University, Atlanta, Georgia.

Holman, M. Carl. Interview with Jed Dannenbaum and Kathleen Dowdey. Ralph McGill Papers.

Jenkins, Herbert. Interview with Thomas H. Baker. Atlanta, Georgia, 14 May 1969. Lyndon Baines Johnson Oral History Collection, Lyndon Baines Presidential Library.

Jenkins, Herbert. Interview with Jed Dannenbaum and Kathleen Dowdey. Ralph McGill Papers.

Johnson, LeRoy. Interview with author. Atlanta, Georgia, 13 November 1990.

King, Lonnie. Interview with Jed Dannenbaum and Kathleen Dowdey. Ralph McGill Papers.

Massell, Sam. Interview with author. Atlanta, Georgia, 3 December 1990.

Morris, John. Interview with author. Atlanta, Georgia, 12 December 1990.

Pauley, Francis. Interview with author. Atlanta, Georgia, 9 November 1990.

Pauley, Francis. Interview with Jed Dannenbaum and Kathleen Dowdey. Ralph McGill Papers.

Pendergrast, Nan. Interview with author. Atlanta, Georgia, 17 December 1990.

Pendergrast, Nan. Interview with Jed Dannenbaum and Kathleen Dowdey. Ralph McGill Papers.

Scott, C.A. Interview with author. Atlanta, Georgia. 29 February 1991.

Shipp, Bill. Interview with Jed Dannenbaum and Kathleen Dowdey. Ralph McGill Papers.

Sibley, Celestine. Interview with Jed Dannenbaum and Kathleen Dowdey. Ralph McGill Papers.

Smith, Benny T. Interview with author. Atlanta, Georgia, 18 December 1990.

Vandiver, Samuel Ernest. Interview with Jed Dannenbaum and Kathleen Dowdey. Ralph McGill Papers.

Zinn, Howard. Interview with Jed Dannenbaum and Kathleen Dowdey. Ralph McGill Papers.

PAPERS AND ARCHIVAL COLLECTIONS

Bullard, Helen, Papers, Woodruff Library, Emory University, Atlanta, Georgia.

Calhoun, John H., Papers, Woodruff Library, Atlanta University, Atlanta, Georgia.

Clement, Rufus E., Papers, Woodruff Library, Atlanta University, Atlanta, Georgia.

Congress of Racial Equality Papers, Martin Luther King, Jr. Center for Nonviolent Social Change, Atlanta, Georgia.

Episcopal Society for Cultural and Racial Unity, Papers, Martin Luther King, Jr. Center for Nonviolent Social Change, Atlanta, Georgia.

Hamilton, Grace Towns, Papers, Atlanta History Center Library and Archives, Atlanta, Georgia.

Hartsfield, William B., Papers, Woodruff Library, Emory University, Atlanta, Georgia.

Jenkins, Herbert, Papers, Atlanta History Center Library and Archives, Atlanta, Georgia.

King, Martin Luther, Jr., Papers, Martin Luther King Center for Nonviolent Social Change, Atlanta, Georgia.

McGill, Ralph, Papers, Woodruff Library, Emory University, Atlanta, Georgia.

Paschall, Eliza, Papers, Woodruff Library, Emory University, Atlanta, Georgia.

Pauley, Francis, Papers, Woodruff Library, Emory University, Atlanta, Georgia.

Rich, Richard, Papers, Woodruff Library, Emory University, Atlanta, Georgia.

Rothschild, Rabbi Jacob. Papers, Woodruff Library, Emory University, Atlanta, Georgia.

Sibley, John A., Papers, Woodruff Library, Emory University, Atlanta, Georgia.

Southern Christian Leadership Conference, Papers, Martin Luther King, Jr. Center for Nonviolent Social Change, Atlanta, Georgia.

Southern Regional Council, Papers, Woodruff Library, Atlanta University, Atlanta, Georgia.

Student Nonviolent Coordinating Committee, Papers, Woodruff Library, Atlanta University, Atlanta, Georgia.

Walden, A.T., Papers, Atlanta History Center Library and Archives, Atlanta, Georgia.

Williams, Samuel, Papers, Woodruff Library, Atlanta University, Atlanta, Georgia.

Index

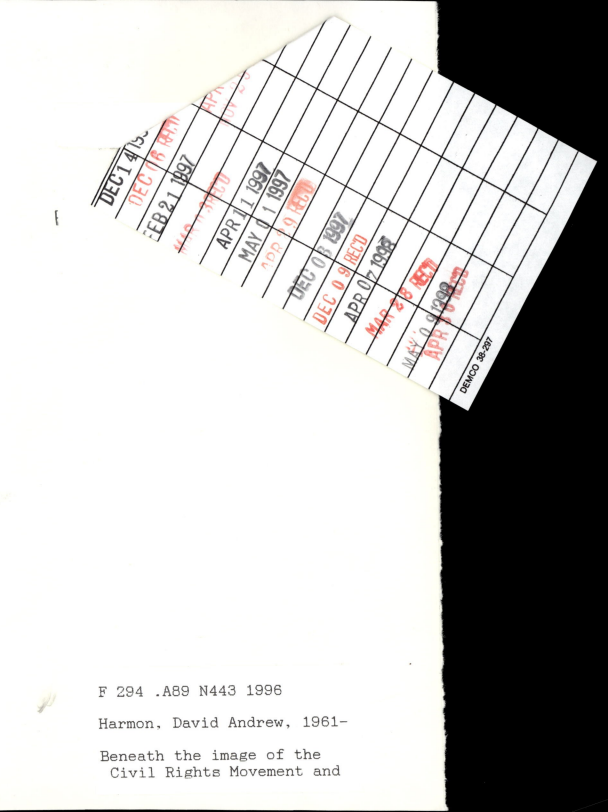